Envisioning Power

Ideologies of
Dominance and Crisis

Eric R. Wolf

UNIVERSITY OF CALIFORNIA PRESS

Berkeley / Los Angeles / London

University of California Press
Berkeley and Los Angeles, California

University of California Press, Ltd.
London, England

© 1999 by
The Regents of the University of California

Library of Congress Cataloging-in-Publication Data

Wolf, Eric R., 1923–
    Envisioning power : ideologies of dominance and crisis /
Eric R. Wolf.
        p.   cm.
    Includes bibliographic references (p.   ) and index.
    ISBN 0-520-21536-2 (alk. paper)
    1. Power (Social sciences)   2. Ideology.   3. Kwakiutl Indians.
4. National socialism.   5. Aztecs.   I. Title.
    JC330.W65   1998
    303.3—dc21   98-23792
                                                              CIP

Printed in the United States of America
9 8 7 6 5 4 3 2 1

The paper used in this publication meets the minimum
requirements of American National Standards for Information
Sciences—Permanence of Paper for Printed Library Materials,
ANSI Z39.48-1984.

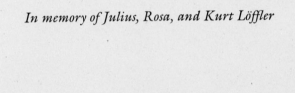

In memory of Julius, Rosa, and Kurt Löffler

Contents

Preface

For some time I have thought that much good work in the human sciences falls short of its mark because it is unwilling or unable to come to grips with how social relations and cultural configurations intertwine with considerations of power. Anthropologists have relied heavily on notions that see cultural coherence as the working out of cultural-linguistic logics or aesthetics. As a result, they rarely have asked how power structures the contexts in which these promptings manifest themselves or how power is implicated in the reproduction of such patterns. I articulated this concern in an address to the American Anthropological Association in 1990, "Facing Power." Yet if anthropologists have favored a view of culture without power, other social analysts have advanced a concept of "ideology" without culture, taking it as ideas advanced by elites or ruling classes in defense of their dominance, without attention to the specificities of cultural configurations.

This book seeks a way out of this impasse. The project for it began with reading and discussion in a workshop on ideology that I conducted in 1984 with students in the Ph.D. Program in Anthropology at the City University of New York. It was then carried forward in graduate courses on the history of theory and on ideology, concluding with a seminar on "Ethnography and Theory" in 1992. I am grateful to the students who took part in these efforts and who made teaching at CUNY a memorable experience. My research and writing thereafter were facilitated by a generous fellowship from the John D. and Catherine T. MacArthur Foundation.

My interest in the Aztecs dates back to my first visit to Mexico in 1951, where I learned much of what I know from Pedro Armillas, Angel Palerm, René Millon, and William T. Sanders. The upheavals produced by German National Socialism provided the main drama of my adolescence and early adulthood and significantly shaped my personal and professional concerns. Work on the Kwakiutl formed part of my anthropological education; as an undergraduate at Queens College I wrote an honors paper on the redistributive functions of chiefship.

I presented initial versions of the material on National Socialist Germany (1991) and on the Aztecs (1992) as Brockway Lectures on the Anthropology of Crisis at the CUNY Graduate Center. More recently I was able to discuss the project before the Research School on Historical Anthropology/Sociology, University of Lund, with Jonathan Friedman as my host (1995); in the Ethnological Seminar, University of Zurich, guided by Jürg Helbling, in the framework of "theoretical discussions in present-day anthropology" (1996); and in a colloquium organized by Anton Blok at the Amsterdam School for Social Science Research (1997).

For advising me on sources or sharing their own writings with me, I am indebted to Johanna Broda (history, Universidad Nacional Autónoma de México), Davíd Carrasco (religion, Princeton University), Enrique Florescano (history and anthropology, Mexico City), Michael E. Harkin (anthropology, University of Wyoming), Thomas Hauschild (anthropology, Marburg), Pierre-Yves Jacopin (anthropology, Neuchatel), Joseph Jorgensen (anthropology, University of California at Irvine), Cecelia F. Klein (art history, University of California at Los Angeles), Ulrike Linke (anthropology, Rutgers University), Alfredo López Austin (anthropology, Universidad Nacional Autónoma de México), Richard A. Koenigsberg (Library of Social Science, Elmhurst, New York), Joyce Marcus (Museum of Anthropology, University of Michigan), Irene Portis-Winner (semiotics, Cambridge, Massachusetts), Kay A. Read (religious studies, DePaul University), Wayne Suttles (anthropology, Portland State University), Pamela Wright (anthropology and linguistics, New York), and Rudolf A. M. van Zantwijk (anthropology, University of Utrecht).

Several friends located materials for me that I might otherwise never have seen. I also want to offer thanks to the many scholars on whose work I have drawn. Special appreciation is due to three demanding and thus helpful critics: Barbara J. Price (anthropology, Columbia University), who read an early draft of my chapter on the Aztecs; Hermann Rebel (history, University of Arizona), who dissected my first efforts to write on National Socialism; and Jane Schneider (anthropology, City University of New York), who read the entire manuscript and clarified some of my arguments. My friend Archibald W. Singham, political scientist-activist, always sure that "the next round is ours," said to me shortly before his death in 1991 that "it was time to meditate."

I dedicate this book to the memory of my second family during my years in the Sudetenland of the former Czechoslovakia (1933–1938): Julius and Rosa Löffler, and their son Kurt. Papa Julius, an itinerant journeyman in his youth, was a master tanner, Rosa an expert dressmaker. When Nazi Germany was about to occupy the Sudetenland Papa Julius offered to hide my parents in his house. Later he stood up to the Gestapo officers who accused him of maintaining friendships with Jews. Rosa never disguised her identity as "a Sozi among the Nazis"; an "Old Catholic," she argued with the archbishop of Austria over her refusal to accept the Vatican doctrine of 1870 on papal infallibility. These two extraordinary people are buried in unmarked graves in Tragwein, Upper Austria. My friend Kurt taught me how to fight and was my companion on many hikes and trips. One of these was a long-distance bicycle tour through Central Europe that took us to Munich in the summer of 1937. There, under the eye of the SS, we watched the processions and parades organized by the regime to celebrate the Day of German Art, and we visited both the approved exhibit of German Art and the disapproved show of "Degenerate Art." The memory of that day remains with me. Kurt hoped to study art and become a painter on glass, but he perished in the final German retreat from Russia in 1945, in a war he did not want.

Without Sydel Silverman, my wife, best friend, counselor, and critic, this project would never have reached its conclusion. I owe more than I can say to her great good sense, her sharp editorial eye for evasions, redundancies, and sallies into baroque prose, and her gift of laughter. Together we finally rolled this heavy medicine bundle into the light of day.

I

Introduction

I want, in this book, to explore the connection between ideas and power. We stand at the end of a century marked by colonial expansion, world wars, revolutions, and conflicts over religion that have occasioned great social suffering and cost millions of lives. These upheavals have entailed massive plays and displays of power, but ideas have had a central role in all of them. Ideas have been used to glorify or criticize social arrangements within states, and they have helped warriors and diplomats to justify conflicts or accommodations between states. Ideas have furnished explanations and warrants for imperialist domination and resistance to it, for communism and anticommunism, for fascism and antifascism, for holy wars and the immolation of infidels. They also reach into our everyday lives: they inform discussions about "family values," prompt some people to scare their neighbors by burning crosses in their yards, cause believers to undertake long pilgrimages to Mecca or Lourdes or to await the Second Coming in a Rocky Mountain retreat.

Nevertheless, an analytic understanding of how power and ideas intermesh has eluded us and remains a matter of debate. Some scholars accord ideas a Platonic existence in human "minds," or endow them with an independent capability to motivate and move people. Others regard them primarily as rationalizations for self-interested conduct or as accompaniments of behavior, lacking significance "in the long run." The long run may be seen as dominated by natural selection, by the forces of the unconscious, or by the ultimately determinant role of the economy.

Arguments about how to think about ideas have marked out the intellectual pathways of American anthropology. Few anthropologists have followed those, such as Cornelius Osgood (1940, 25), who have attempted to reduce everything to ideas, but the field has accorded ideas a dominant role throughout its history. When Alfred Kroeber and Talcott Parsons, the leading doyens of anthropology and sociology respectively in the mid-twentieth century, staked out the boundaries between the two fields, anthropology was assigned the study of "patterns of values, ideas, and other symbolic-meaningful systems as factors in the shaping of human behavior and the artifacts produced through behavior" (1958, 583). This legacy to anthropology strongly reinforced the penchant for mentalistic interpretations.

To counter this "idealist expropriation of culture," the anthropologist Marvin Harris has insisted on granting priority in the study of culture not to ideas but to objectively verifiable behavioral facts recorded by observers employing an operationalized scientific epistemology (1979, 284). Harris did not exclude an interest in what the natives themselves think about their lives, but he treated with maximal suspicion any explanation for behavior derived from putative cognitive rules or guiding ideas. He asserted that "No amount of knowledge of 'competent natives' rules and codes can 'account for' phenomena such as poverty; underdevelopment; imperialism; the population explosion; minorities; ethnic and class conflict; exploitation, taxation, private property; pollution and degradation of the environment; the military-industrial complex; political repression; crime; urban blight; unemployment; or war. These phenomena . . . are the consequence of intersecting and contradictory vectors of beliefs, will, and power. They cannot be scientifically understood as manifestations of codes and rules" (Harris 1979, 285). Perhaps so. Yet "beliefs and will" surely involve ideas that code belief and inform will. How one might conceptualize the relation between ideas and power remains to be more fully specified.

In taking up this inquiry, my aim is not to develop a formal theory of the relationship between two mega-abstractions—something that is probably impossible because ideas come in many different kinds and variants, as does power. As an anthropologist, I believe that theoretical discussions need to be grounded in cases, in observed streams of behavior, and in recorded texts. I want to find ways of interrogating such materials to define the relations of power that are played out in social arrangements and cultural configurations, and to trace out the possible ways in which these relations of power implicate ideas.

Ideas, Power, Communication

If I use the old-fashioned term "ideas," it is not to return to a now obsolete view of ideas as units held and stored in the mind, which replicate within the organism stimuli received from the world outside. Given what we now know about the workings of human neuro-cognitive systems, knowledge can no longer be visualized as a simple "reflection" in the mind of what goes on in the external world. Whether one believes that "minds" (or, rather, human neurological systems that include brains) merely edit what enters from outside or themselves construct cognitive and emotional schemata that can address the world but are not isomorphic with it, we must work with some variant of the neo-Kantian postulate that minds interpose a selective sieve or screen between the organism and the environment through which it moves. This, of course, is rendered even more evident by the work of anthropologists whose studies have taught them that panhuman "minding" is further inflected and conjugated from culture to culture.

Humans inhabit a world, a life space, characterized by imperative constraints and potential opportunities, but the ways in which they adapt to these life spaces is only partially programmed by their biology. They must rely on their nervous systems to construct models of the world and its workings, but these models are not identical with that world, and the connections mapped out between an experienced reality and how it is represented are complex and variable. Thus, any attempt to account for ideas and systems of ideas must juxtapose both dimensions with the aid of theoretically informed guesses.

I speak of ideas in this context because I hope to underline that such mental constructions have content: they are *about something*.

They also have functions; they do something for people. Striving to lay out the features of the world, they seek to render it amenable to some human use. In doing so, they play a part in bringing people together, or—alternatively—in dividing them. Both cooperation and conflict invoke and involve plays of power in human relationships, and ideas are emblems and instruments in these ever shifting and contested interdependencies.

I want to draw a distinction between "ideas" and "ideology." The term "ideas" is intended to cover the entire range of mental constructs rendered manifest in public representations, populating all human domains. I believe that "ideology" needs to be used more restrictively, in that "ideologies" suggest unified schemes or configurations developed to underwrite or manifest power. Equating all ideation with ideology masks the ways in which ideas come to be linked to power. The questions of when and how ideas are thus concentrated into ideologies, and how ideologies become programs for the deployment of power, cannot be answered by merging ideology with ideation as a whole. They demand a separate kind of inquiry.

Conceptualizing power presents difficulties of its own. Power is often spoken of as if it were a unitary and independent force, sometimes incarnated in the image of a giant monster such as Leviathan or Behemoth, or else as a machine that grows in capacity and ferocity by accumulating and generating more powers, more entities like itself. Yet it is best understood neither as an anthropomorphic force nor as a giant machine but as an aspect of all relations among people.

I first encountered this formulation when I heard Norbert Elias lecture in the summer of 1940 at the Alien Detention Center at Huyton near Liverpool in England, where all male Austrian, German, and Italian citizens living within a certain range of London were interned by the British government, as the German armies overran France and an invasion of England seemed imminent. There I not only had my first lesson of sociology but also learned from Elias that "more or less fluctuating balances of power constitute an integral element of all human relations" (1971, 76–77; my translation). Elias likened the shift of power balances to a game: balances may change and produce gains for one set of partners (individuals, groups, or whole societies) and losses for another; a cumulative run of gains may eventually build up monopolies of power yet simultaneously generate efforts to test and disestablish these favored positions. Particular moves in these games can bring on violence and war; but violence and war, too, were to be thought of in relational terms as interdependent phenomena, and not as forms of anomic disorder.

Thinking of power in relational terms, rather than as a concentrated "power-pack," has the further advantage that it allows one to see power as an aspect of many kinds of relations. Power works differently in interpersonal relations, in institutional arenas, and on the level of whole societies. I have found it useful to distinguish among four modalities in how power is thus woven into social relations. One is the power of potency or capability that is seen to inhere in an individual. Power in this Nietzschean sense draws attention to how persons enter into a play of power, but it does not address what that play is about. A second kind of power is manifested in interactions and transactions among people and refers to the ability of an *ego* to impose its will in social action upon an *alter* (the Weberian view). Left unspecified is the nature of the arena in which these interactions go forward. A third modality is power that controls the contexts in which people exhibit their capabilities and interact with others. This sense calls attention to the instrumentalities through which individ- *ways* uals or groups direct or circumscribe the actions of others within determinate settings. I refer to this mode as tactical or organizational power.

But there is still a fourth modality of power, which I want to focus on in the present inquiry: structural power. By this I mean the power manifest in relationships that not only operates within settings and domains but also organizes and orchestrates the settings themselves, and that specifies the direction and distribution of energy flows. In Marxian terms, this refers to the power to deploy and allocate social labor. It is also the modality of power addressed by Michel Foucault when he spoke of "governance," to mean the exercise of "action upon action" (1984, 427–28). These relations of power constitute structural power. Marx addressed the structural relations of power between the class of capitalists and the class of workers, while Foucault was concerned rather with the structural relations that govern "consciousness." I want to trace out the ways in which relations that command the economy and polity and those that shape ideation interact to render the world understandable and manageable.

Ideas or systems of ideas do not, of course, float about in incorporeal space; they acquire substance through communication in discourse and performance. We therefore need to attend also to how ideas are communicated, from whom to whom and among whom. The term "communication"—generating, sending, and receiving messages—was in common usage in the 1950s (for example, Ruesch and Bateson 1951), but it yielded pride of place, after a brief reign, to "meaning." It nevertheless remains a useful term, because it covers both messages expressed through human language and those transmitted nonverbally. Nonverbal communication embraces many modes through which messages can be conveyed. They can be transmitted through human gestures and bodily comportment, and also communicated iconically through displays of objects and representations.

Both modes of communication provide vehicles to convey ideas, but messages have first to be cast into appropriate cultural and linguistic codes. To speak and understand a language, one needs access to its linguistic codes, so as to identify its phonemes and morphemes as well as the syntax through which these elements are formally combined. Similarly, to take part in a ritual, one needs to have a formal script of required acts, set out in the memory codes of participants or in the written instructions handed out to an expectant audience. Codes arrange the constituent elements of the message in particular ways, in order to convey which notion or notions are to be broadcast to an audience and how it should decode the messages heard. There would be no communication without codes, and to the extent that all social relations involve communication, they must also utilize codes and engage in coding and decoding. Thus, this concept of code and codes is applicable not only to language and formalized behavior such as ritual but to other facets of cultural life as well. One can speak, for example, of dress codes, culinary codes, codes of appropriate comportment, or codes that govern gifts of flowers.

Yet these codes should not be understood as fixed templates for how social life is to be lived. They vary with the social contexts in which they are deployed, whether these be on the level of household, family, community, region, or on the level of society at large.

They also vary according to the domain they address—such as economics, politics, or religion—and according to the social characteristics of the parties to the communication process, including their social origins, gender, age, educational milieu, occupation, and class position. Since these social categorizations involve variabilities in access to power, power equalities or differentials are at work in defining who can address whom, and from what symmetrical or asymmetrical positions. The grid formed by these rankings and positions, in turn, sets up the contexts for how things are said or performed and codifies how they are to be understood.

Communicative processes must thus strike a balance between adhering to codes and to the formal properties of codes, on the one hand, and fostering variability in application, on the other. Adherence to rules supports intelligibility and coherence; variability permits communication to be fitted to changing circumstances. Yet these operations of replication or variation do not take place in the minds of isolated individuals. The signs and codes employed possess a tangible, public quality, a reality that anyone attempting to communicate must take into account; no one can simply invent a language or a culture individually. The processes of reproducing or modifying communicative traditions are social, carried on by socialized participants with communicative means and skills deployed publicly in social contexts.

Just as all social arrangements, including those of communication, involve relations of power, so also is that true of ideas. Contrary to the old German revolutionary song that proclaimed that thoughts are "free," ("die Gedanken sind frei"), ideas and idea-systems are often monopolized by power groups and rendered self-enclosed and self-referential. While ideas are subject to contextual variation, moreover, this variation itself encounters structural limits, since contexts too involve social relationships and thus acquire their structure through plays of power. A key question that emerges is how power operates in these contexts to control potential disruption. More concretely, we need to inquire into how conflicts between tradition and variability in communication are fought out.

This kind of inquiry shifts attention away from an internal analysis of how codes are arranged, transmitted, or altered to questions about the society in which these messages are sent and received. Lin-

power is a relation
class is a relation
class is power?   ideas involve relations of power

guistics and semiotics investigate the mechanics of communication that lay the groundwork of signification, but they do not yet address what the communicatory act is *about,* what it asserts or denies about the world beyond the vehicle of discourse or performance itself. Communicative acts impute attributes to the world and convey them as propositions to their audiences. It is part of the ethnographer's task to bring together the different pronouncements thus made, to note their congruence or disjunction, to test them against other things said and done, and to guess at what they might be about. It should also be his or her task to relate these formulations to the social and political projects that underwrite discourse and performance and to assess the relevance of these projects to the contests over power in social relations. These contests involve ideational repertoires; stress on one repertoire over another can affect the outcome of power struggles, opening up opportunities to one set of claimants, foreclosing them to another.

Seeking answers to such questions, however, also requires us to go beyond the ethnographic present—the moment in which the ethnographer collects and records his observations—to locate the object of our study in time. It is not the events of history we are after, but the processes that underlie and shape such events. By doing so, we can visualize them in the stream of their development, unfolding from a time when they were absent or incipient, to when they become encompassing and general. We may then raise questions about proximate causation and contributory circumstances, as well as about the forces impelling the processes toward culmination or decline.

Earlier Explorations

This undertaking on my part may come as a surprise to readers who have understood my work as falling primarily within peasant studies and world-systems research, and who may think that I am now leaving the hard terrain of reality for the shores of fantasy land. I, however, see this endeavor as a continuation of concerns that have engaged me ever since I first heard of anthropology. The very discipline of anthropology had its beginnings in confrontations with then unfamiliar modes of thought and belief, and it set itself the task of recording and explaining their forms and significance. The German ethnologist Adolf Bastian distinguished between *Elementargedanken* and *Völkergedanken,* "universal elementary ideas" and the ideas of particular peoples. Edward Tylor, the doyen of British anthropology, sought to show how the mind evolved through a developing ability to differentiate between subject and object. Numerous scholars hoped to identify the origins and rationales governing "animism," "totemism," initiation, magic, or sacrifice. In these attempts, what people thought and imagined was dealt with as manifestations of their particular mental capacities, as exemplifications of the "mind," without much interest in their links to economy or society.

In contrast to this anthropological absorption in what were then taken as the "absurd beliefs of savages," the protagonists of the developing disciplines of political economy and sociology in the nineteenth century were less interested in the comparative workings of the mind. They downplayed the possible significance of culturally specific ideas as revelatory of peoples' essential cultures and visualized ideas primarily as manifestations of social interests in the operations of civil society. Thus, one set of thinkers fastened on ideas as dimensions of distinctive "cultures" but did not address questions of power, while others in the emerging human sciences stressed the role of power in society but defined ideas entirely as mental precipitates of power games, as "ideology," without much interest in their cultural role as elements of orientation and integration. My present effort hopes to draw these seemingly opposed analytic stances into convergence, by bringing them to bear conjointly upon historically and ethnographically described cases. In many ways, it represents the outcome of several previous explorations in my work and engages their unsolved problems.

I came into the discipline of anthropology at a time when studies of "culture and personality" had won out in the United States over more formalized inquiries into culture-trait distributions in time and space. The guiding idea was that each culture gave rise to a common personality, which was then transmitted transgenerationally through the cultural repertoire of child training. Common socialization and enculturation not only channeled the basic drives but also generated both culturally induced tensions and ways of abreacting these in behavior and fantasy. This model of commonality, it was then thought, would not only apply to small, homogeneous tribal groups but could be extended as well to large and differentiated societies, such as nations.

Speaking as one who for many years earned his keep by teaching courses on culture-and-personality, I would now say that this development within anthropology raised some important questions in asking how people in different social and cultural milieus acquired the knowledge and motivation to be actors and cultural carriers in the societies to which they belonged. In the language of structuralist Marxism, these were questions about how "the subject" is socially and culturally constructed. Yet culture-and-personality studies limited their capacity to find answers by adhering too narrowly to their guiding premises that societies and cultures were mostly homogeneous and that the causes of this homogeneity lay in the prevalent techniques of child training, especially as understood by psychoanalysis.

Today we would pay much greater attention to the differentiation and heterogeneity of social formations and to the multiplicity of social domains beyond the level of family and household. The interest in how "subjects" are formed could also have been more fruitful had it drawn more broadly on other disciplines, ranging from sociology to folkore, in order to grasp the relevant phenomena both processually and in history—to ask how guiding ideas, attitudes, and modes of action were shaped by class rule and hegemony, state policy, law, and public institutions, as well as by child training. One recent effort that moves in this direction is Pierre Bourdieu's adaptation of Marcel Mauss's concept of *habitus*, to show how people acquire "durable and transposable dispositions" through conditioning to the institutional landscape of social settings (Bourdieu and Wacquant 1992, 115–39). These dispositions include the cognitive schemata that order society, which are incorporated into the body until they have "all appearances of objective necessity." This then allows for inquiry into how people deploy their dispositions in daily life and into how symbolic systems can become instruments of domination.

For myself, having grown up in Central Europe, where many national identities, nationalisms, and nation-states were of but recent origin and where antagonisms among ethnic groups, regions, and classes threatened to tear apart even those nations that had been painfully constructed over the course of a century, the culture-and-personality mode of conceptualizing a national totality seemed utterly mistaken. It assumed that a common repertoire of child training would produce a single national character, and it abstracted personality formation from the historical processes that often required the use of force and persuasion to bring differentiated populations under the aegis of unified nation-states.

My own interests turned me toward learning more about these processes. Nations grew over time through intensified flows of capital and labor; through the unification of currencies and measures; through urbanization and migration from the countryside into the cities; through growing participation in politics; through the expansion of formal education, the hegemonic spread of standard languages, and the widening of channels of communication; through universal military training and the establishment of universal codes of law; through the diffusion of new norms of comportment and etiquette relevant to the expanding "civil society"; as well as through elaboration and proliferation of key ideas that celebrated the new collectivities or proved to be critical of them. These activity systems and institutions seemed to me to merit study in their own right. That was also true of the various nationalisms manifested as systems of ideas, and of the programs and visions of nationhood put forth in each particular case.

Yet clearly, the expansion of national life was uneven. Nations were constructed segmentally and unequally, marked by what the German philosopher Ernst Bloch called "the contemporaneity of the non-contemporaneous" (1962). Some people and groups were drawn or propelled into the central orbits of national existence; others were ignored, marginalized, or obliterated altogether. There were winners and also losers, unequally distributed over the national terrain and unequally represented in the symbolizations of the nation. More recently, as nation-states have become partners in wider alliances and participants in transnational networks of exchange and commerce, many of these subgroups and regions have reemerged with claims on their own behalf, testing the limits of integration into nations. None of these simultaneously encompassing and differentiating processes was mirrored in concepts of "national character."

I codified some of these observations early on in an article, "The

Formation of the Nation," published in Spanish as "La formación de la nación" (1953) but never in English. There I argued that the formation of such differentiated and yet stratified societies

involves the growth of new cultural relationships which permit the accommodation of the new groups to each other. The socio-cultural segments of the society must learn them and make them their own. This is true when the ruling segment of one society establishes its dominance over another society. It is also true when culture change within a society causes the emergence of wholly new socio-cultural segments which must establish relations with each other and with the groups which provided the matrix from which they sprang.

Differences in location and timing, as well as in the nature of the sociocultural segments and their activity systems, would render this process uneven and cause it to be shot through with conflicts. It was more likely that the outcome would favor the rise of heterogeneous social arrays than the development of homogeneous national or subnational totalities.

How groups and social segments are drawn into a nation—economically, socially, politically, and in the realm of ideas—was then, and remains for me now, a problem to be explored. My first book, *Sons of the Shaking Earth* (1959a), attempted to depict the historical trajectory of Mexico as a succession of the different ways in which quite varied groups and units were brought into relationship with one another at different phases over time. Each phase, and the integrative processes that characterized it, had ramifying effects on what was to follow. I see much of my work as efforts to amplify this perspective— to think about how different aggregates and organizations of people, operating on diverse territorial and institutional levels, are drawn into more extensive units, only to be then reshuffled and repositioned into alternative arrangements at some later moment in history.

I thought then, and still do, that if we were going to come to grips with such complex and tension-laden processes we would also have to develop a better grasp of how they were rendered and expressed in ideation. My first effort specifically focused on how ideas relate to power was cast in a functionalist mode. An early publication on "The Social Organization of Mecca and the Origins of Islam" (1951) argued that expanding commerce subverted lineage separatism in the city, setting up pressures toward a new form of organization that could transcend the narrowness and limitations of lineage organization. The new form of organization was the community of the faithful (*umma*), built up around the worship of one overarching god. That god, previously only the deity of the non-kin clients of kinship units, was installed as the dominant figure of the entire collectivity, now recodified as a unitary body of believers rather than as members of separate bodies of kin. My article was based on less acquaintance with Arabic and other Near Eastern sources than was required, and I have properly been taken to task for its shortcomings by a number of better-informed specialists (Eickelman 1967; Aswad 1970; Dostal 1991). It was also strongly influenced by British structural-functionalism, and in its own terms was relatively unsophisticated in relating religious phenomena functionally and causally to social structure. Yet it did connect changes in social organization, understood as a structure of distributed rights and duties, with changes in collective representations—in this case the representation of a transcendent "god"—and it did so by paying attention to the particular "form of thought" that inspired that conception.

A few years later I tried to explain the Mexican image of "The Virgin of Guadalupe" (1959b) as a collective representation of Mexican national identity. The icon of the Virgin had played an important role at several junctures of Mexican history. The rebel-priest Father Miguel Hidalgo initiated his movement for independence from Spain in 1810 with an emblem of the Virgin in his battle flag. A hundred years later, during the Mexican Revolution, Emiliano Zapata's agrarian rebels decorated their wide-brimmed straw hats with images of the Virgin. The Catholic Church elevated the Virgin to the status of patroness over all the Americas, and the cathedral housing the image of "the dark-hued Virgin" in Mexico City became a major pilgrimage center for people from all over the country. When I first went to Mexico in 1951, many houses in rural villages bore signs that read: "We are neither Protestants nor Communists—we believe in the Virgin of Guadalupe." In this case the questions were how the icon brought together the sentiments and longings of quite various strata of the population, Indians as well as non-Indians, and how this convergence upon a common symbolism might have taken place. I realized later that the questions, as well as the work based on them, were unusual for their time. They raised issues of differential power at a time when anthropology in general tended to think of native ways in terms of acting out a static "culture." They introduced history as a dimension, calling for us to look at the making of a key symbol as the outcome of processes unfolding over time. They put forth the idea that a common collective representation might be fashioned from very diverse discourses and imaginings of people stationed in different social and cultural positions.

A subsequent, more ambitious experiment (1969) proved unsatisfactory. It tried to construct and then contrast structural "homologies" in society and symbolism on the northern, Christian littoral of the Mediterranean and its southern, Muslim side. This drew some inspiration from the various structuralisms in vogue in the 1960s, such as that of the anthropologist Claude Lévi-Strauss and of the sociologist of literature Lucien Goldmann. My own effort to think in these terms, however, projected an overly abstract and ahistorical scheme of structural oppositions upon very heterogeneous elements and levels of society and culture. The result reinforced the lesson that structural analysis required close attention to the specificity of elements in one structural set at a time. It was not a shortcut to knowledge.

I tried to heed that lesson when I later wrote *Europe and the People Without History* (1982). The title was ironic, the point being that all the people who were drawn into the widening orbit of Europe-centered capitalist expansion *had* histories, indeed that their histories were part of ours and ours part of theirs. To make that point I did pay rather close attention to reports of peoples' concrete lives and fates, especially to emphasize that incorporation into the circuits of capital and labor under capitalist conditions was not a uniform process but was likely to vary according to the circumstances that obtained in different corners of the world.

In characterizing the capitalist mode of production and how it affected the social formations that it drew into its ever widening orbit, I made use of certain Marxian concepts. These concepts seemed to me especially productive in tracing out the lineaments of structural power over how social labor is mobilized and deployed. They continue to be valuable, I believe, for their call to attend to how material production, organization, and ideation intersect, and to how this intersection is not frozen at some moment of history but unfolds in tension-producing changes over time and space. They furthermore raise the question of how the division of labor in society—especially in class-divided society—impinges on the production and distribution of ideas. I became convinced that structural power in any society entails an ideology that assigns distinctions among people in terms of the positions they occupy in the mobilization of social labor.

Some critics argued that by taking this approach I was peddling "cosmologies of capitalism" and that I was underplaying the fact that many groups around the globe cling to their cultural forms and employ them to defend their own ways of life against capitalist encroachment. This may indeed be the case, but it also may not be: the nature of the variable relation between capitalism and the settings it penetrates persists as an open question. There clearly are groups in which one set of cultural understandings remains dominant to the exclusion of others and that refuse any truck with alternatives to their own way of life. Yet there are assuredly others in which people can and do combine diverse lifestyles and modes of thought and learn to negotiate the contradictions. That range of variation demands attention and explanation; it poses problems to be investigated, not certainties to be assumed.

If Marx and Engels retain relevance for us in this endeavor, it does not mean that their work contains the answers to all our questions. Their writings are full of pertinent ideas, along with notions invalidated since ("caduques," according to Maurice Godelier [1970, 110]). While they predicted many crucial aspects of capitalist development, the realization of a socialist future has not corresponded to the ways they imagined it. We also need to confront the fact that the development of linguistics, anthropology, sociology, and neuropsychology in the twentieth century has called into question the modes in which Marx and Engels, like many of their contemporaries, thought about "consciousness." There is a lack of fit between Marxian postulates, however liberally applied, and the ways in which anthropologists have gone about their work of depicting and analyzing other cultures and societies.

Three Cultures

It has been a hallmark of the anthropological approach to submit its presuppositions to the test of direct and intensive encounters with culturally specified populations. This kind of experience has been especially important when the behavior observed in a field location and the utterances recorded there proved to be at odds with the expectations of the investigator. Repeated encounters with cultural differences gave to the anthropological enterprise both caution about rushing to judgment and a measure of willingness to "let the observations speak for themselves"—this despite the understanding that facts cannot find their voice without some assist from a theoretical scheme.

To pursue the problem of how ideas and power are connected, therefore, I will look to three case studies, following the anthropological tradition of trying to relate observed behavior and recorded texts to their contextual matrix. In each of the cases, I will try to trace out the linkage between power and ideation, placing it in relation to the people's history and the material, organizational, and signifying forms and practices of their culture.

The three populations on which I will focus are the Kwakiutl of Vancouver Island in British Columbia, the Aztecs of fifteenth- and sixteenth-century Central Mexico, and the Germans who willingly or unwillingly became members of a Third Reich that was supposed to last for a thousand years but collapsed in fire and ashes in 1945. The Kwakiutl have been categorized as a "chiefdom," the Aztecs as an "archaic" or "early" state, and National Socialist Germany as a distinctive "reactionary-modern" state, combining the apparent modernity of capitalism and technology with a reactionary fascism. This seriation is compatible with an evolutionary sequence, but my aim is not to apply an evolutionary scheme to the study of three sociopolitical systems. Nor am I primarily interested in systematic comparison among the three cases, although I will sometimes juxtapose them in order to highlight contrasts or similarities among them.

My main interest is analytical: I want to find out what we can bring to light by exploring the relation between power and ideas in the cases. I have fastened on these three because each of them is characterized by unusually evocative and elaborate repertoires of ideas and practices based upon these repertoires. Forty years ago, Kroeber suggested that we might come to understand the dimensions and limits of human nature by taking stock, comparatively, of "the most extreme expressions yet found in particular cultures, of the various activities and qualities of culture" (1955, 199). He offered as one such "most extreme expression" the case of human sacrifice among the ancient Mexicans. I present here, as another, the case of National Socialist Germany, because its ideology played a part in the planned slaughter of millions.

I have also added the case of the Kwakiutl. They were one of the groups in Kroeber's roster of "Minor Civilizations in Native North America" (1962, 61), marked by "unusual intensity of cultural activity" (1947, 28). Mauss wrote of their giveaway ritual, the potlatch, that "such a syncretism of social phenomena is, in our opinion, unique in the history of human societies" (in Allen 1985, 36), and he drew on their ethnology for his famous *Essai sur le Don* of 1925 (Mauss 1954). For a long time these giveaways served as type-cases of conspicuous consumption (for example, Herskovits 1940). Ruth Benedict portrayed the Kwakiutl as "one of the most vigorous and zestful of the aboriginal cultures of North America" but also as acting in ways that would be called "megalomaniac paranoid" in our culture; what was abnormal among us constituted, on the Northwest Coast, "an essential attribute of ideal man" (in Mead 1959, 270, 275). These judgments have been called into question for equating ritual displays of antagonism and rhetoric with personal psychodynamics. My interest here focuses precisely on that flamboyant ideology and ritual.

These three cultures represent instances of high drama that challenge the ability and credibility of any observer or analyst. Yet, at the same time, they magnify and display structures and themes that might remain more muted and veiled among peoples who are less assertive in their ways of life. Such a claim is of course open to the charge of being both qualitative and subjective; but it is backed by considerable evidence. One of my tasks will be to evaluate that evidence and to suggest alternative explanations where warranted. Each of the cases will show how the people involved responded ideationally to perceived crises, but I shall also try to indicate how the relevant ideas and actions based on them were embedded in material processes of ecology, economics, social organization, and plays of political power. Moreover, to the extent that crises form part and parcel of everyday life, we must recognize that the generally accepted distinction between periods of normality and periods of crisis is to a large extent fictitious. Hence, ideational responses to crisis are not as divorced and separated from the ongoing traffic in mind-dependent constructions and representations as we have sometimes thought. Thus, these three "extreme" and accentuated cases may not be as removed from our everyday experience as we might imagine and hope.

In taking up each case, I will employ an approach of descriptive integration. I use the term to mean that I locate each case in space and time, bring together extant information to exhibit relationships among the domains of group life, and define the external forces that impinge on the people studied. The notion was developed by Kroeber, who spoke of "conceptual integration" in 1936 (1952, 70–71), and taken up by Robert Redfield as "descriptive integration" (1953, 730). They were seeking a specifically anthropological approach that could preserve the "quality" of phenomena and their relations to each other in time and space, as opposed to generalizing and abstract science. For me, the two endeavors—phenomenal particularism and generalization—are not opposed but rather are different but conjoint ways of addressing the same material. Description and analysis of phenomena necessarily involve selection, which assigns priority to some kinds of information over others according to one's theoretical perspectives. Such perspectives, in turn, are predicated upon generalizations developed within the larger anthropological project of comparison.

There is also, in the three cases, the question of what evidence we can draw on for descriptive integration. Each of the three comes to us through different kinds of records, and each kind requires appropriate handling in its own terms. I believe that this evidence is best interpreted when placed in the contexts of social and cultural life, situated within the parameters of a determinate political economy. Such an analysis should allow us to locate human groupings in the natural world and render manifest the ways in which they transform themselves by transforming their habitats. To see how this is accomplished, we must pay attention to who commands the labor available to the society and how this labor is marshaled through the exercise of power and the communication of ideas. Each of the cases could be analyzed by focusing exclusively on observed behavior, but much would be lost if we were not able also to talk about the motivating affect embodied in ideas, the mind-dependent constructs that drove people to engage in the potlatch, in human sacrifice, or in celebrations of "racial superiority." These ideas take on forms of their own that are not directly deducible from material or social facts, but they are implicated in material production and social organization and thus need to be understood in such contexts.

I write these lines as an anthropologist, albeit as one who sees his discipline as a link in the more encompassing effort of the human sciences to understand and explicate the multiple human conditions. Historically, anthropology owes its position to the fact that it occupied itself primarily with peoples who for a long time were wrongly thought to be marginal and irrelevant to the pursuit of civilization. This experience allowed anthropologists to take up a privileged vantage point in looking comparatively at peoples across the board, both inside and outside the boundaries set out by the spokespersons for progressive modernity. The other main determinant of anthropology's special role among the human sciences has been its method of going out to live, for prolonged periods of time, among the people to be studied. This enabled anthropological investigators not only to obtain more rounded views of how people lived their lives but also to confront the discrepancies between announced purposes and de facto behavior. Behavior often fails to follow the scripts laid out in discourses and texts; often too it obeys covert reasons that do not answer to ideal goals. Experience of such discrepancies has caused many anthropologists to be professionally dubious about stereotypes of other cultures sometimes advanced uncritically by their colleagues in allied disciplines.

Yet, while shrewd in these matters, anthropologists have also exhibited an obtuseness of their own. Cleaving to a notion of "culture" as a self-generating and self-propelling mental apparatus of norms and rules for behavior, the discipline has tended to disregard the role of power in how culture is built up, maintained, modified, dismantled, or destroyed. We face a situation of complementary naïveté, whereby anthropology has emphasized culture and discounted power, while "culture" was long discounted among the other social sciences, until it came to be a slogan in movements to achieve ethnic recognition.

This state of affairs has a history. The chapter that follows, "Contested Concepts," examines how this past has contributed to shaping our theoretical capabilities in the present. I there consider the historical background that first gave rise to our theoretical constructs and delineate the circumstances that sometimes rendered them fighting words of political and intellectual contests. I then turn to the three cases. Readers with an interest in the history of ideas will want to follow the arguments in "Contested Concepts"; others may wish to go directly to the case studies. How the chapters are ordered does, however, pursue a purpose. If, as Karl Marx wrote, "the tradition of all the dead generations weigh like a nightmare on the brain of the living" (1963, 15), that holds for anthropologists as much as for the people they study. Understanding whence we have come sets the terms for how we work through our case material and for the conclusions we draw from it.

2

Contested Concepts

Seeking to relate ideas to power, we enter an intellectual terrain that many others have already charted, albeit in response to purposes other than our own. These past endeavors have left us a stock of concepts, some of which we can appropriate and use, others of which may no longer be helpful. Legacies are always problematic, and they must be sorted out to answer to new undertakings. Anthropology, for example, has understood "cultures" as complexes of distinctive properties, including different visions of the world, but for long without attention to how these views formulated power and underwrote its effects. Other social sciences have taken up that issue under the name of "ideology," treating culture and ideology as opposites, not as complementary. In this contrast "culture" was used to suggest a realm of intimate communitarian ties that bind, while "ideology" conjured up scenarios of factional strife among self-seeking interest groups. Thus, "culture" received a positive evaluation, while "ideology" suffered a change in meaning for the worse. Others of our relevant concepts have undergone related transformations.

Such shifts in meaning and valuation have a history, which needs to be spelled out in order to clarify the intellectual issues at stake. A use of terms without attention to the theoretical assumptions and historical contexts that underlie them can lead us to adopt unanalyzed concepts and drag along their mystifying connotations into further work. Tracing out a history of our concepts can also make us aware

of the extent to which they incorporate intellectual and political efforts that still reverberate in the present.]

Three interrelated issues have persisted in the history of concepts
significant for this inquiry. The first is the counterposing of a vision
of a march of <u>humanity toward a universal reign of</u> Reason, against
an emphasis on the significance of distinctive ways of being human,
which ruled people through emotion rather than intellect. This issue entailed a second: if <u>human life was so dominated by tradition
and custom, what then was the relationship</u> between cultural ideals
and <u>actual behavior</u>? How could it be the case that tradition demanded one course of action, while behavior took a different turn?
This question raised a third issue: how were human minds constituted to deal with experience? Were ideas "the atoms and molecules
of the mind," compounded into images through a "mental chemistry" from sensations received from the outside world (Popper and
Eccles 1983, 194)? Or were human minds so tutored by custom that
external stimuli could only manifest themselves in behavior after
passing through the cognitive detectors of language and culture,
which processed them into templates for action?

Anthropology confronted these issues in a sequence of historical encounters, and it assembled its stock of working ideas accord-
ingly. Each encounter provoked reactions that later informed the
positions taken during the next turn. The issue of <u>Reason</u> against
<u>Custom</u> and <u>Tradition</u> was raised by the protagonists of the Enlight-
enment against their adversaries, the advocates of what Isaiah Berlin
called the Counter-Enlightenment (1982). In the wake of this debate, Marx and Engels transformed the arguments advanced by both
sides into a revolutionary critique of the society that had given rise
to both positions. The arguments put forward by this succession of
critics in turn unleashed a reaction against all universalizing schemes
that envisioned a general movement of transcendence for humankind. This particularism was directed against Newtonian physics,
Darwinian biology, Hegelian megahistory, and Marxian critiques, on
the debatable premise that they all subjugated the human world to
some <u>ultimate teleological goal</u>. The main target of this reaction was
Marxism, which invited attack both for its scientism and for its pre-
diction of a socialist overturn of prevailing society.

Some of these critiques took the form of a refusal to have anything to do with "metaphysics." These protesters wanted to counter

the seduction of abstract theorizing and to return to basics, to a more "natural" and "immediate" relationship with the facts of "real life." Others refused to countenance any application of the methods drawn from the natural sciences to the study of history, literature, and the arts. They insisted that these disciplines dealt with "mind," and hence with phenomena that were irregular, subjective, and colorful. Such phenomena, it was argued, were not amenable to the objectifying, emotionally neutral, and generalizing procedures of the natural sciences but required appropriate methodologies of their own.

This discussion takes up the arguments successively advanced by each "turn" and explores some of their implications. It begins with the conflict between the Enlightenment and its enemies, because the anthropological discipline as a whole owes its very identity to the antinomies then laid out. Indeed, it has drawn the bulk of its energy from efforts to negotiate between these distinctive modes of comprehending the world.

The Enlightenment

The Enlightenment, a philosophical movement in late-seventeenth- and eighteenth-century Europe, arose as an effort to shake off the weight of institutions and ideas that had immersed the continent in brutal religious and political conflicts and to renew hope by advocating a new vision of human possibilities. In contrast to earlier views that understood the human condition as tainted by "original sin," the Enlighteners saw humans as neither good nor bad but as perfectible. They spoke in favor of rationalism and empiricism, and they subjected social and political arrangements to skeptical analysis where they appeared to fall short of these ideals. To improve humanity, they advocated new forms of nontheological learning as avenues of reform. They were opposed by numerous movements that arose in the late eighteenth and early nineteenth centuries to counter these assertions, together with the intellectual and political styles associated with them. We owe the notion of "ideology" to the Enlightenment; the concept of "culture," as well as that of "society," derive from efforts to reverse the effects of that movement.

The Enlightenment envisaged the past and the future of the world in terms of such powerful yet abstract concepts as Reason and Progress. Its proponents spoke in the name of a common and universal humanity. They hoped to dispel the darkness of the Middle Ages by exposing consciousness to the clarifying light of reason and to free natural instinct and talent from the bonds of accumulated cant and hypocrisy. "Écrasez l'infame!" cried Voltaire, and meant by it a call for the destruction of religious dogma and superstition, the abolition of error, and the installation of a regime of truth based on reason.

The leaders of the Enlightenment did not all think alike, and the movement took variant forms in different regions of Europe. Some of its advocates, such as Condillac and Rousseau, even combined arguments both for and against it in their own work, as did some of the later Romantics who would become their opponents. Thus, Condillac saw reason as fundamental to both human nature and language, but he also gave support to the antagonists of universalism by stressing "the culture-bound quality of national languages" (Aarsleff 1982, 31). Rousseau focused most of his work on elucidating the general predicaments of being human, but he also made much of historical and cultural particularisms, as when he represented himself as a "Citizen of Geneva" in his project for a Corsican constitution and in his plan for the creation of a government in newly independent Poland (Petersen 1995). Conversely, the English and French protagonists of the Enlightenment strongly influenced their German counterpart Immanuel Kant, as well as the nationalist philosopher Fichte (called by some the first National Socialist) and the linguistic relativists Herder and von Humboldt, who came to see in language the quintessential expression of a *Volksgeist*. Some Enlighteners saw reason incarnated in logic and mathematics; others envisaged a return to Nature through a schooling of the senses. Some looked to education as the chief instrument for the correction of "error," while others wanted to install the truth by ending the domination of society by "tyrants and priests"; where the true workings of reason were obscured by oppressors, its light could be rekindled by removing these princes of darkness. Still others identified the cutting edge of reason with the novel machine invented by Dr. Guillotine.

Yet all would have resonated to Kant's slogan of *sapere aude,* the call to take courage in using one's own reason to gain and apply knowledge. As Kant saw it, the Enlightenment would permit humanity to shed its immaturity, which had been fostered by dependence on the guidance of others, and bring on a real maturity grounded in the autonomous use of reason. This meant in practice that humans could now break through the limits erected by cultural tradition and political domination and could confront the world rationally, choosing the most efficient means to achieve posited ends.

The appeal to reason, however, entailed consequences. One must not forget to ask who is using reason, rationality, logic, and emotional neutrality to do what to whom. As states and enterprises around the world incorporated the Enlightenment appeal to reason to enhance their managerial efficiency, the application of instrumental logic often exacted an exorbitant price. Rule by reason appealed most directly to state managers and private entrepreneurs and to scientists and intellectuals. Adopted by these strata, it invested them with a professional sense of superiority, which they could direct at the unenlightened obduracy of others. Those charged with dispensing reason can readily tag others as opponents of progress. Down to the present, the protagonists of reason have seen themselves as apostles of modernity. They have advocated industrialization, specialization, secularization, and rational bureaucratic allocation as reasoned options superior to unreasoned reliance on tradition.

One of the ideas that came out of the turmoil produced by the Enlightenment was "ideology." The term actually had an inventor in Antoine Destutt de Tracy (1754–1836), who saw himself as the intellectual heir of the eighteenth-century philosopher Étienne Bonnot de Condillac. Arguing against Descartes's acceptance of "self-evident truths," Condillac had championed "the testimony of the senses" obtained through observation and experiment, as advocated by the British empiricists Francis Bacon and John Locke. In the wake of the French Revolution, in 1795, Destutt de Tracy was asked by the Revolutionary Convention to create a research center for the "analysis of sensations and ideas" within the newly founded Institut National. Destutt de Tracy defined ideology as the *"science des idées"* (Barth 1974, 9); his book on the *Éléments d'idéologie* of 1801 (1824–1826) envisioned the research program of the new center as an effort to study ideas naturalistically, indeed as part of zoology. In the service of this goal one of the members of the institute, Joseph-Marie Degérando (1772–1842), drew up a very modern-sounding study guide for an ethnography of Australian natives.

It soon became evident, however, that the "ideologues" pursued contradictory goals (Hall 1978, 10). On one level, they wanted to understand how people perceived sensations, transformed them into ideas, and then communicated these ideas to others. On another level, they hoped that such inquiries would not only illuminate processes of thought but also produce theories that could free thought from "the yoke of prejudices." The study of ideology thus embodied from the start a wish to subject ideas to the dispassionate eye of science, and another wish to define the really *true* ideas that could found a just society and magnify human happiness. The contradiction soon evoked the wrath of no less a critic than Napoleon Bonaparte. Napoleon had joined the institute enthusiastically in 1797, during the years of his ascent to power. Yet, once embarked on his imperial career and faced with renegotiating relations with the Catholic Church, he began to see the freethinking and republican "ideologues" as obstacles to his assumption of imperial authority. Accusing them of grounding the laws of men in "gloomy metaphysics" instead of basing them on "a knowledge of the human heart and of the lessons of history," he disbanded their research section in 1803. They became for him major imaginary enemies bent on his undoing. In the wake of the disastrous Russian campaign in 1812, he even denounced them as the chief cause of "all the misfortunes which have befallen our beloved France" (in Barth 1974, 27).

The Counter-Enlightenment

In the wake of the French Revolution, marked first by the Terror and then by French military expansion, many followers of the Enlightenment deserted its cause, convinced like the Spanish painter Francisco Goya that the dream of reason breeds monsters. Other protagonists of the emerging Counter-Enlightenment were true reactionaries who set their faces against any party that advocated universal liberty, equality, and fraternity for all humankind. They felt most directly threatened by the revolution in France, which at one fell swoop abolished distinctions between aristocrats and plebeians. Still others sought to defend feeling, faith, and local tradition against the encroachment of Reason proclaimed by the Enlighteners. At the roots of this reaction lay the protests of people—self-referentially enclosed in the understandings of localized communities—against the leveling and destruction of their accustomed arrangements. Together these varied conservative responses to change ignited the first flickering of the relativistic paradigm that later unfolded into the key anthropological concept of "culture."

These conservatives were soon joined by recruits from the new cadre of "nationalists," who came to resent the ways in which revolutionary France expanded its sway and influence abroad. These new nationalists protested the surging conquests of the revolutionary armies, as well as French claims that they were dispensing freedom by abrogating local custom and installing new civic legal codes premised on teachings of the Enlightenment. The anti-French reaction grew especially strong in the Germanies, primarily in the regions associated with Prussia, although groups in other regions too, such as the Rhineland and Bavaria, long sympathized with the revolutionary cause. The conflict between the Enlightenment and the Counter-Enlightenment in the Germanies is often portrayed as a battle for the German spirit fought out between France and the true German patriots; but for some decades attitudes were not that clearly polarized. Thus, Kant, Hegel, and Fichte all greeted the advent of the French Revolution with enthusiasm, and they all owed much to Rousseau. Herder, who became a major defender of national identities, was influenced by Condillac, while Wilhelm von Humboldt, who became a leader of the Prussian movement for renewal, spent years in Paris, in association with Destutt de Tracy's ideologues. Some influential individuals, such as the Baltic "Sage of the North" Johann Georg Hamann (1730–1788), were Enlighteners in the first part of their lives and enemies of the movement in the second. French and German identities certainly came to be locked in opposition, but this was the outcome of a long process of political change, and not—as nationalists on both sides have depicted it—the result of an instantaneous cultural repulsion.

Viewed in broad outlines, where the Enlightenment celebrated reason the Counter-Enlightenment affirmed a belief in faith and in the primordial wisdom of the senses. Hamann proclaimed that God was "a poet, not a mathematician," that reason was "a stuffed dummy," and that Nature was not a repository of primordial virtue but "a wild dance" (Berlin 1982, 169). Where the Enlightenment projected the ideal of a common humanity with universal goals, its opponents exalted differentiation, particularism, and parochial identities. The émigré Savoyard aristocrat Joseph de Maistre (1753–1821)— a founder of sociology, as well as arguably a precursor of fascism (Bramson 1961; Berlin 1990)—rejected human universalism outright: "The constitution of 1795, just like its predecessors, was made for *man*. But there is no such thing as *man* in the world. I have seen Frenchmen, Italians, Russians. . . . But as for man, I declare that I have never met him in my life" (in Berlin 1990, 59). Others, notably the East Prussian Johann Herder (1744–1803), undertook to write a universal history of humanity but transformed the project into a synthetic presentation of the multiple histories of particular peoples.

Herder read the language and folklore of each people as expressions of its unconscious inner genius, its characteristic Volksgeist. This drew on Condillac's idea that "each language expresses the character of the people who speak" (in Aarsleff 1982, 346). This formulation could be employed to modify Enlightenment universalism in order to envisage a pluralistic assembly of particular peoples, each seen as imbued with a distinctive "spirit." One outcome was a fateful conflation of linguistic studies with an ethnically based psychology (Whitman 1984). This orientation was even more evident in the linguistics of Wilhelm von Humboldt, who reinforced the notion that the inner organizational form at the root of each language was neither static nor passive but constituted "a spiritual driving force" (Verburg 1974, 215). Subsequently, as Prussian minister of education, Humboldt channeled the German educational system into *Bildung,* the schooling of the academically educated elites toward a neohumanist revival of the classics, including studies in philology and psychology. As the nineteenth century grew ever more nationalist, this fusion of disciplines equipped German nationalists with a new "spiritual" weapon to combat materialism. It also produced a new science of ethnic psychology (*Völkerpsychologie*), which strove to demonstrate that "the *Volksgeist* was the unifying psychological essence shared by all members of a *Volk* and the driving force of its historical trajectory" (Bunzl 1996, 28). This echoed, a half-century later, Destutt de Tracy's project to establish a science of human ideas, yet it transformed that science from a universal project of humankind into a psychology of national identities.

"Culture" stems from this orbit of German usage. The term was originally processual, being drawn from "cultivation," or agriculture, and then applied to *cultura animi,* the cultivation of young minds to aspire to adult ideals. In this later sense it came into Germany in the seventeenth century. There in the eighteenth century its meaning was extended from the development of individuals to include cultivation of the moral and intellectual capacities of nations and humankind (Kroeber and Kluckhohn 1952, 18–23). The shift in emphasis from "culture" as cultivation to culture as the basic assumptions and guiding aspirations of an entire collectivity—a whole people, a folk, a nation—probably occurred only in the course of the nineteenth century, under the promptings of an intensifying nationalism. Then each people, with its characteristic culture, came to be understood as possessing a mode of perceiving and conceptualizing the world all of its own. For a time ethnologists modified this view by insisting that the components of any one culture were rarely homegrown but rather were assembled over time from many sources and articulated in diverse ways. Yet increasingly, the question of what made the sum of these culture traits cohere was answered by claiming that the aggregates of culture traits from hither and yon were worked into a common totality by the unifying "spirit" manifest in each particular people and in that people alone. Fortified by that inner unity, each separate and distinctive people could resist the universalizing claims of enlightened Reason.

The concept of "society" was transformed in similar fashion. In the first flush of the Enlightenment, people imagined that a new "civil society" would pack off kings and emperors into exile, disband the royally protected social and political corporations, and disassemble the hierarchical arrangements of precedence and privilege. Yet as revolution after revolution leveled gradations and perquisites of rank in one country after another, many began to ask where this process of decomposition would stop and how any kind of integral social order could be restored. How were citizens, now stripped of the robes of status and expelled into the faceless crowd, ever to regain a stake in the new arrangements, a sense of belonging, a foothold in secure and collectively shared values? The search for answers prompted the development of sociology, conceived as a new science able to provide "an antidote against the poison of social disintegration" (Rudolf Heberle, in Bramson 1961, 12). Perhaps social order could once again be

stabilized by building up face-to-face social interaction and association in primary groups and by reinforcing these linkages through appeal to common values.

Marx and Engels

This vision of society was challenged from the 1830s on
by two kindred spirits from Germany: Karl Marx, a journalist from
the Rhineland, and Friedrich Engels, the scion of a family of textile
entrepreneurs from Westphalia. They combined in a new way the intellectual tradition of the Enlightenment with critiques of the dissolution of institutional ties, as advanced by conservatives (Bramson
1961, 21). The two friends followed the Enlightenment in the convic-
tion that reason could unmask falsehood and proclaim truth. They
believed that employing reason would help uncover the sources of
human misery, which—like many conservatives of their time—they
located in the emergence of individuals disconnected from any web
of mutual rights and obligations through the breakdown of older
communal ways of life. They further held that humans could reach a
greater realm of freedom through reliance on their own efforts, including the use of reason, without invoking the consolations of religion. They did not think, however, that such a transformation could
be accomplished by the force of ideas alone, or that the envisioned
change would come about by spreading truthful ideas through education. They insisted that human life was shaped not by the workings of the "Spirit" embodied in reason but through production:
human practice in transforming nature to answer human needs, by
means of tools, organization, and the employment of "practical reason." Practice does not merely contemplate and observe the world;
it works to alter the world, using reason to further the process and
evaluate its results.

Marx and Engels were convinced, moreover, that the prevalence
of misery and untruth among humans was due neither to original sin
nor inherent human incapacity but to a class society with a social system that severed people from communities and interdicted their access to resources. Under these circumstances, the dispossessed were

forced to hire themselves out to members of another class who benefited from this transfer of labor, and who developed rationalizations
purporting to explain why this state of affairs was to the advantage
of possessors and dispossessed alike. Marx and Engels were to call
these rationalizations "ideology."

By the time they adopted the term, "ideology" had lost the initial meaning of a "natural history" or "science" of ideas that Destutt
de Tracy had bestowed on it and had come to mean thought formulated to serve some particular social interest. In 1844–1845, in Paris,
Marx took notes on Destutt de Tracy, as well as on the materialists
of the radical Enlightenment Paul d'Holbach and Claude Helvetius
(Barth 1974, 74, 303). At this time he also noted that "ideology" had
been transformed from a positive term into one of denunciation.

Marx and Engels adopted this reformulated concept of "ideology" and connected it with their own analysis of capitalist class society. The term "class" to denote a segment of society was then also
new in English usage. It derived from the Latin classics of antiquity,
where it designated classes of draftees in the call to arms (Quine 1987,
23). In English usage it first meant a cohort in school. Yet references
to "lower classes" appeared in England in 1772; "higher classes" and
"middle" or "middling classes" followed in the 1790s; and "working
classes" appeared in about 1815 (Williams 1959, xiii). Equivalent terms
became popular in France in the 1830s (Hobsbawm 1962, 209). A
song called "La Proletarienne" appeared there in 1833, together with
a call to arms—"Aux armes, Proletaire" (Sewell 1980, 214). By 1837
Marx was writing to his father about the proletariat "as the idea in
the real itself" (Bottomore 1983, 74). In 1845 Engels published *The
Condition of the Working Class in England* (1971), based on two years
of experience in Manchester, and in 1845–1846 the two together
wrote *The German Ideology* ("abandoned to the criticism of the
mice" and not published until 1932) (Marx and Engels 1976), in which
they addressed both their political economic theory of the working
class and the issue of ideology. In that work they also formulated
their view that "the ideas of the ruling class are in every epoch the
ruling ideas: i.e. the class which is the ruling material force of society is at the same time its ruling intellectual force" (in Sayer 1989, 6).

In this initial axiomatic statement on ideology, Marx and Engels
followed the promptings of the Enlightenment to interpret the "rul-

ing ideas" as forms of "interested error," presented as ostensible truths intended to mystify the people about social reality and thus wielded as instruments of domination over hearts and minds. Unlike other Enlightenment thinkers, however, they did not ascribe this form of "interested error" either to the workings of a universal human nature or to agents of darkness trying to exploit it. For them humans were "corporeal, living, real, sensuous, objective beings," able to acquire real knowledge of the world by acting upon it, even if by that same token they were also "suffering, limited, and conditioned" creatures (Marx 1844, in Ollman 1976, 78, 80). Mastery of the world through labor, together with the capacity for language developed in the course of laboring together with their fellows, would multiply human knowledge and expand the human grasp upon the world. Practical engagement with the world would produce realistic thought and an "increasing clarity of consciousness, power of abstraction and of judgement" (Engels 1972, 255) while driving out "fantasies" that took no tangible object and only filled the mind with apprehension and fear.

In this perspective ideology was made to resemble religion, because—like religion—it mystified the real capacity of humans to change nature through active material practice and because it accentuated human dependence upon forces beyond their control. For Marx and Engels such mystification was due not to human nature or human weakness but to the connection of ideology with the contradictions posed by class society. Class society fostered illusions precisely because it was riven by the social polarization into the many who labor and the few who dominate the productive process. To deny or veil the resulting tensions, such a society produced ideology as "a particular, distorted kind of consciousness which conceals contradictions" (Larrain 1979, 50). Marx and Engels thus hoped that reason and political action based upon it could lift the veils of misrepresentation and allow knowledge to go forward unhampered by figments of the mind.

This phrasing of ideology as "the ruling ideas of the ruling class" is useful for its grasp of social realities, but its authors did not specify how it was to be understood. Do managers of the ruling class hire intellectual agents to produce ideas that exemplify their interests, or did they mean that the asymmetrical structure of society determines the conditions under which ideas are produced and propagated? Did their notion of ideology imply that the ruling ideas "reflect" or "mirror" the real power of the ruling class? Marx and Engels used these metaphors frequently. Alternatively, they spoke of ideas as "corresponding" to certain conditions "most appropriate" to them, as when Marx says that Protestantism, "with its cult of abstract man," is the most "suitable" (*entsprechendste*) form of religion for simple commodity producers exchanging equivalents of abstract labor (1923, 42). These terms resemble Max Weber's later concept of "elective affinity" (*Wahlverwandschaft*) between ideas and group interests, but Marx and Engels did not lay out how social relations were connected with particular ideational representations. Their language suggests a field of force, undergirded by productive relations, setting the terms for how people are to comprehend their world; but they left open the question of how particular forms of ideation arise and how some kinds of representation achieve precedence and power over others. The search for an adequate answer to that question continues in the present.

Soon after Marx and Engels advanced the notion of a link between ruling ideas and ruling classes, this theme vanished from their writings (Balibar 1988). It was replaced in 1867, in *Kapital*, by a new mode of analysis focused on "the fetishism of commodities." This phrasing appeared in the context of the notion that things produced for the market—commodities—embodied human labor deployed and allocated under the auspices of capitalist social relations. In this mode of production, human labor power, purchased by the capitalist in labor "markets," is incorporated into commodities. The workers then lose any connection with what they have produced, which belongs to the capitalist who paid them wages for their labor power. The goods are placed upon "commodity markets," and the proceeds from their sale belong to the capitalist. Thus animate human labor, which is a physical and cognitive attribute of people, and inanimate commodities produced by that labor are treated as if they belonged to the same category.

The merging of these qualitatively different entities, according to Marx, masks the real social relations that govern the way people are harnessed to the production process. Moreover, when worker-producers of commodities and buyers of commodities are equated, the social relations among workers, employers, and buyers are all made to look like relations among the commodities themselves. "It is nothing but the definite social relations between men themselves which assumes here, for them, the fantastic form of a relation be-tween things." Just as in "the misty realm of religion . . . the products of the human brain appear as autonomous figures endowed with a life of their own. . . . So it is in the world of commodities with the prod-ucts of men's hands" (Marx 1976, 165). This notion does not rely on a model of ideology as distortions and errors promulgated by a rul-ing class; rather, it traces the source of deception to a particular kind of social reality, that of capitalism. That reality mixes what is real with fictions; as a result, the participants in the transactions are deceived about the reality of capitalist social relations.

Marx drew the concept of fetishism from studies of religion. The term came from the French scholar Charles De Brosses, who de-scribed in his book on the *Culte des Dieux fétiches* (1760) the behavior of West African carvers who supposedly first sculpted wooden images ("a thing made," *feitiço* in Portuguese), to then treat them as if they were divine beings. De Brosses, like others after him, saw in this "fe-tishism" evidence of primitive, nonlogical modes of thought. Marx, however, applied it to the structural effects of a particular mode of mobilizing social labor—that of capitalism.

Marx applied a similar logic to characterize the structure of non-capitalist social formations, where—as he understood it—a chief or despot, standing above individuals or communities, embodied the sway of an encompassing community or state, thus making that wider entity "appear as a person." This interpretation has been revived in modern Marxian anthropology. For example, Jonathan Friedman used it to characterize the role of the chief in Southeast Asian tribal groups as representative of the higher unity, exemplified in sacrifices to the territorial spirits (1979). Pierre Bonte applied it to the "cattle complex" in African pastoralist societies, where cattle constitute the subsistence base, wealth that underwrites descent marriage, and of-ferings to the supernaturals: "cattle fetishism is thought of and jus-tified as reproducing the supernatural order" (1981, 38–39).

In the end, Marx's efforts left open the question of just what it may be in "human nature" that prompts the recurrent emergence in human doings of "phantasmagoric forms." Since Marx and Engels both saw human consciousness as determined primarily by the historically installed mode of production, they would have been loath to trace fetishism to any proclivities of human minds or to the neuropsychological architecture of the human organism. Yet it has been plausibly argued that humans share general tendencies to engage objects in the world as if they were human and to endow them with human desires, will, and capacities (Godelier 1977, 169–85; Guthrie 1993). These tendencies were abetted by the human possession of language, which postulates abstractions that can then be treated as animate beings and analogically endowed with humanlike capabilities. From this perspective, fetishism represents an escalation of animism, in which entities are treated as animate and superior to humans yet amenable to human entreaties to engage in transactions (Ellen 1988). Therefore, one might rephrase the issue of fetishism in cultural terms and ask which entities come to be selected for this process, under what circumstances, and why. Of special interest would be to ascertain how fetishes, already raised to a position of superiority, model relations of asymmetrical power in society. It may be possible, therefore, to combine Marx's suggestion that the crucial nexus of structural power governing social labor will produce characteristic representations or misrepresentations in thought with an anthropological analysis of ideational complexes such as fetishism.

Reactions against Metaphysics and Teleology

While the opposing parties of the Enlightenment and Counter-Enlightenment disputed the political and intellectual terrain between them under the flags of Reason, Revolution, and Science against Faith, Tradition, and Poetic Subjectivity, a cohort of new protagonists, pursuing a different interest, would alter the terms of the debate. One way they did so was by attacking as "metaphysics" all efforts to subsume human behavior under general laws. Metaphysics was said to pile abstract theory upon abstract theory, until theorizing itself seemed to impede any connections with "real life." These critics were especially opposed to "grand" theories that they accused—sometimes mistakenly—of trying to tie human fate to a central teleological dynamic. Among the teleologies thus denounced, favorite targets were Hegel's unfolding of the workings of a world spirit; Marxism, treated as a form of economic determinism; and Darwinism, interpreted as an evolutionary teleology that favored the victors in the "struggle for existence." The antidote to such universal scenarios was thought to lie in sound, practical, and down-to-earth methodology, without recourse to metaphysics of any kind.

This apotheosis of methodology above theory first took the name of "pragmatism" (Charles Peirce, William James), although a proliferation of intellectual currents added "empirio-criticism" (Ernst Mach) and "logical positivism" (G. E. Moore, Rudolf Carnap, Karl Popper) to the antimetaphysical repertoire. The search for a more immediate contact with "real life" caused some of these critics to associate their perspectives with Darwinism and thus reintroduce biological theorizing through a back door, but all embraced the notion that ideas were usable only if grounded in acceptable methods. When it entered anthropology in the early twentieth century, this "pragmatic turn" prompted a decisive move toward fieldwork as the central methodology capable of yielding adequate knowledge about human doings.

REAFFIRMING "MIND"

Another critical response to "metaphysics" did not reject it entirely but opposed efforts to apply the methods of natural science to the study of history and the human sciences. The "subjectivists" thought it was necessary to "declare war on science" (Wilhelm Windelband), since approaches drawn from the natural sciences could not do justice to human vitality in passion, imagination, energy, and will. Science, it was argued, was unsuited to the study of human minds, subjective and autonomous entities that operated through language and culture. Minds had to be studied in the plural, and not as instances of a universal human mind. Therefore, it was also necessary to abandon evolutionary attempts to trace the development of humankind as a whole and to end efforts to define a "psychic unity of man." Above all, these critics hoped to specify the varied forms through which the mind "apprehended" the world and imposed order upon it. In anthropology, beginning with Bastian and

Boas, such attitudes underwrote a "mentalist turn" that emphasized the diversity of culturally constituted "minds." This programmatic shift focused on language as the major vehicle for human communication, seeing language not as unitary but as manifesting itself in a plurality of languages.

This shift drew in large part on the German reaction against the reign of universal reason preached by the Enlightenment, but it was reinforced as well by political and economic motivations. Early in the nineteenth century, the advent of capitalism had been hailed by many as a breakthrough to a new freedom. Markets were increasingly freed from monopolistic governmental controls and interference, and industrial development promised liberation from tributary dependence and toil; the diffusion of "free" thought held out prospects of delivering the multitudes from the fetters of absolutism and religious orthodoxy. By the end of the century, however, intensifying capitalism had revealed a darker side. Increasingly social critics, both socialist and conservative, pointed to the numbers of people who had been stripped of rights to the resources of field and forest upon which they had once relied for a livelihood, to the uncertainties in industrial employment associated with the business cycle, and to the frequently exploitative character of industrial employment itself. At the same time, increasing numbers of people became aware of the terror and brutality associated with imperialist expansion abroad.

The entrepreneurial class and its supporters came under attack from both the Left and Right, as much for its dedication to Mammon as for its acceptance of the status quo now that its own privileges had been assured. There were reactions against "materialism," understood as a growing proclivity to luxuriate in material well-being. Other critics feared the spread of equality, which they associated with a loss of recognition for individual capacity and achievement. Still others bemoaned the weakening of the sense of heroism and sacrifice once associated with the military aristocracy, the rationalization of social life through the growth of bureaucracy, and the dismantling of comforting traditions.

These various changes made the future seem less promising, sometimes positively threatening. There was widespread concern among the literate about biological and psychological "degeneration," issuing in Germany in lamentations about "cultural pessimism." Increasingly this mood called into question the promises held out by the advocates of Reason. The Romantics had already challenged Enlightenment values by questioning the claims of Reason, and these claims had been shaken further from within the camp of Reason itself. The early Enlightenment understood Reason as the strategic cognitive faculty that would reveal the truth of Nature kept hidden by error and superstition; thus stripped bare, Nature would show itself as an orderly system of prudent imperatives. As "the great infidel" Scotsman David Hume pointed out, however, we lack a convincing basis for testing what goes on in our minds against an orderly and causally determined sequence of facts in Nature: all our thinking is "derived either from our outward or inward sentiment." As a result, Hume asserted, Reason could not guarantee a reliable picture of Nature, and hence one could not derive any rules of ethics from the workings of Nature: "It is not irrational for me to prefer the destruction of half the world to the pricking of my finger" (in Solomon 1979, 73, 76). The Romantic Johann Georg Hamann used Hume to argue that, in the absence of certain and reliable knowledge, any correspondence between Reason and Nature had to be based on "faith." Thus, as Ernest Gellner put it, Reason "cut its own throat" (1988, 135).

Hume had argued that all our ideas and memories are not "truths of reason" but merely matters of "habit." As the universal values of the Enlightenment were increasingly challenged by defenders of local and national traditions, such habits came to be understood as variable both in the course of history and among different groups around the globe. This stripped "habits of the mind" of any claim to universal dominion or validity, rendering them instead historically and ethnologically particular and relative. As cultural groups began to look inward and to ask what made them distinctive, furthermore, they began to stress differences in the qualities of their minds, the nature of their special kind of "spirit," their distinctive kind of subjective "consciousness."

THE NEO-KANTIANS

This psychological "reorientation" had a specific impact on Wilhelm Dilthey, who sought to replace natural-science models in the writing of history with a phenomenological approach that could delineate meaningful patterns of thought. Dilthey's concerns were taken up in turn by various schools of "neo-Kantians," who sought to sharpen the distinction between the natural sciences as nomothetic and the cultural sciences as idiographic. They came to define these idiographic sciences as the study of the mental categories that permit people to construct their distinctive life worlds, and they devoted their energies to developing strict interpretive methods for this kind of study. They accepted Kant's insistence that the human mind was not a tabula rasa on which perceptions were recorded as on a "white sheet of paper" but an organ that possessed a priori the ability to construct mental categories and thus make knowledge possible. For Kant, as for the neo-Kantians, these categories were not innate in themselves; what was innate was the human requirement for categories in order to inhabit this world, whatever particular conceptual schemata might specify these categories.

How we structure our knowledge of the external world also became a central problem for the anthropologist Franz Boas. Boas, who read Kant in his igloo in Baffin Land in 1883 as the outside temperature hit forty degrees below zero, moved from a "rather hirsute" materialism (Stocking 1968, 140) toward a neo-Kantian conception of culture as a study of "the human mind in its various historical, and, speaking more generally, ethnic environments" (p. 160; also pp. 143, 152). This neo-Kantian emphasis led Boas to a form of ethnography that differed from that of the British functionalists. Where the functionalists emphasized behavior in the genesis of social and cultural forms, Boas saw culture as ideas in action. This understanding was to shape his study of the Kwakiutl, to whom he devoted a major part of his anthropological efforts.

The neo-Kantian movement developed numerous variants, but its two most important "schools" were centered respectively at the University of Marburg and in the Southwestern "cultural province of the upper Rhine" (Hughes 1961, 46), at the universities of Freiburg, Heidelberg, Strassbourg (then in German hands), and Basel. The Marburgers focused on the origins and development of scientific knowledge. Their most notable exponent was Ernst Cassirer (1874–1945)— the first Jewish rector at a German university—who charted the changes from substantial to relational concepts in European thought from the late Middle Ages to the present and who later focused on the role played by language in the formation of scientific knowledge. In contrast to the Marburgers, who looked to science as the proto-type of knowledge, the Southwesterners insisted on drawing a sharp line between the nomothetic acquisition of knowledge in the natural sciences and Dilthey's idiographic method for study of the "sciences of the spirit" (*Geisteswissenschaften*) that embraced history and the humanities.

WEBER

The most important figure influenced by the South-western neo-Kantians was the sociologist Max Weber (1864–1920), who studied at Heidelberg. Although he achieved considerable intel-lectual and political prominence in Germany during his lifetime, his work came to be known outside Germany only by slow increments, through translated papers and essays (with his political writings ex-cluded). His major book on *Wirtschaft und Gesellschaft* (*Economy and Society*) was not translated into English in its entirety until 1968.

Weber's politics crucially influenced his interests and choice of top-ics. He was born into a Germany unified by Bismarck, whose power base lay in Prussia. The state was governed by an alliance of Junker landowners with civil bureaucrats and army officers, many of them recruited from Junker families. This class alliance set the new state on the road to industrialization under capitalist auspices, but—in contrast to England, the leader in capitalist development—it did not grant the class of capitalist entrepreneurs a role in managing the af-fairs of state. Weber wanted a strong Germany, able to play its part in "the eternal struggle for the maintenance and cultivation of our national integrity" (in Giddens 1972, 16). In his estimation, the tra-ditional classes leading Germany were unsuited to the task of build-ing a successful industrial society, while the ascending class of the liberal bourgeoisie and the new class of proletarians were unqualified for political leadership. Thus, his famous work *The Protestant Ethic and the Spirit of Capitalism* of 1920 (Weber 1930) not only was in-tended to demonstrate the importance of religion in economic de-velopment but was written to "sharpen the political consciousness of the bourgeoisie" in Germany (Giddens 1972, 12). To advance Ger-man development, Weber said, it would be necessary to break the political power of the Junker class, control the state bureaucracy, and reform the parliamentary system of the state in order to draw the socialist working class into participation in government and to support capitalist development. This, however, would also require separating the workers from their Marxist-inspired Social Democratic leaders, whom he characterized as petit bourgeois innkeepers and revolutionary visionaries, likely to amplify bureaucracy and thus choke off industrial growth.

Weber's sociology played out a number of neo-Kantian themes. Weber rejected any kind of general causal theory, especially the economic determinism then preached by the Social Democrats, who predicted an inexorable forward march of world history based on the development of the economy. Instead, he always concentrated on the study of particular cases. Sociology might recognize repetitive patterns or variations on common themes and propose "hypothesis-forming models" (Kalberg 1994, 12). Such models might draw on a wide range of comparative studies, but they were merely "ideal types," to be used to examine particular cases, not to chart any law-like unilineal process. While Weber saw rationalization—the imposition of a means-ends calculus upon relations—as a recurrent trend in the world and feared that bureaucratic rationalization would enclose the human spirit in an "iron casing" (the usual translation as "iron cage" is in error), he "always refused to present rationalization as the self-unfolding logic of history" (Arato 1978, 191–92).

Weber further denied universal and dominant power to the economic factor: economics was likely to play a major role in framing the possibilities of any concrete situation, but it would co-occur always with multiple other social and ideational factors. Methodologically it was always necessary, Weber held, to investigate the "meanings" that action held for the acting individual, and not to understand people simply as products of social forces. Following the lead of Dilthey, he saw such investigation as involving *Verstehen*, empathetic understanding reached by putting oneself in the position of others, in order to comprehend how they themselves define their situation and the purposes of their actions. Many of his treatises dealt with ideas that shaped the characteristic orientations to religious or economic action. These orientations always addressed particular social contexts; they defined the "meaning" of action for individuals and underwrote their ability make "sense" of the world. Weber's study of such orientations and their "carrier" groups retains an enduring importance for our understanding ideas in relation to the conditions of specific social groups. Yet he saw that relationship as potential but not determined, and he refused to develop any general theory of how ideas were shaped in interaction with economy and society. In his most general statement on the matter, Weber opined: "Not ideas, but material and ideal interests directly govern man's conduct. Yet very frequently the 'world images' which have been created by 'ideas' have, like switchmen, determined the tracks along which action has been pushed by the dynamics of interests" (in Gerth and Mills 1946, 63–64).

Combining Marxism and Neo-Kantianism

Understanding how Weber related to Marx has long constituted a cottage industry in the social sciences. Some scholars have stressed Weber's tragic vision of human life as fatefully threatened by rationalization. Others have cast him as a precursor of National Socialism in his views about the need for a state based on concentrated power and his call for a mobilization of the working class on behalf of national capitalist development. For some sociologists, like Talcott Parsons, Weber offered an alternative to Marx. More recently, as time has passed and the passionate disputes of yesterday have become muted, it has become easier to recognize the ways in which the Marxian and Weberian legacies converge and intersect (Turner 1981; Sayer 1991). My own sense is that Marx and Weber complement one another, each addressing a different level of relationships. Even in the period around World War I, however, when the issues underlying their differences still provided flammable tinder for politics, some major figures worked to combine their apparently divergent perspectives and to bring them to bear conjointly upon social science.

With the rise of Marxian methods of inquiry, there developed Marxian variants that attempted to combine Marxism with approaches influenced by neo-Kantian thought. Two of these focus on the relationship between ideas and power and are especially pertinent to anthropological understandings. One is represented by the work of Karl Mannheim (1893–1947); the other, by that of Antonio Gramsci (1891–1937).

Mannheim was destined to become one of the "free-floating" intellectuals he later described. Born in Budapest, he joined the radical "Sunday Circle" that included Gyorgy Lukács; and, like Lukács, he fled to Germany in the wake of the failed Hungarian revolution in 1919. Hitler's grasp for power in 1933 then forced him to move to England. While in Germany, he—like Lukács—came into contact with Max Weber, then intent on developing his neo-Kantian approach to a systematic sociology, and both Lukács and Mannheim would attempt to combine Marx with Weber. In *History and Class Consciousness* (1971), Lukács used Weber's concept of "objective possibility" to endow the Marxian proletariat with a "potential" (as opposed to an empirical) class consciousness. Yet where Lukács then opted for communism, Mannheim moved toward sociology.

Mannheim accepted the hypothesis of a link between forms of knowledge and social groupings, but he also insisted in Weberian fashion that class intersected with many other memberships in generational cohorts, status groups, professions, and elites. His methodology, used to demonstrate the ties between social entities and ideas, was "essentially anthropological" (Wallace 1970, 174). His essay on "Conservative Thought" in Germany (1953) pointed to the declining nobility as the main social base of support for an intelligentsia that produced conservative theories. The work also exemplified Mannheim's major concern with the social role of intellectuals. In a second work, *Ideology and Utopia* (1936), Mannheim counterposed varieties of ideology that supported the status quo, as against forms of utopian thought that envisioned alternative futures. He delineated different kinds of utopias: the orgiastic chiliasm of Thomas Münzer's Anabaptists; the liberal-humanitarianism of the Enlightenment, which embraced the idea of rational progress as well as German pietism's faith in progress under the stewardship of God; conservative counterutopias; and socialist-communist utopias. In Mannheim's method, each of these perspectives was to be depicted in its own terms, as a prerequisite for an eventual evaluative solution (1936, 98). His great hope was that sociology would affect politics by communicating to the contending participants the sources of their modes of action and would thus facilitate negotiations among them.

Gramsci combined Marx and neo-Kantianism in a different way, developing an approach to understanding how ideas are generated and distributed within a field of force. Born in Sardinia, he went on to study linguistics in Turin, where he was drawn into politics and became a leader of Italian communism. Arrested by the fascist regime in 1926, he was sent to prison, where he died in 1937.

A major influence on Gramsci was his intellectual engagement with the philosopher, historian, and political figure Benedetto Croce. Croce's historical work focused primarily on Italy, but he was strongly influenced by Dilthey and fused his vision of a psychological and phenomenological history with the Italian idealist tradition. Croce intentionally neglected the social and economic side of history and wrote Italian history as a political quest for moral consensus and liberty. Gramsci criticized Croce for his idealism but sought to translate his "ethico-moral moments of consent" into Marxian terms. He did this through his writings on the concept of "hegemony," in which he argued that class domination and influence did not merely rest on the formal political system and the state-operated apparatus of coercion but spread beyond state and politics into the social and cultural arrangements of daily life. "To win hegemony, in Gramsci's view," writes Terry Eagleton, "is to establish moral, political and intellectual leadership in social life by diffusing one's own 'world-view' throughout the fabric of society as a whole, thus equating one's own interests with the interests of society at large" (1991, 116).

The concept of hegemony has political roots. Initially used by Lenin to refer to political domination, it was elaborated by Gramsci to suggest that in the capitalist societies of the West—contrary to what might be true in Eastern Europe—political power could be gained through the construction of a predominant consensus rather than through revolutionary violence. In the West, states did not preempt all social arenas, relying instead on managing society through social and cultural influence; this, in turn, would allow opposition parties to resist this influence by developing counterhegemonic forms of their own. The balance between hegemony and counterhegemony would always be in flux. Thus, hegemony was envisaged not as a fixed state of affairs but as a continuous process of contestation.

As a political leader in a country only recently unified and marked by strong local and regional traditions built up around numerous towns, each surrounded by its own rural dependency, Gramsci was keenly aware of the sterility of a class-oriented politics anchored in a paradigm of a generalized working class conscious of universal interests. His political project was therefore to draw into an alliance segments of the working class, peasant groups, artisans, white-collar employees, and fractions of other classes. Such an alliance would then function as a "historic bloc"—unified politically as well as "culturally" under the leadership of the Communist Party and its allies.

Perhaps because Gramsci did not want to attract the attention of his prison guards, he was never explicit about how he envisaged the interplay between hegemonic processes and the state. Yet as Mussolini's chief political captive he surely did not think that state power could be won through song and dance alone. Once it is acknowledged, however, that hegemony must always be projected against the backdrop of the state, it becomes possible to identify hegemonic processes not only in the sphere of civil society outside the state but within state institutions as well. The state manages "ideological state apparatuses," such as schools, family, church, and media, as well as apparatuses of coercion (Althusser 1971), and state officials contend over policies within these institutional precincts. They do so, moreover, in interaction with society's open arenas. A number of different studies have exemplified these processes in the fields of education (Ringer 1969; Bourdieu 1989), in the social management of the state (Corrigan and Sayer 1985; Rebel 1991), in penology (Foucault 1977), and in military doctrine (Craig 1971). Anthropologists have made use of the notion of hegemony as well, though all too often stripping it of its political specificity and intent (Kurtz 1996).

Drawing on Italian history, literature, and folklore, Gramsci sought to identify the social groups and cadres that "carried" the hegemonic process, as well as the centers and settlement clusters that took leading roles in the production and dissemination of hegemonic forms. In adopting this perspective, he was strongly influenced by his training in the Italian neo-linguistic (or spatial) school developed primarily by Matteo Giulio Bartoli at the University of Turin. These neo-linguists described language change as a process whereby dominant speech communities built on their prestige to influence surrounding subaltern settlements (Lo Piparo 1979). Anthropologists familiar with the diffusionism of the American culture-historical school will recognize parallels with the idea of culture centers, sites of unusually intense cultural productivity that transmit traits and influences to the surrounding culture areas. Like these ethnologists, Gramsci did not see such relations as merely linguistic but as involving other aspects of culture as well. At the same time, he differed from the American scholars in clearly understanding that the hegemonic process did not move by its own momentum. It summoned up and employed power to produce and distribute semiotic representations and practices, favoring some and disfavoring others. Its effects would thus be <u>uneven in form and</u> intensity, affecting classes and groups differentially. Drawing distinctions among locations and groups of people, the process produced tensions among them, as well as between the hegemonic center and the groups within its sphere of influence.

In identifying the cadres at work in cultural dissemination, Gramsci was especially interested in how intellectuals, whom he saw as ideological specialists in formulating and explaining bodies of ideas, interacted with the carriers of what he called "common sense," the general understandings current among the popular masses. He saw this interaction as dynamic, with donors and recipients of ideas engaged in active interchange, each motivated by their own interests and perspectives. Since such interchanges were always contested, they gave rise to "unstable equilibria" between superordinates and subalterns.

Both Mannheim and Gramsci sought to combine Marxian grand theory with the local, regional and national particularism demanded by the neo-Kantians. For both men, this took the form of arguing that class was a major determinant of social alignments but that it was <u>only one such determinant</u> among many others. Both Mannheim and Gramsci related modes of ideation to the role of particular classes and groups, and both thought that common ideas might have a role to play in the rise of wider movements. Gramsci's work, in particular, offers a perspective on how such coalitions, organized to expand and solidify cultural influence, connect with power. Both figures were also concerned with how ideas were generated and disseminated, an interest that underlies their efforts to comprehend the role of intellectuals. This interest focused explicitly on the group affiliation and activities of particular kinds of "brain-workers." Yet it represents an advance from the mere charting of the relationship of ideas to interest groups, toward understanding *how* in fact ideas were constructed and propagated.

Pragmatism in Anthropology

Pragmatism had already scored major victories in the last quarter of the nineteenth century, but its impact on anthropology came later, in the period in and around World War I, and at first affected England primarily. There British functionalism—associated with the names of Bronislaw Malinowski and A. R. Radcliffe-Brown— began to insist on looking at systems of ideas in terms of their practical contributions to activity systems and societal arrangements. This stance excluded a concern with understanding ideas in their own right. Such a practice-oriented approach appealed to Marxists, especially those who preferred to regard ideas as epiphenomena of a determinant economic base. This pragmatic view of ideas was reinforced further by the rise of logical positivism—less a philosophy than an attitude of distrust of abstractions—which was ready to relegate all statements that failed to pass the test of logical consistency and empirical verification to the scrap heap.

The ascendance of these new perspectives yielded both benefits and losses. Tying ideas to their social context challenged scholars to go beyond seeing ideas as the abstract musings of the Spirit and to grasp their connections with the world. Discounting the influence of ideas and ideologies, however, also exacted a political and intellectual price, in that it caused the followers of pragmatism to neglect the significance of ideas in rousing and mobilizing people for action. Thus, many a well-intentioned rationalist simply would not believe, until it was too late, that scientifically unverifiable and irrational ideas could yet appeal to large numbers of people, and that beliefs in witchcraft, eliminationist anti-Semitism, or millenarianism could be taken seriously by apparently reasonable persons.

The new intellectual pragmatism proved extremely influential in anthropology, initially with markedly positive results. By emphasizing practice over ideation, stressing what was done over what was thought and said, functionalists and Marxists—each in their own way—scored important theoretical and methodological points. They educated anthropologists to separate statements of rules about what ought to be done from descriptions based on the observation of actual behavior, and they encouraged them to think about how rules related to action as a problem to be explored and not taken for granted. Until World War I, generations of anthropologists and folklorists had simply assumed that in studying "customs" they were also studying, simultaneously, ideas and the ways in which they were carried out in daily life. For them custom was "king"—"the tyranny of custom" confined behavior within prescribed limits. The new pragmatists, who preached "going to the people" or doing "fieldwork," challenged the unquestioned axiom of uniformity and its transgenerational replication through custom. Asking questions about the interplay of rule and behavior, pattern and action, structure and agency thus goes back in anthropology some sixty years.

Also long with us has been the related issue of how we are to imagine the unity of a "culture." Despite their announced refusal of metaphysics, many pragmatists in fact relied on theoretical premises to guide their work, and this was true also of anthropologists who preached the virtues of fieldwork. Malinowski followed Mach in understanding science as a practical human adaptation to nature, which enhanced the chances of biological survival, and he understood psycho-bio-cultural integration as functional in the pursuit of "life." Radcliffe-Brown, in turn, followed Émile Durkheim in projecting the image of "society" as a solidary whole, pivoted on a social structure that provided a scaffolding for the allocation of jural rights and duties. Yet as soon as account was taken of the discrepancy between rules and behavior, it became evident that cultures and societies were internally differentiated and that this heterogeneity might give rise to very different concerns and expectations. Social and cultural arrangements varied by gender, birth order, generation, kinship, and affinity; by position in the division of labor and in the allocation of resources; by access to knowledge, information, and channels of communication; by accidents of the life cycle and life experience. There was a diversity of rules, as well as a diversity of behavior. Yet if this were so, how were such diversities brought together into unifying systems? That question has not yet received a satisfactory answer.

The pragmatic turn accentuated the difference between what was stipulated in rules and codified in ideas and what was actually done. It also initiated studies of how different activity systems in culture and society—and the ideas connected with them—were orchestrated in order to provide solutions to the practical problems of life. Considering how ideas fitted into social relations was clearly a gain, although looking at *how* imaginings function in group life furnishes no answers to *why* the relation obtains. Indeed, functionalism was intended explicitly to avoid "why" questions about origins, causes, or possible alternatives.

Developments in Linguistics

Each phase in the formulation of concepts aimed at explicating humankind, either in its universal aspect or in its national particularities, entailed notions of the role of language in shaping human minds and actions. During the Enlightenment, Condillac shifted interest away from efforts to define the fundamental logical structure of the mind toward a concern with how language grasped sensations and experience by means of signs. Prominent at the time was the thought that laying bare the roots of words could reveal how the human experience of interacting with nature might first have suggested signs to protohumans. Then the increasingly nationalist nineteenth century generally abandoned such inquiries into the panhuman origins of language and turned instead to the study of particular languages.

These studies were formulated along two different lines. One took its lead from Humboldt, who understood each language as an expression of vital *energeia*, motivated by each people's drive to express its spirit through a particular "inner form" of language. This approach converged with the neo-Kantian effort to render manifest the categories of thought informing the idiographic history of particular peoples. It came to influence American anthropology through a line of investigators that extends from Humboldt to Heyman Steinthal

(Humboldt's literary executor and one of the founders of Völkerpsychologie) to Franz Boas (Kluckhohn and Prufer 1959, 19), Edward
Sapir, and Benjamin Whorf. These scholars all built upon Humboldt's
strong linguistic relativism, while demurring from his occasional suggestion that some languages might have achieved a higher state of
perfection than others.

The other mode of inquiry, a comparative philology associated primarily with the name of Franz Bopp, sought to reveal historical linkages among languages by tracing similarities among formal patterns
of grammatical elements, as well as by noting continuities in meaning. The efforts of these comparative philologists to recover a common Indo-European protolanguage contributed to the development
of historical linguistics. With its intense formalism, their research
avoided any attempt to explain the relationship of language to mind,
but it did emphasize the autonomy of language in setting up "the
formal patterns of grammatical elements through which words are
linked and differentiated" (Culler 1977, 61).

From 1860 on, a strong reaction developed against both "the German mystical school" and Bopp's formalism. Scholars such as the linguist Michel Bréal and the historian-psychologist Hippolyte Taine
argued that there was need for a return to the eighteenth-century
Enlightenment view of language as a human activity (Aarsleff 1982,
290–91, 293–334). That new linguistics was subsequently formulated
by the Swiss scholar Ferdinand de Saussure (1857–1913), who heeded
Bréal's call for the study of language as an activity that "has no reality apart from the human mind" (in Aarsleff 1982, 382); but he combined this perspective with insights derived from the German neo-
grammarians, who strongly emphasized the intrinsic patterning of
grammar. In his courses in Paris and Geneva (1881–1891, 1907–1911),
as well as in the posthumous *Cours de linguistique générale* (1916),
edited by some of his students, Saussure argued that language was
neither the expression of a Volksgeist nor a set of independent forms.
In place of a concept of language that supplied words as tags for sensations received from the external world, Saussure defined language
as a purely internal mental "faculty governing signs" (1983, 11), free
from any involvement with an "informing spirit." With that faculty,
humans could create self-regulating systems of signs in the mind and
thus prove able to convey and receive information by arranging and

rearranging linguistic signs in purely formal ways. The systems created by this internal faculty he called *langue,* language. Each such langue could be characterized by rules, which arranged the elements available to it and maintained the formal relationships thus constituted. A language was able to reproduce itself as long as these relationships obtained.

The corollary of this new understanding was that ideas or knowledge structures could no longer be understood as having a stable content and significance in their own right but were merely temporary effects of particular ways of using language and employing signs. The "true nature of things may be said to lie not in things themselves, but in the relationships which we construct, and then perceive, *between* them" (Hawkes 1977, 17). Saussurean linguistics thus abandoned any notion of an immediate encounter with the world through language and began to treat reality as portrayed selectively by humanly imposed codes. This move, however, severed any physical or psychological link between the linguistic indicators (signifiers) and what they indicated (the signified). The indicators were no longer connected with their designata by any intrinsic relationship with reality. What seemed firm and stable now became merely provisional and contingent; the link between signs and what they "stood for" became arbitrary. The forms produced by this arbitrary connection had to be learned anew in each generation, by children from parents, and by linguists and ethnologists from their local tutors.

For Saussure a langue was a system located in the mind that made speech (*parole*) possible. Because the system of langue was for him closed, homogeneous, and self-regulating, it would also constitute an appropriate object for scientific inquiry, while parole, speech, was not properly part of the language system. It consisted for him merely of the heterogeneous and unpredictable ways in which individuals, differentiated by motivation and temperament, actualized or "executed" that system across a wide range of circumstances. This treatment of language did not have its source in neo-Kantianism as such, although his concept of the linguistic community was influenced by the work of Durkheim, who may be read as the protagonist in an ongoing argument with Kant. Durkheim's conclusion to *The Elementary Forms of the Religious Life,* first published in 1915, agreed with Kant that human ideation was governed by "permanent moulds for the mental life" that "are not made only to apply to the social realm; they reach out to all reality" (Durkheim 1947, 440). But it disagreed with Kant's locating the forms taken by these categories in the individual: the idea of *all* at the root of classifications could not have come from the individual, but only from society (p. 441). Saussure's linguistic categories, like Durkheim's "collective representations," were attributes of a collectivity, through a "faculty of mind" at work in that collectivity. Saussure, like the neo-Kantians, therefore accorded precedence to mental schemata over experience in dealing with the world, contributing to the forcefulness of the mentalistic turn.

Yet if Saussure's structuralist view of the workings of langue constituted the main strength of his approach, his view of speech as a domain of free variation through individual choice has proved the weak point of Saussurean linguistics. As such, it has invited criticisms, and also theoretical modifications and alternatives. One source of criticism was from linguists who agreed with Saussure that the gift of language resided in the mind but who thought that he had not gone far enough. Thus, Noam Chomsky took him to task for restricting langue to a system of static grammatical properties and for failing to recognize that grammatical rules also governed the creative construction of sentences uttered in the language of everyday life (1964, 59–60). Yet in making this critique, Chomsky himself revived the Saussurean dichotomy of langue and parole, now rebaptized as "competence" and "performance," with "competence" defined as the proper arena of linguistic concern and "performance" accorded only secondary status.

A quite different kind of critique raised questions about the relationship of langue and parole to variation in external social contexts. Three such critical stances bear particularly on the question of the relationship between ideas and power. One was that of Malinowski, who described himself as an "ethnographic empiricist." Malinowski elaborated his influential perspective on language and linguistics on the basis of field materials gathered in fieldwork in the Trobriand Islands between 1914 and 1918. He acknowledged that language had structure but at the same time distanced himself from Saussurean structuralism by asserting that language was "a mode of action, rather than a counter-sign of thought" (Firth 1964, 94).

Another critique of Saussure's langue was put forward by the Russian linguist Valentin N. Vološinov, who in 1929 published *Marxism and the Philosophy of Language,* which combined the perspectives of Marxism and linguistic structuralism. After it appeared in English translation in 1973, a review noted that it practically predated "all contemporary interests ranging from semiotics to speech act theory" (Yengoyan 1977, 701). The book is also notable in that its authorship remains uncertain; it may have been written in whole or in part by Mikhail Bakhtin and published, for political reasons, under Vološinov's authorship. For Vološinov/Bakhtin it was crucial that language was lived out socially, by different cohorts of people interacting in different social contexts. He criticized the assumption that signs were univalent within any speech community and varied only through individual choice in the course of speech. Instead, he argued, signs were likely to be emitted with "accents" that varied by social categories, such as gender, generation, class, occupation, or status or by different interpretations of tradition. Such "multiaccentuality," he noted, could turn communication into "an arena of struggle" (1986, 23) rather than a chorus of concord.

A third approach to language that went beyond the Saussurean model derived from the American pragmatist and logician Charles Peirce (1839–1914), whose work became important in semiotics in the 1960s. Peirce had argued that "the study of language ought to be based upon a study of the necessary conditions to which signs must conform in order to fulfill their function as signs" (in Parmentier 1994, 11). If no inherent causative relationship exists between an indicator and what it "stands for" in the world, then their mutual association has to be explained, justified, and certified on other grounds. According to Peirce, every linguistic and cultural sign or set of signs that ties an indicator to its designatum must come accompanied by another sign, which refers to the previous sign and defines and explicates it. This sign he called the "interpretant" (Peirce 1955, 100). Each sign functioning as an interpretant requires still another interpretant and sign to define it in turn, thus making semiosis "an infinite process," "an endless series" (in Parmentier 1994, 27).

In the wake of such critiques, there developed in the 1960s and 1970s various efforts to modify the picture of langue advanced by Saussure and to question the dominant role of grammar defended by Chomsky. The aim of these endeavors was instead "to develop a theory of language in its social context, rather than a theory of grammar," to delineate which elements of the social context affect the production and understanding of language in natural settings (Lavandera 1988, 6). Focusing on speech in context could, in turn, inform us about who is using and manipulating cultural and linguistic forms, in relation to whom and under what circumstances. Such efforts to consider how language and culture are caught up, implicated, and deployed in social action also open up possibilities for investigating the contextual role of power in language use.

Signs and Power

The study of signs began with linguistics, which initially defined signs as elements deployed in the system of langue. Yet it soon became apparent that gestures, colors, tones, apparel, or foods could also serve as signs in appropriate contexts and that, in fact, anything and everything could assume the function of a sign in human communication. The study of language could thus be seen as part of a more general science of all kinds of signs and sign-functions, semiotics.

This expanded interest in signs suggested to some that the notoriously ambiguous concept of "culture" could be made more precise in semiotic terms. One way this was pursued was by drawing on Peirce. The Italian semiotician Umberto Eco took Peirce's approach to signs and related it to the workings of culture. Accepting the premise that signs do not exist in natural reality, Eco pointed out that they depend for their formulation and function upon the network of practices and communications we call culture. In such networks they appear always with other signs, which relate to one another through likeness or contrast. The dimensions of similarity and difference are also defined culturally. The relation of signs to one another and to the contexts in which they may be used further requires an "interpretant" (in Peirce's terms), which clarifies what a sign is about by adducing further signs that place it into the web of culture of which it forms a part (1976, 67).

Signs that assume the function of interpretants have a special role in the exercise of power, because the capacity to assign cultural significance to signs constitutes an important aspect of domination. Power can determine ("regulate") the interpretants that will be admissible, emphasized, or expunged (Parmentier 1994, 127–28). It not only certifies that a sign and its denotatum are cognitively appropriate; it stipulates that this sign is to be used and who may so use it. It can also regulate which signs and interpretants are to be accorded priority and significance and which are to be played down and muted.

The exercise of power over interpretants and their use is clearly a social process that requires study in its own right. To that end, Pierre Bourdieu has suggested the utility of thinking about communication as operating within linguistic fields or "markets." In these fields not all participants exercise the same degree of control over the processes of communication. Speakers address each other from different social positions, and their differential placement determines how they do so. For Bourdieu, "language is not only an instrument of communication or even of knowledge, but also an instrument of power. One seeks not only to be understood but also to be believed, obeyed, respected, distinguished. Whence the complete definition of competence as *right to speak,* that is, as right to the legitimate language, the authorized language, the language of authority. Competence implies the power to impose reception" (in Thompson 1984, 46–47).

Not all individuals are equally competent in pursuing their interests in the exchange of linguistic actions and counteractions. Some people excel in the knowledge of what can be appropriately exchanged with whom; others lack that knowledge. Nor do such transactions go forward automatically and without conflicts of interest. Power is involved in deciding who can talk, in what order, through which discursive procedures, and about what topics. As Lamont Lindstrom has put it in the context of a field-based study in Vanuatu, "Control of the questions—even more than control of the answers—maintains social inequalities in that such control helps frame and make sense of felt desire." In this way, "the powerful set the conversational agenda and, by this means, establish inequalities more difficult to perceive or challenge" (1990, 13).

When we combine the insights from semiotics that point up how priority is accorded to some interpretants over others with an understanding of how differential controls operate in the communicative process, we are led to ask how ideologies can be derived from the general stock of ideas. I earlier defined ideology as a complex of ideas selected to underwrite and represent a particular project of installing, maintaining, and aggrandizing power in social relationships. The selection and management of interpretants and control over verbal communication are strategic operations in ideological construction.

Frequently, these functions are assigned to "intellectuals," part-time or full-time specialists in the communication process, a theme addressed by Mannheim and Gramsci. It may be that human minds or neural systems are constituted to avoid incoherence and to resist "cognitive dissonance" (Festinger 1957); yet it also seems to be the case that not all people are equally concerned with creating cognitive coherence (see Fernandez 1965). Some take on the special role of exercising such functions; this is the case in societies at all levels of complexity.

There is an "intellectual politics in the creation of culture" (Verdery 1991, 420), especially salient in situations where the exercise of structural power is based on the control of culturally available knowledge. Katherine Verdery has stressed the importance of communicative competence in socialist societies, where "language and discourse are among the *ultimate* means of production" (p. 430). Verdery describes these societies as characterized by states that depend on a mix of coercion and symbolic consensus, but her point applies as well to those marked by weak states or lacking states altogether, where performative speech-acts often play a major role and where words are thought to convey effective power. Performatives are utterances that do something, that accompany an action "not to report facts, but to influence people" (Austin 1962, 234); they promise something, issue orders, warn of trouble, or initiate a change of conditions, such as declaring someone to be married or installing a personage in a seat of power and prestige (Austin 1976). Bourdieu has rightly cautioned against the tendency of speech-act theorists to assume that the power of performative speech derives from language itself. He stresses that the speech-act lacks power and validity unless it is institutionally authorized and carried out by a person with the appropriate cultural credentials (Bourdieu and Wacquant 1992, 148). Thus, competence in enacting performative speech is both a source of power and a demonstration of it.

What has been said about ideology in communication, including the role of intellectuals, applies to nonverbal as well as verbal communication. An important contribution of semiotics is its emphasis on the fact that cultural mandates are not only coded into verbal linguistic forms but are all-pervasive in humanly constructed worlds.

The built environment can be shaped semiotically to condense the verbal interpretants around certain emblems and thus convey imperative messages to the beholder. This is seen in such modern phenomena as the Colonial Williamsburg restoration (Parmentier 1994, chap. 6) and the orchestration of Baroque art with music, massed processions, and elaborate ritual performances (Turner 1988) and also in the great prehistoric sites of ancient megapolities like Teotihuacan or Borobudur. Similarly, ideological condensation of interpretants marks particular art forms, such as Mozart's operas that comment on the contradictions of the Enlightenment in Austria (Till 1993), Richard Wagner's myth-making *Gesamtkunstwerk*, and Leni Riefenstahl's film "Triumph of the Will" celebrating a National Socialist party congress. All ideologies enshrine an aesthetic of sign communication in their very mode of construction.

A special vehicle of ideology that usually combines verbal and nonverbal communication to generate messages in condensed form is ritual. Maurice Bloch has described ritual as a mode of performance in which propositions are muted and played down, while the force of illocutionary speech and performatives is magnified. The addition of dance and music to speech heightens the emotional impact of performatives still further, while diminishing the cognitive component in communication (1974, 1977). In the ritual process, the participant enters a spatially and temporally structured environment and moves through it guided by a prescribed script that dictates bodily movements and emotional responses. In the process, ritual reshapes bodies and minds through the performance itself (Bell 1992, 98–101). Participation in ritual, Roy Rappaport has argued (1979, 194), also obviates discussion of belief and publicly signals adherence to the order in which one participates. Requiring people to take part in ritual or abstaining from ritual thus signals who has power over whom.

Ideas in Culture

In contemporary anthropology, conceptions of the relationship between power and ideas are embedded in approaches to culture. A central question in how culture is to be understood is whether priority in explanation should be accorded to material or to ideational factors. This issue has surfaced repeatedly, with "materialists" and "mentalists" locked into arguments about the validity of their respective stances. The present inquiry takes the view that materiality and mentality need not be opposed, and it draws theoretical insights from both camps.

Among the major contributors to these debates, Marvin Harris holds a strongly materialistic position. Harris has resolutely defined the premise of his explanatory strategy as "the principle of infrastructural determinism." This principle joins Marx with Malthus and accords priority in explanation to observable behaviors in both production and reproduction. Since production and reproduction are "grounded in nature they can only be changed by altering the balance between culture and nature, and this can only be done by expenditure of energy" (Harris 1979, 58). Harris acknowledges the legitimacy of a concern with mental constructs; indeed, he readily grants the possibility that subject-dependent "emics" may be studied objectively "by relying on an operationalized scientific epistemology" (p. 35). Yet for him "thought changes nothing outside of the head unless it is accompanied by the movement of the body and its parts," and ideas are consequences of energy-expending body activities that affect the balance between population, production, and resources (p. 58).

If Harris downplays the ideational realm, the French anthropologist Louis Dumont has set aside behavior in the material world to focus exclusively on "systems of ideas and values" (1986, 9), on "ideological networks" (p. 24). He uses the term "ideology" for ideas in general, in the tradition of Destutt de Tracy, rather than taking the later sense of the concept as ideas placed in the service of power, and he sees himself as carrying on the work on "representations" of Durkheim's student Mauss (Dumont 1986). Dumont speaks of "the global ideology" of "a society, and also of the ideologies of restricted groups such as a social class or movement," or of "partial ideologies" characterizing a subsystem of society, such as kinship (1970, 263). His major concern is with ideological systems at the level of entire societies, and he sees them as "central with respect to the social reality as a whole (man acts consciously and we have direct access to the conscious aspect of his action)" (pp. 263–64). At the same time, he holds that ideology "is not the whole of society" and needs to be placed in relation to "the non-ideological aspects." These two aspects may turn out to be complementary; how they are actually related is a matter of finding evidence, producing "proof" (p. 264).

To ascertain the nature of ideologies central to whole societies, Dumont has proceeded comparatively, first investigating ideology in India principally on the basis of Brahmanic texts, then—more recently—using the writings of major political economists and philosophers to define the ideology of Western economics. This project has led him to counterpose one ideology to the other in terms of a generalized contrast—between a *homo hierarchicus* of non-Western societies and a supposed *homo aequalis* of the West. In the course of these studies, Dumont has offered valuable insights on particular ideological themes. Bruce Kapferer (1988), for example, has used Dumont's ideas selectively in his insightful comparison of two nationalisms, one derived from a hierarchically conceived cosmology in Sri Lanka and the other from the egalitarian cosmology of Australia. My own work on National Socialism has benefited from Dumont's studies of German ideas. In practice, however, Dumont neglects alternative voices and traditions that competed with the exemplary protagonists he chooses to discuss, and he concentrates on ideas without reference to the patterns of behavior that helped institutionalize these ideological forms. In this emphasis, ideal patterns of thought seem impelled by an internal logic of mind.

Where Harris privileges behavior over ideas and Dumont studies systems of grand ideas to the exclusion of behavior, Clifford Geertz has focused on questions of meaning. Citing Weber's belief "that man is an animal suspended in webs of significance he himself has spun," Geertz defines culture semiotically as "those webs of significance" and sees his task as "an interpretive one in search of meaning" (Geertz 1973, 5). Anthropology must attend, he argues, to how interacting people interpret and construct their own actions and the actions of others. They do so through recourse to symbolic models or blueprints, culturally available "symbolic templates" for action and of action. In a discussion of "ideology as a cultural system," he decried studies of ideology that did not take account of the "figurative language" of culturally significant symbols. Ideologies, according to Geertz, can be due either to "strains" in the fabric of society or to efforts to assert a group interest in the face of opposition, but neither "strain" nor "interests" will be understood unless they can be rendered into culturally specified symbolic templates or models (1973). Geertz's contribution lies in this emphasis on how understandings are "envehicled" in symbols, in the course of social action. That, however, is only a first step. What remains problematic in Geertz is how we are to think about these symbolic vehicles. Do some have more bearing on the exercise of power than others? Are some more resistant and enduring, others more evanescent and secondary? How are they "carried" into social life and by whom? How and in what contexts are they foregrounded, reproduced, and amplified?

Geertz drew some of his inspiration for a symbolic approach to action from Weber, but Weber's interest lay in developing an objectifying sociology that could provide "causal explanations of action" (Kalberg 1994, 49). Weber did indeed take account of how subjective motivations and evaluations of meaning orient people toward action, but the thrust of his work was directed at showing how subjective assessments led people to take up patterned courses of action, which then caused them to participate in a social order in certain ways (pp. 23–49). In contrast, Geertz defined his own project not as a search for cause and effect but as enhancing the understanding of other cultural milieus through the "explication" and "translation" of significant symbols (1973, 408). His metaphor for "culture" was not that of an interconnected system of variables but that of the loosely jointed and easily disjointed octopus (p. 408).

As a result, Geertz moved from a more directly objectifying Weberian approach, evident in his *The Religion of Java* (1960), toward more literary readings of the ethnological evidence. This led him to favor "thick description" of symbolic actions in the immediate context of their occurrence and away from trying to comprehend these contexts as scenarios within larger structures. He thus raised our awareness of symbols in social action, while rejecting efforts to understand such action in relation to economics and politics.

Other scholars, however, have taken on such efforts, attending to symbolic action but framing it within cultural or political histories that pay heed to the larger dimensions. Two may be mentioned by way of example. Sherry Ortner has traced the monastery-building movement among the Sherpa of Nepal to enhanced merit making by "big people" trying to compensate for a loss of political influence and to gains made by "little people" through wage labor and entrepreneurship. In the course of this movement, she argued, people drew repeatedly on culturally available schemas to enact culturally typical relations and situations. Such cultural schemas are "durable" (1989, 61).

Richard Fox has analyzed Mohandas Gandhi's efforts to challenge Britain in the struggle for Indian independence and to use the resulting confrontations to move the country toward his own vision of spiritual and humane renewal. Focusing on Gandhi's "experiments with truth," Fox wrote a "culture history" of how individual intentions interacted with the contingent workings of cultural hegemony, which sometimes allowed room for action and at other times shut the door on new possibilities (1989). For Fox, "There is no weight of tradition, only a current of action" (1985, 197). Culture is not a given to be reenacted but is "always in the making," "the sum and state of social confrontations at the particular moment or the moment just past" (1985, 206).

Fox emphasizes the play of contingency in cultural innovation or constraint; Ortner stresses cultural replication. Hence, Fox calls approaches such as Ortner's "culturology" (1985, 106), while Ortner accuses Fox (and me) of holding that cultural structures exist "external to actors" (1990, 84). The approaches seem opposed, but they are so only to the extent that they allow generalizations to cover phenomena that are themselves heterogeneous and contingent. Individual and group contestation is clearly important, but participants rarely come to it without previous entanglements. They always bring "scripts" that shape their understandings of their situation; yet these scripts are never free of contradiction. Moreover, cultural hegemony is not a seamless web of domination but a panoply of processes of varying intensity and scope. Whether the structures of communication are negotiable or completely closed is not predictable in advance but becomes apparent only after the skirmishing has begun.

Going well beyond the Geertzian emphasis on "characteristic symbolic forms" or Ortner's "cultural schemas," Marshall Sahlins has applied Lévi-Straussian structuralism, premised on the supposed operations of the mind, to define the cultural structures at work in particular societies. In contrast to Lévi-Strauss, however, Sahlins used structuralism to engage history. To visualize the continuity of structures, he borrowed from Fernand Braudel the notion of structures lasting through the *longue durée* (which Braudel had applied mainly to the enduring dimensions of geography and ecology) but extended it to cover the mental structures of whole cultures. He thus defined, for Hawaii, an overall structure that opposed two contrastive sets of elements: on one side, heaven and sea, gods and chiefs, and masculinity and male generativity, which are associated with foreign invaders who come by sea, take wives from the natives of the land, and implant culture by introducing the customs of sacrifice and taboo; and, as its opposite, underworld, land, commoners, femininity and female powers, wife-givers, natives of the land, and nature (1977, 24–25). At the same time, he argued that these elements were historically combined or opposed in different ways and were adjudged differently when viewed from different positions within the system, thus opening up the total structure to possibly "unstable and meaningfully negotiable" permutations (1977, 25). On top of this, the entire Hawaiian structure was challenged by the advent of European seamen, traders, and missionaries, who imported alternative Western structures into the novel "structure of conjunction" (also a Braudelian term). In seeming paradox, therefore, Sahlins holds that such systems maintain themselves precisely through reconstruction and accommodation; the structure is said to maintain itself by changing. Even though critics have interpreted Sahlins as essentially concerned with the persistence of an unchanging cultural structure over time, his central concern has been to ask "how does the reproduction of a structure become its transformation?" (1995, 8).

Yet laying out the cultural structure can only be a first step in comprehending how "native" categories partition the world into oppositions and levels of oppositions. To grasp what these categories and oppositions imply, one must go beyond the structuralist method to ask questions about the structure itself, especially how it came to be and what role it played in founding and sustaining the differential powers and inequalities that flowed from it. That would involve stepping outside the structure, to view it comparatively in the perspective of another structure or in a longue durée of successive structures in history. Furthermore, it would be important to consider how the structure worked to contain its own contradictions, especially since

Hawaiian sociopolitical organization itself habitually set successors in the direct line of chiefs against collaterals (Valeri 1990, 173). How the structure "works," in other words, requires knowing what the structural categories and their organizational logic are "about." It may be the case that power is always exercised through culturally particular categories and meanings, but how power comes to control social labor must be formulated in other terms.

Sahlins holds that neither Hawaiians nor any other people can step outside their cultural categories to deal with reality, for "material effects depend on their cultural encompassment. The very form of the social existence of material forces is determined by its integration in the cultural system" (1976, 206). In contrast, Roy Rappaport insists that anthropology can adopt both an "etic" approach whose frame of reference is the community of science and an approach that engages the subjective understandings, the "emics" of the people themselves. As an ecological anthropologist, Rappaport began by attempting to trace "the effects of culturally informed behavior on biological systems: organisms, populations and ecosystems" (1971, 243); at the same time, and contrary to Harris, he argued that native understandings have a part to play in activating ecosystemic variables, which can, in turn, be stated in the etic terms of the scientific observer. For Rappaport, therefore, how the "cognized environment" (as understood by the people studied) intersects with the "operational environment" (the model of reality constructed by the scientist) remains an open problem, where Sahlins denies the validity of this kind of distinction.

Rappaport has also contributed a scheme for studying the natives' "cognized models." For him, such models have a structure, an architecture grounded in "ultimate sacred postulates" which, in turn, support understandings about the nature of entities in the world, rules for dealing with them, ways of registering fluctuations in the conditions of existence, and schemata for classifying the beings encountered in everyday life. In contrast to symbolic approaches that confine themselves to the study of culturally specific metaphors, Rappaport's scheme suggests that it may become possible to compare cognitive models cross-culturally. However, in its present form, it probably works best for systems that ensure stability through ritual but is less applicable to arrangements in change that rely on power.

Discussion

In following the contestations between the proponents and opponents of Enlightenment through Reason, and their after-effects, it becomes clear that these were not abstract theoretical debates. The affirmations of utterly opposed claims to the truth became arguments and counterarguments over power and status advanced by contending interests. While increasingly assertive commercial classes allied to expanding rationalizing states presented themselves as the party of the future, besieged social classes and locally based political elites countered this claim by exalting tradition, parochialism, true inner spirit, the social bonds of intimacy, and local knowledge. Many of the foundational concepts of the social sciences were hammered out in such contests over the control and distribution of power and bear the imprint of their political affinities. Revolutionary and Imperial France asserted dominance over Europe in the name of rationalism, secularism, and equality; the Germanies responded with traditionalizing and "spiritual" countermovements in the name of "culture."

At the same time, both cohorts of interlocutors were locked into a common field of social and political interaction and were speaking to the same issues, although one did so from a position of strength through victory and the other from a position of defeat and victimization. Thus, one side accentuated the promises held out by the rationalist vision, while the other focused on the ways in which rationalist techniques would suppress parochial interests and loyalties by installing regimes of more perfect domination. As a result, the concepts put forward—reason and ideology, culture and society, practice and metaphysics—were not only placed in opposition but were reified as emblems of contrasting orientations, each concept objectified and animated as a bounded and holistic entity endowed with a capacity to generate and propagate itself.

When the sets of opposing arguments are placed in their social context, however, they can be seen to intertwine. When Reason is no longer abstractly set off against Culture, one can visualize how it is activated or resisted, in culturally specified ways, within institutional settings such as scientific laboratories, administrative offices, and schools. In this way, phenomena once set apart by absolute distinctions can yield to more integrative understandings.

The same point may be made about the counterposition of "class" and "culture." When first introduced in their present-day senses, these concepts appeared to be wholly incompatible, especially when deployed in political discourse. Yet they do not exclude each other; they occur together and overlap in various ways. Both terms, in fact, claim too much and also too little. They suggest that "classes" or "cultures" represent totalities in their own right—homogeneous, all-embracing entities, each characterized by a common outlook and capable of collective agency.

The advocates of "class" assumed that a common position along a gradient of control over the means of production entails a common interest shared by all members of the class and, hence, common propensities for action. Yet class and classness are better understood in terms of relations that develop historically within a social field. That field subsumes diverse kinds of people, rearranges them, and causes them to respond to new ways of marshaling social labor. One can then speak of the "making" of a class (as did E. P. Thompson in *The Making of the English Working Class* [1966]) out of disparate groups of people, who bear diverse cultural heritages and yet must adjust them to the requirements of a new social order. Similarly, a class may be "unmade" and its members scattered and reallocated to different groupings and strata.

The advocates of "culture," for their part, have generally thought that whatever underlies cultural commonalities—be it language, upbringing, customs, traditions, race—will produce sentiments of identity, social solidarity, love of country, and aversion to cultural "others." Yet, as with class, the forces postulated as generating culture were never strong enough in and of themselves to produce the envisioned unifying effects. Historically, both classness and culturehood needed to be mobilized and reinforced to come to fruition: in many cases, the requisite energies emerged from the turmoil of politics and war.

If class can be wedded to culture, then culture too needs redefinition. The initial use of the concept in the service of the Counter-Enlightenment stressed a supposed inner unity, marked by a continuity through time from primordial beginnings. A "culture" was

thus conceived as the expression of the inner spiritual force animating a people or nation. This understanding was carried into anthropological usage, together with the implicit or explicit expectation
that a culture constituted a whole, centered on certain fundamentals
that distinguished it from others. It was also seen as capable of reproducing and regenerating itself and as able to repair any tears in
its fabric through internal processes.

Once we abandon this view of a culture as a reified and animated
"thing," the problem of how to understand cultural phenomena
must also change. What comes to be called "culture" covers a vast
stock of material inventories, behavioral repertoires, and mental representations, put in motion by many kinds of social actors, who are
diversified into genders, generations, occupations, and ritual memberships. Not only do these actors differ in the positions from which
they act and speak, but the positions they occupy are likely themselves to be fraught with ambiguity and contradiction. As a result,
the persons who occupy them may be required to act and think in
ambiguous and contradictory ways. This becomes most obvious
when people must confront changes imposed from outside, but it is
likely to mark any situation of social and cultural change.

Given this differentiation, neither a language-using community
nor a body of culture bearers can share all of their language or culture,
or reproduce their linguistic or cultural attributes uniformly through
successive generations. As Anthony Wallace has pointed out, social
relations depend not on a "replication of uniformity" but on "the
organization of diversity" through reciprocal interaction (1970).
Culture is not a shared stock of cultural content. Any coherence that
it may possess must be the outcome of social processes through which
people are organized into convergent action or into which they organize themselves.

These processes of organization cannot be understood apart from
considerations of power, and they may always involve it. One must
then attend to how that concept is understood. To think of power
as an all-embracing, unitary entelechy would merely reproduce the
reified view of society and culture as a priori totalities. It will be more
productive to think of power relationally, but it then follows that different relationships will shape power differently. Power is brought
into play differently in the relational worlds of families, communi-

ties, regions, activity systems, institutions, nations, and across national boundaries. To conflate these various kinds of power would lead us into the trap of national character studies, which saw socialization and its effects on personality replicated in every domain and on every level of a national society. At the same time, how power operates on different levels and in different domains, and how these differences are articulated, becomes an important research question—something to be demonstrated, not assumed.

The same caveat is in order as we try to understand how power in social relationships works to draw cultural and linguistic forms into coherence. If it is no longer possible for us, as it was for our predecessors, to assume that culture and language replicate themselves through the impersonal force of "custom" or through some hypothetical human need for cognitive consistency, then we must try to identify the instrumental, organizational, or ideological means that maintain custom or underwrite the search for coherence. There may be no inner drive at the core of a culture, but assuredly there are people who drive it on, as well as others who are driven. Wherever possible we should try to identify the social agents who install and defend institutions and who organize coherence, for whom and against whom. And if culture was conceived originally as an entity with fixed boundaries marking off insiders against outsiders, we need to ask who set these borders and who now guards the ramparts.

We thus need to make our received concepts more flexible and operational, but we must not forget the relational value of concepts like culture, which—whatever its limits—sought connections among phenomena, in contrast to the earlier "custom." Similarly, Marxian concepts have always seemed to me productive, because they broke down the dividing lines between history, economics, sociology, and politics from the start. Relational approaches are especially important when we deal with ideas, an undertaking that always threatens to divorce mental constructs from their historical and physical contexts. These approaches will guide the case studies on Kwakiutl, Tenochca (Aztecs), and National Socialist Germany that follow, to show how culturally distinctive patterns of ideation interdigitate with material and organizational processes.

'Nakwaxda'xw Chief Tutlidi giving away a copper in honor of his son
at Fort Rupert, 1894. A segment of the copper has been broken off
in the manner prescribed for distribution. Photograph by O. C. Hastings.
(American Museum of Natural History)

3

The Kwakiutl

If the connections between power and ideas can be unraveled by focusing on instances in which both dimensions are dramatically evident, one promising scenario is offered by the people long called Kwakiutl by anthropologists, as well as others. The Kwakiutl have furnished a type-case of a "chiefdom," a term applied to societies that are neither simple nor lacking in social stratification but are without the complex architecture of states. They are headed by personages endowed with managerial authority, "chiefs," who can overrule segmentary interests yet are not able to marshal their subjects with a fully fledged apparatus of coercion that can compel obedience. Chiefs usually derive this authority from a culturally constructed connection with supernatural forces, and they are thus in a position to endow their political functions with a unique cosmological aura.

The name for the people that became known to outsiders as Kwakiutl was used by Franz Boas and George Hunt in their inquiries in the field, as well as in their writings, and thus passed into general use in both professional and popular writings. The people now want to be known as *Kwakwaka'wakw*, speakers of the *Kwakwala* language, of whom the four tribes of Kwakiutl who inhabited the village of Tsaxis adjacent to Fort Rupert form a part. For clarity's sake, I shall refer to this group as Kwakiutl or Tsaxis Kwakiutl, and to the Kwakwala speakers in general as Kwakwaka'wakw. Expunging "Kwakiutl" from the literature altogether seems counterproductive.

Examining the case of the Kwakiutl will involve us in ethnography, to detail some of their unfamiliar characteristics, but I shall also try to be historical, to highlight changes in their society and culture. These changes often responded to influences stemming from the larger social fields in which they were involved. Finally, this account will rely on general ethnology, as we draw out the major organizing themes of Kwakiutl culture through analytic concepts that build on the comparative study of many cultures. My aim is to use this historically oriented ethnography and this analytic ethnology to explicate the particular links between power and ideas in a salient case derived from the anthropological inventory.

In anthropology, the Tsaxis Kwakiutl or "Fort Ruperts," as they also came to be known, occupy a special position. As the principal group studied by Boas, who is often spoken of as the founding ancestor of American anthropology, their example had considerable influence on the field after Boas's time. Their culture also became known to nonanthropological audiences, because Ruth Benedict portrayed it, in her widely read *Patterns of Culture*, as striving to annihilate "the ordinary bounds and limits of existence" (1934, 72). In this depiction, she drew on Friedrich Nietzsche's vision of ancient Greek art, which he saw as marked by a central contradiction between the Apollonian search for measure and limits and the Dionysian will to break through the boundaries of the self in ecstasy and intoxication. To Benedict, the people of Zuni pueblo were Apollonian, the Kwakiutl their Dionysian antithesis. In this interpretation, the Zuni walked with care along the well-delineated pathways of life; the Kwakiutl sought instead to break through the boundaries of mundane reality. Apart from Benedict's depiction, the Kwakiutl came to be known to museum visitors through their art, including their dramatic carvings and evocative masks.

Finally, the great public displays and giveaways of wealth of the Kwakiutl, the so-called potlatches, drew the attention of economists and sociologists, among others, because of their apparent nonconformance to "Western" canons of economic rationality. Some European intellectuals, such as Georges Bataille (1967), even celebrated the Kwakiutl as a dramatic example of how humanity might recover in the quest for excess the strength and purity of dynamic vitality.

The Kwakiutl reside on the northern Pacific coast of North Amer-

ica, one of the "First Nations" present there before the coming of
the Europeans. Anthropologists include them—along with Tlingit,
Haida, Tsimshian, Nootka, and the Coast Salish—in an area of similar cultures grouped together as "Northwest Coast." This cultural
belt runs along the rainy, heavily dissected and forested coast from
Yakutat Bay in Alaska south to Kato, near Cape Mendocino in Northern California. The Kwakiutl live along the northern coast of Vancouver Island and along the bays and inlets around Queen Charlotte
Bay, from Smith Sound inlet in the north to Cape Mudge in the
south. A high range of mountains, traversing Vancouver Island, separates them from their southern neighbors, the Nootka (now known
as the Nuu-chah-nulth).

Kwakiutl speak Kwakwala, one of six languages of the Wakashan
language family. This language family is grouped into two categories:
northern Wakashan, including Kwakwala, Bella Bella (Heiltsuk), and
Haisla; and southern Wakashan, made up of Nitinat, Nootka, and
Makah. Although there were cultural exchanges between Kwakwala
speakers and both Heiltsuk and Nootka, their languages are not mutually intelligible. Bella Bella and Haisla are divided from the other
Wakashan-speaking groups by the Bella Coola (now Nuxalk), who
speak a Salishan language. I want to underline that these named
groupings all refer to languages, not to "tribes." Speaking one of
these languages may underwrite an acknowledgment of common
identity that can be expressed in common ritual performance and
myths, but it does not translate into sentiments of political unity or
common organization. In all these groups the basic social unit was
the localized community, often distinguished by dialect from its nearest neighbors. It is still unclear whether all these languages stem from
a common linguistic stock that later differentiated or derive from
different linguistic backgrounds.

Similarly, it is not yet certain whether the Kwakiutl differentiated
culturally from a basic pattern laid down some seven thousand years
ago or whether the northern Tlingit, Haida, and Tsimshian and the
southern Kwakwaka'wakw and Nootka are descendants of people
that were organized rather differently, both socially and culturally
(see Adams 1981). Rubel and Rosman argue persuasively that the social organization of the northern groups resembled that of neighboring Athabascan-speaking food collectors on their northern and

eastern periphery, reckoning descent matrilineally and divided into exogamous moieties and clans. In contrast, the southern groups, including the Kwakiutl, reckoned descent ambilaterally through both fathers and mothers. This produced lines of descent with overlapping memberships and crosscutting marriages, for which exclusive rules of exogamy or endogamy were irrelevant. They share these characteristics with the inland Salish-speaking people inhabiting the Thompson and Fraser River valleys of interior British Columbia (but not the Coast Salish); these inland groups lived in bands that were not based on exclusive criteria of descent, accorded recognition to individuals of wealth and influence, but lacked hereditary chiefs and nobles. Rubel and Rosman postulate that the Bella Coola, Nootka, and Kwakiutl once shared a common social organizational pattern with these peoples, and then developed bounded kin groups with fixed group claims to resources and social hierarchies of rank, hereditary leadership by chiefs, and differential privileges for senior and junior lines when they moved to the coast with its more abundant resources (Rubel and Rosman 1983; Rosman and Rubel 1986).

Scattered reports on the Kwakiutl were collected throughout the nineteenth century, and a number of field studies were carried out in the twentieth century (notably by Helen Codere, focused on the ethnohistory of the Kwakiutl associated with Fort Rupert, and by Ronald and Evelyn Rohner, on the tribes of Gilford Island). The bulk of what we know about them, however, comes to us from the work of Boas, aided by his local assistant George Hunt. Boas visited the Northwest Coast first in 1886 and for a last time in 1930; in all he made twelve field trips to the Northwest Coast, totaling twenty-eight and one-half months (White 1963, 9–10). Together Boas and Hunt are responsible for many thousands of printed pages, in a collaboration that spanned forty-five years. The most recent of the texts dealing with their Kwakiutl materials is Boas's *Kwakiutl Ethnography*, left incomplete at the time of his death in 1942, then edited by Helen Codere and published in 1966.

Following Boas's definition of culture as a manifestation of the mental life of man, the Boas-Hunt texts focus on myths and rituals, especially on those elaborated between 1849—when the Kwakiutl moved to the vicinity of Fort Rupert—and the time of the ethnographic inquiry. Much of the materials on ritual drew on native reports; some Boas observed himself, especially in 1886. Given Boas's major concern with language and linguistics, native texts were recorded in Kwakiutl, then translated, and published in both Wakashan and English. Since controlling and enacting myths and rituals were largely the prerogatives of chiefs and nobles, what these texts reveal to us is primarily the discourse of chiefs and nobility, and to a minimal degree the doings of commoners. This bias was due not to neglect on Boas's part but to the difficulty of obtaining information on commoners. When Boas urged Hunt to collect data on the names and rights of common people, because "they are just as important as those of people of high blood," Hunt replied that this was "hard to get for they shame to talk about themselves" (in Berman 1991, 45).

The texts are also minimally informative about the lives of Kwakiutl women. Guided perhaps by the then-prevailing concept of culture as a homogeneous body of customs and ideas, these texts note gender differentiation in activities but leave them unexplored. They chart the distinctions in the social division of tasks, as well as customs surrounding female puberty, food taboos, ritual work in food processing, and female roles in arranged marriages. They speak of women, fictitiously defined as males, holding positions of authority until their successor was old enough to take over (Boas 1966, 52), and they mention that women with the appropriate privileges performed dances as part of the retinue of the major spirit-figure of the ceremonial season. But what women did and thought was not explored in their own terms, and their informal roles received no attention.

Although the materials collected constituted the cynosure of Boasian anthropology during its first decades, the texts themselves—along with Boas's famous typewriter with Kwakiutl typography—were long neglected, because they did not easily fit with subsequent theoretical paradigms. More recently, they have served as the basis for new interpretations. One set of such studies has sought to move away from representations of the First Nations of the Northwest Coast as inhabitants of an unchanging and timeless "ethnographic present" and to demonstrate native involvements in local, regional, and global changes over time. Others have begun the difficult task of analyzing Kwakiutl religion and cosmology, relying especially on the original Kwakwala texts translated and transmitted to Boas by Hunt.[1]

The Kwakiutl in Time and Place

As significant as "the Kwakiutl" have been for anthropology and for popular audiences, we must not fall into the trap of thinking of them as bearers of some primordial culture, frozen in a moment outside ordinary time. Such an image has tempted the human sciences since the early nineteenth century, when the notion that each people had a distinctive culture of its own first achieved widespread popularity. It is especially ironic for the Kwakiutl to be depicted as unchanging, since Boas selected them for study as much for the fact that their "newly acquired customs had assumed novel significance" as "because they were less affected by the whites than the other tribes" (Boas 1908, in Wike 1957, 302).

To think of Kwakiutl as bearers of a changeless cultural pattern is particularly inappropriate, since their existential conditions have changed in major ways since the times of first contact on the coast in 1774, when a Spanish ship encountered Haida off the Queen Charlotte Islands. James Cook explored Nootka Sound on his third Pacific voyage in 1778; George Vancouver was the first ship captain to meet Kwakiutl in 1792. In the initial years of the nineteenth century fur-trading companies intruded into the region overland, but systematic collection of furs in the Kwakiutl region began only in 1821. In the two decades thereafter, the Hudson Bay Company installed forts and collecting stations along the coast, and in 1849 it received a royal charter to establish a colony on Vancouver Island. The first company settlement on the island was Fort Victoria, founded on the island's southeastern tip in 1843, which soon became Victoria, a sizable city that attracted Indian laborers and settlers as well as Europeans. Coal mining had begun in Kwakiutl territory in 1830, and the company founded Fort Rupert there in 1849. Fort Rupert remained the company's main post until it yielded influence in the 1870s to Alert Bay "as the principal focus of the White economy on northern Vancouver Island" (Galois 1994, 210).

By midcentury the British government had begun to make its military power felt in the region. In 1843 the chief trader at Fort Victoria had discouraged a Songhi attack on the fort by demonstrating the effectiveness of cannon, but the natives continued to think, with good reason, that their bows and arrows outperformed European muskets in forested and accidented terrain (Fisher 1977, 40). Naval vessels were often sent out to pacify Indians along the western coast of Vancouver Island (Fisher 1977, 149). In 1850 and 1851 Nahwitti, an Indian settlement at the northern tip of Vancouver Island, was twice taken and destroyed by naval assault in response to the murder of deserters from a Hudson Bay Company ship. In December 1865 a landing party and cannonades from HMS *Clio* attacked the Kwakiutl village of Tsaxis at Fort Rupert, to impose colonial justice upon a local dispute. Many houses were burned down and a large number of canoes destroyed. The village studied by Boas and Hunt was thus the Tsaxis rebuilt in 1866 (Galois 1994, 214–15). Warfare among Indians intensified in the 1850s and 1860s, not least because the Kwakiutl at Fort Rupert were warring on rival groups in order to consolidate their position as middlemen in the fur trade (p. 58). Yet in the early 1870s Indian warfare and slave raiding diminished again, probably due as much to growing Indian involvement in the expanding money economy of the region as to efforts by outsiders to settle disputes by discussion instead of by war.

By 1858 governmental powers were transferred from the Hudson Bay Company to the government of British Columbia, and in 1871 British Columbia joined the Canadian Confederation. Until 1864 Governor James Douglas followed a policy of purchasing land from Indians where needed to facilitate European settlement, while otherwise remaining mindful of native interests. With the Terms of the Union of 1871 drawn up between British Columbia and Canada, however, native peoples became a "responsibility" of the federal government and thus of governors "less concerned than their predecessor [James Douglas] about Indian rights regarding land" (Fisher 1977, 160). In 1879 government commissions and agents began to allot the Kwakiutl to restricted reserves, and in 1881 the government Kwakewlth Agency was established at Alert Bay. Although the Kwakiutl were unusual among Kwakwaka'wakw tribes in having some of their claims to settlement and resource sites confirmed by treaties (Galois 1994, 198–203), alienation of village precincts and locations for fishing, hunting, and gathering went on apace. When Kwakwaka'wakw applied for additional lands in 1914, 109 of 195 tracts were listed as "alienated." The Kwakiutl headed the list of the tribes listed as claimants (Galois 1994, 60). As government reinforced its grip on native life Royal Mounted Policemen, missionaries, and schoolteachers were called on to intensify their zeal in applying the laws against potlatching and winter dancing passed in 1888. Government representatives and missionaries saw the ritual displays and distributions of the potlatch system as "wasteful" and the winter ceremonials as "barbaric." Although the direct impact of missionaries on the Tsaxis Kwakiutl remained limited, their evaluation of the "atrocities" and "superstitions" of the Indians—"overwhelmingly shocking to behold" (Missionary William Duncan, on Fort Rupert, in Fisher 1977, 127)— strongly influenced the tone of relations between the indigenous groups and new settlers.

These events affected Kwakiutl life in major ways, but the Kwakwaka'wakw communities did maintain a measure of autonomy even in the face of increasing interference of traders, officials, and missionaries. This autonomy owed much, initially, to their sheltered location along inland waterways, a zone they had occupied by driving out other peoples either just before or just after initial contact. At the same time—and in contrast to the riverine peoples of the North and of the Pacific outer coast—this location put them at first only at the periphery of the ocean-borne commerce in furs. The inland straits they had occupied did not support sea otters, initially the main target of that maritime trade. The Kwakwaka'wakw settlements also lacked direct access to inland waterways and to the major trade routes that connected the coast with the interior. By the 1830s, forty years or so later, however, they had become traveling middlemen between the landings and posts of the Hudson Bay Company to the north and northwest and the camps of fur hunters and trappers scattered through the hinterland. Although in the 1840s the Hudson Bay Company tried to cut out Indian middlemen elsewhere in order to monopolize the trade itself, the establishment of Fort Rupert in Kwakiutl territory in 1849 reinforced the middleman role of these Indians. The fort was originally set up to protect the local coal mine rather than as a post in the fur trade, but the company may have permitted the Tsaxis Kwakiutl to settle there and to expand their trading activities in exchange for a role in protecting the fort against Tsimshian and Haida raiders.

At the same time, the Kwakwaka'wakw—like other peoples along the coast—were affected by two major transformations. One was caused directly by massive demographic changes; the other was due to their inclusion in a capitalist economy and their incorporation into an occupying state.

In contrast to earlier estimates that set the precontact population of Kwakwaka'wakw at about 4,500 (Kroeber 1947, 135), recent studies put it as high as 19,000. According to Robert Boyd, the population fell to around 8,500 in 1835, declined further to 7,650 in 1862, and fell precipitously between 1862 and 1924 to little more than 1,000 (Boyd 1990; Galois 1994). This demographic disaster was caused by the impact of repeated epidemics and infectious diseases (first small-pox, then measles, followed by venereal disease and tuberculosis) on an immunologically defenseless population. The epidemiological effects were intensified by the widespread sale of cheap alcohol to the native population. Population loss was further exacerbated through outmigration. This population decrease coincided with the burgeoning of the money economy introduced by the Europeans. European immigration and settlement on Vancouver Island also proceeded apace, until the non-Indian population began to outnumber the Kwakwaka'wakw in their own territories shortly before World War I (Galois 1994, 63).

Such a catastrophic loss of population put severe pressures on the Kwakiutl social and cultural system, which was organized around carefully delineated hierarchies of rank and which required that these rank positions be filled in dependable ways. As epidemics killed off increasing numbers of legitimate incumbents to political and ritual positions, the enhanced opportunities and burdens of rank intensified pressures and tensions among the survivors. More recently, the population has begun to rise again, and it now stands at approximately 3,500.[2]

Other transformations stemmed from major shifts in the political economy of the region. Until 1858 Indian hunting, trapping, and marketing of fur-bearing animals served as the economic mainstay of British Columbia, but even then some Indians had taken employment as casual laborers on Hudson Bay Company posts and ships, in transport, and on company farms. Some also worked independently in panning for gold, mining surface coal, logging, and longshoring. Women found employment in housework and as sex workers in Canadian settlements, such as Victoria. From 1870 on, rising numbers of men, women, and children took jobs in the increasingly mechanized canneries and on fishing schooners. The growing demand for cheap protein on the part of the British working class supported a steadily expanding market for canned salmon, much as it did around the same time for corned beef in cans from Argentina (McDonald 1994, 163). Seventeen canneries were established in Kwakwaka'wakw territory between 1881 and 1929 (Galois 1994, appendix 4). From the last quarter of the nineteenth century on, "wage labour was clearly of importance to many Indian families" (Knight 1978, 21). Young people, especially noninheriting younger sons or women hoping to escape parental control and arranged marriages, found emigration to work sites outside Kwakiutl territory attractive. Cannery work also produced a cohort of Indian labor recruiters who acted as intermediaries between factories and workers in the communities, identifying workers and advancing money against repayment from future wages. One of these was the Kwakiutl chief Charles Nowell, who described his activities between 1905 and the late 1920s in his autobiography (Ford 1941). Work in the fisheries and canneries also produced serious labor troubles and strike activity in the late nineteenth and early twentieth centuries. From 1870 on, Indians owned or operated stores, small farms, and sawmills, as well as packing outfits and charter services. By 1900 "a number of Indian men were skippers and mates of larger steam vessels" (Knight 1978, 12). One such skipper and later owner of a fleet of seiners was the later Kwakiutl chief James Sewid of Alert Bay (see his autobiography in Spradley and Sewid 1972). Today most Kwakiutl depend for a living on the mechanized commercial fishing industry and are subject to the technological and organizational changes demanded by the world economy of which that industry is a part.

If the capitalist sector of activities was under the command of regional entrepreneurs and colonial agents, the native resource areas and settlements remained the home sites of Kwakwaka'wakw people trying to continue a way of life governed by their own rules of social and religious organization. In these home sites they were able to keep up their traditional subsistence. They fished for salmon, especially abundant in the waters around Tsaxis and Fort Rupert, as well as herring, candlefish, halibut, and cod. They collected fish spawn

and shellfish; hunted seals and porpoises along the shore and mountain goats, elk, and deer inland; and gathered roots and berries. The
supply of fish and wild plant food was generally plentiful, although
it varied by season and location. Periods of relative abundance al-
ternated with times of shortage and occasionally even of hunger
(Suttles 1962, 1968; Piddocke 1965; Donald and Mitchell 1975; Ames
1994). Yet in the last two decades of the nineteenth century the rising circulation of money also enabled some Kwakwaka'wakw to buy
dried fish or eulachon oil for cash instead of relying on supplies
drawn from resource-procurement sites in tribal territory (Galois
1994, 59).

Most food was obtained in the period from spring to autumn when
people dispersed to temporary camps near fishing and collecting
sites. This season the Kwakiutl called *baxus*—secular, mundane. In
late autumn people repaired to sheltered winter villages along the
beach for the winter season, a sacred and liminal time called *tseka*
(pl. *tsetsequa*), probably meaning "imitation," referring specifically
to imitating, simulating, enacting the roles of supernatural spirits
and powers (see Berman 1991, 691). This temporal span involved a
major change in social organization and attitudes: it was an appropriate season for ceremonial exchanges in connection with the trans-
mission of dancing privileges; it was also the time when the relationship between humans and supernaturals had to be enacted in the
sacred performances of the Winter Ceremonial. Inevitably, however,
such attempts to maintain the traditional alternation of secular and
sacred activities under the governance of their legitimate chiefs invited the censure of colonial institutions, imposed from the outside,
that called these efforts into question and created problems for their
continuance. Whatever we know of Kwakiutl society and culture
must therefore be visualized in the context of destabilizing demographic and political economic pressures emanating from the larger
encompassing system.

The two sectors of the economy and society—one of capitalist
entrepreneurship and the other populated by native maritime food
collectors—were not divided but closely implicated in each other's
activities. From the 1820s and 1830s on, the Hudson Bay Company,
with its trading posts and forts, built up contacts with local people
all along the coast. Like other Northwest Coast peoples, the Kwa-

kwaka'wakw were drawn into the processes of an evolving "Euro-
Canadian frontier society" (Knight 1978, 19). A rising stream of cash
began to flow into the local economy, allowing new contenders to
compete with the traditional chiefs for precedence and position.
This caused competition over rights to privileges to intensify in the
late nineteenth century, and it increased the quantities of goods offered at such public ritual distributions of wealth.

The realization that Kwakwaka'wakw life has undergone major
transformations since the time of first contact has made it necessary
to reexamine many facets of this culture, especially our rather static
understandings of Kwakwaka'wakw motivations in art and religion.
We have also come to realize that this culture—indeed any culture—
was much more heterogeneous in both practices and ideas than was
thought to be the case as long as cultures were thought of as homogeneous and self-replicating wholes. In this earlier perspective, the
Kwakwaka'wakw seemed to all conform to the same cultural patterns,
whether they were chiefs or commoners, women or men. Yet not
only did the members of these tribes respond differently to changing inputs over time, but they were differently involved in the displays of status and precedence of the dramatic potlatches that so fascinated earlier investigators. Later appraisals also increased our
awareness that both Boas and Hunt—who was raised at Fort Rupert
as the son of a Tlingit noblewoman and an Englishman who ran the
Hudson Bay Company store at the fort—focused mainly on the patterns of the Kwakiutl nobility, to the neglect of "the patterns and
behavior of the lower classes" (Ray 1955, 139).

If we want to know how the Kwakiutl elite deployed power
through the use of ideas as expressed in myth and ritual, however,
the texts recorded by these pioneer investigators do have a special
value. Hunt collected much information relevant to this purpose because he was himself a participant in the Tsaxis status system and was
strongly motivated to fortify his position among people who often
questioned his efforts to seek rank and recognition among them (on
Hunt, see especially Berman 1991, 15–36). As son of an English father and a Tlingit mother he was marked out as a "little northerner,"
an outsider, but he was included in Kwakiutl rituals from the age of
nine, because his Tlingit great-uncle had helped make peace between
the Tongass Tlingit and the Kwakiutl. Though Hunt spoke Tlingit

as a child, he learned Kwakiutl and absorbed Kwakiutl forms of oratory. He married into the upper ranks of the Kwakiutl elite, acquired ceremonial privileges, and sponsored ritual distributions and winter ceremonials in his efforts to gain rank. The Boas-Hunt texts on initiations into the *hamatsa* (cannibal) cult during the Winter Ceremonial were based on the initiation of Hunt's son David, and in 1900 he was himself put on trial for (and absolved of) having taken part in a hamatsa episode in which a body was supposedly mutilated. He also learned how to be a shaman. In his reports on the Kwakiutl, Hunt focused on mythology, language, and art, precisely the areas of knowledge that he needed to control "if he and his heritage were to be presented, recognized, validated and legitimated" (Cannizzo 1983, 54). His expert knowledge of "myth-history" came to be recognized by many Kwakiutl, who relied on him for information on the details of their family histories and names.[3]

If Kwakwaka'wakw society and culture have varied over the course of historical time and have also shown the internal variability due to social differentiation at any one time, then it has also become less easy to speak of one cultural personality, once thought common to the entire Kwakwaka'wakw population. This has cast doubts on Benedict's characterization of the Kwakiutl personality as "megalomaniac paranoid" (1934). Like other investigators, she drew on the observations and texts collected by Boas and Hunt to construct her picture of the Kwakiutl as Dionysians. Many of these texts do record displays of antagonistic rivalry, which Benedict interpreted as projections upon the world of an aggressive Kwakiutl personality "writ large." Boas himself, however, was prompted to say of her interpretation, "The words are those of the Kwakiutl, but they have nothing to do with the Indians that I knew" (in Goldman 1975, 146). Later investigators have challenged Benedict's approach in both general and specific terms. Generally speaking, it is no longer valid to draw direct causal connections between imputed psychological impulses and culturally standardized patterns of behavior. In the particular case of the Kwakwaka'wakw and the Tsaxis Kwakiutl, it is hazardous to relate the formalized etiquettes of antagonism used in public rituals to affirm status differentials directly back to aggressive drives supposedly stemming from a generalized Kwakiutl personality structure (Drucker 1951; Codere 1956; Barnouw 1980).

Sociopolitical Structure

Whenever we examine some feature of Kwakiutl society or political relations we quickly discover how much the sociopolitics of rank, hierarchy, descent, and succession were intertwined with transfers of ceremonial titles and privileges at marriage and with the ritual distributions of wealth that memorialized the transfers of these prerogatives from one party or generation to another. These events, in turn, would be accompanied by recitations and performances that connected the mundane happenings of the world with supernatural doings in the past and present. The French anthropologist Marcel Mauss called this interweaving of religious, legal, moral, economic, and aesthetic aspects within a social fabric *total* social phenomena (1954, 1). Although we should not equate this multiplex interweaving with the assumption of an all-embracing *totality*, we must keep that simultaneity in mind, as we fasten separately now on one, now on another guiding thread within these webs of connection. I shall first outline the basic units of this society. I will then look at how it passed on rights of succession and chiefship, follow this by examining patterns of marriage, and end by dealing with potlatching, the ritual giveaways for which the Kwakiutl became widely known. Since all of these patterns of ordering society found expression in narratives and performances that sought to anchor them in ontogenetic understandings about how they came to be, the discussion will bring in, at several points, their cosmological premises and implications.

The basic sociopolitical body, then, in the life of the Kwakwaka'wakw was the unit that Boas called *numaym* (plural, *numayma*), a term that may be glossed as "a group of fellows of the same kind" (Berman 1991, 69).[4] These numayms, in turn, made up tribes. The four confederated Tsaxis tribes were made up of twenty numayms in all. The Gwetela (also known as Kwawkewith or True Kwakiutl) included eight such units, the Komoyoye (Kwiahka, Kweha) six, the Walas Kwakiutl six, the Komkyutis three (Galois 1994, 206–7, 217, 220). Each numaym comprised one or more houses erected in a winter village, and consisted "of families embracing essentially household groups and the nearest relatives of those who married into the household groups" (Boas 1966, 48). During the summer season, these household units dispersed to their fishing grounds, shellfish tracts, hunting ranges, and berry patches, but they came together in a common winter village at the onset of that season.

The organizing principles structuring the numayms have long/ been in dispute, partly due to the misapprehension that all truly primitive peoples are inherently egalitarian, partly to the notion that all significant relations among primitive folk are predicated exclusively upon kinship. Even today, it is a widespread belief that all North American Indians lived in egalitarian groups mainly defined by kinship (for a critique of this view, see Legros 1982; Donald 1990). Yet Kwakwaka'wakw and Kwakiutl numayms were neither egalitarian nor made up wholly of kinfolk. Boas was one of the first to point out that

numayms are not to be considered as blood relatives (except members of the nobility) and that the various numayma of a tribe are in many cases unrelated except by later intermarriage. The members of the numaym excepting the chief's family are not necessarily conceived as descendants of the ancestor . . . it seems fair to assume that the direct descendants of the ancestors form the nobility; others, accepted as members, form the common people, also called "the house-men" (*bEqwi'l*) of the chief. (Boas 1966, 44)

In fact, as the population declined in the course of the nineteenth century, individuals were increasingly able to exercise options in attaching themselves to chiefs who could offer them advantageous terms of economic support and security (Hazard 1960, in Harris 1968, 306, 313; see also Kobrinsky 1975, 38; on the Nootka, Drucker 1951; on the Tsimshian Gitskan, Adams 1973).

Furthermore, the numayms were stratified into aristocrats, nobles (*noxsola*), or "simply, chiefly class" (Rohner and Rohner 1970, 79, fn.3), commoners (called sing. *bagil*), "man of the house," or *baganamqala/baganamqal'am*, "only a man, entirely human" (Berman 1991, 71), and slaves. One common metaphor used to represent the numaym envisaged it as an animal "of which chiefs and nobles constitute the head and the foreparts, commoners the hind parts" (p. 79). Membership in the class of nobles was defined in terms of proximity to the senior line of chiefly succession. The first four sons of a chief and their descendants were aristocrats; the fifth brother and his line were sloughed off as commoners (Boas 1921, 1097; 1940b, 361).

Nobles were the "real people" of the numaym (Boas 1921, 357), indicated by the suffix -!am, or "real, original, thoroughly, completely" added to the name of the numaym, while numaym membership for commoners carried no such suffix (Berman 1991, 72). Some of the commoners were indeed downgraded collateral relatives of the chiefly lines, while some were incorporated into the numaym by means other than kinship. Slaves were either bought or captured in warfare and may have made up as much as a fourth or fifth of the population. They were seen altogether as "outsiders" who belonged to no local kinship group, and they were ranked below commoners. As "outsiders" so specified, they were apparently treated as a form of "storable" wealth (Mitchell 1984, 46) and were held as workers or as porters in overland transport, as symbols of status, and as disposable valuables that could be exchanged, ransomed, or sacrificed.

A numaym was therefore not a kinship unit in which members could demonstrate connections through descent or affinity. What gave it definition was succession in the chiefly "status lineage" (Goldman 1975, 40) that bore the name of the founding ancestor, surrounded by associate groups and segments of groups, as well as by clienteles consisting of commoners of diverse origins. Affiliation with the core lineage was neither exclusively patrilineal nor matrilineal but could be obtained through either parent. What was crucial was connection with the founding apical ancestor of the core lineage and the subsequent bestowal of names belonging to the numaym upon the candidates for membership. These names are "fastened on" the recipient in appropriate distributive events—potlatches—implying that reproduction, descent, and succession are assured through "asexual propagation" achieved in ritual carried on by men, not by women producing babies after sexual congress (Goldman 1975, 140; see also Shore 1989, 186–87). We can also find here one important reason why Kwakiutl so resisted the abrogation of potlatching, since ritual bestowal of names and titles was crucial in defining and constructing social identities.

After trying in vain to define the numaym organization through ties of kinship, Claude Lévi-Strauss decided to call them "houses," on the model of the aristocratic houses of medieval Europe (1979). Like these medieval houses the Kwakiutl numaym upheld succession to an apical ancestor, strove to keep up an enduring inventory of ecological resources, drew privileges both from the core lineage and affinal lines connected by marriage, and guarded its collective point of honor. The cross-cultural comparison is apt, as long as one remembers that the Kwakiutl "houses" were internally stratified into different categories of people who shared a multiplicity of links but *not* the ties of common kinship exhibited in a genealogy (on "The Newer Lévi-Strauss," see Adams 1981, 368–70).

There has been an ongoing argument over whether these strata constituted classes or merely marked different positions on a continuum of rank. If we take a strict Marxian position that classes are determined by their differential relation to control of the means of production, then the nobles constituted a chiefly *class*, since the chief and his senior heir were the acknowledged owners/managers/stewards of numaym claims to subsistence-producing resource areas, entitled to a stipulated part of the product caught or collected. In contrast to societies based on a "mature" capitalist economy, however, these entitlements were based not on the accumulation of capital won in "a market situation" (Max Weber) but on criteria of descent and hierarchically organized "status" that drew up trenchant distinctions between chiefs, members of junior "cadet" lines of chiefly descent, "the next ones" or commoners—"just ordinary men"—and slaves. Indeed, when chiefs relinquished their position of chiefship to their named heir, they became "commoners," albeit accorded special recognition for their past position. These social distinctions of rank and privileges were, in turn, "cosmological," since they were understood as attributes of more general differentials and inequalities among the living creatures of the world, animals and people included. For Kwakiutl, as Stanley Walens has aptly put it, "there are no equalities, only comparisons" (1981, 30). No term available to us in the repertoire of social science adequately portrays this array of distinctions. The term "estate" (Weber's *Stand*) that has come to be used to designate collective distinctions of status in medieval and early modern Europe fails us in a case like that of the Kwakiutl, because it depended on categorical assignments by a superordinate political authority. We may thus want to categorize the distinctions among chiefs, nobles, commoners, and slaves among the Kwakwaka'wakw as "status classes," in the process of being undermined and rearranged under the pressures generated by the new political economy based on capitalism within the coastal region.

Boas described the Kwakwaka'wakw as divided into twenty

"tribes" (1966, 38–41). These are best understood as local groups, made up of a number of numayms and settled in a common village during the winter season. There has been a debate (Galois 1994, 47–50) on whether the Kwakwaka'wakw people had winter villages before the time of contact or lived dispersed in settlements close to their strategic resources, or whether these patterns were subject to local variation. Around the time of contact, however, winter villages appear as a dominant form of settlement, each taking a sociopolitical identity through adherence to the line of chiefs of the highest-ranking numaym in a ranked set of numayms. That senior line of tribal head chiefs asserted connection to a mythical apical founder and donor of privileges, as was the case with numaym chiefs, without invoking any criteria of common descent. Some tribes were composite, consisting of lines derived from a common ancestor as well as of "individuals of different descent who at an early time joined the ancestor. . . . In other cases there is no such relation, the lines representing disconnected local groups" (Boas 1940b, 359).

These tribes and their component divisions were not stable and enduring units: behind a facade of apparent stability we discern the tumultuous play of kinship politics. Thus the Gwetela, the first of the Tsaxis tribes, consisted of a senior lineage, the descendants of Matagila; lines derived from Matagila's second son; two lines that had "come down," made the transition from supernature into this world separately; two lines that joined later; and still another line of recent refugees from the Walas Kwakiutl. The Walas Kwakiutl themselves merged with the Komkiutis after their move to Tsaxis. The line deriving from Matagila's third son split from the parent body early in the nineteenth century in a dispute over witchcraft, called themselves the Matilpi, and embarked on a separate course of conquests. In the 1890s the Matilpi joined the tribe of the Tlawitsis. Another of the Tsaxis Kwakiutl tribes, the Komoyoye/Kweeha, split early in the nineteenth century. One segment joined the tribe of the Lekwiltok, who moved south and east along the Inside Passage in search of new fishing grounds and opportunities to raid for slaves among the Coast Salish of the Gulf of Georgia and Puget Sound. The other segment joined the Tsaxis Kwakiutl in their move to Fort Rupert (Boas 1921, 938–51; 1966, 39; Goldman 1975, 34; Galois 1994, 168–77, 223–35, 250–51).

Tribes formed local social arenas for rank orderings, for marriages, and for ritual distributions. In addition, however, thirteen of these tribes came to recognize a more embracing unity, called by Goldman the Kwakiutl "ritual congregation" (1975, 31–33). Eventually, the tribes making up this congregation strove for precedence of rank along a scale of differential prestige, intermarried with one another, and engaged in formalized distributions of wealth. This congregational circle was not, however, ancient but arose out of the movement of the initial four Kwakiutl tribes to Tsaxis. "Before that time," Helen Codere points out, "there is nothing in the family histories to indicate that there was a Kwakiutl-wide system of socially ranking the various villages, the numayms that made them up, or the individual standing places in the numayms" (1961, 466). There was also "nothing to suggest that the four Tsaxis tribes were the first ranking and the greatest among all the people before that time. What seems to have happened is that the wealth they were first to get among the people because of their new location at the fort established the claim that they were the greatest of all" (p. 467).

What was ancient was the principle of drawing distinctions among the members of a numaym by rank. When the four tribes gathered at Tsaxis, they were able to gain precedence in rank over other groups because their geographical placement gave them access to ample supplies of salmon, as well as the advantageous position of middleman between the Hudson Bay Company post at Fort Rupert and people in the hinterland. At first they confined their ritual distributions to each other, developing a pattern of cross-matching individuals and groups as appropriate competitors of approximately equal rank at each level of structure from the numayms through tribes and confederacies (Kobrinsky 1975, 41–42, and fn.14). During the decade from 1870 to 1880 the Tsaxis Kwakiutl, intermarrying with the Mamalilikulla (Mamaleleqala), the Nimpkish, and the Tlawitsis (Rosman and Rubel 1971, 143), also began to invite them frequently to witness succession rituals and take part in religious ceremonies (Drucker and Heizer 1967, 43). Rank orderings emerged as these events were held among an expanding number of participant tribes.

A parallel effort to rank tribes in relation to each other and to crossmatch status-equals qualified to compete in ritual contests and distributions developed among the Tsimshian tribes that assembled around Fort Simpson near the mouth of the Nass River (Drucker 1963, 139–40), apparently due to a similar need to manage widening relations among autonomous tribes in the absence of an overarching authority. In these resulting contests, some groups were inevitably winners while others lost out, at least temporarily. Thus, when at Fort Rupert Nimpkish and Mamalilikulla vied for fifth place in the ranking series by distributing wealth to the Tsaxis Kwakiutl, the latter declared that the Nimpkish "had not yet earned their right to change their position" (Ford 1941, 20–21). The Tsaxis Kwakiutl continued to occupy the four top ranks, but the relative rankings of tribes positioned below were subject to reshuffling. As a result the rank orderings of tribes collected among different groups often differed from each other and were revised as tribal segments split off from their original home groups and joined new host communities. In the second half of the nineteenth century, moreover, lower-ranked groups increasingly used the new wealth funneled through the expanding capitalist economy to gain higher status by outbidding competitors in redistributive events (Kobrinsky 1979, 170). The distributive events of 1895 witnessed by Boas involved a rivalry between the highly ranked Kwakiutl and the low-ranking Koskimo (Codere 1961, 473).

CHIEFSHIP

According to the prevailing cosmological schemata, the Kwakiutl chiefs were the first-born in a line of first-borns tracing their descent back to the founding ancestor and donor of the original estate of the numaym. This estate comprised a material resource base, as well as properties such as houses, crests, masks, feast dishes, narratives of myth-history, and songs, which symbolized the reincarnation in the rightful successor of ancestral and supernatural donors. Until the mid-nineteenth century, also, the right to "invite the tribes," to "give away property among the tribes" in an event of ritual distribution (potlatching) was the prerogative of chiefs (Kobrinsky 1975, 40). Furthermore, among the important nonmaterial rights pertaining to a numaym was the "table of organization" that ordered positions of rank within the unit. Each of these positions was defined by a "seat" or "standing place" that defined the sequences of precedence among rank holders. As Boas phrased it, one might "consider the numayma as consisting of a certain number of positions to each of which belongs a name, a 'seat' or 'standing place,' that means rank, and privileges. Their number is limited, and they form a ranked nobility. . . . These names and seats are the skeleton of the numayma, and individuals, in the course of their lives may occupy various positions and with these take the names belonging to them" (1966, 50). The order of "seats" refers literally to the order in which people took up their seating positions at feasts and ritual distributions and to the serial order in which they received food or gifts on these occasions.

To move into a position of rank and occupy the seat that signaled that rank, a man had to receive a name that carried with it these rights to be seated. These names, given to people sequentially in the course of their lives, were not personal designations but structured attributes of membership in a numaym—"names are eternal and . . . although the holders of a name may live and die, the name goes on forever" (Walens 1981, 63). This was true not only of names bestowed on people but also of the names given to places, villages, houses, canoes, boxes, or feast dishes, whose names would go on even if the objects disintegrated and needed to be replaced. When a person or object was given an inherited name, its use invoked and re-created the initial condition of the Kwakiutl world. Bestowal of a name marked accession not only to a particular position but also to the ancestral spiritual power inherent in both name and position. Names were thus thought to be animate, charged with power and vitality, possessing weight and mass. Animate power and vitality were also embodied materially in piles of skins or blankets or in wrought sheets of copper offered at ceremonial distributions. In addition to inherited names, chiefs could gain other names—feast names or warrior names—through marriage or warfare.

To succeed in the chiefship and inherit its perquisites, therefore, the aspirant did not have to demonstrate actual descent from the preceding chief and the mythical founder of the numayms. Ideally a candidate for the position by primogeniture, he had nevertheless to be literally *named* to the chiefship by his predecessor, and this bestowal of the chiefly name had to be witnessed and legitimized by participants in a ritual giveaway. If the predecessor had no male heir of his own, he could—through a strategy of bestowing appropriate names on the children of a daughter who had married into another numaym—bring in one of these appropriately named children to inherit the chiefship and hold a ritual distribution to confirm this event. Succession by descent was stipulated by appropriate naming on either the paternal or the maternal side.

As manager of the productive resources of the group, the chief controlled the fishing grounds and fish weirs, the hunting territories, shellfish beds, and berry patches of the numaym as a legatee of the ancestral spirits. He could rally people to defend these resources, since an attack on the resource base was as much an assault on the link connecting the numaym with its founding supernatural as an act of interference with its economic or political rights. As representative of the supernatural founder of the numaym, a chief could claim rights to all seals hunted, leaving only one to the hunter; to half of all mountain goats taken and to a third of all bears and sea otters; to a fifth of the salmon caught; to a fifth of dried berry cakes; and to all long cinquefoil roots. Traditionally, chiefs were also exempt from drawing water and collecting the wood supply, fishing, and hunting. Since not all numaym members were linked through egalitarian ties of kinship, members other than the chief had access to these resources by virtue of their hierarchically organized relationship to the chief, rather than because of any presumption of equal rights through common membership in a corporate landholding group (Walens 1981, 76). At the same time, there were limits to a chief's exactions. Thus he was not supposed to take more than half of the catch (Boas 1921, 1333–34).

These specifications of rights and obligations also throw light on how transfers of goods and services from numaym members to the chief might have been understood ideationally. As managers of the resource base, the chiefs were also the executors of rights in the group emblems deriving from the ancestral donors. In implementing these rights, they impersonated the original supernatural donors. This grant of privileges entailed obligations. At the point in cosmological time when humans separated from the animals, these ancestral donors had entered into pacts with the spirit chiefs of the animals. In these agreements the animals consented to furnish people with food in return for the proper ritual treatment of their innards, bones, and blood, ritual that would guarantee their resuscitation. In his capacity as ritual performer, the chief was also guarantor of these original compacts.

In this manner the chief was conceptualized as prior to people, both as controller of resources and as ritual communicator with the world of the animals. We do not know, however, how this double role of the chief shaped his intra-numaym relationships with fellow nobles and with commoners. Heirs to the chiefship were enjoined to be generous and helpful to their dependents, but normative statements are no guide to the course of actual behavior. It is likely, however, that Philip Drucker's comments on the Nootka (Nuu Chah Nulth), who neighbored the Kwakiutl on the ocean side of Vancouver Island, applied to the Kwakiutl as well. Thus, one may presume that "the chief's house" included two kinds of "commoners," one consisting of collateral kin who lacked noble status yet received preferential access to goods and services in order to tie them more closely to the chief's person, the other made up of transients whose labor was important to the chief. The latter presumably needed the chief's consent to settle in his numaym but were free to leave again to join other numayms if not offered good treatment and requited periodically by chiefly generosity. Thus, neither chief nor commoners were in a position to unilaterally dictate the behavior of the other, hence ensuring some measure of give-and-take on both sides. Common participation in feasts and ritual distributions served to build ties of mutual recognizance for both chiefs and people (Drucker 1951, 278–80), as well as a way for recruiting additional labor (Kobrinsky 1975, 38). This reciprocal dependence of chiefs and commoners enabled the numayms to raise the supplies to hold ritual distributions, to sponsor the carving of crest-bearing poles, construct houses, and build canoes. At the same time, the chiefs never relinquished primary control over the food supply, and they continued to monopolize the production of the appropriate ceremonial foodstuffs offered to witnessing guests at distributional events. Holding on to the supply of ritually sanctioned feast foods gave the chiefs control of an important lever of power and influence, and they retained this down to the 1930s, even when the growing involvement in the capitalist market had weakened their hold on valuable goods to be offered in the potlatch (Kobrinsky 1975, 38).

Another lever of chiefly authority was the chief's ability to mobilize sorcery against real and potential enemies. Each chief "owned" a "head shaman" who occupied a hereditary role in his numaym and "protects his master by throwing disease into his enemy, while the shaman of his adversary's chief tries to counteract the attack" (Boas 1966, 146). When the Kwakiutl moved to Fort Rupert, however, the head chiefs sought to keep the peace by countering such sorcery, through interference with the spells cast (Codere 1961, 477–78; on chiefly efforts to contain sorcery as an asocial and antiestablishment pursuit of supernatural power among the Heiltsuk, see Harkin 1996, 303).

A notable feature of succession to the chiefship was that each successive bestowal of the chiefly name and title on a new incumbent meant that the donor of the name had to divest himself of that name in order to transfer it to the recipient. In conferring a chiefly name upon this successor, a chief thus declared his retirement from the chiefship. Relinquishing his name and title, he also dismantled his house and gave away its planks. The name of the house and the vital power associated with it were then transferred to a new house, now occupied by the heir to the chiefly name. Former chiefs did, however, receive special seats in recognition of their past standing (Hunt, in Rosman and Rubel 1971, 136–37).

In discussing the relation between nobles and commoners, one should take note of the large numbers of people in Kwakiutl society who became qualified as "shamans," part-time or full-time specialists thought to be able to both cause and cure disease. I have already referred to the hereditary shamans of chiefs who were always nobles. There were, however, many other kinds of shamans (Boas 1966, 120, 146–47), many of whom were clearly commoners. The main significance of these commoners in the present context is that they not only received payment for their services but were allowed to "give potlatches" (Boas, in Goldman 1975, 206). Under certain circumstances commoners could give feasts to chiefs, though their names would not be called on such occasions (p. 241). One is left to guess whether the heavy toll of illness that befell the Kwakiutl in the nineteenth century might have produced an increase in the number of shamans willing to offer their services and whether their income might have played a role in the commercialization of distributional events.

Nobles always remained the preferred heirs of names and rights to rank, but—especially after 1835—as disease began to decimate the traditional elite of title-holders, some commoners came increasingly to acquire privileges and rise in rank. As population declined, both Kwakiutl men and women found increasing opportunities for employment in the capitalist sector of the economy. When the resulting flow of money and commodities multiplied, traditional title-holders found themselves confronted by a demand for rank and privileges by newly mobile non-noble claimants. This competition produced a complex and contradictory internal politics, well analyzed by Vernon Kobrinsky in his perceptive paper on the "Dynamics of the Fort Rupert Class Struggle" (1975). On the one hand, the Kwakiutl kept the number of existing numayms at about 100 and the number of original names at 658; on the other hand, population decline and outmigration produced vacancies in many names and associated seats within these units.

Sitting chiefs were thus in a position to promote possible supporters of their choice to occupy vacant seats. They could sponsor politically advantageous marriages and move their own offspring into strategic positions; or they could throw their support to people of dubious parentage (Adams 1981, 367–68). Indeed, some investigators have suggested that through such political strategies ritual distributions functioned to redistribute people among the numayms. Moreover, chiefs could unite to create new positions, such as the twelve new "Eagle" (*kwik*) titles for "nouveaux riches chiefs of low ranks or commoners who wanted to participate prominently in the potlatch and who were able to curry favor with the real chiefs so that this special privilege became hereditary" (Drucker and Heizer 1967, 89). These Eagles obtained the right to receive potlatch prestations before traditionally legitimized chiefs, even though—like eagles—they could also be seen as scavengers, preempting the rights of people without appropriate heirs (Walens 1981, 107). They "made no pretense at claiming tradition-hallowed names or crests, but assumed or tried to assume invented names that referred in some way to the privilege that they hoped to acquire—that of precedence in receiving gifts before the real nobles" (Drucker 1963, 139). Some of these newly created Eagles "were backed by certain chiefs who recognized them as potential tools to assist in the downfall of some high-ranking rival"

(p. 139). Yet chiefly sponsorship of wealthy and socially mobile commoners also embodied a contradiction. Not only did it bring hitherto socially devalued players into the status game, but it also "risked
de-valuing the cosmological relation attached to each seat within the
ranking system, jeopardizing the entire mytho-social order" (Masco
1995, 64).

If on some occasions the sitting chiefs favored newcomers, at other
times they colluded to ruin the prospects of ambitious aspirants.
Near the end of the nineteenth century high-ranking chiefs united
to force aspiring commoners of whom they disapproved to abandon
their efforts at potlatching. When one of the newly created Eagle
chiefs wanted to collect his gift on the day before the ritual potlatch,
they had him killed (Drucker 1963, 139). Chief Walas Kwaxilanokume
of the Mamalilikulla (ranked fifth as a tribe in the "ritual congregation") threatened to kill Wamis, a commoner, to end his efforts at
potlatching and forced him to yield up his copper, his assumed name,
and his seat (Boas 1925, 97). Walas Kwaxilanokume also ended the
potlatching career of Hayatkin, a commoner who had obtained the
name Wanuk from his wife—a chief's daughter—and had underwritten his potlatching career with wealth drawn from informant
fees paid by Boas, with income from prostitution, and with a copper
received from a friendly chief. Kwaxilanokume defeated Wanuk by
outbidding him in ritual contest, destroying three coppers valued at
39,000 blankets (Boas 1921, 1115–16). In dispatching these two commoner rivals, the victorious chief ended up with five seats in four different numayms; three of these seats included numaym chiefships
(Kobrinsky 1975, 49). Walas Kwaxilanokume also routed Sexuqala, a
commoner, who had a copper paid for with money earned in prostitution by his common-law wife and three stepdaughters (Boas
1925, 93; Kobrinsky 1975, 60). There also circulated stories about the
slave and commoner origins of lineages that discredited aspirants
who wanted to distribute property by pointing to their illegitimate
births (Boas 1921, 1093–1104).

In this way, throughout the second part of the nineteenth century,
the solidary relationship of chiefs to their tribes and numayms increasingly yielded to "individualized" coalitions of hereditary chiefs,
newly enriched and mobile chiefs, and assorted clienteles of followers (Mauzé 1986, 37; for Tlingit parallels, see Oberg 1937). This fur-

thered the self-oriented promotion of individual personages, family lines, and followerships, while loosening the collective bonds previously linking chiefs and the "fellows of the same kind" in the numayms. Visible expressions of such new alignments were the publicly installed "totem poles," really "politicized statements, allowing individuals to publicly declare their hold on certain crests by inscribing in wood a specific mytho-historical family history" (Masco 1995, 61). The first of these carved heraldic tree trunks in a Kwakwaka'wakw village apparently dates to 1873 (p. 60).

This enhanced "individualization" put a premium on the acquisition of the new kinds of wealth made available by the encompassing capitalist economy, even while growing external involvement and intensified outmigration lessened the ability of chiefs to command the labor of their numayms and to control the marriages of women. It advanced potlatching by placing more capital wealth in the hands of would-be participants, but at the same time it caused others "to cease potlatching, again narrowing the circle of people involved and further divorcing the potlatch from its ancient economic significance" (Wike 1957, 312). Simultaneously, the changes and accommodations in polity and economy also undermined the cosmological preeminence of the chiefly role. "After 1849 . . . the original covenant between chiefs and the animal world, which served to legitimate the symbolic domination of the ranking class, was no longer the only basis for explaining material success" (Masco 1995, 64). The cosmological understandings of chiefship were reconfigured into a political ideology that emphasized the role of chiefs as *gigami'*, "standing at the head," "(the one) alone at the front" (Berman 1991, 71), even as their material control of their world diminished.

MARRIAGE

The pressures emanating from the increasingly significant external political economy also affected the system of marriages and the ritual distributions associated with them. Marriage patterns among the Kwakwaka'wakw and Kwakiutl allowed the rights and prerogatives passed down through patricentered succession to be supplemented by privileges drawn from the maternal side. Marriage among Kwakiutl nobles widened the network of social relations by intertwining lines of descent, and it simultaneously transferred rights to names and initiatory privileges from noble fathers-in-law to noble sons-in-law, and thus from numaym to numaym. The institution thus lent a special strength to the position of the Kwakiutl chiefly class, without invoking or creating superior authority over the various constituent tribes.

The marriage system set off members of the chiefly families from commoners. Chiefs were "the real people," the ones with names and the privileges that came with those names. Chiefs sought to find suitable marriage partners in other groups, in order to draw from them valued objects—houses, house posts, crests, feast dishes, shell ornaments, coverings, coppers, canoes, and slaves—as well as the incorporeal prerogative to encounter the spirits in the Winter Ceremonial and to impersonate them in costume and performance. Marriage proposals and negotiations were represented metaphorically as forms of war; to obtain a wife and the objects and prerogatives she would convey to her husband-to-be, the chiefs "make war upon the daughters of the tribes" (Boas 1966, 53). Correspondingly, members of the bride's group and the party of the groom would engage in sham battles. The antagonistic discourse and pantomime symbolized and marked a structural gap between social units to be crossed; yet the actual terms of the marital transactions were negotiated peacefully.

The expectation was that the partners to a marriage would be of equal rank. "The ideal marriage, in the minds of the Indians," says Boas, "is that of a man and a girl of equal rank, particularly that of a man and a girl both of the line of primogeniture and of different numayma" (1966, 53). This implies, in turn, that the chiefly stratum in any one numaym was ideally linked through class-based norms of endogamy to other chiefly families in other numayms, thus keeping both ancestral privileges and rights acquired through affines under chiefly control (Kobrinsky 1975, 47). Compared with these chiefly concerns, the unions of commoners were of "no account," affairs of "the little ones who have no names," who "stick together like dogs." In fact, "Kwakiutl deny marriages to commoners, thus clearly defining marriage as a peculiarly spiritual relationship irrelevant for those who lack full spiritual qualities" (Goldman 1975, 74).

The class-specific, chiefly marriage process involved three steps, each marked by holding a distributional event to witness the step taken. First, the fathers of the bride and groom met to discuss the marriage payment to be made by the groom's family to the bride's. In the second step, the "bride price" or "bride gifts" were actually paid to the family of the bride, and she then moved from her father's house to the house of the groom. In doing so, however, she did not relinquish her membership in her natal numaym.

The third step was called "repayment of the marriage debt," the payment being made by the wife's family to the family of the groom. It was tendered several years later, frequently after the birth of a child, and involved a transfer of valuables many times greater than the bride gift initially paid by the groom's family. Crucially, it included not only tangible assets but also the incorporeal rights to initiation into the sodalities that performed dances and rituals during the Winter Ceremonial. Thus the chief of the Tlawitsis gave his son-in-law the hamatsa dance and the name T'saxwaxstala; the thrower dance and the name Great-Supernatural-One; the chief-fool dance and the name Umakwulala; the grizzly-bear dance and the name Fearless-Companion (Boas 1921, 951–1002). This bundle of rights was then held in trust by the woman's husband and bequeathed to their sons in her new domicile.

The marriage repayment might also contain names for the couple's children, gifted by the wife's father, which potentially gave both his grandsons and granddaughters positions of membership in their mother's natal numaym. The grandchildren could use these names to move to that numaym; or, alternatively, that numaym could call on them to join at some future point. This was especially important if the chief in the mother's numaym had no heirs of his own and sought a proper replacement among his daughter's children, a condition that must have become increasingly common as population sank to ever new lows.

It requires emphasis that marriages created ties not only between a husband and a wife, and between paternal and maternal in-laws, but also between the numayms involved. These relationships gave the offspring the option of taking up rights and privileges in the numayms of both the mother and the father. A new baby was not automatically assigned to either the paternal or the maternal numaym but had to await the bestowal of an appropriate name in a festive distribution, which then legitimized the affiliation that went with that name. Membership in a numaym could also be acquired by receiving the right to a seat in that numaym as a gift; by laying claim to a name associated with another numaym to which one could trace an ancestor; or even by seizing a numaym name by killing its owner (Rosman and Rubel 1971, 132). In all cases, however, the granting of a name had to be publicly witnessed and legitimized in a distributional event, before invited guests.

Equally significant was the fact that repayment of the "marriage debt" was a "repurchase" of the woman that effectively terminated the marriage. If the husband wanted to renew the marriage, the entire marriage process had to be gone through again. Every such annulment of a marriage—whether to the same man or another— added to the reputation and value of the woman and her children; a woman married and repurchased four times had the right to the title of *u'ma* and to wear a painted hat and abalone earrings (Cole 1991, 152). Serial marriage thus allowed—indeed required—the repetitive redistribution and circulation of valuables and privileges in successive ritual events.

The marriage system equipped chiefs and nobles with portfolios of a number of numaym memberships and enabled them to pursue alternative marriage strategies. The main goals of these strategies were to obtain "progeny to carry on one's line, to continue one's numaym, and to maintain and, if possible, raise the status of one's children" (Rosman and Rubel 1971, 156). In that sense, the marriage strategies were strategies for investment (Suttles 1991, 117). Multiplying polygynous marriages could be a way of building renown through alliances with numerous groups of relatives or of accumulating multiple bridal gifts to use in potlatching. Other strategies allowed a man to raise his own rank or the rank of his children. Alternatively, a wealthy and important chief could marry off his daughter to a man of lower rank in order to acquire a son-in-law as a dependable client and then strengthen his case by acquiring the couple's children through a high payment at marriage repurchase. The son-in-law might in turn welcome such a transaction, since a high payment at repurchase would give him the means to raise his rank by intensifying his sponsorship of distributional events. In all cases, marital options taken up in one generation affected the numaym options open to the next generation (Rosman and Rubel 1971, chap. 6).

The custom of serial marriages was, of course, at odds with Christian beliefs, and Canadian government officials and missionaries vehemently opposed it and the marriage system as a whole. Government officials argued that the system favored prostitution, allowing wives to earn money to finance the potlatches of their men; that it permitted parents to arrange the serial marriages of their children without their consent; that the parents could pressure their daughters to leave husbands who could not contribute money to potlatches in favor of those who could. They also recognized that the system worked against the marriages of young and poor men and favored the old and wealthy. Yet what they opposed most strongly was the ways in which the system of marriages contributed to the continued florescence of the potlatch. In the words of George DeBeck, Kwakewlth agent from 1902–1906, this system acted "as a feeder to the Potlatch," "as the main spring" of the interwoven complex of marriages, feasting, and potlatching (in Cole 1991, 150). In this they were indeed correct, because marriage negotiations, payments of marriage gifts, and repurchases of wives were all marked by ritual distributions. Marriages were also the conduits for the transfer, from father-in-law to son-in-law, of ownership rights and rights to the winter dances, for the missionary William Duncan a "horrid fabrication of lies." Finally, the majority of marriages, transfers of rights to dance, and ritual distributions took place in the winter season, thus strengthening the supernatural connotations of these practices. In 1885 the Canadian government outlawed the potlatch and what was legally referred to as "the tamanawas dance," the hamatsa ritual of the Kwakiutl Winter Ceremonial.

Cosmology and Ceremonial

We have already taken note of the Kwakiutl division of the year into two different seasons: the "secular" time of baxus in the spring, summer, and fall and tseka, the "sacred" season of winter. The two seasons were thought to be qualitatively distinct. Baxus was the season for hunting and gathering food, and thus for human predation upon animals and fish; it focused on relations between humans and the creatures of the spirit zone beyond the area of human settlement. Some of these spirit creatures would enter the human zone and permit themselves to be taken, offering their fleshy coverings (their "masks") for human consumption in return for the ritual treatment of their uneaten remains that would ensure their magical resuscitation. This relationship between humans and animals was necessary for human survival and existence in society, but it also posed the cosmological problem of how human predators were to deal with victims that were at once prey and congeners, cosubstantial with themselves. In tseka the roles were reversed; now "spirits are hunters and humans are the food" (Berman 1991, 109).

Tseka invited supernatural forces into the community and simulated their presence in the ritual performances of the Winter Ceremonial. The spirits seized humans, whom they devoured as their "gutted salmon" or "dried meat," but the ritual transformed the crisis of seizure into an initiatory experience for the victims. One of the central events of that ceremonial was the entry of young men— usually the heirs of chiefs and chiefs-to-be—into the hamatsa or cannibal-dancer society, in which the initiands "disappeared" into the "house" of Baxbakualanuxsiui'—"the spirit that eats humans at river's end"—then "went through" and reemerged as initiates who were no longer "entirely human." Ever afterward, "a vestige" of tseka power "will remain with him and his descendants" (Berman 1991, 687). Since this initiatory sequence was confined to high-ranking participants, it can also be interpreted as a process of sacralizing the heirs and aspirants to membership in the chiefly class.

MYTH

Many investigators have commented on the seemingly unsystematic and contradictory nature of Kwakiutl myths (for example, Boas 1897, 395–96; 1935, 177; 1940c, 377; 1940f, 447–48). In part, this impression derives simply from the fact that Kwakiutl numayms each held and elaborated its own particular origin myths and family histories:

Lacking political centralization, the Kwagul [Kwakiutl] nobility nevertheless played out their social, political, economic and religious life within a common political arena. Each rank-holder, each player in the

arena, required a history and a set of authentic, myth-chartered prerogatives that were at one and the same time distinct from those of other
rank-holders, and yet recognizable and acceptable within the overall system. Since there were, in the 19th century, close to a hundred namimuts
[numayms] of varying size and importance, such requirements led to an
enormous proliferation in the supernaturals encountered in myth.
(Berman 1991, 129)

Kwakiutl cosmological narratives, however, do reiterate recurrent
themes in the ontogeny of chiefly power. These themes focus, in sequence, on the change from chaos and disorder to an order of structured distinctions; on the simultaneous emergence of distinctions
among animals and humans, as well as reciprocities between them;
and on the prioritizing of the chiefly role in these transactions.

In Kwakiutl ontogeny, the "world" exists originally in a primordial
state of chaotic coalescence (Kobrinsky 1979, 164). This condition is
shattered by various transformers, such as Raven (among the northern neighbors of the Kwakiutl) or Mink (among the Kwakiutl themselves), who differentiate chaos by setting up dualities of darkness
and light, fire and water, humans and animals, males and females, life
and death. The terms of the oppositions produced are mutually dependent, yet antagonistic toward each other. Their simultaneous in-
terdependence and opposition generate time and its ceaseless transformations into days and seasons, on the one hand, and antagonistic
hierarchies of predators and prey, on the other.

The actions of the transformers arouse other myth-people to action in turn. These spirit-beings were referred to by the Kwakiutl as
"people of myth" (*nuxnimis*), which Hunt translated as "history
people." That term covered "all the different kinds of quadrupeds
and all the different kinds of birds and all the different crabs, when
they were all men, and the trees and all the plants" (Boas 1921, 622),
as well as marine mammals and fish, mythical thunderbirds, and
the wild, inland-dwelling spirit-beings called *Dzonoquas* (Berman
1991, 120). The animals were once human in nature, but they also
shared a substance of being with animals. Now animals and humans
differentiate.

The ancestors of the future numayms descend from the sky or
emerge from the sea; their arrival at particular locations then gives
them charter rights to territory and resources at these sites. They have

great supernatural power; they wear the large cedar-bark headrings that constitute the characteristic headgear of the cannibal dancer in the winter ceremonies, and they perform the Winter Ceremonial continually. Some ancestors remove their "masks" and become humans; the crests that humans retain and exhibit in their numayms continue to depict the ancestor in this "animal connection," his cosubstantiality with animals. Others who do not take off their masks remain animals on the outside but are humanlike on the inside. These ancestors possess supernatural power (*nawalak*) and deal in supernatural valuables, *tlogwe*. Still others emerge from beneath their animal coverings and become natural animals; these are the animals whose skins will circulate as wealth (Goldman 1975, 185–86).

The term "mask" requires further explanation. It is not equivalent to masks donned to disguise the face and identity of the wearer in Euro-American tradition but refers to the entire "fleshly covering" of a human or animal that includes "*both* head and body" (Berman 1991, 89). These masks are removable, so that animals can take them off to reveal their substance, cosubstantial with humans beneath. Humans can skin animals and eat them, but they must assure through proper ritual treatment that the creature will resuscitate. There is a continuity of life, an "iteration" (Berman 1991, 92) of life-forms through the generations.

In Kwakiutl ontogenesis, after humans and animals separate, each kind goes to its own village—birds into the sky, land animals onto the land, sea creatures into the water. The different kinds of animals have chiefs or are represented by type-figures that stand for the multitude. A Head-Wolf represents the wolves as a whole; the supernatural birds of the sky are headed by Thunderbird, the birds of the lower world by Eagle and Woodpecker; the salmon people live in a village of their own under the sea.

The ancestors of humans create people over whom their descendants will have jurisdiction as chiefs. Social hierarchies are established between the generative ancestor and the people at large whom he generates. Qanekilak causes people to issue forth from his house posts to become his followers; the Gwasila ancestor creates men and women from gulls' eggs and shells; another Gwasila ancestor carves them out of alder bark and animates them; the Dzawadenox ancestor transforms his second-ranked younger brother into eagle down, to become future people; Ha'na Lena sees people drifting by on logs—he saves them and they become his "tribe" (Boas 1966, 44). Since chiefs are represented as "iterations" of the founding ancestor or donor, they are equated with the creators or progenitors of the human groups over whom they exercise authority. Because the original donor or ancestor first occupied the resource area that will subsequently be utilized by his group, the chief is also "owner" or manager of that resource base. Since the original donor was endowed with valuables—houses, crests, masks, songs—the chief also keeps and wields these perquisites.

Now that people have separated from animals, they begin to hunt and kill their animal congeners. Yet, "if the substance of animals is human, the flesh that men eat is by analogy human also" (Goldman 1975, 183). Predation is reciprocal: many crest animals, like bears, eagles, killer whales, and wolves, eat humans in turn. Moreover, humans must nourish animals when they die; corpses are exposed to be dismembered by ravens. This is said to be the real or ultimate cause of death. Ravens, cosubstantial with humans, also feed off common substance. The food-collecting season, baxus, thus sets in motion an array of beings, all connected and yet differentiated into various kinds. These kinds relate to each other through mutual predation. Metaphors of incorporation or assimilation through eating or being eaten are salient in Kwakiutl texts and ritual performances, depicting the universe as a place where some beings are eaten by others and some beings must die so that others may feed on them and live (Walens 1981, 12).

If Kwakiutl cosmology envisaged comparisons but not equalities and saw relationships among humans and spirits, humans and humans, humans and animals, animals and animals as actively antagonistic, this meant that comparisons entailed demonstrations of antagonism. In Kwakiutl myth and ritual this basic understanding of antagonisms is expressed as an opposition between strength and weakness (Goldman 1975, 144). Strength is celebrated, weakness derided. Strength has supernatural power, nawalak; weakness lacks it. Yet their mutual definition also depends on context: sometimes the strong encounter forces stronger than themselves; sometimes, as in tales of cunning orphans that prove victorious, the seemingly weak can overcome the seemingly strong. In Goldman's words, "life and death, vigor and illness, victor and victim, killer and killed, devourer and devoured are permanently bound in restless opposition. The pattern of opposition is permanent, but the figures change constantly, yielding and then regaining cyclical ascendancy" (1975, 145).

In this world "red in tooth and claw," organisms compete and ensure their survival at the expense of other organisms. What has been said of other hunter-gatherers was true of the Kwakiutl as well: they "are constantly dealing in death. . . . Death is for them a way of life" (Woodburn 1982, 187). Yet hunters and fishermen also understand that they are dependent on their prey and that dependence is emphasized in myth and ritual. In Kwakiutl cosmology both humans and animals are seen as caught up in the alternation of life and death. When humans die, they become food for ravens, who free their spirits by consuming their bodies. When humans hunt animals, that animal must be willing to die, but it will do so only on the condition that humans kill and process its body in the appropriate ritual manner so as to allow the animal spirit to resuscitate. The acquisition and consumption of food thus come to be hedged about by etiquettes that make eating properly a moral responsibility. Killing, processing, and eating become "ritual labor," for which the chiefs as executives of food rights granted to their original ancestors bear a special responsibility. Since the chief represents the supernaturals among humans, "there is a fundamentally sacramental character to the entire food collection and distribution process" (Walens 1981, 77). In carrying out ritual, as in his prayers, the chief is guardian of the proper balance between humans and animals and thus is responsible for success or failure in the quest for food.

After the humans separate from animals, they encounter spirit-forces that pertain to particular domains of nature: the Thunderbird is associated with the sky; the Dzonoqua with the forest; the spirit Komokwa and the dreaded double-headed serpent Sisiutl with the sea. These spirit-forces favor humans by giving them names. The names will be inherited, passed on in marriage, or transferred in distributional events, but they are connected to the supernatural. An ancestor says: "These will come to be the names when I come to take my place in this world, when I come being a man in this world coming down here" (Boas 1935, 66). Chiefs will later announce their names at distributions, assigning them mass and weight: "This is my name; this is the weight of my name. The mountain of blankets rises through the heavens" (Boas 1897, 349).

THE WINTER CEREMONIALS

The Kwakiutl chiefly class and nobility not only claimed supernatural powers through association with ancestral lines; they also sought access to spirit power through dramatic encounters in the Winter Ceremonial. Among many North American Indian peoples, seekers after sacred power had visions in which they entered into contact with guardian spirits, who bestowed on them both supernaturally charged objects and instructions, and visionary encounters with spirits who endowed their clients with such powers were widespread on the Northwest Coast. The essential plot of the Winter Ceremonial conforms to this pattern in that a spirit kidnaps and consumes the initiand, and in so doing grants him supernatural powers; it then releases him back into normal life as a person transformed by that experience. Unlike the vision in much of North America, however, in the Kwakiutl ceremonial this visionary experience was neither open to all nor specific to the individual visionary. It was confined to sets of people who had acquired the prerogative to enter a sodality that impersonates the supernatural in question, and that prerogative was acted out in a highly standardized and impersonal form, within an organized framework of impersonating performances.

Boas suggested that ceremonials such as those of the Kwakiutl represented an accommodation of individual experience to hereditary rank (1897, 336). Indeed, it may be possible to trace out some of the steps in this "accommodation" through comparative ethnography. Among the Salishan-speaking peoples around Puget Sound, south of the Kwakiutl, seekers after supernatural power enacted their spirit encounters in the winter season, with each performer singing and dancing in his or her own way, without any overall organization. However, among the northernmost Salish of the Georgian Strait (Comox, Pentlatch), closest to the Kwakiutl, these enactments represented not personal and individualized meetings with spirits but hereditary and standardized impersonations of the experiences undergone by a common ancestor of a set of bilateral descendants (Barnett 1955; Jorgensen 1980, 259–60). Among the Wakashan-speaking peoples the most systematically arranged, hierarchically organized, exclusive, and hereditary ceremonial sodalities with rights to particular winter dance cycles occurred among the Northern Kwakiutl (Heiltsuk/ Bella Bella, Xaihais, Haisla, and Wikeno). It was probably these people—especially the Heiltsuk—who originated hereditary and organized winter dancing in the area in the protohistoric period (Jorgensen 1980, 259–60; Harkin 1997, 1–2). The organizational model of dancing sodalities and the cultural performances associated with them, together with their Heiltsuk names, then diffused outward, reaching the Tlingit in the north only in the recent historic period. They were also adopted by the Southern Kwakiutl, including the Tsaxis tribes, who organized them into one all-encompassing cycle of performances.

These dances and spirit impersonations were, among the Kwakiutl, graded into two categories, one superior to the other. The superior category was called *laxsa,* which translates as "gone through" or "gone into the house" but also as "to go through to the other side" (Goldman 1975, 118) or "dying" (Boas, in Goldman 1975, 243). The house is that of Baxbakualanuxsiui', "the spirit who eats humans at the river's end" (Berman 1991, 56–57) and his ferocious "brothers" or companions. In the Winter Ceremonial the initiand meets Baxbakualanuxsiui', is first possessed by him and then devoured. Eaten by the spirit, the initiate becomes the cannibal dancer or hamatsa, ferociously pursuing victims in search of human flesh. Being eaten by the man-eating spirit consumes his body, yet releases its vital energy for further transformation. During baxus humans have hunted animals; now the initiate offers himself up to requite the debt, "an earnest" to show that "he who wants to get food must become food" (Reid 1979, 256). He then reenters the human world, where he must be pacified gradually and returned to a second childhood. As a quasi-child he must be resocialized, emerging then as a responsible person in control of his drives.

Contrary to past interpretations that have represented the "spirit at the river's end" as the ultimate and most awesome predator, Berman points out that in Kwakiutl mythology the river's end is the point where the salmon leave their home in the zone of the spirits and are born into the world of humans. In the Winter Ceremonial, the spirits enter the zone of humans to capture them, drag them off to their spirit homes, and eat them. In the course of the ceremonial the laxsa disappear into the woods and are taken to "the end of the river." This is the place where salmon enter this world, and, in analogy of humans with salmon, where humans, "consumed by predatory spirits, are then restored to life" (1991, 688). Transformed by being eaten and given access to the spirit zone, they return purified and empowered by knowledge. In contrast to the laxsa, who have thus "gone through" to meet the spirit in the woods, all other ceremonial dancers are *wixsa,* who have "merely leaned against the front of the house" (Boas 1966, 174).

The original meanings of the dances are unclear. It may be, as Boas believed, that the prototypical Kwakiutl spirit quest originally bore "a close connection" to war (1940a, 383). It was thought that a killing could bring on a Winter Ceremonial in the midst of the summer season, while killing someone and appropriating his name and ancestral privileges, or assaulting a supernatural, were still mentioned as ways of gaining status in Boas's time. Furthermore, the spirit Winalagelis, Making-War-all-over-the-World, who can both grant war powers and heal, was considered "the bringer of the ceremonial" (p. 383). He appears in the Winter Ceremonial as the younger brother of "the spirit who eats humans at the river's end." It may also be relevant that the Heiltsuk were an aggressive group, heavily involved in warfare with the Tsimshian, the Bella Coola, and the Xaihais, as well as in raiding for slaves (Ferguson 1984, 307). According to Boas, both the Tsimshian ("not before 1820") and the Tsaxis confederates ("around 1830") adopted the Heiltsuk ceremonial pattern of killing and eating a slave as part of the Winter Ceremonial (Boas 1940a, 383).

We know that the central dance and performance cycle of the Kwakiutl Cannibal Society was taken from the Heiltsuk by force in 1837 and brought to the Tsaxis Kwakiutl before they moved to Fort Rupert (Berman 1991, 259). Presumably, also, knowledge of the dance was conveyed to the Kwakiutl by intermarriages with the Bella Bella and the Wikeno (Rivers Inlet tribe) (Boas 1966, 258). The acquisition may have resonated with a Northwest Coast thematics of cannibalism already present at the time of first contact, which defined human life as a valuable to be consumed as part of the perquisites of status (see Wike 1984). Before the advent of the new Man-Eater wrested from the Heiltsuk the Kwakiutl Winter Ceremonial had featured an older man-eating-spirit-of-the-woods, the *Hamshamtses*. The Hamshamtses dance, however, was the privileged possession of a particular numaym, "bound to the numaym chieftainship as was the privilege of inviting the tribes" (Kobrinsky 1975, 47). It did not represent a spirit who encompassed the initiatory system in its entirety. The dances featuring the new Man-Eater not only displayed a spirit being both more dramatic and more violent than the Hamshamtses, but they were not tied to any particular numaym. Indeed, "the ability of these dances to circulate, and serve the established chiefs as a floating screen for admission to chiefly status (a back-up to marriage regulation), may account for their rapid climb to ceremonial primacy" (p. 48). In this way Baxbakualanuxsiui' replaced his predecessor as the focus of laxsa initiation, while Hamshamtses was relegated to the position of one of his companions, and from then on was danced by women.

There is thus also a clear link between initiation into the circle of hamatsa initiates and the institution of chiefship. Initiation as a hamatsa was "the exclusive prerogative of the highest-ranking chiefs" and their heirs apparent (Goldman 1975, 110; also Boas 1897, 411, 418; 1921, 1176; Codere 1961, 474). By meeting the Man-Eater they acquired both supernatural treasures and powers; they embody life: "I have the magical treasure / I have the supernatural power / I can return to life"; "The Cannibal spirit made me pure. I do not destroy life. I am the life maker" (Boas 1897, 373; 1966, 253).

This is a ritual that conforms to Maurice Bloch's notion of "rebounding violence" (1984, 4–7). Attempting to define the "irreducible core of the ritual process," Bloch lays out a characteristic sequence of performances. First, there is a devaluation of the here and now. Second, the initiates are symbolically killed, ritually negating their earthly condition. Third, they move into the supremely valued world of the transcendental, where their own vital drives are mastered and transformed. They yield to a double violence: violence first abrogates their ordinary vitality, then replaces it with a purified vitality supplied by contact with the transcendental. "Going through" the hamatsa ritual substitutes for the ordinary drives of the initiand the transformed motivations of the initiate, who returns to the here and now purged and disciplined by his otherworldly experience in the house of the man-eating spirit. Yet if initiation into the dancing sodalities was the prerogative of the highest-ranking chiefs, the candidate who is enabled to "go through" was also seasoned and prepared to become a chief, an exemplary controller of ordinary people and a manager of the relationship between people and animals.

There is a third facet to this initiation: theatricality. Many students of Kwakiutl culture noted that its ceremonial seemed secular and formalized, rather than informed by a devotion of heart and mind. Its performances relied strongly on staging and impression management, including the use of mechanical aids to produce desired effects. It is also likely that what may once have been actual acts of cannibalism in the hamatsa performance became in the course of the nineteenth century theatrical simulations (Codere 1961, 448, 474–75).

Boas relates the Kwakiutl term for the period of the Winter Ceremonial (tsetsequa) to a root *ts!a'ga*, to be fraudulent or to cheat, and suggests that it "is clearly and definitely stated that it is planned as a fraud" (1966, 172). Goldman argues that this rendition is too strong—that the theatrical effects and impressions were used to evoke the return to a prototypical condition when present realities came into being: "what was real then is simulated now." Berman furnishes strong support for the idea that Kwakiutl myth and ritual "imitated" an original condition or state of being through carving, singing, dancing, and elaborate theatricals. The thought is to *follow* the original pattern correctly, to endow the reiteration and reenactment of past "myth-historical" events with political and moral meaning. To follow correctly is "to obey"; "to disobey" is "to fail to follow" (Berman 1991, 87). Thus, Goldman can say that "the impersonations are artifice, but the powers brought by the spirits is genuine" (1975, 103, 104). Anyone familiar with the Catholic Baroque in Europe can certainly testify to the fact that theatricality is no impediment to religious devotion. Susan Reid adds a further insight: the novice undergoes the experience of death and release at the hand of the Man-Eater but also discovers that the experience is stage managed. In his resocialization after the experience, he learns that he must accept the simulation as part of his return to the society of humans. Acceptance is "helping the novice to find his way out of the myth" (Reid 1979, 268). Yet more is involved, I believe, than a simple acceptance of a human lot. Since the initiate will return to society as an aristocrat or chief, he will also qualify for that position by the political knowledge that it takes stage management to project reality.

A fourth facet of the Winter Ceremonial is that it displaces the sociopolitical structure active in the profane season and replaces it with the different alignments of sacred time. The profane season was dominated by the structural arrangement of the numayms, each centered upon its particular chief, legitimized by its special names, legends and privileges. With the onset of the sacred season, the participants who are members of the nobility change from their summer names to their winter names (Rosman and Rubel 1990, 624). The structural alignments of the numayms yield to those of the ceremonial dance sodalities. Numaym membership remains relevant to the ceremonials only residually, because the roles of the ceremonial assistants to the initiates are inherited patrilineally, as are the rights to dance some of the minor dances like Fool and Bear.

Each dance sodality brings together the initiates of a particular spirit, regardless of their sociopolitical membership (see the diagram in Walens 1981, 42). Thus, members of the most prestigious of the dance societies, the hamatsa, were seen as "all related to the Cannibal spirits, especially to Man-Eater. Rules of kinship have no influence on the relationships of these men" (p. 43). Yet, if we are attentive to ways in which politically charged ideas mask the class stratification of Kwakiutl society, we may note that the change from baxus to tseka also entailed a shift from numaym solidarity to "the class-determined arrangements of dancing societies" (Kobrinsky 1975, 47). Moreover, initiation into the Cannibal Society created crosscutting ties among chiefs as initiands. It reinforced the role of marriage ties as links among the numayms and reminded the initiands that their supernaturally legitimized privileges of "going through" derived from the marriages of their parents, who were themselves born into different numayms.

What this shows is that the chiefly role involved both a symbolic identification with the founding ancestor and a special kind of sacralizing socialization. These symbolic assets then proved useful in controlling upstarts and retaining dependents, even as the transformations caused by the pressures of a capitalist political economy weakened the material underpinnings of chiefly power. Seen in that context, we can also begin to understand why both potlatching and winter dancing might have had symbolic value in warding off the intensifying European encroachment on the native way of life. Joyce Wike was perhaps the first to suggest that these rituals harbored a nativistic element, despite the apparent paradox posed by the fact that the cultures of the Northwest Coast emphasized the manipulation of wealth, "while other embattled American Indian groups responded with religious revivalism." What needed to be recognized, she argued, was that "this manipulation was an earthly manifestation of supernatural powers and related to supernatural power," a point easily "lost sight of," when Northwest Coast uses of wealth were misinterpreted due to "our own cultural values" (1952, 99).

Potlatching

As noted, the displays and giveaways of valuables at distributional events have often been misunderstood as patterns of accumulation and exchange that obtain under capitalism. The "wealth" demonstrated in these ritual affairs was not capital in the modern sense, and the valuables offered or received as gifts were not primarily commodities, not even when the capitalist economy had begun to swamp native society. Related to this misunderstanding was another one: if the wealth and valuables activated in the potlatches were seen as capital and commodities, then giving them away or destroying them without thought of adequate compensation seemed economically irrational and improvident. This was the reasoning of the Canadian authorities when they forbade potlatching in 1888 as a "foolish, wasteful and demoralizing custom" (in Fisher 1977, 206). In a different kind of misunderstanding, an overwrought romanticism interpreted such supposedly wanton disregard of rationality as the unleashing of untrammeled passions in the service of liberation from social restraint (see, for example, Bataille 1967, 120–39). As a result of such misunderstandings, potlatches came to be seen primarily as ostentatious occasions for "conspicuous consumption," the term with which Thorstein Veblen (1899) stigmatized the improvident expenditures of an unproductive leisure class. This placed the emphasis on the wasteful use of resources in sumptuous feasting. Yet not only are feasting and potlatching not the same thing (Suttles 1991, 104), but Kwakiutl socialization strongly emphasized restraint and sobriety in the intake of food and frowned upon shows of gluttony and careless waste.

What came to be called "potlatching" did involve feasting and gift giving, but its central feature lay not in lavish expenditures but in the display and affirmation of privileges and in transfers of valuables in the presence of witnessing guests. These displays and transfers marked important changes in "the life cycle of persons and the cycle of the seasons. They are interlocked with birth, with the stages of maturation, with adolescence, with accession to rank, with marriage, with succession to chiefship, and with death" (Goldman 1975, 125). The custom of giveaways clusters around critical points of social and cosmological transformations. Each transition in the identity of persons and each alternation of baxus and tseka seasons demanded a change of name; each such change required a display of inherited privileges before groups and individuals invited to witness the events, accompanied by donations to the guests and counterofferings to the hosts. Every transgenerational bestowal of a privilege triggered an outflow of goods to the members of other groups in attendance. Distributions accompanied the specific rituals to mark a girl's puberty or the bestowal of a name upon a boy, to commemorate a marriage, to mourn a death, to celebrate the construction of a house, to invest an heir, to transfer a valued copper, to hold Winter Ceremonial dances, and to display newly acquired supernatural properties. Originally, each kind of distributive event bore a different name that distinguished among events organized "to give away presents," to offer "feasts," or to do both. The designations for giveaways distinguished among those that involved giving blankets to one's relatives, to one's tribe, and to many tribes and set these off from giveaways of various kinds of property from father-in-law to son-in-law. Feasts were also differentiated by whether they featured salmonberries, eulachon oil, cranberries and eulachon oil, seals, or the stomach fat of mountain goats (Berman 1991, 53). For this reason, Goldman has argued that there "never were, at least in precontact days, such events as 'potlatches.'" The general term "potlatch"— supposedly derived from *patshatl*, to give, in the Chinook trade jargon used up and down the coast—became popular only in the period between 1860 and 1870 (1975, 131, 245).

Although Boas may have been ill-advised in using the term to cover all kinds of giveaways, its wide employment by scholars as well as in general discourse is justified by a basic resemblance among the various distributive events. More significant, however, has been the growing recognition that this general pattern itself has been subject to major changes over time. We are indebted to Helen Codere (1950, 1961) for systematic exploration of these quantitative and qualitative changes. She defined the founding of Fort Rupert in Kwakiutl territory in 1849 as the watershed event between a Pre-Potlatch period from 1778 to 1849, when the potlatch existed "as an institution but in competition with other institutions on a fairly equal basis," to a Potlatch Period proper, when "the potlatch came to be the central and all-encompassing institution" (1961, 434). This period ended, for Codere, when the Canadian government, long hostile to potlatching and ceremonial winter dancing, confiscated masks and other valuables after Chief Dan Cranmer's potlatch of 1921. Yet redistributive events continued to be celebrated clandestinely even later, and potlatching was revived in the course of ethnic renewal in the 1960s. A modified form of the ceremonial has been held every year since 1963.

Codere's periodization may be overly precise, but her analysis helps us to understand the forces at work in the transformation of Kwakiutl society and culture. The founding of Fort Rupert 1849 was certainly pivotal, in that it furnished the incentive for the four tribes of the Gwetela, the Komoyaye, the Walas Kwakiutl, and the Komkyutis to move from their villages on the Clio Channel to Tsaxis at Fort Rupert. This moment signals a transition from smaller to larger potlatch donations, a change in the nature of the goods distributed, and a moment in the widening of the potlatch circle.

The move to Fort Rupert came at a time when independent raiding and warfare by Indian groups suffered a decline. By the mid-1850s, the unregulated and often amiable accommodation of European fur traders to Indian requirements began to yield to demands for protection by permanent settlers on Vancouver Island. The fur traders had already begun to limit Indian warfare, since it clearly interfered with business. The government moved to further discourage Indian raiding in the 1860s. Raids and wars did not disappear entirely, but they decreased in number and intensity. The escalation of ritual distributions coincided with this diminution of warfare.

Some investigators have seen enhanced giveaways as a direct cultural substitute for the pursuit of prestige through warfare. In support of this view, they point to the frequent employment of warlike metaphors in the native characterization of distributive events (Boas 1940e, 234). Warfare was certainly of much greater importance than many scholars have allowed (Ferguson 1983, 1984). However, both warfare and slave raiding declined as sources of chiefly wealth in the first half of the nineteenth century, while access to European money and goods grew ever more significant, in both production and distribution. At the same time, opportunities for ritual distributions to a widening circle of participants increased apace, especially between 1870 and 1880.

The rising scale of ritual donations is clearly seen in the family histories analyzed by Goldman (1975, 131 and appendix 4). In the first half of the nineteenth century the average distribution featured fewer than 300 "blankets," about half of them low-value cedar-bark blankets given to commoners. In some instances, all the visitors together received only 50 animal skins (see also Codere 1961, 446). The largest distribution known before 1849 involved 320 blankets. The earlier distributions featured primarily animal skins; blankets made of fur, mountain-goat hair, and cedar bark; canoes, boxes, and dishes; and food, slaves, and coppers. Distributions after 1849 included diminishing numbers of skins and ever more Hudson Bay blankets, by the thousands, and hammered copper shields that stood for multiples of thousands of blankets. A potlatch held in 1869 featured a distribution of 9,000 blankets; another, held in 1895, 13,000 blankets. Cranmer's great distributive event in 1921 involved the giving away of more than 30,000 blankets (Codere 1961, 467). The number of events in which coppers were offered increased dramatically after 1849, and so did the value of the shields transferred (p. 468). By 1893 the copper called Maxtsolem ("All other coppers are afraid to look at it") was valued at 7,500 blankets, Laxolamas ("Steelhead salmon") at 6,000 (Boas 1966, 84). Distributions also featured increasing quantities of European-made goods. People "were able to raise the always increasing amounts necessary both by earning more wealth and by lending what they had to one another at high rates of interest. The development of the concept of interest and interest rates and of a credit potlatch economy ensued" (Codere 1961, 468).

The circle of ritual distributions among participating tribes at first encompassed only the Tsaxis groups themselves. Then, probably between 1870 and 1880, the Tsaxis confederates began to invite Mamalilikulla, Nimpkish, and then Tlawitsis to take part in large distributions as entire groups (Drucker and Heizer 1967, 43). Widening distributive opportunities may have responded to several class interests. They brought together different resource-owning groups and consolidated relations within the class of chiefs (Adams 1981, 373). The corollary of this strategy was to extend the range of marriages among the leading families of diverse groups (see, for example, Goldman 1975, 35, 235). This strengthened the position of chiefly families through preferential endogamy. It simultaneously facilitated access to material resources and to supernatural privileges through donations from the affinal line, precisely at a time of diminishing opportunities for predatory warfare. The government certainly discouraged raiding and war; but the impetus to replace "rivers of blood by rivers of wealth" may have come as well from the chiefly elite itself. As one Kwakiutl phrased it, "In olden times we fought so that the blood ran over the ground. Now we fight with button blankets and other kinds of property and we smile at each other! Oh, how good are the new times!" (Boas 1966, 119).

The expansion of ritual distributions also generated a search for more ample funding of the distributional events. A misunderstanding drawn from his attendance at such events in 1897 caused Boas to err in thinking that all gifts made had to be returned at 100 percent interest. This misperception made him believe that continuing distributions would lead to geometrically increasing burdens of debt. Loans requiring a double return did exist—first in blankets, later in money, and on occasion in eulachon oil—but no rates of return were stipulated for offerings in the ritual distributions as such (Charles Nowell and Ed Whonnuck, in Drucker and Heizer 1967, 55; Drucker 1963, 55–66). However, this does not mean that the giveaways operated completely outside the market economy. Loans for interest did become more prominent as the Kwakiutl increasingly drew cash from the burgeoning commodity and labor markets of the nineteenth century. People preparing for a ritual event sometimes forced loans on clients to induce them to contribute to the occasion or called in loans to finance the events. Cash earnings from a variety of sources underwrote the efforts of aspirants to rank, whose names were, as Hunt said, "made up" (in Goldman 1975, 56). Unregulated credit appeared in the acquisition of copper shields, but defaults on these loans caused the chiefs to discontinue the practice in 1921 (Drucker and Heizer 1967, 66). A growing demand for loans, as well as insistent requests for repayment, played a part in the upward spiraling of giving and receiving at ritual events, at the same time making people ever more dependent on the external economy and its changing conditions.

Quantitative escalation in ritual distributions within a widening circle of participants must thus be placed against the backdrop of an intensified relation with the capitalist political economy surrounding the ritualists. It must also be projected against the disastrous demographic decline that ravaged the population as a whole until the initial decades of the twentieth century. The joint effects of these trends gathered significant momentum in the period between 1860 and 1880.

Until that turning point, the main actors—and perhaps the only ones—privileged to distribute and receive wealth had been the senior chiefs. These chiefs, as we have seen, held their positions as the named stand-ins for the initial founders of their corporate groups and were thus repositories of that initiatory supernatural power; but, as ever more mobile and quantifiable wealth flowed from the outside world into all domains of Kwakiutl life, the traditional power of chiefs over resources and labor diminished. The entry of new aspirants into the competition for the statuses and privileges vacated by the dead raised the stakes for all participants, senior chiefs as well as holders of second-ranking positions. Moreover, the title-holders increasingly had to contest rival claims to precedence in situations where no prior rule clarified how the deceased incumbents were to be replaced. By 1888, George Dawson reported that "The rules governing the potlatch and its attendant ceremonies have grown to be so complicated that even those persons most familiar with the natives can scarcely follow it in all its details, and it is sometimes difficult for the natives themselves to decide certain points, leaving openings for roguery and sharp practice with the more unscrupulous" (in Wike 1957, 303). Thus, two of the twenty-one coppers whose history Hunt recorded were forgeries produced between 1864 and 1869; they continued to circulate thereafter (Codere 1961, 468–70).

In the 1960s, ecological anthropologists interpreted potlatching primarily as an adaptation to the natural environment. They argued that the maritime resources available to the peoples of the Northwest Coast were generally plentiful but that seasonal and geographical variations produced repeated local shortages and even episodes of scarcity. This threat of scarcity could be averted through the development of distributive mechanisms that drew on plentiful supplies in one location to counteract shortages in another. The institution of chiefship, in this view, fulfilled a pivotal role: by amassing resources for potlatches, chiefs could concentrate needed resources, only to pour them out again in redistributive giveaways to assemblies of guests. The benefit for the redistributing chief would be a gain in renown and prestige, but this manifest function merely served a more important covert function, that of leveling access to available supplies in order to even out life's risks.

There is indeed evidence that resources were variable and that groups with a more assured resource base were accorded higher ranks than were poorer groups (Piddocke 1965; Suttles 1968; Donald and Mitchell 1975). It is also true that Indian groups argued with the Canadian government that an end to potlatching would mean that people would not have enough to eat (Petition of the Mamalilacala [Mamalilikulla], 1889, in Fisher 1977, 208). Yet a comparative statistical test failed to confirm the hypothesis that greater long-term variability in the availability of salmon correlated with increased participation in distributional events (Donald and Mitchell 1975). There are also problems with establishing how much food chiefs collected from their followers and how much was actually redistributed. Careful planning must have been of the essence, since chiefs were required to repay communal services with food. Perhaps it was not need in times of scarcity that propelled the intensifying redistributions, but the need to accumulate liens on labor, at a time when commoners could opt for new opportunities and required incentives to stay. This also means that potlatching at this time set the chiefs in competition with each other over followers and clients. John Adams has argued that chiefs always strove to be the largest contributors to their distributive events because they sought to reduce the influence of contributors who, with each contribution, gained liens over the disposal of the returns (1981, 372).

There also remain questions as to the amounts and kinds of food distributed at such events. The standard ceremonial foods included dry salmon; rendered fish oil ("grease," namely eulachon or candlefish oil, or whale oil); crabapples, viburnum berries, soap berries, and dry berry cakes; and short and long cinquefoil roots. Seal meat was reserved for the highest chiefs, as were halibut skins, winkles, salmon cheeks, a mix of currants and salal berries, and long cinquefoil roots (Walens 1981, 94). (Walens says that venison was not eaten, because it was thought to induce forgetfulness [134, 135]). Discipline in eating was rewarded, and gluttony was deprecated. Etiquette demanded that one not ask for food; portions were usually small and limited to one course; there were no second helpings. Vomiting carried positive supernatural connotations of transformation and rebirth (Goldman 1975, 150; Walens 1981, 146–47).

Finally, on general grounds, we know that the effects of a system are not the same as its causes (Orans 1975), and any ecological outcomes may well have been side effects of other, more proximate causal factors. Moreover, a purely ecological explanation does not specify who was invited to these events and for what reason (Rosman and Rubel 1971, 178–79). Choice of distributional partners and invitations to guests involved politics, both the politics of renown and the politics of political alliances. Ecological considerations thus raised important questions and generated interesting answers, but further, complementary approaches are required to explain the cultural role of potlatching as such.

Such approaches must include the realm of Kwakiutl ideas—for present purposes, particularly those ideas that sustained the power of chiefs and aristocrats. The assertive and aggressive ways in which Kwakiutl chiefs faced each other during ritual distributions enacted the ideological dimension of chiefship. Since all ranking involved gradations of superiority and inferiority, all gains or losses of rank entailed contests, which were fought out in terms of both the natural political economy and differential access to supernatural power. "What observers have usually taken to be rivalry over rank," says

Goldman, "are in fact, invidious demonstrations of supernatural powers—of *nawalak*. . . . They manifest aggressive hostility against rivals to demonstrate that the capability of destroying is one of the attributes of *nawalak*" (1975, 181).

Nawalak was "the general term for the supernatural, the wonderful" (Boas 1940d, 612). It came from spirit donors, who granted visions or bestowed names. Chiefs faced each other as agents of the initial supernatural event and depended for their right to do so on having authentic names received from spirit donors, not names just "made up." Names were charged with nawalak; nawalak endowed them with mass and weight; goods offered in distribution stood for that mass and weight. When chiefs offered piles of blankets, they materialized the weight of their name; piling on valuables in marriage exchanges made the bride "heavy with wealth." Symbolically, blankets also fell from the red cedar neckrings that initiates wore in the sacred Winter Ceremonial. When a bridegroom faced the father of his wife-to-be to receive the winter dance privileges, the father-in-law took on the supernatural dimension of a "power-granting donor."

Just as masks were not facial disguises, so "wealth" in the form of these valuables was not capital. Until the use of money—with its own magical property as a universal common denominator—became widespread on the Northwest Coast, valuables in all their particularity as blankets, canoes, boxes, door posts, feasting dishes, and rights to dance or to use specific masks were thought to convey some quantum of supernatural energy, some vital force, in and of themselves. They were also tokens of evidence that their managers or "owners" were recipients of some supernatural gift or reward themselves, whether that gift was obtained by legitimate succession to the privileges of an original supernatural donor or was wrested from a supernatural by force. These attributes of things and privileges gave a person nawalak and underwrote his ability to expand that power further by becoming a donor in turn, making gifts and transferring vital forces to others.

The ability to acquire wealth objects and to give them away in displays of the powers of one's name was thus not only political and economic but derived from transactions with supernatural power. Festive foods offered to guests, like food in general, implied supernaturally grounded contracts with the animate spirits of animals and plants. Wealth objects in the form of containers, such as canoes, boxes, and dishes, were thought to embody vital forces granted by spirits and ancestors. Animal hides may similarly have been regarded as containers of vital energy, perhaps by drawing an analogy between containers and the skin as containing the vital principle of the animal within (Walens 1981, 150–53).[5] It is also relevant that humans and animals were regarded as cosubstantial beneath their skins, with animals retaining their skins except when at home, while the original donor-ancestors had doffed their coverings in taking up their careers in the human domain. Giving and receiving coverings thus appears to have implied a giving and receiving of quanta of vital forces.[6]

As the capitalistically oriented outer world increasingly encompassed the Kwakiutl in the mid-nineteenth century, the earlier hide or skin coverings (*naenxwa*) distributed at these events gave way to woolen blankets (*pelxelesgeme,* "fog coverings") purveyed by the Hudson Bay Company. The introduction of these blankets contributed to the development of uniform quantitative standards in evaluating wealth, and they became the universal "currency" utilized in distributive events during Codere's Potlatch Period, from 1849 to 1921. The increasing use of Hudson Bay Company blankets also affected the other major valuables used in potlatching events, such as the worked shields of copper that were given away or destroyed in the course of distribution events. These shields came to stand for large multiples of blankets. There is some question as to whether both the form and the meanings of the copper antedate contact with Europeans. Excavations at Ozette in Makah territory have yielded stone artwork some 500 years old that strongly resembles coppers from the nineteenth century (Adams 1981, 381). These valued objects were probably originally connected with head-hunting and slave-raiding, standing for heads taken or slaves killed and placed under the house posts or crest-bearing poles of ancestor-based "houses." Native copper may have been worked to make shields before contact, but none has survived; all extant coppers were derived from material obtained from the sheathing of ships or through commerce.

Much more needs to be known about skin coverings, blankets, and coppers to fully understand their role in potlatch transactions. It is clear, however, that chiefs heaping blankets upon their guests took a doubly aggressive role in doing so: they "made good" their own names in contest with the recipients, and they demonstrated their qualifications for precedence over them, even as they conveyed vital forces to them. Bestowal of vital forces upon the recipients was expressed in metaphors of ingestion—they "swallowed up the tribes" to whom they distributed or "vomited" out offerings (Boas 1966, 192–93). Ideologically, the chief aggressively and demonstratively made "great" his name, while multiplying vital energies for all.

The same motif of status antagonism was enacted in distributions featuring the vaunted coppers. Widerspach-Thor argues that coppers replaced real human beings as warfare and slave-raiding ebbed over the course of the nineteenth century (1981, 166–70). By the time Boas and Hunt did fieldwork, they carried metaphorical meanings beyond these earlier functions. Their reddish color associated them with light, the sun, and the sky, but also with the sea and with salmon. At the same time, supernaturals, ancestors, and initiates were believed to travel between the realms of sky, earth, and sea over copper poles, copper ladders, or copper mountains. Copper shields thus metaphorically linked the different levels of the world and connected multiple kinds of life. These shields were equated with hundreds and thousands of blankets in distributive events, but they reached an evaluative climax when they were ritually destroyed or thrown into the sea. Throwing a copper into the sea transferred vital force to the fish-people. Melting down a copper in fire conveyed vital energy to the sky spirits. "Killing" a copper by breaking it up simulated the death of the vitality contained in it; riveting the pieces together once more, however, was understood as a transformation that multiplied its power to redistribute vital forces among human beings (Walens 1981, 60–61). Transfers or sales of coppers usually took place during the sacred winter season, as a prelude to a high-status marriage. In all of these transfers and movements, coppers traveled metaphorically across boundaries—cosmological boundaries in space and social boundaries between groups. When the Tsaxis tribes expanded their circles of ritual distributions to embrace new partners, coppers also began to circulate more widely among these participants in trade and marriage.

Thus, during the period characterized by the dominance of the four Kwakiutl tribes at Tsaxis, Hudson Bay blankets circulated first in the hundreds and later in the thousands, and coppers gained in value each time they moved among contestants, as well as each time they were "killed"—broken up—and then resurrected by resoldering the pieces. The fact that blankets were readily available and could be acquired for money by commoners and second-ranking nobles in search of rank diminished the hold of the great chiefs over the distributive rituals and permitted these newcomers to enter the distributive contests in increasing numbers. Yet the standardized character and accessibility of the new blankets conveyed little of the connotations and interpretants implicit in the traditional use of animal hides. The case makes one think of Walter Benjamin's argument (1969) that mechanical reproduction stripped works of art of their "aura" and makes one wonder whether such "secularization" (Wike 1952, 98) may not have affected the rationales behind potlatching as well. Walens has suggested (but without any references to supporting material) that, as potlatching went forward at a time of great demographic and cultural crisis, many Kwakiutl came to believe that the ever-increasing number of their dead "were being taken to vivify the bodies of an ever increasing number of white men" and that it was their responsibility to "reincarnate all those Kwakiutl who had died and not come back to life" (1981, 154). Kobrinsky has pointed to the paradoxical role of the Hudson Bay Company blanket as "the symbolic hide of the white man" that "became the new standard of chiefly power because Whiteman now *was* the power," even as it impaired "the credibility of the ancestral legends" (1975, 43). If there is some validity in these speculations, they suggest that both Hudson Bay blankets and coppers may have retained connotations of connections with vital forces, while serving as ready means of circulation and mobility, much as heads and scalps taken from enemies and hides taken from animals had once been understood to multiply vitality in the communities of their captors. Thus, one may imagine that potlatching during the decades of intensifying crisis continued to combine two sets of values, one drawn from the capitalist economy of commodities, the other from a culturally constructed economy dealing with imaginary quanta of spiritual energies.

In pursuing this double course, the traditional chiefs fought a losing battle, since their cosmological weapons could not ward off the further penetration of capitalism. Yet, paradoxically, their fight enabled the potlatch to survive even when outlawed by Canadian law.

The course of the battle greatly altered the means by which the chiefly families asserted their dominance, together with the rationales invoked to explicate and legitimize their preponderance. The way in which this confrontation was fought out also allowed the chiefs to bequeath to their people some of the cultural emblems of potlatching and winter dancing that had served to project their power and influence in the past. In the present, under changed circumstances, these forms have been taken up once more. The Indian Act of 1951 dropped the prohibition against potlatching, and ritual distributions, accompanied by dances in the appropriate emblematic paraphernalia, are again being held in Kwakwaka'wakw territory. Even the hamatsa and the masked dancers representing the servants of Baxbakualanuxsiui' have returned to dance, in what has been for many participants "the proudest moment of the whole potlatch" (Webster 1991, 238). Refashioned and revaluated, these activities and objects now serve to define and display a reformulated Kwakwaka'wakw cultural identity. At stake is no longer the maintenance of a precontact cosmology that authorized and legitimized the hierarchically organized worlds of the numayms and their chiefly class but the movement of the First Nations of the Northwest Coast to reassert their cultural identities as a prerequisite for political recognition under Canadian law.

Discussion

The Kwakiutl case material, as presented here, is an account above all of the efforts of a chiefly elite to retain and fortify its power against the forces that weakened its hold and threatened to undermine it. In this struggle a central role—as instrument and weapon—was played by ideology, ideas drawn together into a coherent configuration, which served to underwrite and manifest the power of the title-holding chiefs. The available material does not allow us to trace in detail the advent of this ideology in the initial stages of its formation, but we can see it in full play, and we can detect efforts to make it respond both to the changing needs of the chiefs over time and to the claims of new aspirants to chiefly power.

We have referred to the concept of the "chiefdom" as an arrangement that could sustain an order of social stratification, not through decisive force concentrated in the institutions of a superordinate state but through a mix of material, organizational, and ideational features and sanctions. Although the concept has been criticized for trying to cover too many forms varying widely in complexity and scale, it does underline that ideational representations are essential in making such arrangements possible.(The Kwakiutl exemplify how, in such a case, material and organizational power is interrelated with ideas about the constitution of the world.)Kwakiutl chiefs belonged to specially marked status lineages that set off the line of aspirants to the chiefship from other nobles, as well as from commoners. Within the group, a chief scheduled its activities and orchestrated its resources, but his capacities were represented as outcomes of a cosmic transition from primordial conditions to socially organized time. Chiefly continuity was envisaged not as the perpetuation of a common biological substance through sexual reproduction but as the sequential bestowal of names and thus of rank and privileges, bestowals that had to be exhibited and legitimized in public ritual displays and distributive events.

In this configuration, ongoing events were continuously referenced to cosmological premises and rationales. This involved, in the first place, recourse to myths and rituals to portray how the world of humans came to be. In ritual, internally within the group and externally in relation to other groups, the chief incarnated the original group founder, the founding spirit-animal, and perpetuated, down through myth-historical time, both the privileges accorded them by the founder and ancestors and the obligation to guard and execute the compacts and requirements imposed on humans through the original donations.

Since in Kwakiutl ontogeny beings are conceived as dual, with an outer-body "mask" covering an inner-body "substance," this idea was extended to characterize the relation of the chief to people within the numaym itself. The chief is the bearer of the "mask" that generated the numaym, and thus its head. His house stands metonymically for the entire numaym, and his line and noble kin, carrying the privilege of holding numaym names and seats, constitute the substance of the numaym. Thus, the chiefly seats "were linked to social stability and continuity" (Berman 1991, 73). The death of a chief threatens the numaym with disintegration, to be allayed only by installation of an heir to replace him.

The cosmological referencing of chiefly power demanded that the social order specified in the ontogenetic account be maintained through repeated reenactment, including ritual representations of the temporal sequence in which beings first made their appearance. That sequence gave first place to animals; then to people and ancestors; then to chiefs, followed by commoners who "watch" and "obey" (Berman 1991, 87). Thus, the cosmological ontogeny is duplicated socially in a hierarchy of prerogatives and obligations imposed upon people. Kwakiutl oratory constantly insisted "that the speech and action are nothing newly invented, that it goes back to the time 'when light came into our world' and that the right and duty to use these forms was inherited from their fathers, grandfathers, and remote ancestors" (Boas 1966, 353).

At giveaways called to mark the assumption of new names announcing changes in status over the course of a person's life, these chiefs—acting in concert—transferred goods to each other in repeated cycles of prestations and acceptances. How are these circulatory transfers to be explained? A key issue is precisely whether the power to distribute depends in some way on ideas, or whether ideas are only epiphenomenal effects and rationalizations of relations established on other grounds.

There is a long history of debate over this issue in the anthropological literature. In his essay on *The Gift*, Marcel Mauss (1954, 1) raised the question, "what force is there in the thing given which compels the recipient to make a return?" His answer was that each gift embodied supernatural force, "a spirit of things," which made the recipient beholden to the donor and demanded requital through repayment. This answer has been hotly disputed, because it touches on basic anthropological premises about how social realities are to be explained. It stems from the Durkheimian view that modes of thought originated in society: since primitive man was supposedly unable to separate his person from the object it had possessed and then gave away, each object contained a charge of supernatural energy or *mana;* society was then produced in collective ritual in the very act of circulating the imaginary person-dependent charges of mana (Crapanzano 1995). Marshall Sahlins argued, in turn, that Mauss's invocation of the spirit inherent in gifts merely explained why gifts were repaid but not why there was an obligation to give and receive in the first place (1972, 150). Sahlins also showed that Mauss was wrong ethnographically in his use of Maori data by imputing a "spirit" to objects given, yet—paradoxically—correct in understanding that gift exchange avoided a Hobbesian "Warre" of all against all by drawing the partners into a social contract and political consensus based on exchange (169–70).

This insight, as Sahlins understood and Goldman came to emphasize (1975, 123), still left unanswered the question of what does "compel the circulation" in the first place. For Goldman, the circulation was rooted in "a cosmological conception that postulates an eternal circulation of forms of being" (p. 124). Giveaways are synchronized with successive and cumulative shifts in identity, as persons acquire new names when they change from one socially recognized phase of life to another, and as groups change from the secular names and identities of the summer season to the sacred names and identities of the winter season. What is at stake in these rituals, however, is not merely the advancement of particular individuals through the stations of life but the fundamental relationship of humans to animals. In myth, animals offer themselves as food and make gifts of their skins and animal qualities to humans. In the giveaways the chief acts as mediator of the animal realm in relation to humans: in these contexts, the chief displays and represents the foundational ritual compact that sets out the terms of "life" and that secures these terms.

Chiefly power was greatly enhanced by the forcible acquisition of the hamatsa ritual from the Heiltsuk in 1837. That ritual brought together the actual or potential heirs to the autonomous chiefships in a ritual sodality that crosscut the numayms and then subjected the initiates to a common sequence of death, revival, and transformation that imparted special qualities to them. Standing for "life," the chief must also confront the dimension of entropy and death, symbolized in the winter-season ritual journey to the house of the "spirit that eats humans at the mouth of the river." In the summer months humans hunt and eat animals; in the winter season the roles are reversed: "the eater becomes the eaten, the aggressor the victim" (Berman 1991, 690). The agents in this reversal are the nobles, especially the chiefs' sons, "who accomplish this by offering up their own persons to the predatory spirits" (p. 692). By "going through," the initiates are transfigured and return to ordinary life imbued with supernatural power. They will never be "entirely human" again; they have been tempered by this experience for their special role as mediators between ordinary folk and transnatural powers. In contrast, commoners remain "only humans, entirely human" (Berman 1991, 687). This encounter with death and transfiguration corresponds to Bloch's "construction of rebounding violence," in which the biologically based cycle of life is socially reversed by visiting violence and spiritual death upon the human subject; this transforms it into "a permanently transcendental person" who will return to the here and now, able to control it and to mediate between life and death in the world of the living (1984).

If oratory repetitively invoked cosmological sanctions to sustain the order of status classes and ranks, material and organizational features dovetailed and articulated with the cosmological understandings. The numayms—together with their resource sites, names, seats, and emblems—were conceptualized as eternal units. A head-chief derived power from his apical role in administrating such an enduring monopoly. Class-based "ownership" of the natural resources of his numaym, together with control of the emblematic valuables delegated to him by his ancestral donors, put him in a position to take part in public demonstrations of his own standing. Since he stood for the numaym at large, he also asserted the prerogatives of his numaym. In displaying publicly his rights to privileges through descent and succession, he legitimized at once his own perquisites and the chiefly claims of others, thus validating chiefship as an institution in general. As chiefs, the heads of numayms and tribes organized the ritual distributive events held when persons of appropriate standing within their groups assumed or relinquished statuses open to members of their class. At the same time, these ritual distributions of goods, assets, and privileges conveyed vital forces from numaym to numaym through the interactions of chiefs with chiefs. Marriages, too, moved women and the privileges they carried with them from one chiefly house to another.

If we follow Lévi-Strauss's suggestion that these modes of circulation are also modes of communication, we can see how the chiefs exercised a near-monopoly over not only assets but also the channels of the communication involved. They exercised control over the circulation of "messages" by acting and speaking for society at large in the ritual displays and formalized rhet ›rical presentations of their myth-history. Simultaneously, we can recognize the coercion implicit in ritual as it scripts a sequence of physical movements in a structured environment that emphasizes, validates, and extends the schemes being communicated to the participants (Bell 1992, 109–10). Like a Christian mass, a ritual distribution among the Kwakiutl followed a culturally validated script not open to alternative modes of expression (Bloch 1974). To the extent that oratory and ritual accompanied most public events in Kwakiutl life, they also disprivileged the ability and motivation of others to be recognized and heard, a condition evident in the unwillingness of commoners to talk to George Hunt, "for they shame to talk about themselves" (Berman 1991, 95).

Nevertheless, the chiefly class was ultimately the loser in "the Fort Rupert class struggle" (to use Kobrinsky's term). In the initial period of the maritime fur trade, title to the chiefship and the right to engage in redistributive events had been the undisputed privilege of the highest-ranking chiefs of the noble houses. With the acceleration of capitalist development, capitalist accumulation in expanding markets, coupled with population loss, cumulatively subverted the structural conditions that had underwritten this earlier concentration of chiefly power. Opportunities for raiding also decreased, and "fighting with property" grew more important. Population loss and the advent of alternative ways of gaining wealth undermined the controls over labor and resources that had sustained the chiefs until the 1850s. At the same time, repeated epidemics reduced the number of legitimate claimants to titles and to the chiefship, and access to new sources of wealth allowed new aspirants to validate spurious claims to privileges through participation in giveaways and feasting. These newly rich also gained entry into the Kwakiutl system of multiple marriages, benefiting from the fact that the Kwakiutl transferred titles and privileges from the kin of the bride to the kin of the groom through the marriage process, in contrast to other groups on the Northwest Coast that passed on titles, emblems, and privileges at the time of death.

In this context the increasingly dramatic portrayals of antagonism

at distributive events by traditional chiefs who affirmed supernaturally instituted privileges can be seen as displays aimed at turning back
the efforts of questionable challengers. Such challenges "primed the
potlatch inflationary cycle" (Kobrinsky 1975, 41). The entry of new
claimants equipped with additional resources produced a cumulative rise in the number of giveaways held, as well as an expansion in
the quantity of goods placed into redistribution.

Furthermore, as population fell and as commoners with new
claims to status entered the competition for ranks, seats, and the
right to potlatch, the class of chiefs not only lost its monopoly over
the circulation of goods, valuables, and marriageable spouses but also
faced a diminution of its control over "messages" about the state of
the world through the recitations of myth-history. The stock of ideas
underwriting chiefly power lost credibility and relevance, as claims
to prerogatives and valuables bestowed by supernatural donors entered into competition with demands posed by the spread of the
pound sterling or the "almighty" dollar. As Weber showed, the new
capitalist order could also attribute success in amassing wealth to
proper connections with the supernatural, through the "Protestant
ethic." Had it been introduced among the Kwakiutl, it would have
challenged the arrangements that underwrote chiefly power in redistribution, in marriage strategies, and in the celebration of the
hamatsa ritual. This may be why the Kwakiutl chiefs long resisted the
encroachment of missionaries.

Yet inevitably, pressures from both inside and outside began to
undo the connections that linked the internal ideology of sociocosmic ontogeny and hierarchy to the workings of economy and society, which became increasingly "individualized." Traditional relations between chiefs and their numayms gave way to market-oriented
relations between chiefs and followings, based on more entrepreneurial combinations of external and internal sources of wealth.
Concomitantly, a cosmology that once operated within a closed system of communication was transformed into an ideology that invoked supernatural connections in an effort to fortify the claims of
the chiefly stratum in the contested and changing present.

The anthropological texts from Boas's time and later thus portray
the political project of a class of former power holders under conditions of decline. This decline was occasioned by changes that altered

the social and cultural contexts under which power related to ideas. It produced escalating differentiation and opposition among individuals and groups, in a process similar to that described by Gregory Bateson as "schismogenesis" (1972, 68, 155). In those terms, Kwakiutl distributive events grew increasingly schismogenic.

The cycle of escalation eventually came to an end. One factor was surely the decision by the government to prosecute the participants in the great potlatch of 1921. But this intervention took place in the midst of changing political-economic circumstances. Redistributive events began to absorb credit that might have been used to buy fishing nets and boats, an especially important consideration for Indians who were losing out to Japanese and Anglo-White maritime enterprises. Chief Assu of the Lekwiltok decided to end his participation in the potlatch, to redirect funds to civic projects such as building houses, the introduction of electricity, and the construction of an adequate water supply (Cole and Chaikin 1990, 163–64). As the depression of the 1930s advanced, fewer people were able to pay off their debts and disappointed their creditors. Young people increasingly came to see "the potlatch system" as a source of their difficulties (Codere 1961, 483). When the potlatch eventually reemerged, it did so in a new context, that of Indian identity politics.

Although the chiefs lost out in the struggle to retain their traditional holds on resources and labor, their efforts to do so through control of ritual, myth-histories, and emblematic art had lasting effects. They helped to preserve some of the memories and knowledge of families, great houses, and communities, as well as material objects and regalia that had been used to display their claims and underwrite their privileges. Carvers and makers of button robes also maintained some of the artistic traditions connected with this past, and they increasingly found outlets in upscale markets for their art.

Fort Rupert is today a small settlement of about 500 people, but political and economic changes have given rise to a renewed sense of identity among Kwakiutl/Kwakwaka'wakw, as among many of the First Nations all along the Pacific coast. Increased recognition of native rights by the Canadian government led to abrogation of the punitive laws against potlatching in 1951, and in 1979 objects seized at Chief Cranmer's last potlatch (and not sold off) were returned to be housed in two new tribal centers. Government encouragement of the tourist trade has further underwritten efforts to enhance and display the "cultural resources" of the area through sponsorship of native crafts for sale, dances and ritual performances, and museum exhibits. These activities have not reversed the asymmetrical relations of power between the native population and the rest of society in British Columbia, but they have widened the opportunities available to native groups and allowed them to be more assertive in staking out their own demands. Since the 1960s potlatches have again been held publicly on Vancouver Island, and it has become possible once more to perform a (modified) hamatsa ritual. The change in the political atmosphere was clearly signaled when, at the opening ceremony of the Commonwealth Games held in Victoria in 1994, Chief Adam Dick, bearer of the name Kwaxistala ("the smoke of the big house reaches around the world") reenacted in song and dance the primordial ancestor of his tribal entity, the Tsawataineuk, in confirmation of his rights to the Kingcome River and his obligations to it.

The frontispiece of the Codex Mendoza depicts the founding of Tenochtitlan and (below) the Tenochca conquests of two cities. The leaders
of the Tenochca surround the eagle whose appearance upon a cactus has
led them to the site. (Bodleian Library, Oxford)

4

The Aztecs

If the Kwakiutl are most often thought of in terms of the potlatch, our second case brings to mind human sacrifice. This is the case of the Aztecs, who came to dominate Central Mexico in the fifteenth century, until they were conquered by the Spaniards led by Hernán Cortés and their Mesoamerican allies in 1521. Human sacrifice was in many ways central to Aztec political and ritual life, and any discussion of that life must come to grips with this phenomenon. In engaging this issue, I intend neither to denigrate the Aztecs in order to justify their conquest by the Spaniards nor to defend them against accusations of cruelty and inhumanity. Many Spanish conquerors did see the Aztecs as spawns of the devil, but others thought of them as merely misled and hence capable of salvation. "Never was there a more idolatrous people, or one so given to killing and eating of men" wrote Cortés's secretary and chaplain Francisco López de Gómara in 1552 (in Keen 1971, 83). In contrast, the Franciscan friar Gerónimo de Mendieta believed that they showed "in their works . . . more signs of virtue and Christianity than are found in many of our own nation" (in Keen 1971, 126). These contrary arguments have been taken up in the present century, with the same kind of partisanship. Some, like the Mexican historian and archaeologist Eulalia Guzmán (1958), have represented the Aztecs as democratic, communal, and monotheistic, wisely led by wise men who sacrificed only young turkeys and not children and who ate only amaranth-seed cakes and not human flesh at their supposedly cannibalistic feasts. Others, like the Mexican poet Octavio Paz, point to the Aztec hall in the National Museum of Anthropology as a latter-day apotheosis of the centralized and autocratic modern Mexican state. Repeating the theme of "the stepped pyramid and the platform of sacrifice," the hall celebrates, for Paz, "the survival, the continuance in force of the Aztec model of domination within our modern history" (1972, 153-54).

The anthropologist's task should be neither to exalt nor to condone but to explain. Viewed purely in their own terms, Aztec ontology and cosmology provide us with a view of one kind of human possibility—a possibility that came to be realized in history. From a comparative perspective, the Aztecs are an instance of state building in one of the major civilizational orbits of the world; it should be interpreted in comparison with other cases of state making in class-stratified, politically centralized societies not only in Mesoamerica but also on other continents (for such comparisons, see Steward 1949; Adams 1966; Wright 1977; Kurtz 1981; Blanton 1996). In general, to the extent that we can come to understand something about this unusual ideology, we shall ask more insightful questions about the relationship of ideas to power. This discussion will pursue especially the connections that might obtain between Aztec ideology and the structural power that governed social labor in that society, one predicated on relations between primary producers of tribute and tribute receivers. I will try to show how Aztec understandings of the world were embedded in these relations, and how they were implicated in the ways power was concentrated and deployed.

What we know about the Aztecs must rely on very diverse kinds of sources. A great deal can be learned from the work of archaeologists who have explored the physically evident relationships obtaining between culture and the built and cultivated environment of the Valley of Mexico. But for how the Aztecs behaved and what they may have thought we must rely almost entirely on the reports of Spaniards who came to conquer the land in 1519 and were motivated to write about their experiences. A few Amerind documents did survive the conquest or were produced shortly afterward by scribes responding to the requirements of the new conquerors. Among these documents are pre-Hispanic or early colonial manuscripts from Central Mexico on ritual, divination, and the Mesoamerican calendar, such as the Codex Borbonicus and the Tonalamatl Aubin; the Anales de Tlatelolco transcribed into European script in 1528; and the historical-economic Codex Mendoza, prepared soon after the conquest for the Emperor Charles V by an Aztec scribe working with a Spanish friar. We also owe numerous direct accounts to interested friars, soldiers, and administrators. Among the friars, the most notable interpreters of Aztec thought were the Franciscan Bernardino de Sahagún (1499–1590) and the Dominican Diego Durán (ca. 1537–1588). Sahagún enlisted a cohort of Mexican court nobles and wealthy merchants to record, in both Nahuatl and Spanish, their knowledge on a great many topics for inclusion in an encyclopedic *General History of the Things of New Spain.*[1] Diego Durán, who lived in Texcoco as a child and later moved to Mexico City, authored a *Book of the Gods and the Rites and the Ancient Calendar,* as well as a *Historia de las Indias de Nueva España y islas de tierra firme.*

Such written sources on the Aztecs represent almost entirely the perspectives of their elites, a social stratum that was committed to predatory warfare and the exploitative extraction of tribute. This record was further shaped by the fact that the most important texts were gathered and reedited by the Spanish friars, agents of the spiritual conquest of Mesoamerica. However, theirs was not a simpleminded, Eurocentric project. Many of the early friars were millenarian dissidents in their own society. They aimed to rescue the Indians from the grasp of the devil, but they also saw them as god-given instruments in the building of a new, less corrupt Christian social order. They wanted to learn what they could about preconquest lifeways from indigenous informants, in order to be able to preach convincingly in the Nahuatl language of the Aztecs to their potential converts. Modern linguists and ethnohistorians have looked again at these texts in both Nahuatl and Spanish, now setting them more carefully in their social and cultural contexts and clarifying how the Nahuatl texts were Christianized and the Christian texts Nahuatlized. They have explored new ways of looking at long familiar materials and raised new questions, even about sources that were thought to be already well understood.

Other disciplines have also enriched our knowledge of this society and its culture in recent years. Archaeologists have uncovered the ecological underpinnings of Mesoamerican civilization and have gone on to examine its economy and politics. Their efforts have been advanced considerably by the excavations of the Great Temple in Tenochtitlan, begun in 1978. Ethnohistorians have studied the extant texts on a whole range of issues, from kinship to the political functions of ritual, but they are now also working with new sources such as land records and wills. Art historians and anthropologists have studied Aztec aesthetics, costume, and iconography. Archaeoastronomers, long fascinated by Mesoamerican concerns with astronomical phenomena, are now exploring the representations of these understandings on the ground as well as in documents. And scholars are once again delving into the rich storehouse of myth and folklore, now often aided by a familiarity with comparative studies of religion as well as by a more sophisticated command of Nahuatl linguistics. This array of available sources allows us to approximate, with some degree of assurance, what the Aztec elites thought they were doing and what they were saying and then to relate this to what is now known about Aztec society and polity.[2]

In speaking of the Aztecs, I will refer to them by their Nahua name for persons from Tenochtitlan—singular, *Tenochcatl;* plural, *Tenochca*—perhaps meaning "Cactus Stone People." They might have called themselves Culhua Mexica, when emphasizing the putative Toltec descent of their rulers through the royal dynasty of the city-state of Culhuacan; but they called themselves and were called by others Tenochca, when the reference was to the inhabitants of the city of Tenochtitlan. Tenochtitlan constituted one city-state among many in the Valley of Mexico around A.D. 1500, and even at the height of its power it entered into alliances with other city-states, such as Texcoco and Tlacopan. However, it came to be the largest and most populous of these entities, as well as the highest-ranking political power in the region. As such it is the best described city-state in the Valley of Mexico and will therefore serve as our major point of reference in this discussion.

The Tenochca in Time and Place

To properly understand this people, we must place them in history, tracing their course from humble beginnings to their emergence as the core of an expansionist state. This account will sketch out the major changes in the organization of state and society, and it will highlight some of the sources of difficulty and disorder that attended these transformations. It will then look at the ways in which the available texts portray the centering of the cosmic order upon Tenochtitlan and follow out some of the important ideological implications of this portrayal. In particular, it will try to explicate the ways in which ideas formulated the relations between class and power in this society.

BEGINNINGS

Before the Tenochca ever achieved ethnic or political identity, Mesoamerica had already witnessed several cycles of population growth, settlement expansion, and political centralization followed by demographic decline, settlement contraction, and political dismemberment. The Tenochca proper appeared in the Valley of Mexico in the wake of the disintegration of the military "Toltec" polity after A.D. 1000. It must be emphasized that the Tenochca did not constitute any kind of pristine tribe or state, nor were they the egalitarian barbarians envisaged by Lewis Henry Morgan and Adolphe Bandelier. Rather, the people later designated as Tenochca had formed a composite and subaltern component of the Toltec domain centered upon the city of Tula (Tollan Xicotitlan). From this association they derived a Toltec model of political-cosmological order, including its solar cult and sacrifice by heart excision. Their social organization was clearly stratified, and they were acquainted with the Mesoamerican technology of cultivation and water control (Zantwijk 1985; Boehm de Lameiras 1986). As the Toltec polity broke apart, it splintered into political-military units of much smaller scale, commanded by war leaders who initially identified themselves as descendants or representatives of the Toltec god Quetzalcoatl, in his warlike incarnation as Tlalhuizcalpantecuhtli, "the dawn warrior" (López Austin 1989, 168). Making and engaging in war reinforced the military character of these groupings, while a common interest in obtaining booty united warrior aristocrats and commoners. To cope with political interregnum and greatly diminished control over resources, many of these groupings developed or adopted a pattern of charismatic command by god-imbued leaders (*hombre-dioses* or man-gods), whose authority derived from their abilities to communicate with tutelary deities and to execute their orders (López Austin 1974b, 1989). The Tenochca would follow this pattern in adopting the guidance of the god Huitzilopochtli, as communicated through inspired "god-carriers" and spokesmen.

During the period of Toltec disintegration, between A.D. 750 and 1200, the Basin of Mexico itself had been relegated to a position of secondary importance within Mesoamerica. By 1200, however, its population began to grow again, and cultivation expanded all around the shores of the valley lake system. These developments, in turn, set the stage for political reconsolidation. By the late fourteenth century, sustained infighting among the epigonal Toltec domains of the valley had produced some forty small polities, whose rivalries were exacerbated by their rulers' competitive claims to divine guidance and precedence. In the resulting conflicts, these micropolities often formed temporary and unstable alliances, but these were riven by factionalism and frequently subverted by assassination and usurpation.

This was the context in which the Tenochca made their initial appearance, albeit in an inferior and dependent role that contrasts sharply with their later claims to have been the Chosen People of their tutelary god Huitzilopochtli, who destined them for universal dominance. At this time, the Tenochca comprised eleven separate units with distinctive leadership and patron deities, allied under the aegis of Huitzilopochtli (Tezozómoc, in López Austin 1989, 171). They were of composite ethnic origins, as were their leaders (Zantwijk 1985, 83), and their survival depended wholly upon their ability to offer their services as clients to one or another paramount ruler and to shift their allegiances among them (Price 1980, 164–65). In a myth calculated to exalt their rise to Manifest Destiny from these modest beginnings, they later insisted that they had arrived in the Valley of Mexico over the course of a long and arduous migration, always guided by Huitzilopochtli, from a point of origin in a cave located in a mythical northern land called Aztlan. It is more probable, however, that they had previously inhabited ecologically marginal lands to the northwest of the Toltec capital at Tula (Price 1980; for a contrary view, see Smith 1984). There is also good evidence that the concept of Huitzilopochtli was compounded of various elements, which included the deities of their epigonal Toltec overlords in the city-state of Culhuacan (Zantwijk 1985, 53–55; Brotherston 1974; Brundage 1979, 128–52). He may originally have been a real person—"only a common man, a human being" (in Brotherston 1974, 157)—later deified through his role as hombre-dios, spokesman, and representative of a divinity.[3]

In the mid-fourteenth century, these congeries of people—propelled by the twin forces of demographic increase and horticultural intensification throughout the valley (Price 1980, 164–67)—moved to islands off the western shores of the valley lake system. There they attracted immigrants who then adopted the ethnic identity of the community's ruling lineage and the cult of its patron deity (Smith 1984). From early times on, however, they were not only cultivators but also engaged in trade, especially after a crisis in the hydrological system brought on floods in 1382–1383 (Calnek 1972a). In their new locations, they laid the bases for two distinctive political domains, located in close proximity to one another: Mexico-Tenochtitlan (the Tenochca proper) and Mexico-Tlatelolco. The inhabitants of these two towns were both called "Aztecs" and shared a myth of common descent and provenience from Aztlan. Yet they were always at loggerheads and parted ways in the first half of the fourteenth century in a dispute over the distribution of land (Davies 1980, 39). Each became a separate city-state. Tlatelolco emphasized commerce, became the site of a great market, and grew into a major center of mercantile economic and ritual activities, while Tenochtitlan intensified its commitment to making war. Initially dependent on other powers in the basin, both city-states accepted rulers from more powerful neighbors: Tenochtitlan's first *tlatoani* ("speaker" or ruler) came from Toltec Culhuacan; Tlatelolco received its first ruler from the Tepanec dynasty at Atzcapotzalco. In the last quarter of the fourteenth century both Mexico-Tenochtitlan and Mexico-Tlatelolco came under the domination of Atzcapotzalco, then a rising power in the valley, and the nobles of both client towns were included in the ranks of the Atzcapotzalcan elite in return for their military services (Calnek 1974, 201–2). Half a century later, in 1428, however, the Tenochca, as well as the Tlatelolca, rebelled against this hegemonic center, appropriated its resources, and utilized this newly gained wealth to underwrite their separate political careers.

ROADS TO EMPIRE

Atzcapotzalco means "place of the ant heaps," Ant-Heap City, most likely a metaphor used to describe the crowded and busy life of what was then the largest city in the vicinity (Durán 1967, 2: 101). The Tenochca conquest of Atzcapotzalco was probably motivated by the growing scarcity of resources within their delimited island domain, as well as by their desire to shake off Atzcapotzalcan domination and to appropriate the land and wealth of their overlords. It was triggered by the death of the paramount ruler of Atzcapotzalco and by the disputes over his succession that followed. In the course of conflicts among interested factions, the Tenochca king Chimalpopoca was assassinated, either by one of the heirs to the kingship of Ant-Heap City or—more likely (Davies 1980, 61)—by his own uncle or cousin Itzcoatl, who advocated Tenochca independence from Atzcapotzalco. The war against Atzcapotzalco was launched by a troika of generals—Itzcoatl and his two nephews Motecuzoma Ilhuicamina ("He pierces the sky with an arrow") and Tlacaelel—against the opposition of the common people and amid fears of internal dissension due to divided loyalties (Brundage 1979, 77). The people had already decided to signal their subjection to Atzcapotzalco by transferring the image of their god Huitzilopochtli to the threatening capital, when the military troika spoke out against surrender. The rebel leaders' proposals for resistance and victory in war carried the day, underwritten by the offer that if they were defeated the common folk, the *macehualtin,* could eat the flesh of the military nobility "on broken and dirty pottery." In the event of victory, however, they promised to be loyal servants. The textual phrasing of this "social contract" resembles the pledge of surrender offered in 1429 by the town of Xochimilco to the victorious Tenochca (Durán 1964, 78–79); it may well have incorporated a general formula for submission. Mario Erdheim notes that such a contractual quid pro quo entails the proposition that while victory secures legitimacy, defeat abrogates it. He supports this conclusion by pointing to what happened when the Tenochca reconquered Cuetlachtlan [Cotaxtla] after that city-state had revolted against Aztec rule, encouraged by nearby Tlaxcala. In that case the Cuetlachteco commoners successfully averted the slaughter of all of the city's inhabitants by arguing that their lords were "accursed thieves" who deserved to be killed, while they themselves were but "simple and ignorant folk, without malice and intention" who only paid tribute, "all created by means of their labor and sweat" (Tezozómoc, in Erdheim 1973, 77).

Success in the war against Atzcapotzalco had signal consequences. In the past these developments have frequently been explained as accompaniments of a supposed evolutionary transformation that changed Tenochca society from a primordial, kin-based *communitas* to a *societas,* characterized by a full-fledged state. Yet we need to remember that there were states in Mesoamerica a thousand years before Atzcapotzalco. The Tenochca saw themselves as inheritors of the obligation to maintain the cosmos, and thus also as heirs to their Olmec, Teotihuacano, and Toltec predecessors. When they reconstructed the Great Temple of Tenochtitlan in the mid-fifteenth century, they filled it with buried offerings that derived from these older Mesoamerican traditions (Broda 1987a, 213). They employed Toltec themes in their own political and cosmological representations, followed the city plans of Tula and Teotihuacan in laying out their own lacustrine city (Umberger 1996, 89), adopted Toltec patterns of clothing (p. 105), and drew on Toltec models of statecraft to set up their own form of state domination. (On a possible Tenochca identification with the anti-Quetzalcoatl political strategy at Tula represented by Huemac, see Zantwijk 1973, 1985, 95–97.)

The victorious generals and their trusted companions appropriated rights to land, labor, and tribute payment in the defeated Ant-Heap City domain (Tezozómoc 1944, 35–37; Zantwijk 1985, 117). This provided the upper aristocracy with a resource base that was independent of its home station in Tenochtitlan. Their preponderance in landholding was strengthened further by conquests in the fertile lacustrine zone of the southern valley, including the city-states of Coyoacan (1428–1429), Xochimilco (1429), and Cuitlahuac (1429–1430). Both land and titles were distributed among the twenty-six chiefs and warriors who had distinguished themselves in these military operations (Zantwijk 1985, 114–24). From this period on, the right to distribute lands in conquered domains passed into the hands of the paramount ruler. This gave him a considerable measure of independence from the consent of the governed within Tenochtitlan. It also restructured older forms of reciprocity between ruler and ruled. Rulers could now make distributions of rewards and gifts to warriors within Tenochtitlan more directly dependent on victory in war; they could also place greater reliance on the mandatory exaction of tribute from external political domains, instead of accepting more intimate offerings of "gifts" as a sign of political subjection (for this contrast, see Hicks 1988). At the same time, the increased ability of the ruler to use resources to reward both nobles and meritorious commoners allowed him to build up an elite that owed resources and loyalty directly to him (Hassig 1988, 146).

The conquests of the southern lakeside further enhanced the Tenochca food supply (Calnek 1972b). This was the fertile zone of *chinampas:* rectangular platforms constructed to grow crops along shallow lakeshores. They were built by driving posts into the lake bottom and connecting them with a plaited mesh of vines and branches. The resulting enclosures were then filled with layers of fertile lake mud and anchored in place by planting trees along their perimeter. Chinampas were resistant to frost; as long as they received adequate supplies of water they could produce high yields year-round and year after year. To underwrite these productive possibilities, however, waterworks were extended over some 10,000 hectares of swampland in the chinampa zone of the southern valley, and additional thousands of hectares in the southwest were subjected to hydraulic controls (Sanders, Parsons, and Santley 1979, 176–77). The lake system of the Valley of Mexico consisted of bodies of water that stood at different altitudes; these differentials threatened floods and inundations. Moreover, the waters of Lake Texcoco in the eastern part of the valley were heavily saline and detrimental to horticulture. Making the valley safe for cultivation therefore involved not only terracing the surrounding mountainsides but also building dams, canals, and aqueducts to keep water levels steady in order to avoid drowning the chinampas and to shield them against the inflow of saline waters from Lake Texcoco.

The victory over Atzcapotzalco put the Tenochca ruler in a position to begin construction of such a hydraulic system to control the lacustrine water supply (Palerm 1975, 72). Capture of the southern chinampa zone then meant that Tenochtitlan could rely on it for nearly two-thirds of its food supply (Parsons 1976, 254). Finally, control of the lake system implied control of the lacustrine system of transport and the many thousands of canoes that made it possible. Canoes could ferry foodstuffs and other resources to the capital from any part of the Valley of Mexico and convey goods from the capital to the lakeshore. Control of the lakeshore brought the landing docks on the shoreline within the carrying range of porters from the regions of Puebla, Morelos, and Toluca, located beyond the mountains that ringed the valley (Hassig 1985, 60–66). Enhanced control of the lake system through hydraulic cultivation and transport by water further unified the basin and provided the ecological bases for Tenochca expansion.

Eventually this shift to external sources of supply affected the nature of the victorious city, rendering it much more cosmopolitan than the city-states that surrounded it. Although additional hydraulic works were built to secure the subsistence base for a growing conurbation, the number of specialists dedicated to different crafts and administrative services grew at the expense of the number of cultivators. This, in turn, strengthened the interests driving the expansion of craft production and commerce and reinforced the political-military impetus to enlarge external sources of supplies and raw materials (Calnek 1976, 290–91).

CONSOLIDATION

The victors of Atzcapotzalco also effected internal political changes. To begin with, they changed the rules for succession to the Tenochca rulership. Where previously the title of tlatoani would have passed to the descendants of Chimalpopoca in the direct line of fathers to sons, the rebels excluded this line of succession, while widening candidacy for rulership to the remaining collateral lines of the royal lineage. In practice, this legitimized succession from within the immediate entourage of the ruler. Itzcoatl ("Obsidian Snake"), the leader of the war against Atzcapotzalco, was elected as the first paramount, even though, as the son of a slave woman, he might previously not have been admitted to such an exalted position. Where his predecessors still wore rawhide capes and royal rosettes of scarlet macaw feathers and sat on seats consisting of bundles of unwoven green reeds, Itzcoatl now assumed turquoise ornaments and took his position upon a seat of woven reeds with a backrest, suggestive of "consolidated power" (Sullivan 1980, 234). Administration, law, and military policy were concentrated in his hands; he was aided by an advisory council of four close relatives, one of whom was normally chosen to succeed him.

The circle of candidates for rulership was also reinforced through limiting marriages to agnates, "so that rulership would not go elsewhere" (Relación de la geneología, sixteenth century, in Carrasco 1984, 57). This created a pool of potential successors who shared descent through both fathers and mothers and tied them to the throne as possible appointees to key positions. That core of high nobility (*tlazopipiltin*)—"great lords, of whom there were up to twelve" (Durán 1984, 2: 212)—could then draw in other nobles; they were recruited in the kinship idiom from the numerous descendants of the original Tenochca tlatoani, Acamapichtli, who had consolidated his position by marrying daughters of all the leaders of groups that formed the original Tenochca congery. Itzcoatl's successor, Motecuzoma I (1440–1468), later enlarged the pool of potential functionaries for the growing state by legitimating noblemen born to slave or servant mothers. Thus, a cohesive ruling elite, interconnected by ties of kinship and affinity, came to occupy the helm of the increasingly centralized Tenochca state (Rounds 1982).

At the same time, the central descent group was enabled to use marriages strategically to create alliances with subordinate lords in other city-states. Marrying off daughters to less powerful rulers elsewhere was a well-known Mesoamerican device for the formation of desired affinal bonds. Such alliances, in turn, allowed the descendants of these unions to inherit rulerships in other polities and thus attach them to the Tenochca cause (Carrasco 1984, 57). The marriages were accompanied by exchanges of luxury goods and periodic feasting, which promoted "social solidarity within the geographically dispersed noble class" (Smith 1986, 75). As Tenochtitlan began to widen its political range, it could also use these ties to incorporate new domains into its structure and to employ local aristocrats as administrators and tribute-collectors on their imperial behalf. Equally important, this network of marriages produced an extensive regional elite of ruling families, which were linked in various ways to the royal palace in Tenochtitlan and became players in its orbit of influence (Calnek 1982; Smith 1986). Judicious marriage strategies thus connected the ruling strata of Tenochtitlan with dominant elites else-where, to form an overarching Central Mexican upper class, based on "the nobles' control over land, labor, and government" (Berdan and Smith 1996, 211).

Significantly, the victorious tlatoani Itzcoatl ordered the destruc-tion of past calendric records: "It is not necessary that everybody know the black ink, the red ink [the painted books]. He who is car-ried, he who is borne on the back [the people] would fare badly, and the earth would only be replete with intrigues. Because many lies were invented and many have been taken for gods" (Sahagún MC, in López Austin 1989, 175; my translation). New codices were painted to portray a suitably revised depiction of the Tenochca past and fu-ture. Such revisions were not unusual in Mesoamerican history (Mar-cus 1992, 146–52); in this case they probably responded to quite spe-cific motives. One purpose seems to have been to fortify the new rules of royal succession against the claims of rivals, such as the de-scendants of the assassinated Chimalpopoca. Another was likely the desire to silence the voices of god-imbued leaders by concentrating calendric ritual in the hands of the victorious junta (López Austin 1989, 175). A third motive was to efface the subservient past of the Tenochca and to represent them as predestined to dominate the Mesoamerican world, as forecast by their super-god Huitzilopochtli. This related to a fourth motive, that of advancing the claims of Huitzilopochtli, the supernatural advocate of the Tenochca cause, above those of the god Quetzalcoatl. Since Quetzalcoatl was de-picted as the apical ancestor of the nobility that had come to lead ri-val political-military groups after the fall of the Toltec polity, deem-phasizing Quetzalcoatl also weakened the ability of his numerous progeny to claim access to power. Itzcoatl, now tlatoani and spokes-man for Huitzilopochtli (Chimalpahin, in López Austin 1989, 173), was not prepared to share that power with alternative claimants (see López Austin 1989, 170–77). Whatever the motives involved, an en-during effect of Itzcoatl's revisionism is, of course, that many details of Tenochca history remain thoroughly obscure.

The successful ruler also sponsored the renewal of the Great Temple in his capital city of Tenochtitlan. That temple has recently been excavated, revealing that the structure was built in phases. The first two phases antedate the Tenochca conquest of Atzcapotzalco and witnessed the construction of a pyramidal platform, crowned by two shrines. Itzcoatl's reconstruction probably involved the third phase, and each king thereafter rebuilt the temple anew. In these constructions the Tenochca gave material form to a paradigmatic Mesoamerican "vision of place": the capital city was made to represent the center of the cosmic order, the point at which the four cardinal directions intersected with the vertical axis that united the tiered heavens, the surface of this world, and the underworld below.

The art and architecture of the central ceremonial district was intended to convey in various ways the foundational myths of creation (Carrasco 1982, 160–70). Adopting design features drawn from Teotihuacan, Xochicalco, and Tula, the Tenochca rulers signaled their continuity with polities and ruling elites of the past, a claim furthered by their including caches of offerings from the relics of long-extinguished Mesoamerican cultures. Items of marine fauna from the Pacific and Gulf coasts served to link the temple complex with the sea walls, which were thought to connect either shoreline with the heavens. (On the symbolism of the temple structure and offerings, see Broda 1987a; Broda, Carrasco, Matos Moctezuma 1987; Matos Moctezuma 1987; Umberger 1996.)

The two separate shrines that crowned the platform of the temple pyramid were dedicated respectively to the god of earth and rain, Tlaloc, and the warrior god Huitzilopochtli. Tlaloc's shrine may have represented his "sustenance mountain," the storehouse from which the super-god Quetzalcoatl stole food crops for humans to use in the cycle of the Fifth Sun. The shrine to Huitzilopochtli, now elevated from the status of hombre-dios to that of a divine "son" of Tlaloc, represented the mythical Hill of Serpents, the Coatepec. This was the site of Huitzilopochtli's bloody victory over his rival sister, Coyolxauhqui (Face Painted with Bells), and hence by metaphorical extension made to stand for Tenochca victories over all efforts to create internal dissension.

Itzcoatl was followed by Motecuzoma I, whose half-brother Tlacaelel was made imperial chief administrator, or *cihuacoatl*. Motecuzoma began his rule by initiating a rebuilding of the Great Temple in Tenochtitlan, inviting contributions from the lords of the nearby towns—a request that represented as much a test of political allegiance as an act of piety (Hassig 1988, 159). All but Chalco and Tlatelolco complied. Having secured his political base, the new tlatoani first proceeded to consolidate the conquests of his predecessor in areas outside the Valley of Mexico. Then he turned on the Chalco confederation within the valley and overcame and incorporated this rich chinampa domain piecemeal between 1456 and 1465. The other nonparticipant in the construction of the Great Temple—Tenochtitlan's refractory neighbor, Tlatelolco—was conquered by Motecuzoma I's successor, Axayacatl, in 1473.

The Tenochca Hegemonic Order

If Itzcoatl was the initiator of political consolidation around the pivotal figure of the central ruler, Motecuzoma was its main architect. Above all, he sacralized the person of the ruler: "Although thou art human, as we are, although thou art our friend, although thou art our son, our younger brother, our older brother, no more art thou human, as are we; we do not look on thee as human" (Sahagún 1950–1969, 6: 52). This ascription of divinity did not make the paramount ruler omnipotent, but it installed a distinction between the physical and mortal person of the ruler and the enduring structural position of rulership within the order of society. As in the cases of "divine" kings elsewhere in the world (Feeley-Harnik 1985), endowing the position of the tlatoani further with a supernatural aura also placed the status and role of the "speaker" outside and above the conflicts and contradictions that necessarily attend the exercise of power. When the tlatoani then spoke or acted, he did so as a representative of the gods among humans: "You are the substitute, the surrogate of Tloque Nahuaque, the lord of near and far. You are the seat [the throne from which he rules], you are his flute [the mouth through which he speaks], he speaks within you, he makes you his lips, his jaws, his ears. . . . He also makes you his fangs, his claws, for you are his wild beast, you are his eater of people, you are his judge" (Sahagún FC, in Sullivan 1994, 117–18).

The installation ritual specified the privileges and responsibilities of the ruler. He was addressed as *iyollo altepetl,* the heart of the city, the term also directed at the tutelary god of the city-state. As such, he was "like a great tree full of branches, a great tree full of leaves, thus he rules over people"; "he bears people, he leads them along the way, he governs people, he guides people" (Sahagún FC, in Sullivan 1980, 226). To do this he had to foster the cult of the gods, promote cultivation (*tlalchioaliztli*), carry on war (*teuatl tlachinolli,* literally holy water, or blood, and fire), and implement justice (Sahagún 1950 – 1969, 6: 72). As tlatoani, in announcing his decisions and in exhorting the multitudes he spoke as the representative of the gods.

The administration of justice was represented metaphorically as a devouring beast with claws (Sahagún 1950 –1969, 6: 72). A hierarchy of courts was staffed by "the fangs, the claws" of the city, which administered law that severely punished treason and disobedience on the battlefield, homicide and personal vengeance, property damage and theft, infringements of the sumptuary restrictions, drunkenness and adultery. There were special courts for the nobility, enforcing laws that were more strict and punitive than those in force for commoners. There were also autonomous law courts for merchants.

After the rulership was sacralized, the tlatoani could appear in public only rarely and had to be approached with head bowed and eyes lowered. As stand-in for Tloque Nahuaque, who was synonymous with the god Tezcatlipoca, the ruler also received from him the primordial powers of the Old God—the God of Fire (*Huehueteotl-Xiuhtecutli*)—the progenitor of all the gods before the present epoch of the Fifth Sun, together with the right to wear the turquoise ornaments associated with that deity (Sullivan 1980, 233). Since the Tenochca deity Huitzilopochtli was regarded as one of the manifestations of Tezcatlipoca, upon investiture the tlatoani donned clothing that identified him with Huitzilopochtli. When he died he was dressed in the robes and regalia of the gods Huitzilopochtli, Tlaloc, Yohuallahuan (another name for Xipe Totec), and Quetzalcoatl (Brundage 1985, 198).

Motecuzoma also set up a sumptuary code to regulate clothing, insisting on different styles and materials for royal councillors and noblemen, for different grades of warriors, and for commoners. The motive for this codification of distinctions, according to Durán, was that Tenochtitlan now included "strangers as well as natives and citizens" and that "decorum and good manners, regimen and order . . . in so great a city" demanded that "all might live in their status" and "pay respect . . . to the authority of his person and to the great lords of the kingdom" (in Clendinnen 1991, 41). Only nobles were allowed to wear cotton clothing; commoners had to confine themselves to maguey fibers and rabbit fur. Nobles alone could wear gold bracelets, gold headdresses with feathers, and jade; warriors could sport lip plugs and earrings of bone and wood and wear eagle feathers; commoners had to content themselves with obsidian earplugs. Unauthorized use of royal, noble, or military insignia and clothing was punishable by stoning to death (Alba 1949, 18). In the presence of the ruler, only his chief administrator Tlacaelel was allowed to wear shoes in the palace; all others had to go barefoot.

THE IDEOLOGICAL ROLE OF WAR

The ruler was, above all, chief military commander. One of his first obligations following his installation was to go to war, return victoriously, and bring back enemy prisoners to be sacrificed. He was also responsible for military preparedness. To shape his army into a more effective fighting force, Motecuzoma set up schools for military training in each subdivision of town. Military prowess was further maintained by participation in the ritualized "flowery wars" (*xochiyaoyotl*). Such wars, which dated back to the earliest Tenochca ruler in the fourteenth century, became a part of Tenochca military strategy. They were fought over the course of many years with evenly matched city-states that were too strong to be conquered outright yet not strong enough to constitute a major threat. In practice, they honed military skills and provided captives for sacrifice. As a form of low-intensity warfare, these military events did not absorb great quantities of energy and resources, and they permitted the parties to seek more extensive conquests elsewhere (Hassig 1988, 128–30).

Courage and positive performance on the battlefield were rewarded with appropriate decorations. At Tlacaelel's insistence warriors were no longer allowed to buy their jewelry and feathers in marketplaces but were given them as gifts from the ruler (Durán 1984, 2: 236). This centralized the system of military and political rewards in the ruler's hands. The palace received fine cloaks and feather work in the form of tribute. Feather workers then embellished military outfits and shields with designs to exhibit distinctions of category, rank, and emblems (Broda 1978). The ruler subsequently disbursed these valued objects as rewards for military prowess.

Assignment of rank depended primarily on the number of captives a warrior had seized on the battlefield; each additional captive taken was reflected in the mantle and clothing, face paint, haircut, jewelry, insignia, and armor bestowed on the captor. After a warrior brought in four captives, the bestowal of any additional honors depended on the origins of the captive. Prisoners from the city-states of Atlixco, Huexotzinco, and Tliliuhquitepec, located in the Puebla-Tlaxcala region to the east of Tenochtitlan, were held in especially high regard, and every additional capture of a prisoner from these sources was rewarded with further titles, items of clothing, and emblems (Hassig 1988, 39–40). These towns often formed alliances with Cholula and Tlaxcala against the Tenochca and frequently arranged to fight "flowery wars" with the Tenochca. At the same time, they shared myths of a common origin with the Tenochca, in the mythic source of Nahua-speaking peoples in Aztlan or Chicomoztoc. In contrast, prisoners from other regions were not valued as highly. Tlacaelel did not regard the people of Michoacan, of Yopitzingo on the Pacific coast, or from the Gulf Coast as fit food for the supernaturals: "Our god does not like the flesh of those barbarous peoples. They are yellowish, hard, tasteless breads in his mouth. They are savages and speak strange tongues" (in Durán 1964, 141). Huastecs from the eastern coast were held in especially low esteem. They were stereotyped as drunken, unwarlike, and steeped in eroticism; their capture as prisoners went unrewarded (Hassig 1988, 39–40). These invidious comparisons show that not all prisoners were equally suitable to be food for the gods: common descent and language, as well as common patterns of military demeanor and behavior, made some groups superior to others as offerings to repay the supernaturals for their gifts of life.

In general, nobles were more likely to capture prisoners and reap the associated esteem than were commoners. Nobles received better military training in their separate *calmecac* schools and were probably better equipped than commoners, who attended training centers in their neighborhoods. They could also draw on the military experience of their fathers and relatives, and they benefited from the assistance of veteran warriors when going into battle. More than four captives brought in entitled a man to entry into the military orders of "eagles" and "jaguars," regardless of whether he was a noble or commoner. Commoners thus could also win the right to wear clothing usually worn only by nobles and to dine at the palace, keep concubines, and eat human flesh and drink maguey beer (pulque) in public. Nevertheless, their lowly descent was not forgotten. In battle they were required to wear war suits made of animal skins, while "true" nobles donned war suits made of feathers sewn on fabric (Hassig 1988, 88). The top four military titles were reserved for the kinsmen of the ruler who manned the royal council. The other grades of army commanders and war leaders, however, were open to nobles and commoners alike, as long as they were acknowledged captors of men.

Although Tenochca myth-history and ideological propaganda made much of the procurement of prisoners for sacrifice as the central motivation for making war, the custom is better understood as one military element—though an important one—among many. Engagement in "flowery wars" featured stylized modes of individual combat with thrusting spears, swords, and clubs. In contrast, wars aimed at conquest involved gathering intelligence, advance planning and preparedness, mobilization, and deployment of large organized armies in space and time. Attacks began with a hail of arrows and slingshots unleashed systematically by bowmen and slingers. Projectile fire was followed by the advance of the military orders and succeeded by the organized units of the army. The formations moved in orderly fashion, each following the bearer of its unit's standard and responding to signaling by drums and trumpets, until they closed with the enemy. Hand-to-hand combat allowed some warriors to take captives and pass them on to support personnel, who bound the prisoners with ropes for the march home and eventual sacrifice (Hassig 1988, 300).

Within this sequence of organized violence, the capture of prisoners may not have been decisive in influencing the origins and outcomes of battle, but it did play a major role in heightening the commitment and motivation of the participating warriors. That commitment had its source both in subjective attitudes and in objective considerations. The Tenochca warriors surely responded to the appeal to live up to the expectations set by Huitzilopochtli and to gain undying fame through deeds of valor. Engaging in battle and taking captives demonstrated a warrior's capacity to fulfill Huitzilo- pochtli's promise that war would bring the Tenochca tributary goods "without number and without limits." Success in war also brought renown and the opportunity to exhibit one's fame and finery in pub- lic. In this context the warrior was not only seen as heroic but also as beautiful, enacting aesthetic patterns that associated war and suc- cess in war with the beauty of flowers. Tenochca nobles always car- ried bundles of aromatic flowers. Tenochca texts (recorded by Saha- gún, translated by L. Schultze-Jena, in Erdheim 1973, 47–53) speak of "flowery wars," of warriors as "dancing flowers," of blood as "flower-water." Captives destined for sacrifice were "flowers of the heart"; taking captives in battle made a man "rich in flowers, the true ones in this world." Upon death warriors became humming- birds or butterflies, sucking "the different flowers . . . the choice ones, the flowers of joy, the flowers of happiness; to this end the noblemen go to death—go longing for, go desiring [death]." Prayer implored the god Tezcatlipoca to let the warrior "long for the flowery death by the obsidian knife. May he savor the scent, savor the fragrance, sa- vor the sweetness of the darkness."

The beauty of these warlike flowers was celebrated in song, which spoke of how "the flowers of war will never decay, they accompany the course of running water. Yet the shining blossom of the warrior himself, imbued with courage like the jaguar, armed with his shield, will be stretched out overnight into the dust." Erdheim has noted, further, how all that glory-seeking after "flowers and song" of the successful warrior was also tinged with the melancholy expectation of an early death: "verily, oh friend, we will one day have to take leave of our flowers, our song." If humans themselves are mortal, how- ever, the songs and tales of their valor will render them immortal— their fame will live forever.

At the same time, these sentiments have their objective, structural side. Success in gaining prisoners largely determined how an aspir- ing Tenochca could obtain social prestige and trade it for tangible rewards in public acclamation, gifts from the ruler, and advancement to position of authority and influence (Erdheim 1973, 72–76).

Making war and capturing prisoners for sacrifice constituted the guiding theme of public rituals, but it was embedded in a cyclical or- chestration of displays that insistently recapitulated the imagery of cosmic order, which the Tenochca ruler was required to uphold. Drawing on the information provided by Hernando Alvarado Tezozómoc about the dedication of Ahuitzotl's reconstructed Great Temple in Tenochtitlan, Rudolf van Zantwijk has shown that just as the layout of the temple was made to correspond to the layers and directions of the cosmic order, so the different groups of participants were positioned to represent their functions within that order. Ahuitzotl, the ruler, and his invited royal guests began the round of sacrifices, which was then taken over and completed by groups of priests associated with the various temples (1985, 200–220).

PRIESTHOOD AND CALENDRICS

The available sources deal warily with the role of the priesthood, and much is still to be learned about it. In the early Aztec period the number of religious specialists seems to have been restricted to a handful of "god-carriers" (*teomama*), each of whom held converse with his particular god in trance and visions. As the polity became more centralized and consolidated in the second half of the fifteenth century, the priesthood became larger and much more highly specialized and hierarchical, both to serve a growing number of different supernaturals and to carry out different kinds of tasks (Katz 1969, 371–76). Various kinds of priests organized and officiated at rituals, including those featuring human sacrifice; managed the wealth that was accumulating in temple treasuries; taught school; and took confession and prescribed penance.

Such a listing does not, however, exhaust a discussion of priestly functions in the workings of Tenochca society. Although priestly routines were formalized and assigned to particular domains, they also touched at many points on major systems of activities that affected the society as a whole. While each sequence of ritual involved the priests of a particular deity, together with lay groups of religious supporters, the rituals were also coordinated with each other through the operation of the calendric cycle. That cycle, in turn, scheduled the sequence of seasons, the call-up and rotation of groups assigned to public works, the execution of horticultural tasks, and the holding of markets. Archaeo-astronomical research and ethnohistory have shown that ritual sequences were intertwined in complex ways with astronomical observations and a scheduling of events at different

spatial locations of myth-historical importance. Thus, while Tenochtitlan was built to represent the paradigmatic center of the cosmic
order, it also served as the hub of a ritual system covering the entire
valley, activating its local components sequentially in correspondence
with the ritual cycle. The system culminated in the figure of the
sacralized ruler at the sacred center; its components were put into
play by the priesthood in conjunction with local acolytes.

All these activities imparted major ideological functions to astronomical observations and calendric calculations. Integrated with as-
trology and closely tied to the staging of major ritual events, these
"provided those who had access to this knowledge with the ability to
give the appearance of controlling those phenomena and producing
them deliberately. . . . Cult as social action produced a transference
of associations that reversed the causal relationship and made natural
phenomena appear to be a consequence of the proper performance
of ritual" (Broda 1982, 104–5). In this way, the ritual system pivoted
on the calendar, in which the priesthood played a major part, underwrote the political and economic power of the ruling elite.

Calendrics endowed with supernatural references further con-
joined individual and private concerns with the cosmic round, by integrating the day-count of 260 days (the *tonalpohualli*) with the
eighteen-month festival cycle of the solar year. The day-count was
thought to indicate the likely character and fate of people born on
that day. Numerous astrological specialists interpreted and predicted
how a person's day-sign affected his or her life course. However,
"flesh and spirit did not come into being at the same time" (Furst
1995, 66). It was believed that the gods used a fire drill to insert the
"hot" spiritual animating force of the *tonalli* into a child shortly before birth. On the one hand, this act allocated to the neonate a portion of the impersonal animating force that suffused the universe; on
the other hand, this apportionment specified the child's potential
characteristics and destiny for the rest of its life. This component of
tonalli is placed *in* a person, but is not itself personal—it can be
shaken loose from the body in "soul loss" or transferred to someone
else. Thus, in capturing a victim for human sacrifice, the captor also
transferred this portion of the victim's vital force to himself.

Drilling for animating force also operated on the macrocosmic
scale. Every fifty-two years a cycle of time came to an end, and the
people of Central Mexico then extinguished their fires, destroyed

their cooking ware, threw out their hearthstones and household idols, and climbed to their housetops to await the news that a new fire had been drilled. If the drilling for fire proved unsuccessful, all would be turned into mice; if it succeeded, the universe would continue for fifty-two more years. The New Fire was drilled and kindled by the fire priests in the chest cavity of a sacrificed warrior on the hill of Uixachtlan. The fire was then carried by runners to the temple of Huitzilopochtli in Tenochtitlan and distributed from there in hierarchical order, first to the training schools for the nobility, then to the temples in the wards, to the training centers for commoners, and finally to the households of the common folk (Sahagún 1950–1969, 7: 29–30). In these actions, the priesthood not only managed a particularly anxiety-provoking ritual event but also mediated its outcome among the different levels of the social order.

POINTS OF CRISIS

In an immediate sense, the hegemonic order installed by Tenochca might was a great success. Tenochtitlan came to draw tribute from thirty-eight provinces, sometimes directly through officials of its own, more often through the coopted or forced assistance of second-tier paramounts. Yet the system also frequently fell into crisis, and it generated crises of its own. Some were due to uncontrollable environmental conditions; some were due to mistakes in environmental engineering; not a few were implicit in the mode of expansion itself. These points need emphasis, because the Aztec polity is all too often portrayed as a commonwealth unmarked by discord and disobedience.

The Basin of Mexico has been a region of recurrent earthquakes (the latest being the devastating quake of 1985). Nahuatl sources register fifteen quakes between 1455 and 1513 (Kovar 1970; Rojas Rabiela 1987). They also list numerous snowfalls, incidences of frost and hail, and six major floods, as well as incursions by locusts and rodents during the same period. One great earlier flood, in 1385, wiped out the chinampas in the northwestern part of the valley; others hit in 1499, 1500, and 1501. There were also severe droughts. In 1450, 1451, and 1452, the combination of frosts and drought produced the valley-wide Great Famine of One Rabbit, in 1454.

This famine proved disastrous not merely in its own terms but in its effects on the Tenochca leaders, who saw themselves as heirs of Toltec dominion, the collapse of which had been preceded by a four-year drought thought to have been sent by the rain gods to punish the last Toltec ruler (Velázquez 1975, 126–27). Such environmental stress must have reflected on the leadership, who claimed both the right and the responsibility to rule as managers of the Tenochca cycle of time, and called into question the legitimacy of the ruling cadre. These uncertainties may have been expressed in the myths that deal with Tenochca stewardship of the Toltec legacy, especially the narratives about Motecuzoma I's efforts to dispatch his wise men to the mythical cave of Tenochca origins in Aztlan, as well as in the myths that surround the figure of the Toltec god-ruler Quetzalcoatl. Although the myth-histories concerning these figures remain unclear, it is possible that Quetzalcoatl came to represent Mesoamerican ideas about the "ideal" sociocosmic "center," based on cultivation, city life, and wise rulership (see, for relevant interpretations, Willey 1976; Carrasco 1982; Florescano 1995). In that light, invocations of Quetzalcoatl may have permitted an overt or covert critique of policies followed by the Tenochca leadership and raised doubts in the mind of the ruler himself.

As local reserves were used up in the famine of 1454, nobles and commoners alike were affected, prompting the ruler to allow people to leave the city, to search for food on their own in the Totonac-speaking eastern lowlands. Many died of hunger on the road or sold their children into servitude to obtain food.

This was the time when they bought people; they purchased men for themselves. The merchants were those who had plenty, who prospered; the greedy, the well-fed man, the covetous, the niggardly, the miser, who controlled wealth and family, guardians, the mean, the stingy, the selfish. In the homes of [such men] they crowded, going into bondage, entering house after house—the orphan, the poor, the indigent, the needy, the pauper, the beggar, who were starved and famished; who just went to sleep, just so awoke; who found nothing and got nowhere; who in no place found their rest, relief or remedy. At this time one sold oneself. One ate oneself; one swallowed oneself. Or else one sold and delivered into bondage his beloved son, his dear child. (Sahagún 1950–1969, 7: 23–24)

Half a century later, the last Tenochca ruler was still using his treasury to redeem noble children sold into slavery.

The year 1455 produced a bountiful harvest, and a New Fire ceremony was held to inaugurate another fifty-two-year cycle. The Tenochca state strove to cope with its economic problems by stimulat-
ing cultivation and canoe transport throughout the Valley of Mexico
and within the range of the city accessible to bulk transport by human carriers (Hassig 1985, 128). While the state thus strengthened
production and distribution, it also intensified its commitment to
war, partly to extract more tribute and widen the scope of its trade
and partly to bring back more prisoners for sacrifice. The disaster of
the Great Famine of One Rabbit also coincided with the completion
of the reconstruction of the Great Temple of Tenochtitlan, with renewed warfare in the Huastec region, and with the mass immolation
of captives before invited noble guests. This suggests that ecological
and social crisis led to an intensification of ritual, possibly to reassert
the promise of Huitzilopochtli in the face of cognitive dissonance.

Problems in provisioning were related to rapid population increases and urban concentration. Before the emergence of the Tenochca as an identifiable social entity, the population of the Valley of
Mexico as a whole probably stood roughly at 120,000, but it climbed
to about one million between 1200 and 1520. Tenochtitlan had begun as a small settlement, but by the end of Tenochca rule it encompassed an estimated 160,000 inhabitants and may even have reached
as many as 200,000 (Sanders, Parsons, and Santley 1979). As I noted
above, to feed this growing population required that cultivation be
expanded through extensive construction of canals and dams. The
largest of these dams, nine miles in length, was built to hold back the
saltwaters of Lake Texcoco during the initial years of the midcentury
famine, with the assistance of the ruler of Texcoco. Yet an attempt to
build a new dam in 1500 by the tlatoani Ahuitzotl (1486–1502) in order to tap the waters of Coyoacan not only ended in failure, but it
brought on a major flood that destroyed much of the Tenochca capital. The historian Nigel Davies has compared the effects of this disaster to those of the Great Fire of London (1980, 197). The city had
to be virtually rebuilt; what the Spaniards saw when they reached
Tenochtitlan in 1519 was this rebuilt city of Ahuitzotl.

Despite these efforts another two-year famine started in 1502, during the rule of Motecuzoma II. Once again, "the people of Mexico
dispersed everywhere, and there was great suffering from hunger." As
before, "many nobles sold their young sons and maidens," to be ran-

somed once more by the king "with large capes and mantles, and dried maize grains" (Sahagún 1950–1969, 8: 3, 41).

There were poor and destitute people in Tenochtitlan. The available sources note them only in passing, but they mention hungry people offering to sell dried peppers and cakes of salt, people begging for food on festive occasions, and distributions of maize gruel to the hungry on the occasion of the Great Feast of the Lords (Huei Tecuilhuitl) in July, when the new maize had just come in and food resources were especially scarce. The distributions did not meet the needs of all claimants, and those left out wailed about their bad fortune and their hungry children (Broda 1978, 236–37; Clendinnen 1991, 64–67). Inga Clendinnen notes that hunger and poverty must have intensified as the city grew, "when men no longer grew their own sustenance and food had become a precious commodity" (1991, 64). Feasting ceased to be occasions for redistributive "commensalism" but featured instead an invidious display of status. This suggested to Clendinnen "an intensifying imbalance of reciprocities in the urban milieu" (p. 67).

The population of the city increased not only through internal reproduction but also through immigration. Multiethnic in its origins, the city incorporated new groups of people throughout its history. Even before the conquest of Atzcapotzalco, newcomers had responded to invitations to settle and marry in Tenochtitlan. By the time of Motecuzoma I, the state had to stem urban disorder by reorganizing the city's population, which now included numerous immigrants (Calnek 1976, 288). Among these immigrants were groups of specialized craftsmen, such as lapidaries from Xochimilco; merchants (*pochteca*), possibly with ancient ethnic ties to the Gulf Coast (Acosta Saignes 1945); and manuscript painters working in what has been called the "Mixteca-Puebla" horizon style. The city's population was also fed by war refugees from the Basin of Mexico and beyond (Calnek 1978, 289–90). The rapid growth of population and its increasing heterogeneity transformed a small village of mud huts into a large urban center, at the hub of an empire, in the course of only a few generations. As a result, if "Tenochtitlan's sudden wealth earned the envious admiration of outsiders, it also brought internal tensions" (Clendinnen 1991, 37–38).

Still another source of crisis lay in the character of Tenochca em-

pire building itself. Ross Hassig has argued cogently that the Tenochca aimed not at continuous and permanent territorial control
but at maintaining the ability to strike flexibly and with overwhelm-
ing force whenever required (1988). They often had to put down revolts in provinces only recently "conquered" (Hassig 1985, 94). The
comparative study of Tenochca imperial strategies has shown that
the strategists differentiated between provinces that furnished regular tribute of specific resources and products, and provinces that
served mainly as bases for further imperial expansion into tribute-
producing zones or else as ramparts to contain intrusion by foreign
enemies (Hicks 1988; Berdan and Smith 1996). The tribute-paying
provinces, constituting "the economic mainstay of the empire" (Berdan 1996, 135), were managed largely by delegating power to local
elites, under the supervision of tribute-collectors imposed by the
center. The imperial frontiers were guarded either by the forces of
client states, which also furnished military support in exchange for
"gifts" sent out from the center, or by more permanent Tenochca
fortresses and garrisons. Tributary provinces might not always fulfill
their quotas of goods and services, and the guardians along the frontiers of empire might not always watch over these ramparts as single-
mindedly as the Tenochca tlatoani might wish. In either case, the absence of a standing army (Davies 1980, 186–87) put a premium on
keeping military motivation at the center at a high level of readiness
through a continuous celebration of war making as a way of life.

In the end, despite their invocation of Huitzilopochtli's promise
to make them rulers of the earth, the Tenochca did lose wars. They
suffered grievous defeat in their campaign against the Tarascans in
1479–1480, losing some 21,900 men (Durán 1967, 2: 284–85). In
1481 they were forced to a draw by Metztitlan, repeatedly a refuge
for dissident nobles from the Valley of Mexico. They never subdued
Tlaxcala. When the Spaniards appeared on the Mesoamerican scene,
they quickly obtained support from both Tenochca rivals and subjects; the Spaniards' ultimate victory was due as much to their native
allies as to their own force of arms.

Finally, even while the Spanish sources spoke admiringly of the
maintenance of law and order in the Tenochca realm in the years before the conquest, social control sometimes faltered. One important
set of Tenochca texts features the "words of the ancients" (*huehue-*

tlatolli), formal speeches pronounced on public occasions by orators trained in the schools of the nobility. Among the many themes of these orations, they praised the "good ruler," "the good father," "the good wife," "the good merchant" and excoriated the "bad" rulers, fathers, wives, and merchants, who must have been recognizable types for the Tenochca. Laws were harsh and severe, but there were thieves, murderers, traitors, and even corrupt judges who, when caught, were jailed in wooden cages and then executed, "so that the judges might walk in dread" (Sahagún 1950–1969, 8: 42). Supervisors of the marketplace who sold stolen goods and did not inform customers about the source of their purchase were put to death (8: 69). Military trainers who levied tribute "without leave," "who exacted as tribute whatsoever they wished," were strangled, or beaten and stoned to death. "Thus the ruler implanted fear." Tribute gatherers and administrators whose tallies did not "equal the correct count" were executed and their families "cast out" (8: 44).

Warriors were expected to be brave and return with prisoners, but some failed; after two or three unsuccessful tries, they had their heads shorn like porters and were expelled from their training schools. Drinking maguey beer (pulque) was severely censured and was permitted only among certain grades of nobles and warriors on stipulated occasions. Officers in charge of training warriors were barred from drinking, but some did drink and were beaten to death if they were caught (Clendinnen 1991, 117–18). Yet the fact that the longest court oration recorded by Sahagún, which was delivered by the king to an audience of noble men and women, high functionaries, and great warriors, devoted two-thirds of its text to denunciations of drunkenness suggests that this constituted a particularly serious problem (Sullivan 1974, 89). It was "a whirlwind, a cyclone that covers everything with evil, with wickedness" (Sahagún 1950–1969, 6: 68).

The Cosmological Charter for Rulership

Many elements of Tenochca cosmology were shared with other American Indian groups. Widely distributed, they may also be very old. Human sacrifice is "hinted at" archaeologically in

Mesoamerica by 6000 B.C. (MacNeish 1964, 125). The practice has a split ethnographic distribution in North and South America (Rands and Riley 1958), a pattern that supports its considerable age and suggests that it was once much more widespread. It is depicted on monuments dating from 600 to 500 B.C. in San José Mogote, Oaxaca (Marcus 1992, 37), and is now attested in mass burials associated with the construction of the Feathered Serpent Pyramid at Teotihuacan around A.D. 200–300 (Cabrera and others 1989; Sugiyama 1989). Blood ritual and heart excision is rendered explicitly in glyphs and emblems depicted in murals (Berrin 1988, 220–21). Representations related to human sacrifice are known from Post-Classic Cacaxtla in Tlaxcala (Baird 1989, 112–18), Xochicalco in Morelos (Hirth 1989, 75–78), and Tula in Hidalgo. Tula also features a skull rack, or *tzompantli*. Thus, many Tenochca conceptions and practices were undoubtedly ancient in the New World, yet they were readapted to defend and legitimize the social order against the challenges of crisis and change.

THE CREATION OF THE WORLD

The Tenochca rulers and their spokesmen rearranged and highlighted the stock of cosmological ideas at their disposal to explicate their specific role in wielding power over people. Nearly twenty mythic texts narrate the creation of the cosmos, as envisioned by the Tenochca, and delineate the tasks appropriate to gods and humans within it (Moreno de los Arcos 1967). Some of these texts represent the elite version produced by ideological specialists for use in the training schools of the nobility (Nicholson 1971, 397; Gardner 1986, 27). The texts start with narratives of creation, beginning with a cosmic condition in which the world was still shrouded in darkness, things lacked defined outlines and structures, and all was suffused by an inactive, dually sexed principle. This primordial calm then gave way to a process of differentiation, enacted through the unfolding of the original principle into multiple divine forces.

These divine forces were called in Nahuatl *teotl* (plural, *teteo*). The friars rendered this term as god/gods. When Sahagún learned of these strange and unfamiliar gods, he compared them with the Greek and Roman gods of Mediterranean antiquity and recorded the comparisons in his own handwriting on the margins of the texts he assembled (López Austin 1974a, 125). Yet the Mesoamerican deities were not individualized personalities in the manner of the gods of Greco-Roman antiquity (Townsend 1979, 30). Mesoamerican ideas about the workings of the supernatural have distinctive features that differentiate them from traditions prevailing elsewhere.

Mesoamerican cosmology did not draw a neat dividing line between the sacred and the profane; aspects of sacrality were thought to be present in momentary events, in things, in animals, and in people. People shared in the transhuman potency of the sun through the quality of tonalli placed in their bodies at birth, and they participated in the rhythm (*ollin,* movement) of the cosmos through the beating of their hearts. The prefix *teo-* could thus be applied to a wide range of referents. Sahagún noted that this included the sun in its fearsome aspects and even terribly behaved children, "things extremely good or bad" (in Read 1991, 273). Teotl thus denoted a bundle of special potency in "a spectrum of life-forces" (Townsend 1979, 30), some of which were endowed with much greater power and efficacy than were others.

To call forth these powers, one had to name them and activate them by specifying their appearance in particular locations within the calendric round of space-time. The divine forces were subject to the pulsations of time and the workings of the calendar. A series of myths depict how the gods transited from their transhuman reality into the reality of the present world and became time-carrying, time-enacting, and time-dependent beings, and thus subject to the round of calendric ritual.

Calendric reckoning and astronomy have constituted a major focus of interest in all archaic civilizations, but they assumed a role of special importance in the civilizations of the New World. Control of time placed in the hands of ruling elites a major instrument for social coordination and control, and it supported specialists who could interpret these reckonings as cosmic directives for ordering human activities in space and time. The Mesoamerican calendars probably served these ends from at least 600 B.C. on. They associated the sequential intervals of time not only with particular kinds of human action but also with schemata that referred to features of the earth and sky, directions in space, components of human bodies, categories of gender and age, body parts and ailments, kinds of animals and plants, foods and household articles, tools and weapons, and names and colors. Each such combination was linked to segments and cycles of calendric time, which were equated in turn to points and directions in space (Hunt 1977, chap. 3).

A particular combination of elements stood for—indeed, was thought to constitute—a particular transnatural being or force. As entry into the calendar drew the gods into the round of human activities, it also brought them into focus and definition as conveyors of ideas about time. Each of the more than thirty temporal, spatial, and taxonomic combinations of features rendered manifest a divine force, a force that would come into play at a particular moment in a cycle of moments. The ideogram for this concept was the emblem of the tumpline (*mecapalli*), by means of which the divinity carries a segment of time like a human porter; it "carried, set on its path, took with it, and bore the burden [of the year]" (Sahagún 1950–1969, 7: 21; Nicholson 1966, 144).

At the same time, a "god" might sometimes share the attributes of another deity, because they were thought "to occupy the same positions or effect actions that are similar at some point in their existence. A god does not always bear the same emblems and costumes because his composition, actions and circumstances are constantly changing in this world" (López Austin 1990, 177). Gods could combine the attributes of different functional domains, and at the same time divide and subdivide, assuming different characteristics within each context of space-time (pp. 207, 209). Many of them were also dually gendered, appearing now as male, now as female, featured sometimes as husband and wife and at other times as distinctly gendered versions of the same basic combination of features.

Once these extraordinarily potent forces had ruptured the primordial condition, they proceeded to impart structure to the cosmos. First they formed this world and reality (*tlalticpac*) by assaulting the cosmic alligator (*cipactli,* probably a reptilian and male form of the earth-goddess *Tlaltecuhtli* [Klein 1975]). They tore it in half: its upper part became the sky and the upper world, its lower half the earth and the underworld. The sky was to be primarily male, above, hard, and dry; the earth female, below, soft, and moist (Krickeberg 1956). I want to emphasize that this image of duality may express a relationship of complementarity, but it can also be used differentially to justify a cosmic imperative according to which a ruling class, representing the sun and sky, can impose order and direction upon the moist, supine, and structureless earth and upon the people who work it. Moreover, this dichotomous relation was portrayed as the outcome of cosmic violence. This world will end when the layers of the heavens and the underworld fuse again, and the cosmic alligator is again made whole.

Once the cosmos was given structure, it did not remain stable: it underwent repeated creations and destructions. This is the second theme of the elite myths. Mesoamerican myths generally portray a sequence of four successive world creations and extinctions, each world marked out by the domination of a different "sun," each characterized by a different key food, each destroyed by a different element, each ending with the transformation of its inhabitants into monkeys, fish, turkeys, or giants. But to this sequence of four worlds or "suns" the Tenochca added a fifth sun, a fifth cycle, in an account that presents "in both structure and content, an entirely different myth" (Gardner 1986, 27). Its calendric name *Nahui Ollin,* Four Movement, includes the number four as a symbol of completion and the term *ollin* (abrupt movement) from the verb *olini, olinia, olinilia,* which refers to the kicking of the fetus, the throes of abortion, the tremors of earthquakes, and the palpitations of the heart (*yol/ yolli/yollotl*) (Burkhart 1989, 58–59). This fifth cycle will end in earthquakes, and there will be no other. This account of the Fifth Sun constitutes the charter myth of Tenochca hegemony.

The myths now unfold a third set of themes, this time specific to the Fifth Sun of completion, which depict transactions between humans and divine forces wherein the transhuman forces bestow gifts upon humans and humans are expected to requite the gifts. First, new people have to be created to replace the extinct inhabitants of past suns. The super-numen Quetzalcoatl retrieves the bones of the dead from the underworld, sprinkles them with blood drawn from his penis, and produces people. The god gave people the gift of life through autosacrifice; they must reciprocate. Second, the emergent humans have to be fed. Two gods steal the basic food crops from Sustenance Mountain, where they are guarded by the minions of the earth and rain god. This time the key food is not some unsuitable approximation to food, as in the previous "suns," but maize. Again, said the Nahua interlocutors with the Spanish missionaries in 1524 (Sahagún 1949, lines 965–71), the gods "gave us all that one drinks and eats, that which preserves life, corn, beans, amaranth, chia [*Salvia hispanica*]. They are the ones we ask for water, rain, through which things grow in the earth." The gift of sustenance must be repaid.[4]

Third, the divine forces must raise a new sun. They gather at Teotihuacan, around a burning divine oven, and wait until one of them volunteers to jump into the flames, destroying himself in order to then rise as the new sun. A second volunteer, who loses his courage and does not jump first, is relegated to the position of the moon. The courageous godling, transformed into the sun, rises into the sky, yet he stands there, unmoving. To propel the new sun on its track through the sky requires no less than the immolation of the assembled gods. In some versions of the myth, they immolate themselves voluntarily; in other versions, they are sacrificed en masse by one or another super-god. Thereupon the sun embarks on its trajectory. "And when the sun came to arise, then all [the gods] died that the sun might come into being. None remained who had not perished" (Sahagún 1950–1969, 3: 1). In the words of Davíd Carrasco, "it is a myth not just about one sacrifice but about a sudden increment in human sacrifices" (1987, 135). Once the mass sacrifice of the gods at Teotihuacan had set the sun in motion, time too could unfold, with the calendric alternation of day and light, night and darkness, with the oscillation of rainy season and crop time, dry season and warmaking time. The Fifth Sun, the cycle of Tenochca time, had arrived.

This narrative not only locates mass human sacrifice at the beginning of the new sociocosmic order but also charters the prototypical ritual that will ensure its perpetuation. Myth and ritual together announce the role of war-making in furnishing the "sanguinary nourishment of the Sun and the Earth" (Nicholson 1971, 424). In that ideologically constructed world, gods with predominantly military and sanguinary attributes overcome and dominate supernaturals endowed with attributes related to cultivation and craft production (Ingham 1984). The myth foregrounded Tenochca prowess in war through a "propaganda of sacrifice" (Marcus 1992, 373), while masking material reasons of state, such as attempts to occupy land and to augment and secure the flow of tribute. Simultaneously, it celebrated and justified the warrior role in capturing prisoners to sacrifice as the mainspring of political and economic expansion.

The narrative of how the sun rose in the sky and was then set in motion by the collective sacrifice of the gods was followed by another episode of mass sacrifice, brought on this time by the failure of the beings who were supposed to provide the moving sun with its food to fulfill their obligation. The *Historia de los mexicanos por sus pinturas,* thought to reflect the official canonical version of cosmogonic history of the Tenochca elite (Carrasco 1982, 92, 93), related that Tezcatlipoca created four hundred men and five women who would provide food for the sun. In the Codex Chimalpopoca (ca. 1570), it is the goddess Iztacchalchiutlicue who creates an army of supernatural warriors to do the same for their father. In both tales the food providers fail to do so. Four more supernaturals are then generated to slay their errant brothers.

Sacrifice

The gods had sacrificed themselves for humankind, elevated the sun to its rightful place, and set the world in motion. They had bestowed upon humans the gifts of life, food, and time. In doing so, say the interlocutors in Sahagún's *Coloquios* (1949, lines 951–58):

> They were teaching us
> all their forms of worship
> all the ways of honoring [them].
> Thus, before them we touch earth to our lips [in a judicial oath],
> we bleed ourselves,
> we fulfill our vows,
> we burn copal [incense],
> we offer sacrifices.

To honor the gods, people make offerings, either by drawing their own blood in autosacrifice or by carrying out allosacrifice, that is, offering enemies taken in war or immolating impersonators of the gods in calendric rituals.

AUTOSACRIFICE

Autosacrifice, drawing blood by puncturing one's body parts with a maguey thorn or sting-ray spine and depositing the drops upon a grass ball, was incumbent upon everyone—commoners and nobles, rulers and ruled, adults and children—at regular intervals and in situations of personal and social crisis. Nobles were especially enjoined to perform autosacrifice. The "one of noble lineage [is] a follower of the exemplary life," "an adviser, an indoctrinator, a presenter to others of the exemplary life," "a doer of penances" (Sahagún 1950–1969, 10: 19–22; Klein 1987, 354). Nobles were especially obligated to carry out these acts in imitation of the rite performed by the god to bring the "vassals of the gods" to life (Klein 1987, 354). Autosacrifice thus reminded the common people of the debt owed to the creator gods, and it underlined the special qualifications of the nobility in upholding the political-cosmic order. Endurance of pain also qualified a man for war: "he who extracted the most reeds was considered the bravest, the most penitent, the one who was to obtain the greatest glory" (Durán 1971, 191). The paramount ruler, in particular, was required to perform autosacrifice during the events of royal succession. Cecelia Klein, in her study of this ritual, sees it "as a symbolic death substituted for the real thing and, as such, as a debt payment made in return for continued life" (1987, 297).

The manifest purpose of autosacrifice was to repay the gods; a latent function was to reinforce impulse control. People were exhorted "to travel along a mountain peak. Over here there is an abyss, over there there is an abyss. If thou goest over here, or if thou goest over there, thou wilt fall in. Only in the middle doth one go, doth one live" (Sahagún 1950–1969, 6: 101). Body and soul had to be kept in balance, an equilibrium always likely to be upset. One's soul stuff, tonalli, was connected with the sun in the sky and thus was always in danger from supernatural forces emanating from the earth and from cold and water. One needed food to live, but food came from the "heavy" earth and was contaminated with death through the killing of plants and animals. People ate maize, but maize was thought to die every eight years and had to be rejuvenated at the Atamalcualiztli festival (Brundage 1985, 32). Sexuality, too, was desirable and yet problematic, because too much sex, too early in life, at the wrong time, or without orgasm, threatened to decrease tonalli. Thus entropy was at work, threatening and diminishing the vigor of the gods, of people, and of things. The time-bearing gods had to be rejuvenated through human sacrifice. Time, too, was in danger of running down. The solar year ended with five extra days (*nemontemi*) without divine tutorship, a disorderly interval, reckoned unfortunate, and a time for "great penance," flagellation, bloodletting, and abstinence

(Durán 1971, 469). Every fifty-two years, when all possible combinations of the solar calendar and the divinatory calendar had been exhausted, a new fire had to be lit in the chest cavity of a sacrificial victim to ensure the rebirth of the sun and the renewal of time.

The concern with things wearing out, growing heavy with the sludge of life in the very course of living, was summed up in the concept of *tlazolli*. Usually translated as "filth" or "dirt," the term derives from *izolihui*, "for things to get old, to wear out," to become undifferentiated (see Burkhart 1989, 88). Louise Burkhart places it in parallel to what Mary Douglas (following William James) called "matter out of place." Its indices were debris, leavings, secretions, and offal. Defending oneself against impurity meant constant washing, sweeping, and penance. The Nahua, notes Fray Diego Durán (1971, 266), "owed much to water since it washed away their sins and taints." Constant sweeping stood for moral endeavor; brooms were instruments of physical cleanliness and moral purification. Yet brooms also became weapons of aggression, when they were used to sweep impurities into enemy lands. Constant penance ensured an upright life, purged of tlazolli.

ALLOSACRIFICE

Whereas autosacrifice was primarily an offering tended by a person, attempting either to rid himself or herself of tlazolli or to gain supernatural assistance in some moment of person-centered crisis, allosacrifice—the immolation of human beings—was a matter of institutional organization sponsored and implemented by the state and addressed to fulfill public aims, the concerns of the whole social ensemble. Allosacrifice was defined in Nahuatl as the "spreading out of an offering" (Read 1991, 272). The sixteenth-century Franciscan Alfonso de Molina notes two Nahuatl terms for sacrifice in his Spanish-Nahuatl dictionary. The first, *uemanna,* comes from *huentli,* an offering, and *mana,* to spread something out flat and smooth, to pat out tortillas; the second, *tlamana,* is simply "spreading out" (Read 1991, 272; Karttunen 1992, 135). The generic term for priest in Molina's dictionary was *tlamacazqui,* a provider of offerings. Yet these offerings took two forms that need to be distinguished, even though they sometimes overlapped and intertwined. One consisted of sacrificing individuals who were required to impersonate the gods and thereby cause them to appear in public rituals at regular calendric intervals; the other involved the sacrifice by heart excision of enemy prisoners captured in war. The god-impersonator was an *ixiptla,* a stand-in for a god, who was thought to infuse the particular god with energy by enacting him in public. The warrior slated for sacrifice was a *teomiqui,* "he who dies in godlike fashion," and would feed the sun so that it might shine upon the world and keep it in motion. War captives offered in sacrifice were not god-impersonators but were destined to accompany the sun on its way in the form of butterflies or hummingbirds.

The sacrifice of god-impersonators was connected primarily with the Tenochca calendars. In the calendar dedicated to divination each number stood for one deity and each day-sign for another; each date represented the combination of their distinctive powers, which were thought to determine together the fates of people and events associated with that date. In the solar calendar, each monthly segment was connected with a cohort of gods, and it ended with a major public ritual held in cognizance of their divine presence during the preceding interval. The gods could not manifest themselves in their invisible essences within the sphere populated by humans. To move in this sphere required that they take on material form in a gust of wind, a puff of air, in a bird, an animal, or a person. In ritual, they had to be represented materially in a human impersonator, the ixiptla. Completion of their turn of divine duty was then an occasion for the sacrificial immolation of a human impersonator of the dominant deity for that month. Each such performative event and killing replenished the energies of the god.[5]

The core meaning of ixiptla can be rendered as "guise," as in appearing in "the guise of," in the dual sense of donning someone's emblems and clothes and assuming the demeanor that goes with the costume. Coverings and behavioral forms are removable, after the occasion for donning them has come to an end. Thus, the human god-impersonator would don the facial paint and trappings of the god and walk with a distinctive gait to bring the deity into definition. In doing so, it was thought, he not merely playacted the god; "in him the god arises." At the end of each month, he or she was to be sacrificed, "so that his force might be born again with a new potency. . . . If the gods did not die, their strength would decline into progressive senescence" (López Austin 1980, 1: 434). Brundage counted fifty-seven such impersonators of particular gods who were sacrificed in Tenochtitlan in an annual round, a figure that does not include the ixiptlas who were sacrificed in groups (*cihuateteo,* malevolent divine women; *centzonhuitznahua,* the four hundred southerners, companions of Coyolxauhqui; fire gods; *tlaloque,* rain godlings) (1985, 47).

Captives destined for sacrifice either were seized by Tenochca warriors in direct engagements with their enemies or were obtained as gifts or tributary payments proffered by client states (Smith 1996, 148–49). Captives were sacrificed during rituals that recurred annually in ten out of the eighteen months of the Tenochca calendar (González Torres 1985, 124–27) and were also sacrificed in connection with astronomical events, such as the rising of the morning star or eclipses of the sun. Large-scale sacrifices marked special occasions, such as the accession of rulers or the mourning over their demise, the rededication of the Great Temple in Tenochtitlan after reconstruction, or the celebration of the end of the fifty-two-year cycle. Ahuizotl is supposed to have sacrificed 80,400 men to celebrate the completion of the Great Temple in 1487 (Durán 1964, 199); Motecuzoma II sacrificed 2,000 prisoners obtained in his conquest of Teuctepec (453–54).[6]

Each calendric ritual or feast demanded its own modes of immolation, but prisoners were usually sacrificed by extracting their hearts while they were still alive. Heart excision generally followed the decapitation of female god-impersonators and also concluded the proceedings when war captives were subjected to torture or ordeals. The motive was to offer the heart to the supernaturals while it was still palpitating and thus thought able to impart its vibrations to speed the sun on its way.

The divine recipients of these gifts of life were conceptualized as neither good nor bad but above all as hungry and driven by desires. The Tenochca statesman Tlacaelel spoke of the need for "flowery wars" to obtain prisoners for sacrifice so that Huitzilopochtli could find a place "to buy victims, men for him to eat. They will be in his sight like maize cakes hot from the griddle ready for him who wishes to eat . . . soft, tasty, straight from the fire" (Durán 1964, 140). In the version depicting the rise of the Fifth Sun in the Nahuatl Codex Chimalpopoca the sun demands that men be killed—"with this you will serve me food and give me to drink" (Velázquez 1975, 122). The goddess Cihuacoatl "was always famished" (Durán 1971, 217), while

Mictlantecuhtli, the lord of the underworld, is forever "unsatiated . . . coveting . . . thirsting there for us, hungering there for us, panting there for us" (Sahagún 1950–1969, 6: 4). These gods were not content with first fruits or valuable objects; they were desirous of human lives. To satisfy the rain and earth god Tlaloc, children were sacrificed as "debt payments" at openings of the earth filled with different kinds of water (Aveni 1991, 71–72). The teteo did not merely want to be acknowledged and repaid; they had active desires for parts of humans that were thought to be charged with extraordinary energy. These were human hearts, heads, and head hair, as well as blood obtained in heart excision (but not blood extracted in autosacrifice or blood shed in menstruation or parturition [González Torres 1985, 118–19]). The thigh also carried a special value. Hearts (*yol/yolli/yollotl*) contained the animistic vital center of a person, called the *teoliya;* the head and hair housed the tonalli, the "hot" irradiation of the sun and the flux of force connected with a person's day-sign; and the blood was *teoatl,* most "precious water," "our liquid, our freshness, our growth, our life blood" (Sahagún, in López Austin 1980, 1: 179). Offerings of blood were equated with offerings of maize tortillas (*tlaxcalli*); tlacaltiliztli was the act of nourishing the sun or fire with offerings. "While we transmute bread and wine into flesh and blood, reflecting the centrality of man in our cosmology" summarizes Clendinnen, "the Mexica saw human flesh and blood as transmuted into sacred maize and sacred water" (1991, 209). Through the capture of prisoners for sacrifice the successful warrior became "the mother, the father of the sun. He provideth those above us [and] those in the land of the dead with drink, with offerings" (Sahagún 1950–1969, 6: 88). Allosacrifice, whether of prisoners captured in warfare or god-impersonators, thus constituted intensified ways of transferring the energy stored in human bodies to their transnatural recipients.

This paradigm, according to which "people feed the cosmos and its various inhabitants (human and otherwise) and, in turn, the cosmos feeds people" (Read 1991, 287; 1994, 49), collapses complex meanings. It refers to analogies between the growth cycle of plants, especially maize, and that of humans (see, for example, Clendinnen 1991, 181–82, 189, 208–9, 251; Read 1991, 252–54). A connection is also made between destruction and life-giving powers; destruction, acted out in sacrifice, replenishes life. Read has argued that this perception was based on more comprehensive understandings, that all elements and forces of the Tenochca world—gods, spirits, things, and humans—were seen as forever interacting in the course of cyclic processes. In these interactions some died so that others could gain sustenance and vitality from their destroyed substance in a continuous round of death and life, predicated on the proposition that "it was only by the transformative powers of destructive change that creation could occur" (1986, 123). The metaphor for these interactions and transformations was culinary: all the forces of the world, including humans, were seen as feeding on each other, procuring, preparing, eating, and excreting sustenance.

In this perspective, humans might deal with these interacting gods, spirits, and things in the world—and attempt to control them—by bringing them to bear on human concerns through offerings and sacrifice. Contrary to cultures that are committed to setting off the sacred from the profane, the Tenochca brought the sacred into everyday life, in seeking to requite the hungry forces on which human life was thought to depend. If the divine forces make crops and people grow, they must be repaid through "transformative sacrifice" (Read 1986, 115). In Nahuatl the act of sacrificing to divine powers was called *nextlahualiztli*, payment, and the elements transferred were *nextlahualtin*, payments (López Austin 1980, 1: 82–83, 434).

If in functional terms war served to expand control over resources and people, and if capturing victims for sacrifice motivated soldiers for the task, ideologically warfare was represented as a continuous reenactment of the original sanguinary destruction that placed the cosmos of the Fifth Sun under the sign of bloody violence. This initial act inaugurated a cosmos that would be governed by the culinary appetites of imaginary forces for which warfare furnished the means of consumption. It also installed a hierarchical order of things in which gods could feed off people and godlike nobles could consume "the labor and the products or the very lives of those who were lower" (Ingham 1984, 393).

POLITICS AND SACRIFICE

The elaboration of this sanguinary and militarist emphasis owes much to particular Tenochca leaders. One of these was Motecuzoma Ilhuicamina, as tlatoani of Tenochtitlan from 1440 to

1468 the major consolidator of Tenochca state power. Fray Diego Durán reports that he was much concerned with the story of Huitzilopochtli's birth, the prototypical myth chartering the ritual focus of Tenochca state power. He also arranged for a mission of shaman-priests to revisit Aztlan, the mythical origin point of the Tenochca (Durán 1967, 2: 215–24). Another contributor to this ideological intensification—perhaps its major protagonist—was Motecuzoma's half-brother Tlacaelel, another of the three Tenochca leaders against Atzcapotzalco. Durán called him "the greatest warrior," but also "the most cunning man ever produced by Mexico" (1964, 52). Tlacaelel was one of the main advocates for raising Huitzilopochtli to the position of the dominant warrior deity of the Tenochca. Chimalpahin, the chronicler of the Chalco federation, described him as "the one who was always busy demonstrating that the devilish Huitzilopochtli was the god of the Mexicans" (in Brotherston 1974, 159). Tlacaelel was also the primary spokesman for the inauguration of "flowery wars" to obtain prisoners for sacrifice after the great drought and famine of 1450–1455. Moreover, he came to occupy the position of cihuacoatl, snake woman. As such he was "chief of the administration of internal affairs," as well as chief priest. He held this position until his death in 1478.

Tlacaelel's title is also the name of the goddess Cihuacoatl. Durán specifically identified her as the "mother" or "sister" of Huitzilopochtli, ministered to by maidens who served in his cult. She was patron goddess of the economically strategic chinampa region of the southern Valley of Mexico, from where her cult and image were probably brought to Tenochtitlan after the Tenochca conquered that area. Tlacaelel assumed the title with her name after the Tenochca victory over the chinampa towns (Klein 1979). As chief administrator Tlacaelel also headed the prestigious priesthood of the god Tlaloc, the Chachalmecas (Klein 1984), thus representing the dark powers of earth and water associated with Tlaloc. Indeed, the goddess Cihuacoatl, in her aspect as the earth mother Ilamatecuhtli, was regarded as the spouse of Tlaloc (Klein 1980).

As I noted earlier, in Mesoamerican thought sky and earth were conceived as basic oppositions. The sky stood for the light of the daytime sun, for life, for dryness, hardness, and masculinity, for war, for East and North. The supernaturals associated with sun and sky were nonagrarian gods associated with fire, war, and the hunt, among them Huitzilopochtli. The earth stood for darkness and moisture, for death, for female fecundity and reproduction, and for the cultivation of plants. It was represented by the male god Tlaloc and by the female goddesses of fertility and reproduction, Tlaltecuhtli and her "sister-variants" (Klein 1975, 72). It seems probable that in Tenochtitlan, this opposition was played out and symbolized through opposing and yet balancing the role of Cihuacoatl (one of the "sister-variants") as internal ruler with the role of the tlatoani—"speaker," military commander, and external ruler, representing Huitzilopochtli and the sun (Broda 1987a, 244).

This opposition was evoked in myths and rituals that depicted how transhuman forces killed their opponents to feed the sun and the earth. Some of the narratives probably incorporated real political conflicts in mythic form, such as the story that celebrated the victory of the god Huitzilopochtli over his rebellious sister Coyolxauhqui. In Tenochtitlan, Huitzilopochtli's divine slaughter of his sister and brothers was reenacted regularly in the annual calendric rite of Panquetzaliztli (González de Lesur 1966; León-Portilla 1987). The figure of Coyolxauhqui was, in turn, commemorated in art, as in the large stone disk featuring the dismembered goddess that was placed at the bottom of the stairs of Huitzilopochtli's temple, as if to receive the sacrificed prisoners that were thrown down the "jade steps." This image offers a clue to how the Tenochca combined strategic interests with symbolic representations of power.

Coyolxauhqui may initially have represented the leader of an enemy faction related to the Tenochca (Zantwijk 1985, 46–47; Broda 1987b, 78). After the city-states of that area became part of the Tenochca domain, her image was conflated with representations of the earth and fertility goddess Cihuacoatl, worshiped in the chinampa region. Then, in 1473, this Coyolxauhqui/Cihuacoatl was combined further with the goddess Coyolxauhqui worshiped in Tlatelolco. Relations between Tenochtitlan and Tlatelolco had deteriorated. Tlatelolco's ruler, Cuauhtlatoac, had refused to contribute resources to the building of the Great Temple in Tenochtitlan. Tenochca youths raped Tlatelolca maidens, and Tlatelolca carried out attacks on Tenochca (Hassig 1988, 159, 336). Cuauhtlatoac's successor, Moquihuix, had married a sister of the Tenochca tlatoani Axayacatl, but he mistreated her systematically. He then took the opportunity to mock the Tenochca by building in Tlatelolco a temple for Coyolxauhqui, a structure that imitated a similar edifice built in Tenochtitlan to house foreign gods, including the image of Cihuacoatl brought in from the chinampa region. In response, Axayacatl stormed the central temple of the town in 1473, killed Moquihuix, and imposed a Tenochca military governor in his place. For some time, the Tenochca exacted a tribute payment in commercial commodities and in supplies and porters for future military excursions. They asked for the surrender of Tlatelolca land and required the defeated antagonists to sweep out the palaces at Tenochtitlan, as well as to provide slaves for sacrifice (Davies 1980, 131).

The violent death of Moquihuix has been linked further to the completion of the temple to the Tenochca god Huitzilopochtli in Tenochtitlan and to the installation of the monumental stone disk featuring the dismembered goddess Coyolxauhqui. Axayacatl killed Moquihuix before the altar of Huitzilopochtli in Tlatelolco and then threw him down the ceremonial stairs, much as Huitzilopochtli was supposed to have killed Coyolxauhqui and her supporters at Coatepec, near Tula. The Tenochca burned the Tlatelocan temple, transferred its own image of Huitzilopochtli to Tenochtitlan, and placed a large stone disk representing the defeated Coyolxauhqui at the bottom of the stairway to Huitzilopochtli's pyramid, the spot where corpses of sacrificial victims would land after they were thrown from the top of the temple. It depicts Coyolxauhqui as naked, decapitated, and dismembered, her limbs knotted about by snakes. She carries a skull on her back and wears a belt tied like a male loincloth. Emily Umberger (1987, 425–28; 1996, 94–97) points to the Tenochca symbolism of using the sun to represent victory and the moon to represent defeat and suggests that Coyolxauhqui here represents the moon in death and defeat, marked by the skull on her back and made to portray "the humiliation of a captive destined for sacrifice." She also observes that the goddess's male loincloth may have conveyed a standard Aztec insult that equated cowardly or defeated warriors with women, this time addressed to the defeated Moquihuix by inverting his gender. Quite possibly, indeed, Moquihuix may have been buried close to the Coyolxauhqui stone (Umberger 1996, 97). This placement of the goddess's image, however, not only celebrated the Tenochca victory over the Tlatelolca but probably turned Coyolxauhqui into a more universal icon, "the representative image of enemy gods in general" (p. 95).

The entry and departure of the gods were regulated by the calendar, each segment of time being dedicated to a particular deity or two. Each temporal segment was marked by a dominant religious agenda, with ritual sequences dedicated to the forces that governed horticulture and subsistence alternating with those focused on the cult of the sun and war. Tenochca commoners, nobles, warriors, and the ruler might all participate in these rituals and common feasts, while asserting asymmetrical distinctions in their interactions. Similarly, the supreme ruler of Tenochtitlan might invite other rulers to take part in the ritual events in order to demonstrate his power, initiate distributions of tribute, underline a friendly alliance, or convey tacitly a possible threat. While the ritual gatherings and performances were manifestly addressed to the supernatural, they also acted out ritualized political relationships among differentially positioned groups and entities, drawing people together even as they displayed human and transhuman differences in power and wealth (Broda 1978).

In an earlier discussion I underlined the necessity to think of ideas and ideology as coded not only into thought but also into the body. One way in which Aztec ideology was inscribed into the body was through the practice of regular autosacrifice. Participation in repetitive and replicative ritual familiarized Tenochca of all classes with the sequential performances, the odors of blood and incense, the sounds of instruments and songs, the colors of flowers, the details of costuming, and the moods expected and generated as one ritual segment gave way to another. A significant aspect of this bodily absorption in ritual was dancing, an activity in which the Tenochca engaged daily, not only on ritual occasions. Young people met each day before sunset at the local "house of song" in their neighborhood, for long hours of dancing and recitations of songs and orations of Tenochca myth-history. Warriors and young people were exhorted by the ruler to sing and dance at night, clearly to maintain a state of military preparedness, "so that all the cities which lay about Mexico should hear. For the ruler slept not, nor any of the Mexicans" (Sahagún 1950–1969, 8: 57). Dancing accompanied most rituals, causing them to raise "their hearts and senses to their devils," worshiping them "with all the talents of their bodies" (Toribio de Benavente, in Clendinnen 1991, 258). Warriors and nobles danced collectively on many festive occasions, including events linked with military exercises and the distribution of arms and emblems by the paramount (Broda 1976, 41–44). At the conclusion of the process of confirming a new tlatoani, the ruler clad in full regalia joined a synchronized dance of 2,000 noblemen (Townsend 1987, 404–5).

The festivities that celebrated success in war through the sacrifice of prisoners similarly worked their effects on different levels. Prisoner sacrifice was thought to strengthen the ruler. Sacrifices "nourished" him, "by means of them his destiny was fortified [literally: his day-sign was fortified], by means of them he was given new life" (Sahagún FC, in Sullivan 1980, 235). He, in turn, rewarded the warriors who had furnished the victims. For them this meant public recognition of their valor and merit, and it allowed them to display the emblems of the prestige so gained.

The individual warrior who captured prisoners for sacrifice might be motivated by the wish for glory and the hope of political promotion, but his act was performed in service of the larger political community, and to that community he relinquished control of the physical person of his captive (Duverger 1983, 92). Permits to perform separate human sacrifices were indeed given to some social groupings that specialized in the acquisition and processing of luxuries required by the Tenochca elite, such as feather workers or long-distance merchants; but these events were confined to stipulated occasions and performed by sacrificial priests within restricted local precincts (p. 108). The right to carry out general human sacrifice was retained by the state as the party offering the sacrifices and entitled to receive their political benefits in making war and inspiring awe and fear among its adversaries (González Torres 1985, 237–38).

It also requires emphasis that the apparatus of sacrifice required extensive organization. The capture of sacrificial victims on the battlefield did emphasize individual prowess and brought rewards to the individual captor. Once captured, prisoners were restrained and bound by aides who followed the assault troops. They were usually marched back to Tenochtitlan, where they were housed and guarded in groups of twenty to forty in enclosures located in the various sections of the city. Before the sacrifice, the captors cut their prisoners' top lock of hair, thought to be filled with life-giving tonalli and hence a conveyor of vitality, courage, and renown (López Austin 1980, 1: 241–43; Furst 1995, 126–27). The actual sacrifice was then performed by agents of the state—the king, his immediate entourage, and the sacrificial priests. The victims' heads were skinned and mounted on one of the several skull racks of Tenochtitlan. Hearts may have been eaten by the priests, burned, or buried.

Classes

In contrast to the Kwakiutl, where local groups were ranked in relation to one another yet were not subject to an overarching political center, Tenochca society was both stratified into distinctive classes and politically centralized. The classes were set off from each other through rules of descent that entailed a differential allocation of power, privileges, and obligations. Nobles formed a warrior aristocracy, which inherited rights to control land and the labor of people connected with it, as well as privileged access to rulership and the important offices of state and religion. Supporting this stratum with labor and the payment of tribute was a large class of commoners, "the workers in the fields and the water folk" (Sahagún 1950–1969, 4: 124). Intermediate between these strata were the members of groups specializing in luxury crafts, merchants, and commoners who had received special recognition for their performance in war. Below all these classes was a category of "slaves," people who had lost their rights to status for a variety of reasons.

NOBLES

The Tenochca nobles were collectively known as *pilli* (plural, *pipiltin*)—strictly speaking, "young ones," with the connotation that they could trace elite descent from the first Tenochca paramount brought in from Culhuacan. In a wider metaphorical sense, they were called descendants of the god Quetzalcoatl (Sahagún 1950–1969, 6: 83, 141). The title was handed down through both males and females, without any ascriptive privileges of succession to offices or rank (Calnek 1974, 193). Since Acamapichtli had married twenty noble "daughters of the lords of the territory," this stratum grew very large. It also became diversified into the central endogamous lineage of royals that received special tributary rights after the war against Atzcapotzalco, collateral lineages deprived of

royal succession, various secondary sublineages, and affinal or unrelated lineages in control of one or several "noble houses" (*tecpans*).
Lineages were further stratified into senior and junior lines, each line
surrounded by clienteles. There was competition among these
groupings for seniority and precedence, for access to tribute rights,
and for advancement to political and ritual jurisdictions.

As I noted above, the second imperial ruler, Itzcoatl's nephew
Motecuzoma I, formalized the distinctions between the nobility
and the common folk in a code of privileges and obligations. From
their early teens, nobles were obligated to attend special schools in
order to receive training in myth, ritual, and calendric knowledge, in
hieroglyphic writing and the recitation of sacred narratives, in a severe regime of penances, and in the arts of war. At the age of fifteen
they were taken to war by their elders, to earn recognition and merit
badges through the unassisted capture of enemy warriors. The size
of the military nobility shaped by this training has been estimated at
1,600–2,150 men between the ages of twenty and fifty (Hassig 1988,
60), in a city of 150,000 to 200,000 inhabitants (Calnek 1976, 288).
From this group, the paramount drew his administrative cadre.

Nobles, in general, enjoyed preferential access to state positions.
They were exempt from tribute, though they were expected to bring
gifts to the king and to other nobles and received gifts from them in
turn (Hicks 1988). As nobles they received rights to land, labor, and
tribute through state disbursement; and they could—subject to
royal confirmation—hold patrimonial estates. Carrying out their responsibilities was believed to augment their soul stuff, tonalli, and to
build their prestige and reputation. They were entitled to practice
polygyny, were subject to special courts, and were admitted to special quarters in the palace. Only nobles could live in two-story
houses, wear cotton garments of specified style rather than the
maguey-fiber clothing of commoners, exhibit precious ornaments
and wear feathers, drink chocolate, carry certain flowers, and use
certain perfumes. They also had a special role in assuming peniten-
tial duties. Collectively, they were "fathers and mothers of the sun . . .
whose task it is to give food and drink to the sun and the earth with
the blood and flesh of their enemies" (Sahagún 1950–1969, 6: 72,
Spanish text note 20). Their duty was to make war and deliver to the
state prisoners for ritual killing. In carrying out these obligations,
says Durán, they "considered themselves images of gods and any

honor given to the gods was given to them" (1964, 44). As images of the gods, they also had the right to eat the flesh of sacrificial victims.

Although war captives were sacrificed by heart excision, the heart imparting its palpitative beat to help propel the sun on its course, their captors never performed the sacrifices themselves. The task was carried out by state-appointed sacrificial priests, or—on special occasions—by the ruler himself. No individual other than the ruler (including any potential god-imbued hombre-dios) could communicate directly with the gods through such ritual killing. The connection of captive sacrifice with rulership is evident.

The ruler was "the heart of the city," the ixiptla or embodiment of gods. He was "nourished" by sacrifices (Sahagún FC, in Sullivan 1980, 235). The captor yielded up the skull of his captive to the state, to be placed on the skull rack next to the temple, and he offered one thigh—an especially supernaturally charged body part—to the ruler. The second thigh belonged to the captor, to be exhibited conspicuously in his front yard as an emblem to his valor and a relic filled with divine potency (*malteotl*). The rest of the body was his own, to cook up for his guests. The sacrificed prisoner was thought of as a *teomiqui*, one who "dies in godlike fashion." His flesh "was held to be truly consecrated and blessed. It was eaten with reverence, ritual, and fastidiousness—as if it were something from heaven. Commoners never ate it; [it was reserved] for illustrious and noble people" (Durán 1971, 191).

This pattern of obligations and privileges was not exclusively Tenochca; it was shared with the nobles of other city-states. These noble elites interacted politically and economically, through marriages, and through what Michael Smith (1986) calls "periodic consumption rituals." These rituals were usually connected with events that featured captive sacrifice, such as coronations, temple dedications, and funerals. The nobles attending such events were likely to be "sons, grandsons, cousins, nephews, or even brothers of the reigning emperor" (Calnek 1978, 469). Nobles of other city-states were invited to witness these sacrifices and were often asked to bring sacrificial victims of their own or else to witness (in disguise) the immolation of their own warriors. It is said that such guests reacted to these celebrations with fear and horror, but they surely trembled less at the familiar form of sacrifice itself than at its massive intensification at the hands of the Tenochca leaders. Nobles from outside the

Basin of Mexico attended regularly (Smith 1986, 80), and the Te-nochca ruler in turn sent captives to be sacrificed at temple dedications elsewhere. The sacrificial feasts were coupled with large-scale redistributive events that promoted "social solidarity within the geographically dispersed noble class" (p. 75). Even hereditary enemies were invited: though "we wage war, in our festivities we should rejoice together. There is no reason why they should be excluded since we are all one. It is reasonable that there be trust and greetings among the rulers" (Tlacaelel, in Durán 1964, 192). Thus, in the words of Tenochtitlan's last ruler, "the sun, Tlaltecuhtli, the god of battle, feeds alike from both sides" (Tezozómoc, in Brundage 1985, 134).

There is in this amicability among predatory nobles more than a hint of a class consciousness that crosscut the various city-states, a sense of belonging to a superior stratum "to be adored as gods and to be taken for such," as Durán says of the great lords of Tenochtitlan (1984, 2: 211). It bespeaks a pride in descent mixed with a collective responsibility for maintaining the world of the Fifth Sun, a combination of superior privilege with a sense of status obligation.

By capturing enemies for possible sacrifice, the nobles earned merit and glory and built careers, yet with only a slight turn of fate they become food for the gods themselves. Carrying on war to feed the gods and thus sustain the cycle of time made the ruling elite responsible for maintaining the world, a proximity to transmundane powers that presumably also entitled them to practice anthropophagy. Serving the gods in this manner was thus also a matter of status honor, exhibited when the Tlaxcalan captive Tlahuicole turned down Tenochca offers to set him free and insisted on being sacrificed and when the two warriors captured by Cortés were outraged at not being accorded the honor of a sacrifice (Davies 1980, 172). It seems likely that such a sense of common status honor extended to the captured nobles of other polities—similar to relations among enemy nobles in medieval and early modern Europe—and may in fact explain the preference for victims from neighboring Nahua-speaking polities.

Another measure of commonality among nobles is evident in the "gladiatorial" ritual of *tlauauani,* in which "distinguished warriors, lords and captains" taken prisoner were tied to a large round stone and made to fight individually, equipped only with a sword-stick decorated with feathers and four wooden balls, against four warriors armed with obsidian-studded swords. Captive and captor were made to address each other with kinship terms ("father," "son"), and the heroism of the captive was extolled. The greater the courage he showed in the fight, the greater the renown due to his opponents. After the captive was brought low, his heart was extracted, and his blood was painted on religious structures. His body was returned to the captor, who could distribute it as food among members of his household, but he could not partake himself due to the quasi-ritual bond set up with his captive. In such instances, the captor received some of the tonalli of his victim. Yet such beliefs in the transferability of vital forces from victim to captor might also have worked to create a degree of identification among the protagonists in a common lot, ruled over by the god Tezcatlipoca, the Mocker or Capricious Creator. He was, as Clendinnen says, "fickleness personified," introducing anguish, transgression, and illness but also courage, nobility, honor, and wealth (1991, 79). Should the selected victim defeat his attackers, he was appointed governor of a distant province (González Torres 1985, 227).

COMMONERS

Commoners included cultivators, fishermen, and craft workers. They were called *macehualtin* (singular, *macehualli*), from a root *maceh,* a particle cluster that introduces clauses expressing wishes, commands, admonitions. Macehualli refers to a subject, a vassal, a commoner. In this it contrasts with another word that resembles it closely, *mahcehua,* but that is differentiated from it by a glottal stop (Karttunen 1992, 127, 130); mahcehua means both meriting something *and* carrying out an obligation, that is, doing penance or dancing in ritual in order to merit something. This distinction is true also of their derivatives: thus *macehualtia* means to make a person into a vassal, *macehuallotl* is vassalage (Molina 1970, 51). *Mahcehualiztli,* with a glottal stop, means gaining merit, acquiring good fortune. The two terms differ and yet intersect, because a grant of merit always implies *tequitl,* obligation, debt payment, tribute. Thus, when Miguel León-Portilla suggested that macehualli (without the glottal stop) referred to the divine creation of humans for the Fifth Sun by irrigating the bones of past generations with genital blood (1963, 111), his point was well taken, for if the gods are understood to have granted people life, then people owe obligations to them. This phrasing also holds for the relation between commoners and nobles: nobles "govern/lead/carry/cradle" people "on their laps," "on their backs/in their arms" (Sahagún, in Sullivan 1980, 227); thus commoners owe them tribute in kind and services.

Proper fulfillment of one's obligations not only repaid the original gift of life but also enhanced a person's vitality. All humans, nobles and commoners alike, received life forces from the supernatural. One of these was the tonalli, which is located in the head. Tonalli stems from *tona:* heat, light, and—by extension—the day. It connected the person with the sun and lent him or her vigor and the capacity to grow. Tied to the sun, the tonalli also linked one to the alternation of light and day, and thus to the day-sign of one's birth and to one's fate as determined by the calendar. Nobles received a larger charge of tonalli than did commoners and thereby a fate different from that of commoners, but proper comportment enhanced a person's tonalli and "fortified" his fate. Nobles added to their tonalli through showing courage in war and competence in governance, commoners by meeting their obligations in tribute and service.

Ranked directly below the nobility was a status category of commoners whose unusually meritorious deeds in war were rewarded by a royal grant of nobility and inclusion in the "eagle nobles" (*cuauhpipiltin*). They could take their place in the war council and join the military orders otherwise reserved for nobles, and they were allotted land for their use. At the same time, they were not allowed to place tenants on that land or to alienate these holdings to commoners. Their sons could inherit the "eagle" title, but they were never allowed to forget their humble origins. The "eagle nobles" apparently had exclusive rights to furnish the personnel for the positions of military trainer, keeper of arms, and executioner. For a ruler, such a stratum, which owed its titles to him, gave him control over a strategic military group that was independent of other units in society (Hassig 1988, 29, 146).

Commoners gave tribute; royals and nobles received it. This much is clear, but the relation carries ideological implications that invite further attention. On one level tribute was known as tequitl, but that word is polysemic: it can mean both tribute and work. The related verb *tequiti* can also mean "to work" as well as "to pay tribute," and a *tequitqui* is both a worker and a payer of tribute. Furthermore, the word carried extended connotations of "a kind of work," an "office," an "occupation," and even more generally

the obligation that any individual has to contribute something to the society. The tlatoani, the king, had his tequitl, which was to govern; a priest gave his tequitl, religious service; the tequitl of a warrior was to fight, etc. all gave their tequitl. With reference to the organization of the economy, the basis was the tequitl contributed by the great mass of the common people—the producers—for the maintenance of state as a whole or of the members of the dominant class on which they were dependent. (Carrasco 1978, 29–30; my translation)

This meaning thus connected an economic and a moral sense of obligation, a connection that has survived through colonial times into the modern period: *tequio* or *tequitl* is still widely used for work people in Mesoamerican villages are expected to perform for public purposes. Furthermore, the word conveyed a moral obligation that embraced all classes, whether fulfilled by nobles or commoners, or requited by doing labor, offering goods in kind, or paying money. Moreover, it tied that moral sense of obligation to membership in an imaginary corporate political order, defined by a tutelary god and his incarnation in a living surrogate, the tlatoani. One did not offer tequitl as a gift; one performed it by virtue of where one stood in a system of political domination (Hicks 1988; Carrasco 1978, 30). In contrast, goods in kind that were obtained as tribute through coercive relations between conquering Tenochtitlan and conquered populations lacked such connotations of morality. They were called by a different name, *tlacalaquilli*.

MERCHANTS

Tenochtitlan was home also to traders, including a multitude of part-time or full-time petty traders and full-time professional merchants who engaged on a large scale in long-distance trade. The professional merchants or pochteca—more than 10,000 strong (Sanders 1992, 286)—lived in wards and vocational associations of their own that drew members not only from Tenochtitlan itself but also from Tlatelolco, Tenochtitlan's neighbor, which had originally formed an independent city-state with its base in commercial organization. The Tenochca and Tlatelolca associations also

maintained ties with merchant groups in city-states within the Valley of Mexico and beyond it. They owned houses and depots in those
cities and used them as points of departure and return for voyages to
the two coasts and southward, perhaps as far as Guatemala. The voyages were often undertaken in conjunction with merchants from the
other trading towns.

It is likely that pochteca identity and organization predated the
rise of Tenochtitlan. Miguel Acosta Saignes thought they were of
Toltec or even pre-Toltec origin, because they shared many traits with
the cultures of the Gulf coast and maintained organizations in many
towns historically associated with the Toltec (1945). Their role grew
steadily more important as Tenochtitlan expanded its sway, and an
ever-increasing supply of precious feathers, jewelry, decorated garments, and emblems flowed through the hands of the pochteca into
the ruler's coffers in Tenochtitlan, to be parceled out to honor
officials and reward warriors. This pochteca trade in luxury goods
served in the main the palace and the nobility. Yet they not only
dealt in troupial feathers and amber labrets, or capes with eagle-face
designs. They also traded in slaves, and their sacrificing of slave victims in connection with their feasts is specifically noted in the sources.
Motecuzoma II "especially honored the principal merchants, the
disguised merchants [spies disguised as merchants, or merchants
who spied], those who bathed slaves [in preparation for sacrifice],
the slave dealers" (Sahagún 1950–1969, 9: 23). These merchants have
been characterized as "a true middle class" (Sanders 1992, 283), but
they are perhaps better understood as a hereditary professional group
engaged in state-dependent and state-administered trade.

While standing apart from the classes of nobles and commoners,
the merchant associations were stratified internally, ranging from
rich and influential "principal merchants" (*puchtecatlatoque*) to
people in their lowest ranks. Some subgroupings specialized in trading slaves, others in various paramilitary or military functions; their
trading activities in foreign lands were supported and defended by
the Tenochca state. Within Tenochtitlan they were exempt from public labor service but paid taxes in the goods of their trade, and they
administered their legal and organizational affairs autonomously.
They were made responsible for managing the large open market in
Tlatelolco and for overseeing deliveries from the market in times of
war. Although not nobles, they could send their sons to the schools

of the nobility, and they could also use and display luxury goods not allowed to commoners.

Despite these privileges, their position appears to have been problematic and insecure. On the one hand, they were rewarded by the ruler. The tlatoani Ahuitzotl "valued them highly. Indeed, he made them like his sons; their very equals he made them" (Sahagún 1950–69, 9: 19). His successor, Motecuzoma II, "set them right by his side . . . he rendered them honor" (p. 23), "made them like his sons" (p. 32). Yet the merchants also feared "envy" and took care not to flaunt their wealth in public. If "they corrupted their way of life, when they no longer were of good heart," then the ruler was "saddened." He slew the accused and used their holdings "so that by means of [their goods] the shorn ones, the Otomi warriors, the war leaders, might be sustained" (p. 32). (The Otomi warriors and the shorn ones refer to warrior orders that recruited men of especially outstanding military accomplishments.) The textual phrasing thus records not merely the ruler's "sadness" but a policy decision to re-channel wealth from previously favored "sons" to military recipients. The merchants strove to imitate warrior ways and used gift giving and feasting to secure the favor of the ruler and his military nobility, but neither activity dispelled what Clendinnen (1991, 135) calls "the generally beleaguered quality of merchant life in the imperial city."

SLAVES

At the bottom of the social order was a category of people called *tlacotin* (singular *tlacotli*), a term the Spaniards translated most often as *esclavo*, slave, sometimes as *servidor* or *sirviente* (servant). These terms were in fact applied to people of quite different origins and position, and this—I want to suggest—conceals a puzzle. Some tlacotin were domestic servants, while others worked the land. Some married, had families, and even owned other tlacotin. Some were war prisoners who were not sacrificed but given by the ruler to deserving warriors, and some were assigned as helpers to artisans. Some tlacotin were obtained through capture; others became such through impoverishment, having to sell themselves or family members into servitude, as in the Great Famine of One Rabbit, in the mid-fifteenth century. Christian Duverger, following Mireille Simoni-Abbat, has suggested that voluntary entry into slave status was a way of escaping the burden of individual and communal responsibilities altogether (1983, 79). In general, tlacotli-hood (*tlacoyotl*) did not extend beyond a person's lifetime, and his descendants were free; but we also learn of slaves born into households (*tlacatlatoctli*) and hereditary slaves subject to "old" servitude (*huehuetlacoyotl*). People could also be enslaved to settle unpaid debts of their own or of a family member. Gamblers unable to pay their debts were enslaved. Significantly, people unable to pay tribute were enslaved and their purchase price used to pay their tribute. Criminals were enslaved, usually for theft and sometimes for murder. Furthermore, heads of households could sell their disobedient children into slavery, and uncooperative tlacotli could be sold in the market, with failure to improve after three such sales punishable by sacrifice (Duverger 1983, 81).

Such a heterogeneous category is surely suspect: what unifying thread could hold together such a varied array? Cross-culturally, slavery or servitude often accompanies a deficit of economic or social resources, an abrogation of social support. There are, however, indications in the case of the Tenochca that the terms *tlacotli* and *tlacotin* refer rather to some kind of ritual impurity; they relate to *tlatlacoa* (transitive)—to sin, to harm, to damage, to spoil—and *itlacoa* (intransitive), to become corrupt, to go bad, to injure oneself. In Sahagún's text in which he discusses the way people enslaved themselves and their offspring to escape the ravages of the Great Famine, the narrative of events is followed by passages that explain that this happened because

they had incurred sins [*ueuetlatlaculli*]. They had taken unto themselves, and placed themselves in great wrong, through which they went always being slaves. . . . [This was] because they had prepared nothing for themselves, had shown no forethought for themselves; had paid no heed, had lived in negligence, and were disposed to evil before the year sign One Rabbit had begun . . . when it had not yet set in. Thus was it said, that their fathers and grandfathers had succumbed to One Rabbit; hence they took on great sins. (Sahagún 1950–1969, 7: 24)

Burkhart points out that the Spanish friars, looking for a Nahuatl term to translate their *pecado*, rendered *tlahtlacolli* as "sin," whereas in the Nahuatl context it actually covered anything "from conscious moral transgression to judicially defined crimes to accidental or unintentional damage." It referred to the effects or outcomes of an act, rather than to an "element inherent in the act itself" (1989, 28–29). Burkhart thus suggests that whereas the Christian concept referred to an internal moral failure of a person, the Nahuatl idea focused on an infraction of a cosmological order of which individuals and their society formed constituent parts. Such infractions were understood to upset the proper sequencing and interaction of cosmic forces and required acts of "counterbalancing" (Read 1991, 284). These acts could range from autosacrifice in the case of minor transgressions to "enslavement." The infractions that led to enslavement appear to have been connected with a sense that the person's tonalli and other animate forces had become in some way deranged (see the rituals connected with enslavement and liberation from it in López Austin 1980, 1: 402–5). Since the tonalli was connected with one's day-sign, and through the day-sign with the sun and its course through the world, this derangement may have been seen to threaten the proper relationship of forces.

In some way still not fully understood, therefore, tlacotli-hood set apart a ritually marked category of social marginals. Slaves constituted a majority—and apparently an increasing majority—of the human victims sacrificed as deity impersonators in the monthly rituals. Even then they had to be ritually purified, "bathed," to become *xochimique*, "those who are to meet death as captives" (González Torres 1985, 232). Durán provided us with a singular perspective on this dimension when he wrote in 1579: "Many a time I have asked the natives why they were not satisfied with the offerings of quail, turtledoves, and other birds which were sacrificed. They answered sarcastically and indifferently that those were offerings of low and poor men and that the sacrifice of human beings—captives, prisoners, and slaves—was the oblation of the great lords and noblemen" (1971, 227).

Discussion

In examining the case of the Aztecs or Tenochca, we located the nexus between power and ideas in their cosmology, which was deeply implicated in the formation, maintenance, and expansion of their state. That cosmology underwrote the hierarchy of Tenochca social relations, creating a sociocosmic order wherein gods, nobles, commoners, and slaves were arranged in a graduated series, with appropriate rights and obligations allocated to each distinctive grade.

The entity that was to become the Aztec state had its beginnings in a poor and marginal grouping of mercenaries, who traded their military services to more powerful rulers for permission to settle in their territories. From this seemingly inauspicious start the polity developed over the course of a century into a formidable political and military power. The crucial turn in its rise to dominance was the rebellion organized by a military faction of the Tenochca leadership against the ruler of Atzcapotzalco. Its successful outcome placed royal power in the hands of a core group of new leaders, related both by kinship and by a common interest in wielding and expanding sovereign power.

Ideology played a special role in the growth of this centralized and centralizing state. The new rulers rewrote history to prevent the spread of "falsehoods" and to secure a monopoly for elite versions of the "truth." These truths asserted the Tenochca claim to be the heirs of the preceding "Toltec" civilizations of Tula and Teotihuacan. New narratives retold how the gods sacrificed themselves at Teotihuacan to cause the Fifth Sun to rise and move, thus initiating a new cycle of time, and recounted the migrations of the Tenochca from humble origins to a destiny of glory and wealth under the guidance of their ferocious god Huitzilopochtli. These accounts legitimized Tenochca domination and rights to tribute, together with their obligation to reenact the primordial sacrifices and rituals that were thought to ensure the passage of the sun through the cycles of time. The mythic themes were also displayed in the layout of Tenochtitlan and in its public architecture and art, and were re-presented dramatically in calendric festivals and in the mass immolation of captured warriors.

With the accession of Motecuzoma I in 1440 the Tenochca kingship was sacralized, and fictitious genealogies were created to set off from the rest of society an elite of rulers and aspirants to rule. As in other archaic civilizations, the hierarchical order of classes in Tenochca society was connected with the structure of a divinely suffused universe. At each level of the cosmos, supernatural energy was imagined to manifest itself with different intensity and potency: super-gods possessed more than gods, gods more than nobles, the ruling lineage more than other nobles, nobles more than commoners, and all these more than tlacotin or slaves. Differentials of supernatural power corresponded to differentials of function: the gods gave life and food and installed the cycling of time; the nobles managed the exchange of prestations to requite the debt to the gods; the commoners supplied the basic resources for that management. Thus, the postulate of a sociocosmic hierarchy was also phrased as a hierarchically organized chain of gifts and counter-offerings between gods and people, nobles and commoners, superiors and subalterns.

The myths of the Fifth Sun explicated and celebrated the advent of a new and resplendent cycle of time, coming in the wake of four preceding cosmic cycles that had ended in chaos and destruction. These earlier cycles had produced only incomplete kinds of human beings and insufficient means of subsistence. The fifth and specifically Tenochca cycle, in contrast, would bring the sequence of cycles to completion, to inaugurate "the synthesis and 'center' of the four 'earlier' ages" (Elzey 1976). This time the gods would offer humans the gift of time and life, as well as true crops to sustain them, in exchange for reciprocal counter-prestations through human sacrifice.

As I have noted, the Tenochca did not invent the custom of human sacrifice, but they implemented it with unparalleled intensity. This raises the difficult question of how their adoption and use of the custom can be explained. At stake is not merely the nature of the evidence but also the premises on which possible explanations are based. Michael Harner (1977) and Marvin Harris (1977), according priority to material factors, traced Tenochca militarism and the sacrificial complex to a supposed shortage of protein and fat in the Central American diet, a shortage exacerbated over time by an increase in population. Implicit in this approach is the assumption, itself disputed, that the Tenochca engaged in anthropophagy. Some investigators, such as William Arens (1979), deny New World cannibalism altogether, on the grounds that archaeological interpretations are not warranted by the data and that Spanish and Portuguese reports and depictions of the practice are dubious because of the political or religious motivations of the commentators. Others, among whom I include myself, are convinced that these postconquest sources are specific, circumstantial, and repetitive enough to warrant acceptance of anthropophagy as a culinary practice. The case is es-

pecially strong for the Tenochca, for whom Sahagún reported reci-
pes employed in preparing dishes of human flesh with maize (1950–
1969, 9: 67). For those who have accepted the fact of Aztec cannibalism, the question then posed has been whether the eating of human flesh was primarily a response to a putative shortage of protein
in the diet, or whether it was practiced to ingest transnatural power
symbolically, according to cultural imperatives alone (Sahlins 1978;
Sanday 1986).

It has been well argued that the Mesoamerican diet was balanced
enough to obviate significant shortages of protein (Ortiz de Montellanos 1990, 85–119). Furthermore, it is unlikely that human sacrifice would have yielded supplies in sufficient quantity to nourish the
bulk of the population (Garn 1979). However, the sources tell us that
human flesh was consumed primarily by nobles—"the commoners
never ate it, only the illustrious and noble people" (Durán 1971,
191)—and by the *tequihua*, commoners whose exceptional military
record of capturing at least four prisoners entitled them to a share of
the sacrifice. To understand Tenochca anthropophagy, therefore, requires taking account of the wider political economy, encompassing
both eaters and eaten. As Barbara Price has insisted, the whole system of Tenochca food supply was under the domination of an ex-
tractive upper stratum (1978); as in all class societies, relations of
domination intervened between production and distribution. Moreover, population increase was not an independent variable but was
intertwined with elite concerns about horticultural intensification
and the ability to field large armies.

Conversely, an explanation based on the force of cultural symbolism alone would miss the mark if it avoided the issue of how symbolism is embedded in the dynamics of power. In this discussion I
attended to the cultural understandings that informed human sacrifice. I took note of how the Tenochca imagined the supernatural, as
well as of the ways they devised to influence its forces and bring them
to bear on human concerns. The Tenochca comprehended the cosmos as a manifold of forces neither wholly good nor wholly evil, but
as approachable and potentially helpful sometimes, and ambiguous,
turbulent, or even terrifying at other times. To deal with these forces
people employed calendric orderings and forms of ritual, hoping to
bring them into conjunction with human ends through offerings and
sacrifices. According to understandings widespread and probably

old in Mesoamerica, objects and human beings had to be destroyed in sacrifice, if they were to yield renewed and enhanced life. Ritual aimed at inviting participation of the supernaturals thus involved violence in the service of engendering life—"la vida y la muerte son cuates" (life and death are twins, bosom pals) is still a Mexican saying. Yet in the myths of the Fifth Sun the Tenochca elite transformed this general perception of the cosmic flux into a specific ideology, which assigned to them a special role as "fathers and mothers of the sun." In that role, they would escalate violence to repay the debt incurred by the divine gifts of life. The myths legitimizing the role invoked the slaughter of the gods at Teotihuacan and Huitzilopochtli's killing of his sister as rationales for a politics of "transformative sacrifice" placed at the service of Tenochca power.

Some of the themes evident in the Tenochca material resonate with theories about the origin and nature of sacrifice. Thus, gift giving to the gods marks Edward Tylor's first stage in a hypothetical process of moral evolution. Communication between gods and humans through sacrifice is central to William Robertson Smith's interpretation of sacrifice as a totemic feast, in which people killed an animal that stood for their supposed animal ancestor and ate it in a ritual of communion. The theme of enhanced fertility gained through sacrifice underlies James Frazer's explanation of the ritual killing of "divine kings." The notion of sacrificial violence appears in René Girard's postulation, on largely philosophical grounds, of a primordial murder that is endlessly repeated in the course of history. While such evolutionary conceptions of cultural origins have been abandoned, these themes recur repeatedly in anthropological accounts. However, we do not yet have a satisfactory general explanation for the practice.

Another major effort to explicate sacrifice was that advanced by Émile Durkheim's students Henri Hubert and Marcel Mauss. They sought to replace evolutionary theories of origins with a universal scheme of sacrifice. In doing so, they followed Durkheim in his absolute distinction between the realms of the sacred and the profane, and explained sacrifice as a mode for conjoining the two worlds through rituals of "sacralization" and "de-sacralization." This scheme does not account for Aztec sacrifice; the Tenochca did not set off a sacred realm from the profane world but saw the entire universe as constituted by interactive, animate forces—supernatural, human, and inorganic. Luc de Heusch has noted, similarly, that Hubert and Mauss's scheme does not apply to Africa, perhaps because they drew their illustrative material primarily from Vedic Hindu and Greek-Roman sacrifice (1985, 4). He argues convincingly against the pursuit of a single "formal universal schema" at the root of all sacrifice, advocating instead recognition of a plurality of sacrificial patterns. One model might focus on the immolation of animals to restore the socio-cosmological order, another on the ritual killings of sacralized kings (or animal substitutes for them) to ensure fertility, still a third on sacrifice as repayment of a primordial cosmic debt—the pattern that best fits the Tenochca case.

The question remains, however, whether "sacrifice" was ever a unitary phenomenon cross-culturally, characterized by any common features beyond the killing and offering of some plant, animal, or human organism. Instead, the Tenochca material suggests that the very definition of killing—whether in sacrifice, in war, in execution by the state, or in vendetta and murder—depends heavily on the specific cultural symbolics of the society. Any explanation of Tenochca sacrifice must take account of their cosmological understandings about the creative and transformative capacities of violence, as well as of the use made of these ideas in their imperial ideology.

That ideology represented sacrifice not only in its own terms but as a means for securing "life." This evokes an older vitalism, represented in anthropology by A. M. Hocart (1883–1939), which located the rationales of social existence not in practical, jural considerations but in the search for a secure and more abundant life. Drawing on his work in ethnography and archaeology in Southeast Asia and Oceania, Hocart argued that the functions of ritual were prior to functions of government, that political institutions "were originally part, not of a system of government, but of an organization to promote life, fertility, prosperity by transferring life from objects abounding in it to objects deficient in it" (1970, 3–4). The point for the present discussion is not whether ritual has temporal or even logical priority over governmental institutions, but rather that a society constructs and projects ensembles of ideas that strive to connect power with visions of life. The claim of ideologies—such as that of the Tenochca—is that the acceptance and implementation of these ideas will lead to an intensification of vitality, even if the price of doing so is death—whether death dealt out to an enemy or accepted as self-sacrifice so that power may live and beget more life.

The Tenochca case revealed numerous material sources and causes of crisis, ranging from the ecological instability of the Valley of Mexico to the organizational stresses brought about by rapid urban and imperial expansion. The events generated by these crises affected both the society and its leadership, which clad itself in the mantle of Toltec legitimacy and ruled as managers of the Fifth and final Sun. The extant texts convey a prevailing sense of anxiety about whether individual self-control and penance, as well as government policy and public ritual, would ever suffice to maintain personal balance and political continuity. One may surmise that this anxiety was also fed by the calendric system of reckoning time. Since segments of time were connected with many other aspects of the social and cosmic order, uncertainties regarding the passage of time implied other uncertainties as well. Different day-signs were associated with differential charges of tonalli and fatality, and people were forever consulting shamans and priests to elicit diagnoses of their fates. Public rituals celebrated the role of the state in maintaining the cosmos; yet they could become a source of anxiety when their performance was judged to be insufficient or inadequate. Human sacrifice, too, had to be calibrated to assuage the needs of the gods. Finally, anxiety loomed large at the turnover point from one fifty-two-year cycle to another or at moments when the moon eclipsed the sun. When we are told that "the city never slept," that its inhabitants were forever mobilized for collective dances or public festivals, and that much time and energy was devoted to autosacrifice to avert entropy, we may conclude that in "the Aztec arrangement" satisfaction and tension were closely linked, each acting in synergy upon the other.

In 1519 Cortés and his Spanish troops landed in Mexico. Reversing the Tenochca conquests by recruiting Indian allies and laying siege to Tenochtitlan, Cortés entered the city in 1521, over the bodies of inhabitants struck down by war and European-borne disease. The conquerors replaced the Tenochca government with an administrative apparatus of their own, integrating Aztec chiefs and nobles as lower-rank executives under Spanish supervision; Spanish authorities replaced Tenochca tax collectors and tribute-takers, judges and administrators. They razed the great temple of Tenochtitlan and the ceremonial precinct of which it formed part and built the Catholic Cathedral of Mexico on its ruins. They dismissed or executed the priesthood and burned as many of the Tenochca sacred texts and relics as they could find. They utterly destroyed the Tenochca cosmological and liturgical apparatus, including its machinery of sacrifice, and replaced it with the organizations of the Catholic Church. Missionaries spread out across the countryside to propagate the Christian message, sometimes in competition with native prophets and visionaries who strove to perpetuate traditional understandings in the midst of changing circumstances. Eventually the sanguinary shock produced by the conquest subsided, and novel syncretic forms of behavior and ideation, drawn from Mesoamerican and Mediterranean sources alike, began to develop and spread throughout New Spain, to underwrite new patterns of social life and culture.

Still, the memory of Tenochca power persisted, in Nahuatl dirges about lost glories in Milpa Alta (Zantwijk 1960), in performances of battles between Moors and Christians transposed to scenarios in America, in European theatrical plays about the last Motecuzoma, as well as in the writings of antiquarians and scholars interested in their manuscripts, calendars, and monuments. For Europeans of the Enlightenment period, who were laying the basis for new forms of government and law, the Tenochca furnished prototypes either of civilization or of barbarity. Mexico after independence in 1821 combined admiration for the heroes of the pre-Hispanic past with denigration of anything Indian in the present.

The Mexican Revolution of 1910, however, gave rise to the view that the country should turn its back on the legacy of alien and reactionary Hispanic colonialism and instead draw energies from its cultural roots in preconquest Mexico. The resulting *indigenismo* produced an efflorescence of plastic and performative arts that once again exalted the Tenochca cultural legacy. In Mexican immigrant communities in the United States today, Tenochca emblems decorate the walls of meeting places, and Tenochca impersonators appear at rallies and festivals, to underline and display Mexican cultural identity in a strange and often hostile environment. Elements and themes drawn from what was long thought of as a dead culture signal a live presence under new circumstances.

Hitler presides over the consecration of storm-troop eagle banners at the celebration of the Reich's Party Day, Nuremberg, September 1934. (Corbis-Bettmann)

5

National Socialist Germany

Our third case study looks at Germany in its incarnation as the Third, National Socialist (NS) Reich, which was supposed to last a thousand years and ended in destruction and defeat only twelve years after its birth in 1933. When that Reich began, the NS anthem, the "Horst-Wessel Lied," proclaimed that "millions already look full of hope upon the swastika / the day has come for freedom and for bread." When it ended, the German historian Friedrich Meinecke characterized its trajectory from promise to ruin as "The German Catastrophe" (1950).

This inquiry focuses on the ideas that guided this paroxysm of events. The German catastrophe was of course the vortex of other catastrophes: Jewish, French, Gypsy, Polish, and Russian, to name but a few way stations on the descent into hell. What the National Socialists wrought is, without a doubt, a cause of moral outrage, but outrage is not enough. It is vital that we gain an analytic purchase on what transpired, precisely because it embodied a possibility for humankind, and what was once humanly possible can happen again. There is probably no single all-encompassing explanation for the phenomenon, but we can hope to assemble and assess some of the elements for a comprehensive understanding.

I shall argue that German National Socialism is better understood as a movement akin to the cargo cults and ghost dances studied by anthropologists than as a rational deployment of means to pragmatic ends. Its ideology projected the overthrow of the existing order and its forcible replacement by a new regime of "bread and hope." Writing in 1933 on the Hitler Movement "from the perspective of a participant," the German anthropologist Wilhelm E. Mühlmann called it a "chiliastic millenarianism" (1933, 129).[1] More generally, anthropologists have labeled such phenomena as "nativism," "millenarianism," or "chiliasm." Anthony Wallace saw all such movements as efforts at "revitalization," that is, "deliberate, organized attempts by some members of a society to construct a more satisfying culture by rapid acceptance of a pattern of multiple innovations" (1956, 265). Thinking of National Socialism as such an effort is useful because it points us toward questions about the tensions and contradictions produced by antecedent social and political arrangements in the Germanies. At the same time, it was unlike most other efforts at revitalization, in that it aimed to enhance vitality by linking it to apocalyptic visions of racial corruption and sought renewed life for the Germanic few by destruction of the many who were judged to be "subhuman." This ideological vision it pursued with singular tenacity, becoming increasingly lethal, both to its followers and to its victims. It took a world war and the death of millions to halt this homicidal project.

The quantity of material published on NS Germany is enormous and still growing. This is partly due to the fact that we are not yet sure what made the ensemble work, either as a whole or as a sum of its parts. Some believe that it will never be possible to comprehend the realities of the Third Reich; others hold—as I do—that we must make the attempt, even if our efforts prove only partial and inconclusive. It is a way of remembering; it may also help us mark out our directions in the future.

Disagreements on how to understand this virulent Reich abound. There are knowledgeable interpreters who conceptualize "the German catastrophe" as the outcome of a distinctive historical trajectory of German history, the fateful *Sonderweg,* while others see the twelve-year episode as merely a temporary deviation along an otherwise unobstructed autobahn to modernity. Scholars differ further on who supported the NS regime actively, and why, and who only pretended to support it while striving to maintain a measure of distance. Some experts emphasize the "intentions" and actions of Adolf Hitler or his intimate advisors, while others stress the interest politics pursued by particular institutions or the improvised "functional" decision making by lower-level personnel (see Mason 1981). The "intentionalists" believe that war and genocide were planned from the start and that attempts to identify stages leading to the ultimate outcomes are therefore misleading. In contrast, the functionalists discern a sequencing and proliferation of strategies over time and seek to "historicize" their inquiries. Some writers blame the NS leadership and Heinrich Himmler's guard troops or *Schutzstaffel* (SS) for what transpired but seek to distinguish between these organizers of terror and the German army proper. Others point to ways in which all were drawn together into a collective "ideological" war (see Kampe 1987). Furthermore, as the historian Arno Mayer has put it, some investigators are "reductionists" who focus on the making of particular decisions, while others are "extensionalists" who emphasize interconnections among "factors and developments in what they consider to have been a single historical process" (1988, 454). My own judgment is that these various approaches are not mutually exclusive.

Some scholars have interpreted Germany as a capitalist economy, while others have emphasized the primacy of fascist politics over economics. Yet purely economistic and political explanations alike sidestep or underplay the significance of NS racialism and "applied biology." That ideology underwrote actions aimed at separating "life worthy of life" from "life unworthy of life," at assigning conquered populations deemed "valueless" to backbreaking and lethal work; and at exterminating people designated as "subhuman."

An extended listing of writings on National Socialism is beyond the scope of this discussion and would, in any case, soon be obsolete, but I want to indicate some waymarks that have been important for this inquiry. I remain partial to the concept of the Sonderweg, which stresses the historical peculiarities of development in the Germanies, because I think that local, regional, and national divergences matter everywhere. The trajectory of the Germanies did not duplicate what happened in England or France, Russia or Poland, and there is much to gain from trying to define what made the Germans historically "peculiar."[2] It has been common to describe this Germany as "totalitarianism," but I have never thought that this global concept was sufficiently analytic to do justice to the particular mix of "populist" politics and mass party organizations with conservative institutions and capitalist interest groups. The question of whether this was a state at all was raised early on by Franz Neumann (1944); many of Neumann's concerns have been resurrected by Edward Peterson (1969), Hans Mommsen (1976), and Michael Geyer (1984). At the same time, all these works leave unanswered how centralization and polycracy interdigitated within the NS polity.[3]

Of necessity, I have drawn extensively on *Mein Kampf* (My Struggle), which Hitler wrote (or rather, dictated to Rudolf Hess) during the year he was imprisoned in the fortress of Landsberg am Lech for his part in the unsuccessful coup of November 8, 1923. (Hereafter I cite this source as MK, referring to the complete and annotated English translation of 1939.) The book drew together most of the ideological themes that inspired the social and political understandings of the German nationalist Right, but it is especially important because Hitler, as uncontested leader of his nation during twelve fateful years, was in a position to translate that vision into reality. A goal of this discussion will be to locate such views in history, but I do not aim at constructing genealogies of guiding ideas traced back to historical prototypes. My purpose is to show how such ideas relate to particular social, political, and economic arrangements of the past, and how they were caught up in the transformations of those arrangements. While there was considerable divergence and dissonance in the Hitler Movement, these ideas provided a structure of comprehension and imperatives for action that were understood by all.

The Course of the Movement

The National Socialist German Workers' Party (NS-DAP) was organized in Munich in 1920, two years after Germany's defeat in World War I. Like many other organizations that emerged at the time, its program was anti-Marxist, anti-Semitic, antidemocratic, and against something defined as interest capitalism. Its leader, the former corporal Adolf Hitler, had returned from the war to take a job as an agitator for the Bavarian army. By autumn 1923 the party had some 55,000 adherents, and in November of that year it joined in a local demonstration that was supposed to trigger an uprising against the national government. The demonstration was dispersed by police, and Hitler was jailed at Landsberg prison, where he wrote *Mein Kampf.*

After his release from prison, Hitler decided to abandon the attempt to win power through a coup d'état and turned rather to electoral politics, but an electoral politics backed up by the threat of party militias. These formations, which included the storm troops (SA) and Hitler's SS, grew rapidly. The SA numbered 6,000 in 1923, 70,000 by 1930, and 2.9 million in 1934 (Fest 1970, 144; Snyder 1976, 304; Payne 1995, 186). The SS had 300 members in 1929 but 50,000 by 1933 and 240,000 in 1938 (Fest 1970, 117; Snyder 1976, 330; Payne 1995, 186). It needs emphasis that while the National Socialists added greatly to their electoral strength between 1924 and 1933, the party never obtained a majority of the votes cast. Hitler's appointment as Reich Chancellor after the elections of 1933 was the outcome of a negotiated agreement with a group of conservatives who thought they could hold Hitler in check through their own control of key positions in industry, the army, and government. In that election Hitler won 37.3 percent of the vote; even in the next election, after his formal seizure of power, he received only 44 percent.

On February 27, 1933, a fire was set at the Reichstag (Parliament) building and blamed on the communists. Parliament then passed an "enabling act" giving Hitler dictatorial powers. All districts and regions were coordinated under central Reich control in the so-called *Gleichschaltung,* or synchronization. Parties other than the NSDAP were dissolved, leaving the National Socialists as the only legal party in Germany. Trade unions were abolished and their members integrated into the National Labor Front. Opponents were intimidated and silenced by the storm troops. The SA was also responsible for killing more than 500 people during the first nine months of the regime, and an estimated 100,000 were sent to concentration camps, while 50,000 fled the country; some 200,000 others were imprisoned over the next five years, and another 50,000 were confined at the beginning of war in 1939 (Fest 1970, 145; Snyder 1976, 57). The number of concentration camps in the Reich rose from about fifty in 1933 to more than a hundred in 1939 (Kogon 1980, 22, 27). After the outbreak of war in 1939 and German occupation of much of Europe, the number of camps came to exceed 10,000, 5,800 of which were in Poland (Goldhagen 1996, 170–71).

By 1934, however, the storm troops had grown impatient waiting for their reward. Some began to talk about "a second revolution" that could move further in the direction of "socialism" and the formation of a "People's Army," which would grant them greater participation in government and speed up the flow of resources in their direction. To this talk Hitler put a decisive end by calling on his SS guard to liquidate the SA leadership in a three-day massacre. Thereafter, the SS became an autonomous organization; its leader was the colorless chicken farmer Heinrich Himmler, whom Hitler called his St. Ignatius of Loyola.

This point marks the beginning of Himmler's remarkable institutional career. By the summer of that year, he brought under SS control all of the concentration camps in the Reich, thus laying the basis for control of similar camps to be built elsewhere all over Europe under the management of his dreaded Death Head (*Totenkopf*) guard battalions. Simultaneously, he initiated the buildup of the so-called SS dispositional units (*Einsatzkommandos*), which would eventually grow into the Waffen-SS—a full-fledged army parallel to the official army of the Reich, the Wehrmacht. This dispositional army grew from 7,000 in 1935 to 900,000 in 1944 (Wegner 1985, 445, 446). In 1936 Himmler added control over all the police forces of the Reich: the civil police, the secret police or Gestapo, and the party Security Police (SD), which collected dossiers on the entire population.

Yet this was not enough for Himmler. By 1939 he also ran most of the agencies dealing with racial questions: the Central Office for Race and Resettlement; the Ancestral Heritage Office (*Ahnenerbe*), which retrieved "the sunken cultural treasures" of Teutonic folklore and checked on the racial credentials of possible settlers in Eastern Europe; the Well-of-Life (*Lebensborn*) orphanages for "racially valuable" children; and the Liaison Office for Ethnic Germans Abroad. In the wake of the invasion of Poland in 1939, Himmler persuaded Hitler to make him Reich Commissar for the Consolidation of the German People. Each of these agencies proliferated into numerous, often competitive, segmentary organizations. By war's end, the SS also owned forty different economic enterprises, with some 150 plants and factories, covering agriculture, forestry, construction, textiles, and publishing (Wegner 1985, 440). The sociologist Rainer Baum has said, not in jest (1981, 277), that the best preparation for a career in the SS would have been a Harvard Master's degree in business administration.

Two of the major aims of the movement were to rearm Germany and to prepare for the conquest of living space in the Slavic East. Both goals were strongly emphasized in *Mein Kampf.* For Hitler, making war represented "the most powerful and classic expression of life" (in Nolte 1969, 516). In 1936 the Wehrmacht reoccupied the demilitarized Rhineland. In January 1938 Hitler assumed firm control of the armed forces, sacking on trumped-up charges both the minister of war and the commander-in-chief of the army, who had opposed his expansionist drive, and putting his own men in charge. Thereupon Austria was occupied in March 1938, the Sudetenland of Czechoslovakia in September, and the rest of Bohemia and Moravia, as well as the Memel region of Lithuania, in early 1939. In September 1939 Germany invaded Poland, and war broke out with France and Great Britain. Early in 1940 German troops seized Denmark and Norway; France was defeated and cut in half in midyear, and British troops were forced to evacuate the Continent. The Balkans were occupied in spring 1941, and then in June Operation Barbarossa was launched against the Soviet Union. The Germans inflicted heavy losses on the Soviets and thought that the war would be won by winter; but the Russian enemy did not break, and by 1944 the tides of war were reversed. In April 1945 Hitler committed suicide in his Führerbunker in Berlin.

Historical Context

This sequence of events needs to be placed within the larger framework of German history. In order to trace out the relationship between ideas and power, one must look at the sequence of structural contexts in which ideas made their appearance and to which they responded. I emphasize two recurrent themes in this history: the salience of status distinctions within German society and the highly localized scenarios within which the distinctions were played out.

THE GERMANIES BEFORE
THE THIRTY YEARS' WAR

Following the dismemberment of the Roman Empire, a new over-kingdom (*regnum teutonicorum*), was installed in A.D. 800, sometimes referred to as the Old or First Reich. It soon collapsed as a territorially organized entity but survived as a federative association of countries, cities, principalities, and knightly domains of varying scale and size. Under the name of the Holy Roman Empire this association lasted until 1806, serving as a forum for legal and political appeals and for the display of titles.

All these domains, from the minuscule to the large, were in turn crosscut by categorical distinctions among nobility (*Adel*), town citizenries (*Bürger*), and peasants (*Bauern*). These terms, denoting distinctions of relative "standing" (*Stand,* plural *Stände*), are usually translated as "status groups" or "estates," but this rendition omits the German connotations of the terms: of kin-determined membership and exclusive connubium, of hierarchically arranged and fixed social positions and attributes of social honor, and of codified charters of rights and duties that specified parameters of action within the established hierarchies. There were further distinctions within each category: between upper and lower nobility, who were not allowed to intermarry; among town patriciate and guild masters drawn from the leading guilds, masters of the lesser guilds, advanced apprentices, and journeymen; among free peasants and peasants in different positions of dependence. These ordered and chartered hierarchies contrasted with the unlicensed and unchartered sector of society, made up of people lacking local roots, such as wayfarers, *fahrendes Volk;* members of the so-called dishonorable (*unehrliche*) occupations, such as beggars, peddlers, tanners, shepherds, linen weavers, millers, jugglers, musicians, actors, barbers, surgeons, and executioners; and the perennial sojourners in Christendom, the Jews.

This scheme for social stratification was pan-German yet variable by region and locality. Privileges and restrictions were qualified by ecology and geographically differentiated cultural traditions and by whether the people designated were members of autonomous units or dependent upon direct overlords—imperial, princely, secular, or ecclesiastical. Thus, some peasants might be free and have the right to bear arms in one place yet not in another; nobles could marry into town patriciates here but not there; Jews might enjoy considerable latitude under one lord or bishop and be much more constrained under another. These variable abilities and disabilities were codified in local or regional customary law, based not on an overarching Roman law but upon idiosyncratic local statutes, administered by local notables, that went under the name of community law (*Gemeinderecht*), German customs (*deutsche Gewohnheiten*), or local options (*Willkür*) (Gierke 1958; Walker 1971, 38).

At the same time, such statutes had to be negotiated with superior courts or overlords that exercised dominion, *Herrschaft*. This term is usually translated as "domination" but is better rendered as "rulership." The significant cultural sense of Herrschaft entails not merely the exercise of power to extract labor or taxes but a multistranded relation of superordination and subordination, ideologically embedded in a hierarchically ordered and divinely sanctioned scheme of prerogatives and obedience (Sabean 1984, 20–27). For this reason, performance and nonperformance of ritual, such as the taking of communion, could become an index of obedience or disobedience in relation to Herrschaft (pp. 58–60). Taking communion called into question not just the political relation of a subject to his superior but the subject's entire moral being; and it reflected upon the moral standing of the community to which he belonged. This became especially important after the Thirty Years' War between Catholics and Protestants was settled in 1648, when each of three hundred separate rulers was granted the right to determine the religion of his own subjects—*euius regio, euius religio*. Statecraft and obedience to the state then became closely intertwined with religious performance and turned the local pastor and his council of local notables, or the local priest and friars, into the moral watchdogs over community life.

Moral regulation also affected the members of particular corporate bodies. Peasant communities had their special statutes. Guilds maintained distinctive codes, barring members who had not been "procreated by honorable parents in a pure bed." Guild members were barred from relations with traveling folk and members of the dishonorable occupations and were seen as dishonored themselves if they worked as peasants, as servants to nobles, or as factory hands

(Walker 1971). Separately and in tandem, therefore, social, moral, religious, and legal qualifications could be used to disqualify some people and permit the advance of others, to underwrite security of membership for those deemed respectable and deny that security to those considered illegitimate in their claims to social honor. Aristocrats lost status if their descent lines included any plebeians, if they married commoners, or if they engaged in commerce or crafts. These prohibitions persisted into the twentieth century, rendering criteria of descent more important than comportment (Elias 1989, 36).

This prolix structure of particularistic corporations and memberships was strained to the breaking point by the economics and politics of the late modern period, after the Thirty Years' War. Princely absolutisms began to streamline rulership bureaucratically, in order to intensify surplus extraction and obedience. They might do this by raising taxes, by increasing household productivity through strengthening patriarchal control and furthering single-heir inheritance, or by raising the requirements for labor services in place of deliveries in kind or money (Weber 1946a, 1979; Rosenberg 1958, 1978; Rebel 1983, 1991, 1995; Taylor 1994). At the same time, these strategies sought to extract more revenue from an economy that had lost out in competition with other countries. While Brecht's Mother Courage was wheeling her miserable trading cart through the burning towns of the Germanies during the years of religious war, London, Amsterdam, and Bordeaux were setting up trading emporia on American and Asian shores. The Germanies were thus pressed to produce more revenue, even as they were shunted to the semi-peripheries of the newly emerging capitalist world system.

THE RISE OF PRUSSIA

The period after the Thirty Years' War also witnessed, amidst this desolation, the unforeseen development of the state that would become the pivot of German unification, Brandenburg-Prussia. One of a number of statelets organized to hold back Lithuanians and Slavic-speakers along the northeastern frontiers of the Old Reich, it was an unlikely candidate for this role. Located on poor glacial soils in an unpromising land, its transformation from a frontier march into a state has been described as "the triumph of will over nature" (Gay and Webb 1973, 319). In this region a feudal reaction had put an end to town-based commerce and colonist liberties in the fifteenth century and had fortified Junkerdom as an aristocracy living off lands worked by the corvée labor of their bondsmen. The grip of these rural nobles was weakened, in turn, when their holdings were severely devastated in the Thirty Years' War. Paradoxically, these circumstances enabled the Hohenzollern dynasty to begin turning the Prussian marchlands into a bastion of military absolutism, without encountering much opposition from either an urban patriciate or an impoverished nobility. The instrument of this transformation was the Prussian army command, *das Generalkriegskommissariat,* which was put in charge of drawing taxes from the poor country (taxed twice as heavily as was rich France). The taxes were employed to build "the army of a first-rate power on the resources of a third-rate state" (Dorn 1931, 404).

Using this centralized army command, Friedrich-Wilhelm of Hohenzollern developed a unified bureaucracy to administer, tax, maintain law and order, exact obedience, and dispense justice. To man this bureaucratic apparatus he enlisted the Junker nobles, who were induced to exchange their feudal rights to autonomy for secure administrative positions. At the same time, the ruler yielded up his ultimate territorial rights as sovereign and granted his new state servants freedom from taxation, along with quasi-capitalist freehold rights over their landed domains, which they could continue to work with bondsmen and corvée laborers. Furthermore, the nobles retained command over their own peasants as soldiers in the militias, which supplemented the regular army. Thus, the Junkers held on to their traditional role and status honor as lords of men in their localities while accepting a dependent relationship to the state, which enrolled them in a militarized bureaucracy.

When Prussia faced utter defeat by Napoleon at Jena (1806), a set of innovative reformers turned to this same centralized administrative apparatus to carry out "a revolution from above." The reformists introduced universal conscription and opened military and civil careers to commoners as well as nobles. They abolished serfdom, cut back guild controls over production, expanded primary and secondary education, and spurred industrial growth based on wage labor. They hoped to "renew" Prussia by removing many barriers to social mobility and to speed the flow of economic transactions. Some of their policies were turned back not long after they began, but others succeeded in setting Prussia on the road to economic development.

NATIONALISM IN THE WIDER GERMAN CONTEXT

While the defeat at Jena set in motion a process of re-forming the Prussian state, it also transformed many people into nationalists determined to defend German identity against domination by the French. Some abandoned the aristocratic entertainments of riding, fencing, and ball playing, which had been carried out within enclosed spaces restricted to nobles, and joined a Gymnastics Society headed by Friedrich Ludwig Jahn, who saw open-air gymnastics as a means for national regeneration (Eichberg 1986). Jahn also promoted formation of a union of university student fraternities, dedicated to being German in "words, deeds, and life." In 1813–1814, many members of these groups enlisted in volunteer regiments for the Wars of Liberation against France and were joined there by artisans and apprentices, perhaps attracted to the cause by the Prussian reforms that in 1810 ended obligatory guild membership and granted "free" manufacture and movement.

The volunteers returned from the war thinking of themselves as "the nation in arms." In 1817 gymnasts and students together held a meeting at Wartburg Castle that set a pattern for national festivals of the future. They paraded in torchlight processions, sang Protestant hymns, burned "un-German" books, made speeches extolling the *Volk,* and ended with a church service. The speeches also—for the first time—publicly attacked not only foreign oppressors but also home-grown tyrants who had failed to grant liberal constitutions and to work for German unity.

Yet the Germanies long remained parceled out among parochial statelets, and the nationalist message of a common identity had to contend with the reality of barriers posed by territorial boundaries, which often constituted religious boundaries as well. The calls for national unity and for constitutionally guaranteed liberties failed to give rise to a unified nation-state, supported by a free and politically active citizenry. Instead, a loosely knit German federation replaced the defunct Holy Roman Empire in 1815. Each of the component statelets had its own court and dynasty, its own aristocracy and bureaucracy, none of them eager to share power with the mob.

This situation contrasted sharply with the process of nation making introduced in France by the French Revolution. Every Frenchman became legally a citizen, a participant in French political society, but in the Germanies, advocates of political unity had to anchor the national idea in appeals to a historically formed common culture and language as bases for their collective being.

This gap between individuals as bearers of language and culture and as political subjects of states constituted a special problem for professionals who sought careers in government administration, in education and publishing, as medical doctors and lawyers, or in the clergy. These new professionals were united in their use of standard German (*Hochdeutsch*) and by common preferences in literature and the arts, and also by a growing distaste for French culture and language, which until then served as the common hallmark of the nobility in the diverse petty courts. Although sharing similar social positions and patterns of cultural communication, the new professionals experienced politics as the dependent servants of parochial princelets.

To manage this discrepancy, they strove to distance themselves from politics while deepening their "inwardness," either through following a religious calling or—in more secularized terms—by cultivating the self. The name for such self-cultivation was *Bildung*. Usually translated as "education," the term refers rather to the wider and deeper processes of character training in the values of the German *Bürgertum*. This social stratum consisted of people who held political rights of citizenry in the German city-states (not only rights to property) and together formed a "middle" level of society between aristocracy and the common folk. Since the early sixteenth century the Bürgers had accumulated and monopolized a distinctive cultural capital through acquaintance with the "high" canon of German language and literature, and they strove to maintain these patterns of "high" culture throughout the centuries that followed. Relying on their character training to guide their individual "intellectual and moral maturation" (Lichtheim 1970, 88–89), they also claimed authority—as properly "formed" (*gebildet*) people—over the uncultivated mass of inferiors not so formed. Yet concentrating in this way on the interior shaping of the self distanced them from the practical world. Hence, it seemed to many that the German nation "was to be found solely in the heads of its educated members" (Schulze 1991, 47). As Madame de Stael said of the Germans she met in 1813, they "argue amongst themselves with the greatest vivacity in the sphere of Theories, and . . . leave the whole reality of life to their earthly rulers" (p. 47).

Thus, the carrier groups of German nationalism and liberalism were slow to turn their imaginings into practical politics. They faced military interference and repression by the numerous political establishments. They were also slow to realize that they did not always seek the same goals. This became obvious in the Revolution of 1848, when delegates met in Frankfurt to debate the making of a constitution for the entire Reich. Some nationalists hoped for a pan-German, *grossdeutsche* solution that would include German-speaking Austria as well as the Germanies that had entered the federation of 1815; others favored a limited, *kleindeutsches* Germany, without Austria and the Habsburg lands. Liberals wanted new constitutional arrangements but did not necessarily favor political unification, arguing instead for continuation of a customs union among participant states. Yet even while the delegates debated, Prussian troops occupied Berlin and drove members of the Prussian National Assembly out of the city. Austrian troops put down nationalist rebellions among Czechs, Hungarians, and Italians and retook Vienna from its revolutionary "security committee." After the Frankfurt assembly fell apart without reaching final conclusions, a rump parliament convoked at Stuttgart in 1849 was definitively broken up by Württemberg dragoons.

THE IDEAS OF VOLK AND REICH

Despite the immediate failure of 1848, political agitation and the intellectual communication associated with it succeeded in disseminating widely the idea that the Germans were one common people, a *Volk*. This idea built on the long tradition in German usage that distinguishes the Volk as a phenomenon of nature, a natural given, from a "nation" understood as a political and intellectual creation.

Herder (1744–1803) is usually cited as the proponent of the historically particular qualities of each Volk, in opposition to the claims of universal rationalism. For Herder each such Volk had its characteristic spirit, which infused its members with its form and vitality. The ties that linked the individual soul to the collective soul of the Volk were thought to be embedded organically in the wider unities of nature. Herder's inspiration was Albrecht von Haller's "experimental psychology on a vital basis," which envisaged a panoply of vital forces driving physiological and psychological life, binding individuals to the Volk, people to landscape, landscape to nature, nature to cosmos. In contrast to French and English Enlightenment views, "man was not seen as a vanquisher of nature . . . ; instead he was glorified as living in accordance with nature as one with its mystical forces" (Mosse 1981, 15). These organic and vitalistic conceptions of the Volk have informed the stream of German conservative-Volkish ideology down to the present and have surrounded the idea of the Volk with beliefs drawn from religious traditions or occult heterodoxies.

Whereas Herder saw the many Völker "as equal in principle" (Mosse 1981, 15), Johann Gottlieb Fichte spoke for the next generation, one shaped by the defeat of the Prussian army in 1806. When Fichte gave his *Lectures to the German Nation* in Berlin in the winter of 1807–1808, the city had fallen under French occupation. Fichte sounded a new note: the Germans were a primordial and unadulterated *Urvolk* fighting not only for freedom from French subjugation but also on behalf of a universal mission that would make them "the regenerator and restorer of the world." Unity of the Volk had priority over the political organization of states, and the prevailing political fragmentation would yield to an encompassing unity; even Old Prussia would become part of a Reich or Reich-union of all the Germans. Members of all classes listened with rapt attention; but the Prussian court was not pleased, and it forbade the lectures from being read for several years.

In summoning up the vision of a Reich of all the Germans, Fichte invoked an apocalyptic tradition, current since the Middle Ages, which foretold "a world purged of suffering and sin, a Kingdom of the Saints" (Cohn 1961, xiii). In the German lands, this tradition had given rise to the dream of an encompassing empire or Reich, a dream kept alive in popular myths. Some centered upon the figure of

Charlemagne, who would arise from his sleep to smite the infidels. Later emperors asserted religiously inspired powers in order to unify imperial rule, but without enduring success; Frederick Barbarossa perished in the Third Crusade, and Frederick II failed to overcome a papal interdict. Nevertheless, the idea of the empire endured. In the twelfth century the Calabrian abbot Joachim of Fiore prophesied the advent of an Age of the Spirit, which renewed the hope that the world might yet be set right through the resurrection of another Emperor Frederick. A number of resurrected Fredericks then made their appearance. The legend of the sleeping emperor persisted in Thuringia into the fifteenth century, where it may have influenced the Anabaptist rising in the century following (Cohn 1961, 142–48).

The invention of printing allowed geographically dispersed members of a literate elite to communicate over wide areas, and local popular traditions became widely known. Herder built on this growing interest to develop the study of "folk-lore" as a way of capturing the quintessential expression of the genius of each Volk. Fusing literacy and folklore, nation builders and nationalists began to use old myths in political appeals. Norman Cohn has called attention to an early publication of this kind, the *Book of a Hundred Chapters,* written before the peasant risings of 1525 by an anonymous author known as the Revolutionary of the Upper Rhine (1961, 114–23). The tract "is almost uncannily similar to the phantasies which were the core of National Socialist 'ideology'" (p. 122). It projected the advent of an Emperor Frederick at the head of a knighthood that would employ terror to destroy the wicked, hang all usurers and lawyers, install "one shepherd, one sheepfold, and one faith throughout the whole world," banish all Latin peoples, and establish an order of equality of communal ownership for the Germans—for "the Germans once held the whole world in their hands and they will do so again, and with more power than ever." According to legend, the emperor Barbarossa slept on after his death inside the Kyffhäuser Mountain, whence he would reemerge in a moment of dire need of the German people. In 1896, a statue of the German emperor Wilhelm I was placed on a fortresslike structure on top of the mountain, which became the center of major national festivals (Mosse 1975, 62–63). It is relevant that the German plan for the attack on the Soviet Union in 1941, initially called "Fritz," was given the name "Barbarossa."

PRUSSIA AND THE SECOND REICH

Prussia was awarded the West German region of Rhine-Westphalia by the Treaty of Vienna in 1815. The new acquisition connected Prussia with the West, put it in control of a rapidly growing commercialized region with the deposits of coal and iron that would underwrite German industrialization, and made Prussia the most populous power among the German dominions. In Perry Anderson's words, "The military acquisitions of the feudal Prussian state thus came to incorporate the natural heartland of German capitalism" (1974, 273). Fortified in this manner, the Prussian state—now led by the redoubtable Junker Otto von Bismarck—became the predominant power in German politics. In quick succession it defeated the Austrian monarchy in 1866 and France in 1870 and proclaimed the founding of a Second Reich in 1871, thereby making the king of Prussia emperor of Germany. "It is a fact of fateful significance," says the historian Otto Pflanze, "that German national sentiment could gain sufficient momentum to overcome the particularistic loyalties of the German people only in combination with Prussian militarism and Hohenzollern authoritarianism" (1963, 13, 14).

This sequence of successes had major consequences for the Germanies, now united under centralizing Prussian leadership. Elsewhere in Europe political parties were becoming forces in active governance, but in Germany policy continued to be initiated primarily by an imperial civil service built on the foundations of the bureaucracy of the kings of Prussia. Reformed after the Napoleonic wars, this apparatus settled again into the role of a loyal instrument of the status quo and inhibited any turn toward a federative political arrangement such as had been advocated by the revolutionaries of 1848. The aristocratic and plebeian enthusiasts who before 1848 had spoken for a national unity based on liberal and democratic principles now "received the realization of their wishes and hopes seemingly at the hand of their social opponents" (Elias 1989, 123). In installing such a powerful and cohesive administrative machinery, Prussia also underwrote the predominance of the aristocracy. That predominance was not only political but also culturally hegemonic, installing models of comportment that accentuated social inequalities and set aristocratic standards for candidates for bureaucratic or military careers. The outcome was the extensive "capitulation of wide circles of the bourgeois estate before the aristocracy," in the wake of which they traded in "their classic bourgeois idealism for a pseudo-realism of power" (p. 23). It also placed the other German statelets under the aegis of Prussian military power, which began to make its weight evident in international affairs as well as at home. The result was a pronounced move toward the "institutional militarization of the whole social order" (Anderson 1974, 271).

FISSURES IN THE BODY POLITIC

Prussia's rapid rise to political dominance also had destabilizing effects. Peasants and peasant-artisans who could not meet official expectations were expelled from the land; supernumerary sons and daughters lost their claims on inheritance and were forced to seek their livelihood elsewhere. There was a marked turn toward proto-industrialization, sponsored by merchants who invested in local putting-out systems. This led to confrontations between the guild artisans of the towns and the nonguild entrepreneurs, who hired on the very folk whom the guilds held in low repute as rootless, morally loose, and linked to the dishonorable occupations. At the same time, as artisan output declined under nonguild competition, more and more artisan households themselves sank into marginal employment. Thus, an increasing number of paupers fed the growth of the Pöbel, the lowly populace stigmatized as lacking respectability and being "outside the honors of work" (Riehl, in Conze 1954, 52).

The growing Pöbel marked the beginnings of the German industrial proletariat (Conze 1954), emerging gradually and in very localized form with the progress of industrialization. Even as industrialization intensified, the battles over respectability and honor long continued to be fought out in local microcosms. It needs emphasis that the Germanies remained surprisingly rural into the present century, with the bulk of the population living in small towns rather than in cities and dense industrial zones (Moore 1978, 177–81). Although industrial development accelerated greatly in the second half of the nineteenth century, in 1907 industry and mining still accounted for only 27 percent of the population identified by occupation. In that year there were forty-two cities in Germany with populations of 100,000, but less than one-fourth of these urban inhabitants were engaged in industry, mining, or construction. Even in factories employing more than ten people, work was still carried on without the assembly line, in largely artisan-type sequences. As Barrington Moore concluded, "German industry before the First World War was, on the whole, still very much a small-town affair even by the standards of today" (p. 180).

Yet even with industrialization dispersed and localized, the growing working classes began to develop a sense of a common lot and identity. In 1863, a class-based General German Workingman's Society was formed by Ferdinand Lassalle, who hoped to contravene the limits on workers' income imposed by "the iron law of wages" by moving toward worker ownership of large industrial enterprises. This Lassalle sought to accomplish through an alliance with the Prussian state, but such a coalition was politically unrealistic, and it became moot when he was killed in a duel in 1864. It is nevertheless possible that this suggested alliance between workers and the state resonated in Bismarck's own thinking in the 1880s, when he initiated state-sponsored schemes for disability and health insurance for German workers. He spoke of these as "our State Socialism—our practical Christianity," "compassion, a helping hand in distress," but he also understood that it was a way to tie working people to the institutions of government. "State Socialism will make its way," he said. "Whoever takes up this idea again will come to power" (in Hollyday 1970, 59).

Lassalle's followers affected the development of German socialism in identifying it with "welfare legislation extracted from the state" (Lichtheim 1970, 92) and in guiding the movement to look to the national state to underwrite the progress of the working class. This proved true even of the "Marxists" Wilhelm Liebknecht and August Bebel, who organized the Social Democratic Party in 1869. Unlike the Lassalleans, however, Liebknecht and Bebel were strongly internationalist and resolutely opposed to war right up to the beginning of World War I. They thus invited the opposition of the conservative-liberal parties in power, who denounced their socialism as "an invitation to bestiality" and defamed them as "traitors to the fatherland."

These German Marxists differed from the Lassalleans in enter-
taining no illusions about the nature of the Prussian-German state.
They understood that any real progress of working people depended
on breaking the aristocratic Junker hold over the army, the bureaucracy, and the law courts, as well as over the hegemonic canons of
comportment; but they hoped to achieve control of the state
through universal suffrage. In that sense they were the true heirs of
the aborted Revolution of 1848. As believers in what has been called
the "mechanical Marxism of the Second International," they thought
that they represented the future, that capitalism would engender its
own destruction, and that "bourgeois democracy" would reward
their steadfastness by voting them into power. By 1877 they did, in
fact, attract half a million voters. Bismarck in 1878 outlawed the
party, its newspapers, and its meetings, but by 1884 the party again
received nearly half a million votes, and almost a million and a half
votes six years later.

This steady rise in support for the Social Democrats brought
them a sense of success, but it also reinforced the dividing lines in
the German body politic. Secure in their views of the future, the socialist leadership failed to reckon with the growing forces of nationalism that were leading Europe into war, while also underestimating
the opposition to socialism and democracy at home. Until the end
of World War I, antisocialist and antidemocratic politics had its base
in the Prussian court, the aristocracy, and its middle-estate supporters. Unlike England, which had broadened political participation
beginning with the Reform Bills of 1832, Germany expanded voting
rights only haltingly, and this by design. Prussia retained a discrimi-
natory three-tier system of voting rights, which gave different weight
to the votes of aristocrats, property owners, and general citizens, until after World War I, when the Weimar Republic offered voters a new
constitution. Similarly, while Bismarck had engineered general voting rights for elections to the Reichstag in 1871 as a way of tying all
Germans to the Reich, he also made certain that this institution
would never wield any executive powers and that policy making
would remain entirely in the hands of the court and its ministers.
These core institutions of the state grew ever stronger, as the onset
of a major economic crisis after 1873 forced state and industry to
abandon liberal economics in favor of an "organized" capitalism,

based on state-directed banking, the formation of industrial cartels, and the imposition of protective tariffs (Rosenberg 1967).

Bismarck also unleashed the force of the state against Catholic voters. This *Kulturkampf* (culture war) was motivated by his desire to diminish the influence of the papacy while securing the Protestant character of the national bureaucracy, which was tied through Prussia to the Lutheran and Calvinist Churches. In characteristic Bismarckian fashion this anti-Catholic policy was intended at once to counteract the effect of Pius IX's declaration of papal infallibility in 1870, to bind anti-Catholic German liberals more strongly to the cause of a Prussian-led Reich, to weaken the papacy's political influence on the newly formed Catholic Center Party in Germany, to inhibit Catholic support for the Polish inhabitants of Germany's eastern provinces, to lessen support for Catholic Austria in the German south and west, and even to forestall any French and Austrian alliance with the Vatican. However, in this instance Bismarck's political moves backfired, reinforcing opposition to Prussian centralism rather than reducing it among both the Social Democratic working class and the growing Catholic bloc. Both these segments reacted by developing, each in its own way, alternative institutions and visions of "their own future Germany" (Geyer 1992, 81, 82).

Within the Germanies as a whole, unification under Prussian aegis gave rise to a widespread malaise. This mood was cast into analytic terms in 1887 by the sociologist Ferdinand Tönnies, who characterized it as a conflict that opposed *Gemeinschaft,* community, to *Gesellschaft,* society. The experience informing Tönnies's discussion derived from the conflicts of the traditional communities in his home region of Schleswig-Holstein with the imperiously managed, impersonal Prussian state (Mitzman 1973, chap. 6). There seemed to be an unresolvable contradiction between the local life of the Volk and the superordinate, bureaucratically organized state. Similar problems shaped Max Weber's specifically German concerns. If the structures of local life dissolve and the state can do no better than sequester people in "the iron shell" of its soulless, rationalized bureaucracy, the only hope for a new surge of creative energy lay in a breakout, engineered by a charismatic leader supported by a plebiscitarian democracy (Dronberger 1971, 369–70). Had Weber lived long enough, he would have seen this happen.

MILITARIZATION

The state's greatest success was in expanding the machinery of war. State-sponsored industrial efforts strengthened the armed forces, in support of Germany's increasingly active foreign relations. This goal was materially advanced by political means, first by the joining of industrial and agrarian interests in one conservative party and then by tradeoffs between the leading industrialists and the representatives of agrarian interests, notably those of the Junkers in eastern Germany. The industrialists traded tariffs on imported agricultural products, especially grain imports from Russia and America, for support of their program to expand the German navy in order to challenge English predominance on the high seas.

The military, much like the bureaucracy, reaffirmed its recruitment of nobles into the officer corps, yet as the army expanded, the noblemen had to be increasingly supplemented by "educated" reserve officers of middle-class origins. Army service drew these commoners into the orbit of aristocratic modes of thought and behavior. Though commoners were frequently discriminated against by the "true" aristocrats, they nevertheless adopted their noble superiors as role models and made themselves over into a new type of "feudal bourgeois" (Brinkmann 1926).

A parallel process affected university life, as shown in an extraordinary growth of university-based dueling fraternities between 1871 and 1918 (Weber 1946b; Elias 1989, 61–158). These hierarchically organized fraternities brought together nobles and commoners around highly ritualized forms of challenges to honor, fought out in two-person combat with sabers, which awarded social acclaim for courage, steadiness, and the repression of any show of compassion. Participation opened the doors to elite drawing rooms and underwrote the formation of social networks in support of career advancement. Members of social groups lacking in appropriate status honor—and hence thought to be unworthy of defending their honor by dueling—were excluded. This removed them from the honorable *satisfaktionsfähige Gesellschaft*, those social strata that could offer "satisfaction" when their honor was infringed. These rules of exclusion especially affected Jews, who responded by forming their own dueling clubs.

Weber complained that such pseudoaristocratic comportment offered opportunities for advancement to plebeian parvenus, yet that appears to have been one of its major functions. Participation in ritualized violence centering upon honor facilitated the transfer of notions of status honor from the hierarchical structure of corporate groups and estates into novel arenas of associational life. New associational relations, in turn, supported claims to status mobility within a capitalist order yet permitted such successes to be draped in the cultural forms and idioms drawn from aristocratic styles of life (Elias 1989, chap. 1B). These old symbolic indices acquired new functions as previously distinct local and regional elites expanded their ties across the territory of the new Reich. The dueling tradition provided this developing national elite with a common cultural denominator, while allowing it to set itself off from all those judged incapable of "offering satisfaction." In this manner fraternity dueling also drew a line between the protagonists of crypto-aristocratic notions of "honor" and the defenders of values of individual probity associated with the middle-estate Bürgers. With the passing of time, the rules that participants engage in an obligatory number of duels became more uniform among the dueling associations, while the arms used grew heavier and more powerful. In contrast to France, where dueling served primarily to settle interpersonal disputes over honor, among German university students it became "the daily bread" of the fraternity system (p. 376). As the dueling complex spread, it became not only more important socially but also imbued with a warlike aura, which denigrated mediation as weakness and impelled participants to compete with no quarter offered and none given. The outcomes were then displayed for all to see by dueling scars on the face.

WORLD WAR I AND AFTERMATH

World War I brought a new kind of warfare, a form of "industrial killing" (Bartov 1996). Massed battles, fought across a labyrinth of trenches, devoured lives by the hundreds of thousands. It was for many a liminal experience (in Victor Turner's sense), which separated them from ordinary life, shattered their customary ego structure, and reintegrated the initiates into the primary group of fellow soldiers (Leed 1979). This sequence of breakdown and reemergence gave rise to the syndrome of the returning veteran who found himself unable to relate to the people at home. In the wake of German defeat, many continued to fight on, notably against the revolutionary Red Guards in the Baltic countries. Some 200,000 veterans joined the armed bands of the postwar *Freikorps* and became subsidized strongmen for right-wing causes during the Weimar Republic, until they were absorbed into the NS movement. "These people told us the war was over," said the future SA leader Friedrich Wilhelm Heinz. "That was a laugh: we ourselves were the war" (in Waite 1952, 41).

The Prussian-dominated Second Reich prior to the war had already propagated the spread of military ideas and practices into the orbit of civil society. Relations between employers and workers and between authorities and their subjects were modeled on the modes of dominance and obedience in military comportment. The qualities of being iron hard and unshakable were exalted, along with injunctions to avoid pity and emotional indulgence (Elias 1989, 272–73). These demands on people favored the dominance of a character structure first analyzed by Wilhelm Reich (1975), a mode of being and acting that repressed feeling as weak and feminine, was brutal to the self and to others, and was unresponsive to suffering—all traits captured by the term *hart*, hardened and hard. To be hard implied a willingness to use direct physical violence, which would set one off from those too soft, cowardly, and decadent to engage in violent action. The theme of making people hard would reverberate constantly through NS rhetoric: in Hitler's demand for a Volk "hard as steel," a youth "hard as Krupp steel," "a violent, domineering, undismayed, cruel youth, nothing weak or gentle about it. The beast of prey must once more flash from its eyes" (in Fest 1970, 233); in Himmler's praise of the SS, "this has made us hard" (in Höhne 1969, 413); in the appraisal of the SS by a concentration-camp commandant—"we were Germany's best and hardest" (interview with Tom Segev, in Kren and Rappaport 1980, 43).

Defeat in war was followed by revolution. For many veterans their return home was an experience of humiliation: angry mobs tore off their insignia and taunted them with insults. The revolution was put down by the government with the aid of right-wing paramilitary forces, but there was to be no peace in the new Republic. People suffered real hunger and privation, as food relief was withheld in the bargaining over the terms of peace treaties, and the Allied demand for war reparations fueled a burst of hyperinflation that ended only in 1923–1924. Defeat, hunger, and inflation undermined any certainties of social position and status honor that might have survived from earlier times. The sequence of the war years and of the crisis that followed exposed the cohort born during that time to cumulative stresses and may have predisposed many of that generation to the appeal of National Socialism (Loewenberg 1983).

Germany's defeat in World War I ended with territorial losses and the exaction of reparations to be paid to the victorious Allies. The Versailles Treaty ceded Alsace and Lorraine to France, demilitarized the German Rhineland bordering on France, transferred the mines of the Saarland to French ownership, and delegated the governance of this mining region to the League of Nations for fifteen years. East Prussia was severed from the remainder of eastern Germany, and the land in between was ceded as a corridor to reconstituted Poland. In the Baltic the new state of Lithuania occupied previously German-held Memel. Reparations were set at a total of 132 billion gold marks (U.S. $33 billion), in addition to a sum amounting to 26 percent of the value of German exports. Both the territorial cessions and the reparations requirement opened fissures in German society that would not heal. Regular payments proved difficult in a time of enhanced inflation and diminishing opportunities for foreign trade, and delays in payment invited a French occupation of the Ruhr (1923–1925). Costly to France, this occupation also exacerbated German nationalism. Inflation grew rampant in 1922, producing orgies of speculation and destroying social strata that depended on fixed incomes, and also transferring wealth to industrial leaders. "The captains of industry," wrote the economist M. J. Bonn, who advised stabilization, "were staging a capitalist variant of the communist expropriation; they robbed not their 'class enemies' but the broad mass of their supporters" (in Gay and Webb 1973, 970).

The German governments that handled these treaties and their consequences did so through the instrumentalities of a militarily defeated, politically impaired, and only weakly legitimated state. Rightists denounced the German signatories as traitors and reviled the politicians who attempted to steer the defeated state across an unstable political field polarized between the industrial bloc and the trade-union organizations (Geyer 1984). Successive governments managed to work out a modus vivendi of disgruntled cooperation, which permitted the various groups to engage in temporary and shifting alliances and tradeoffs. Yet repeated political uprisings and attempted seizures of state powers, as well as assassinations and frequent acts of paramilitary violence, "hollowed out" the state from within (Elias 1989, 289). Under the strain of hyperinflation in 1923–1924, the efforts at accommodation nearly collapsed, but a renewed truce permitted a return to stabilization and again enabled Germany to attract capital investment from abroad. This "integration of Germany into the international monetary system became the tie that held the alliance of unwilling members together" (Geyer 1984, 200).

With the onset of the world economic crisis of 1929–1933, this fractious alliance dissolved once more, as foreign investors called in their loans and German capital began to flow out of the country. Unemployment burgeoned, and workers who still had jobs faced pay cuts. At this point, neither the army nor the bureaucracy commanded the resources to reorganize the political arena. This, however, the NS party offered to accomplish, by using its power to restructure the state. In contrast to the other political groups that had engaged in tradeoffs under the Weimar Republic, the National Socialists came to their bid for power with the reputation of a movement that had opposed interest-group politics in the name of national revitalization and which could put an end to the mere reshuffling of existing interests by installing a new, Third Reich. As Michael Geyer has noted, "in its own inverted and brutal way" NS ideology offered to replace interest politics with one predicated on moral principles (1984, 202). These principles were framed in a set of distinctive, but linked ideas: Volk, Race, Reich, and Führer.

National Socialism in Power

Hitler made his first appearance in one of the many small counterrevolutionary sects of the time. He initially referred to himself as "the drummer," and only later became the *Führer*. A native of Upper Austria, he was characterized variously as a coffee-house dreamer, a chameleonlike opportunist, a carpet-chewing enragé; but it is clear that he impressed many who had no reason to like him with both his knowledge and his personality. He absolutely dominated his adjutants and generals, had a superior sense for political and military strategy and tactics, and possessed untrammeled concentration of will. Göring declared, "I have no conscience! Adolf Hitler is my conscience." "He who forsakes the Führer withers away," said Göbbels. Himmler saw in Hitler's orders "pronouncements from a world transcending this one" (all in Fest 1970, 75, 90, 122). "They were all under his spell," said Alfred Speer. "They obeyed him blindly, with no will of their own, whatever the medical term for this phenomenon may be" (p. 207). Yet Speer would also confess to what attracted him to the Führer: "In his presence we felt we were lords of the universe" (in Lewin 1984, 31).

Who were Hitler's followers? This query has guided a considerable body of sociological inquiry, but it has not yielded satisfactory answers (Sheehan 1984; Baldwin 1990). One problem is that the use of statistics on party membership misses nonmembers who were nevertheless active in the movement. Many storm troopers did not join the party; even Heinrich Müller, head of the Gestapo, did not become a member until the 1940s. On the other hand, many people voted for the NSDAP but did not join the party. As established parties lost appeal, the National Socialists gained increasing numbers of sympathizers, especially among the young who had never voted before, as well as among the alienated veterans.

Another problem with the use of statistics derived from voting records and rosters of party membership is that numbers as such say little about the motivations that prompted people to join the party or vote for it. Furthermore, successive cohorts of acolytes had different motivations. "Founders, men of the first hour, cadres, early recruits, true believers, mass membership, voters, *Septemberlinge* [Göbbels's pejorative term for people who joined after the elections of 1930 in the hope of future employment], elite stirrup-holders, sycophants, hangers-on, *Konjunkturritter* ['knights of a rising market'], *Märzgefallene,* collaborators: each group had its own relationship to National Socialism" (Baldwin 1990, 7).

The movement gained many votes in small towns, where the party recruited heavily, especially in the crucial period of 1930–1932;

many joined the party for local reasons, to defend "grass-roots social life against national party and class strife" (Koshar 1987, 3) rather
than in support of the movement's national program. Some observers have thus spoken of two fascisms, the local fascism focused

on the *Stammtisch* (the predilect table in the local restaurant) and
that of the party on the national level (p. 5). Regional differences in
religious affiliation also played their part: Catholics, especially in
rural areas, strongly supported Catholic-oriented parties, while a
majority of Protestants voted National Socialist (Hamilton 1982).

Still another unresolved issue concerns the occupational background of members or voters. Sociologists have inquired into this
question, expecting to link voting behavior to class interest. An outcome of such inquiries has been the repeated assertion that the NS
movement was strongly "middle class" in character. This claim may
be correct, but it is not informative. Given the particularism of German development, the term "middle class" misses strong peculiarities. "Middle" class strata differed by locality and region and had
variable histories of provenience and commitment. The "middle"
class was also divided among an old middle class consisting mainly
of small retail merchants, peasants, and self-employed craftsmen, all
of them threatened by economic depression and shrinking markets,
"the historical precipitate of an earlier phase of capitalism"; a new,
salaried middle class, "the offspring of the rise of big government
and big industry"; and members of the "free" professions, both old
(doctors, and lawyers) and new (engineers and technicians) (Moore
1978, 406). According to 1935 party figures and census data, 40 percent of teachers and 25 percent of self-employed merchants were
party members, but the proportion who were party members in the
remaining six "middle-class" categories ranged between 13 and 20
percent (pp. 404–5). In considering the number of teachers who
were National Socialists, it must be remembered that party membership became compulsory for many kinds of public employment.
It does not seem to be the case, therefore, that National Socialism
rested overwhelmingly on the support of middle-class voters and
members.

Workers did generally cast their votes for the parties of the Left,
but they, too, were differentiated by local interests and occupational
histories. The National Socialists had already enlisted some working-class support in their first organizing efforts in Bavaria, and they

later drew working-class voters away from other parties, including the socialists and communists (Rogowski 1977, 399–400; Mühlberger 1980). While the miners remained generally immune to NS appeals, for instance, the party proselytized with some success among the skilled metalworkers, long considered the revolutionary vanguard of the German proletariat. The Left certainly overestimated the cohesiveness of the working class and its willingness to oppose the NS seizure of power through mass action. In fact, workers "in massive numbers went along with the new regime—not only in its early embryonic weeks, but also (and even more so) when it came later to Nazi policies of rearmament and war—and many even joined in the jubilation" (Lüdtke 1995, 200). With the successful blitzkriegs against Poland and the Allies, many workers voiced approval for the victorious regime, and at least the better-paid workers continued to support Hitler down to the war's bitter end (Hiden and Farquharson 1983, 90–91, 106).

There was clearly considerable upper-class backing for the movement. In most large cities, the National Socialists received their greatest electoral support from upper-class neighborhoods, while people in middle-class categories voted Left along with the working-class districts (Hamilton 1982, 387). Elite families also contributed to party membership in disproportionate numbers and became increasingly prominent in the higher ranks of the party hierarchy (Kater 1983). The leaders of business and industry took up strategic positions in the blocs of political and economic power that emerged after the NS accession. They profited from the policies of enforced "labor peace" and military expansion pursued by the regime and adjusted to its dictated "primacy of politics," even when this meant having to transact business with the interference of party bosses and political fanatics.

In the end, neither the rise nor the continuing success of National Socialism can be explained through an analytic approach that relates abstract class position in linear fashion to modes of consciousness. This is particularly clear when the appeal of National Socialism is traced to "middle-class *ressentiment.*" Rejecting this kind of explanation, Barrington Moore attributes support for the movement to attitudes of moral outrage at the collapse of values, especially the bureaucratic values of duty and obedience and the "feudal" values of personal honor and loyalty to superiors (1978, 411). This conclusion may be apt in emphasizing culturally specific considerations, but such values and disvaluations must be set in the unfolding contexts of a much longer history. As we have seen, that history was locally particular, propelled by economic and political forces of varying intensity, and interrupted by failures and crises on the way. As older corporate bodies and estates were dismembered, along with the criteria of social honor associated with them, the outcomes were often experienced as incoherence. A cumulative literature and mythology interpreted such experience as the result of national victimization at the hands of enemies at home and abroad (see Mannheim 1953; Stern 1974; Weiss 1996). These characterizations developed an especially salient form in a rising anti-Semitic rhetoric, which provided an all-purpose diagnosis of what was wrong with the world.

This rhetoric built on experiences of a world turned upside down (Mühlmann 1964), and it was amplified into visions of evil forces that needed to be controlled and bent back. NS propaganda drew readily on this tradition, with its proclivity for conspiratorial explanations of fettered mobility or victimage. The propaganda combined these representations of despair with messages of hope for a better national future with tangible opportunities for steady work and personal advancement. Thus, National Socialism held a measure of appeal to many and diverse groups in German society. Many people, of course, truly believed in the movement, not least because it promised to establish a more popular and plebeian *Volksgemeinschaft* that would honor all participants as members and comrades (*Volksgenossen*) within the racially unified community of the Volk. That community, they thought, would reinstitute lost social distinctions and social honors and accord recognition to their distinctive needs and contributions.

THE THIRD REICH

A significant facet of the NS vision was its emphasis on the polysemic term *Reich* for the German state. The new Reich would bring to fruition the hopes of the Volk and inaugurate a glorious future. This vision had been invoked by the nationalist Arthur Möller van der Bruck in his 1923 book *Das Dritte Reich*. Having already argued for a remaking of the German Volk in the style of the Old Prussia during World War I (1915), he now advocated an end to the party-ridden Second Reich, as merely "intermediate" between the First Reich of the Ottonic dynasty and a Third Reich to come. For him, the idea of a Third Reich was "an old and great German idea. . . . [A] political idea has always lived within it, an idea with ties to the future . . . of the arrival of a German era, when the German people will first fulfill its destiny on earth" (in Hermand 1992, 83).

At stake in this vision of a German future were strategies for incorporating the working class into the social order, the problem that had gone unresolved since Lassalle had raised it with Bismarck. The "intermediate" Second Reich seemed discredited, having failed to unite all the Germans under the aegis of one all-encompassing German Reich and having lost World War I in spite of an enormous expenditure of resources. Moreover, it had failed to address the major "social problem" posed by the continuing division of German society into classes. How that "social problem" was to be managed now became the touchstone of further conservative and nationalist politics. In the past, Germany's exclusive and endogamous aristocracy had been routinely rewarded with honors and positions within the structures of the Reich, but it had been increasingly weakened by social commerce and intermarriage with the merely wealthy. It had lost strength militarily by accepting officers of commoner descent and had mismanaged political opportunities through its stubborn sense of caste, which not only denied the aspirations of the growing working classes but devalued them as enemies of social order. The insurrections of 1918, the renunciation of the emperor, and the establishment of the Weimar Republic had further deepened the gulf between working people and the other classes, especially when the untried managers of the fledgling Republic unleashed the army and the "free corps" soldiery to put down the internal revolts.

In this period of turmoil, Möller acted as a spokesman for a political and ideological current that sought to take over the German Revolution of 1918 and guide it toward a "new" conservatism, one that would forsake its antilabor stance and form an alliance with nationalist leaders of the working class. This would draw the workers away from proletarian internationalism toward a militarized, Prussian-style nationalism. Such a synthesis of "socialist convictions" and the "old Prussian spirit" in order to "bring together the best part of the working class with the best representatives of the old Prussian idea of the state" was also advanced by the conservative and nationalist Oswald Spengler (1919). Even Hitler, who scorned these "fore-runners" for their insufficient political realism, used this language in *Mein Kampf,* suggesting that "the principle that once made the Prussian army the most marvelous instrument of the German people" could be transformed into "the principle of the construction of our whole State constitution: authority of every leader towards below and responsibility towards above" (MK 690). That transformed principle was, in fact, the *Führerprinzip,* Hitler's idea of authoritative leadership.

These ideas also informed the language that characterized the parties of the Right as "national" and "Prussian socialist," as against the Left as "international" and "socialist." The National Socialists first called their party the German Workers' Party, but they changed its name to National Socialist German Workers' Party in 1920. Diverse factions within and outside the party continued to define "socialism" differently. The party program advocated freedom from "interest slavery," confiscation of war profits, nationalization of "trusts," and profit-sharing plans for industry, but how the "community of the Volk," the Volksgemeinschaft, was to be realized proved to be a bone of contention. Many people joined the movement because they understood the "socialism" in its name as a commitment to a national community of mutual protection and support.

Hitler, however, was prepared to jettison these stated goals as unrealistic even before he seized power. The different views of the Volksgemeinschaft surfaced early in the struggle between Hitler and the followers of Gregor Strasser, who not only contested Hitler's claim to absolute leadership but also combined a more pronounced anticapitalist stance with advocacy of an enhanced role for the SA. Strasser regarded capitalism as an international and hence anti-German system, and he advocated instead an autarchic "socialism" modeled on the experience of the mobilization of the German economy during World War I.[4] Others, drawing on older Volkish sources, favored a "third way" based on corporatism, the organization of society into functionally differentiated, hierarchically ordered units administering their own affairs under the authority of the state. Such corporate organization had been instituted in Fascist Italy, and the model found resonance among some German National Socialists (Otto Wagener, for example; see Turner 1985, 116).

Hitler himself was neither a corporatist nor an advocate of industrial nationalization. He claimed his goal was not "to smooth the way for international socialism, much less to preach a new socialist religion. . . . I bring to the German Volk national socialism, the political doctrine of the Volk community, the solidarity of all who are part of the German Volk" (in Turner 1985, 166). He wanted a state that would permit "the free development of the personality" by loosening "the shackles and restraints that hinder the free play of the natural struggle" and "a competitive struggle that is as free as possible, connected purely and simply to the promotion of the commonweal" (p. 116). German renewal would come not through corporate organization of the economic field but through ideological mobilization of the people under his leadership. In his reading what made a people great was its will to sacrifice. He would imbue the Volksgemeinschaft with that will and thus enable Germany to take its proper, dominant position in the world.

It may be that in distancing himself from a communitarian socialism in any economic sense, Hitler was merely trying to convince the German industrialists that they had nothing to fear from an NS takeover, knowing that the coming mobilization for war would in any case subject them to dictation from his government. Yet his commitment to maintaining competition among individuals and groups was also in accord with what has been called his "social Darwinism," his guiding axiom that "struggle is the father of all things. It is not by the principle of humanity that man lives or is able to preserve himself above the animal world, but solely by means of the most brutal struggle" (in Fest 1970, 10). This premise entailed "the obligation" to act "in accordance with the Eternal Will that dominates this universe to promote the victory of the better and stronger, and to demand the submission of the worse and the weaker. Thus in principle it favors also the fundamental aristocratic thought of nature and believes in the validity of this law down to the last individual" (MK 580).

THE FÜHRER

Hitler's maxim of "struggle as the father of all things" applied to struggle among individuals as well as among entire groups and populations. For him, the growth of a movement was a process of assembling "human material" that was differentiated through natural selection. Propaganda would attract followers who exhibited only "a passive appreciation of an idea" (MK 849). Such "recognition in its passive form corresponds to the majority of humankind, which is inert and cowardly" (MK 850). One or two followers would become members "who will fight for it." Success depended on the tight organization of "the permanent, organic, and fighting union of those followers who appear to be able and willing to lead the fight for victory" (MK 850).

As National Socialism moved toward the seizure of power, the followers became *Parteigenossen,* party comrades, while the core of the party differentiated into, first, a largely honorary category of *alte Kämpfer,* the Old Guard, who were granted special civil-service status; second, the cadres of local and regional party groups, as well as leaders of the top party ministries; and, third, the chiefs of the party paramilitary formations, the SA and the SS. The top tier in this hierarchy formed the party elite proper, the so-called *Führerkorps,* which served at the behest of the Führer and competed for his favors.

The concept of the Führerprinzip, the principle of leadership, elaborated by the romantic pre–World War I Youth Movement and reinforced by the war experience, called for a strongman to put an end to the irresolute politics that conservatives associated with constitutionalism. Thus, the poet Stefan George (who had visions of a new aristocracy of the spirit) sang the paeans of a leader to come who "would break the chains, sweep in order among the rubble heaps, whip home those who have lost their way back into the eternal law so that greatness would again be great, lord again lord, discipline again discipline" (in Craig 1982, 70; my translation). (Upon Hitler's accession to power, George left for Switzerland.) Hitler, who had initially defined his role as a mere prophet, was even then occasionally referred to as a "Führer" by others. After he came out of prison, the office of the party Führer was transformed from an elective position into a permanent role and identified with his person. "Heil Hitler!" was made the official party greeting. Hitler himself wrote that the leader must above all "be able to move masses" rather than possess "the talent of shaping ideas" (MK 848). Yet he also averred that "the combination of theorist, organizer, and leader in one person is the rarest thing to be found on this globe; this combination makes the great man" (MK 849).

One of the functions of the Führer was to convey the messages of National Socialism through "the words of the Führer." The movement strongly emphasized the power of oratory over what Göbbels derided as the output of "the knights of the inkpot" (Volkov 1989, 51). As a public speaker Hitler was uncanny, a kind of shaman. "He begins in a low, slow, tenor voice," wrote a contemporary observer, "and after about fifteen minutes something occurs that can only be described by the ancient, primitive metaphor: the spirit enters into him" (Blank 1931, in Fest 1970, 36). Hitler wrote that "only he who harbors passion in himself can arouse passion" (MK 137). He thought the crowd was "like a woman, whose psychic feeling is influenced less by abstract reasoning than by an undefinable, sentimental longing" (MK 56). The mass assemblies at which he unleashed "the magic force of the spoken word" (MK 136) resembled religious revivalist gatherings more than political meetings (Kershaw 1989, 108). Emphasis was on the repetition "of very few points," because the receptivity of the masses "is only very limited, their understanding is small, but their forgetfulness is great" (MK 234). The function of mass assemblies was to make the lonely individual feel part of a greater community and impart to that "great embracing body" the "force of thousands" (MK 715). The psychoanalyst R. E. Money-Kyrle described the crowd at a rally he attended as "an elementary monster": it responded first with "an orgy of self-pity to the evocation of Germany's plight after World War I," then with hatred against Jews and Social Democrats as authors of that fate, thereupon with growing self-confidence to the story of how the party rose from humble beginnings into a powerful force, then sentimentally to a plea for unity; finally, it was "anxious to immolate itself" when the speaker asked for a promise to die so "Germany may live" (in Fornari 1975, 150–52).

In his "messianic" mood, Hitler described himself as an instrument of Providence, predestined to march before all the rest "with the torch of perception" (Turner 1985, 153). "Transcendental inspirations"—a term he claimed to have gotten from Einstein—gave him insights into the law of life. A romantic pantheism had brought many nationalists of the early nineteenth century to visualize the Volk as rooted in the land, thus forming an organic part of nature and cosmos. Hitler, too, placed himself and the party in relation to

Nature, God, or Providence. At a party rally in Nuremberg, in 1936, he invoked a unity among himself, the party leaders, and God: "Now we are together, we are with him and he is with us, and we are now Germany" (Turner 1985, 153).

THE NATIONAL SOCIALIST STATE

Since the NS state had from the beginning a dual organization of party and government entities (Fraenkel 1941), analysts have found it difficult to fit it into social-science typologies of states. It is easier to say what it was not than what it was. It was not a state grounded in a constitutional contract that laid out the rules of negotiation among constituent interest groupings, and it did not charter fixed institutions to implement such a contract. From the first, it was marked by an opposition between the large civil service, trained in Prussian and imperial bureaucratic traditions, and the combative organizations of an unruly mass movement. The latter frequently acted outside the law, unleashing violence against opponents, dissidents within the movement, and people excluded from the community of the Volk. The waves of assassinations and riots that led up to the seizure of power were followed by the imprisonment and flight abroad of thousands. But the violence extended to the party itself, as in the so-called Blood Purge of the SA leadership by the SS in 1934. When it came to power, the new regime installed a large-scale security apparatus to track down and eliminate potential enemies. The party also maintained a powerful internal judiciary, which could control members by threatening loss of employment, social shunning, and even terms in prison. Moreover, the movement intruded on the spheres of the bureaucracy and army, frequently multiplying competing offices and military formations.

While the party called itself "socialist," it did not abjure capitalism. Capital accumulation in business and industry was allowed to proceed, yet basic decisions involving the conditions of production had to be hammered out in dealings with other entities—regionally and functionally differentiated party organizations, branches of the army, institutions of the bureaucracy, units of the security services, the Labor Front, and the Reich Food Estate. According to former Gestapo official Hans Gisevius, it was clear even in 1933 that "our allegedly highly centralized Führer state had already begun to break up into dozens of satrapies and scores of tiny duchies. Each of the Nazi governors interpreted the law according to his own sweet will. These men succeeded in disrupting all local government to an incredible extent and completely ruined the finances of these governments. What kept the state apparatus going—unfortunately—was the indefatigable devotion to duty of the despised bureaucrats" (in Peterson 1969, 103).

Hannah Arendt characterized this as a "system of systemlessness" (1951, 334, 384). There was an extraordinary degree of bureaucratic duplication and confusion of responsibilities, as party organizations were appointed to carry out the same tasks as the institutions of the state. There were also not enough trusted party members with the requisite qualifications to take over governmental tasks. Instead of working through defined institutions, the state allowed the various power blocs—the state security complex, the Labor Front, the party, the armament complex, and the propaganda ministry complex—to compete with each other or to form temporary alliances in pursuit of individual and collective goals.

Viewing the system only as an ad hoc arrangement of shifting alliances does not, however, do justice to Hitler's role as its charismatic concertmaster. NS ideologists recognized that their state constituted a novel political formation. They located its political power not in the institutions or organs of the state but in the person of the leader as the "personification" of the Volksgemeinschaft (Neumann 1944, 469; Caplan 1993, 105–9). The jurist Carl Schmitt agreed that the Führer's command over the part, the army, and the state bureaucracy was "not institutionalized but only personalized" (1939, in Neumann 1944, 469). The fountainhead of political action was "the Führer's will," expressed in the slogan "*Führer, befehl, und wir folgen*" (Führer, give us orders, and we follow). In practice, however, since Hitler often avoided making binding decisions, this gave much latitude to competing parties in a dispute, allowing all to claim they were acting in fulfillment of the Führer's will, and intensified the struggles among them.

Hitler's role was to set general goals and orient people toward them. He did not involve himself in administration and rarely gave orders in writing. He appointed people from different power complexes to carry out the same task, left their powers vague, and let them fight it out. After the parties had worked out a modus vivendi, he might then ratify the outcome as an expression of his own "unalterable" will (Mommsen 1993, 89). This style suited him temperamentally; but it was also part of his insistence that human beings were unequally endowed and that true leaders would emerge only in "the hard struggle for life" (MK 665). While many true believers understood NS "socialism" as a promise of comradeship and mutual support, Hitler himself saw it entirely in terms of the devotion of all to the mission of the Volk. His task, as he saw it, was to forge "a unity of ideology, mind, and will among our people . . . the creation of a new unity of mind and will for our people . . . a general intellectual and moral rearmament of the nation on the basis of the new ideological unity." [5]

The result was an "endemically fragmented political system" (Caplan 1993, 109). Yet because it was ultimately predicated upon avenging past defeat in war, it was also unified by the vision and reality of going to war. Since war was the system's most cogent raison d'être, the Führer could always redirect the energies of the various power domains toward preparing for and staging war and thus rearrange the ground upon which they waged their internecine battles.

At the same time, appeal to the Führer's will projected a magical quality, similar to that of the secret emperor rising from his millennial sleep to succor Germany in its hour of greatest need. Perhaps its invocation—such as the dictum to "act in such a way as that if the Führer knew of your action, he would approve" (Hans Frank, in Caplan 1993, 106)—was inversely related to the real ability of the regime to manage its internal contradictions. Yet fusing the Volksgemeinschaft with the Führer's person and will did mobilize support for the NS leadership, and the imagery was utilized extensively in propaganda throughout the war to sustain belief in the Führer and in his message that "only the strong can stand firm in battles of destiny" (Bartov 1992, 125).

The "system of systemlessness" may help explain the extraordinary rise to power and influence of the SS. Under Himmler that organization always put its weight behind the ideologically most extreme solution of policy or tactics. In this Hitler allowed it a wide margin of autonomy. Its motto was "My Honor Is Loyalty" (*Meine Ehre ist Treue*); but that loyalty was also a passport to success in organizational infighting and in expanding the hegemony of predatory entrepreneurs.

The German refugee scholar Franz Neumann was among the first to argue that if a state was to be defined by "rationally operating machineries disposing of the monopoly of coercive powers" (1944, 467) and if capitalism required a state with a legal system able to guarantee the fulfillment of contracts (p. 443), then NS Germany was not a state. It seemed at that time astonishing to many, including social scientists, that a "modern" and "civilized" society could fall prey to such a violent and unpredictable regime. Neumann called his study *Behemoth*, taking Thomas Hobbes's term for the condition of chaos and anarchy, in contrast to the "Leviathan," a state that installs absolute domination through the rule of law. Neumann's conclusion was that NS Germany was "a form of society in which the ruling groups control the rest of the population directly, without the mediation of that rational though coercive apparatus hitherto known as the state" (p. 470). This broke with modes of analysis that saw the state as a unified machinery of domination, always seen as primary, while politics—the rough and tumble among social groups—was considered as secondary or unimportant. Neumann opened up a more nuanced appreciation of politics in statelike formations that have not adopted the patterns of liberal-constitutional state making associated with the rise of capitalism.

Volk and Race

National Socialism projected the imagery of a new society, a "community of the Volk." As we have seen, *Volk* is usually translated as "people" or "nation," but it stands for more than that: a social entity rooted in space and time and characterized by an enduring inner essence, a spirit or *Geist*, a vital soul, which manifests itself in cultural expressions, language and art, social relations and legal codes, and even economic arrangements.

Invoking the common membership of all Germans in a Volksge-

meinschaft, National Socialism projected a "spiritual revolution" that
"could be supported by all classes without fear and trembling" over
threats of class war and social revolution (Mosse 1981, 292). Using
this notion, Hitler brought together the modes of discourse of the
various currents in the "national movement" of the German Right
(Faye 1972). The Young Conservatives had talked about renewing
conservatism through an alliance with nationalist labor; the National Revolutionaries called for "total mobilization"; still others
advocated anti-Semitic policies to curtail the Jewish role in German
life. In giving vent to and systematizing his own anti-Semitism,
Hitler also laid hold of "a code for the overall Weltanschaung and
style of the right" (Volkov 1989, 43). Still others longed for a charismatic Führer to embody the popular will and steer them toward the
future. Adopting these various projects, Hitler made the idea of the
Volksgemeinschaft central to them all.

Hitler's vision of the Volk-community was not that of a common
kinship but a project to be realized under the guidance of a ruthless
and dedicated elite. True Volkhood was to be achieved only by purifying its racial composition. In this view, Hitler echoed an increasingly widespread set of racist ideas that had gained ground, especially since Jewish emancipation in 1871.

This new raciology drew its inspiration no longer from religious
tenets but from the science of the times. In place of the older views
that all humanity descended from Adam and Eve, the new raciolo-
gists stressed differences among human types and derived from the
observable facts of physical difference their guiding notion that each
"racial type" carried a characteristic portfolio of mental and behavioral traits. These differential endowments were supposedly hereditary, passed on integrally from generation to generation. They could
also be ranked, on the premise that some endowments were superior
to others; and from this it was only a short step to the idea that the
different racial types were locked in an ongoing struggle for precedence. National and imperial histories could be rewritten to justify
the victory of superior elites in the internal struggle of classes, or the
dominance of the better endowed peoples in ethnic conflicts or
colonial wars. In the German context, such scientifically embellished
myth-histories exalted a putative Aryan or Teutonic past and advocated a return to these wellsprings of spiritual strength and purity.

They also furnished support for an evolutionary history of all human-kind, in which "the fittest" were destined to conquer and replace the "unfit," providing the capstone of a seamless rationale for a politics of human inequality.

For Hitler, then, ultimately what mattered was not Volk but race: "all that is not race in this world is trash" (MK 406). The races were there originally, parts of nature, and they retain their original en-dowments, as long as they do not fall prey to race-mixing. There were culture-founding races, culture-bearing races, and culture-destroying races (MK 398). The "founder of higher humanity as a whole, thus, the prototype of what we understand by the word 'man' . . . the Prometheus of mankind is the Aryan" (MK 397–98). "What we see before us of human culture today, the results of art, science, and techniques, is almost exclusively the creative product of the Aryan" (MK 397). The Aryan is able to build culture because he possesses the "will to sacrifice in staking out his personal labor and, if necessary, his own life for others. . . . With him the instinct of self-preservation has reached its most noble form, because he willingly subjects his own ego to the life of the community and, if the hour should require, he also sacrifices it" (MK 407–8). This will to sac-rifice had enabled him to build culture by subduing inferior people and making them follow his bidding. "As a conqueror he subjected the lower peoples and then regulated their practical ability accord-ing to his command and his will and for his aims," thus giving them "a fate which was better than that of their former so-called 'freedom.' As long as he kept up ruthlessly the master's standpoint, he not only remained 'master' but also the preserver and propagator of culture" (MK 405–6). It was Germany's misfortune that "our German Volk-stum is no longer based on a racially uniform nucleus." Instead, it consists of Nordics, Easterners (Ostisch or Alpines), Dinarics (Bal-kan), and Westerners (Westisch or Mediterraneans), "and in between stand mixtures" (MK 597–98).

If the Aryans were the real culture builders, the Jews were as-signed the role of paradigmatic culture destroyers. Whereas the Aryan has the will to sacrifice and offer his life to the community, "in the Jewish people the will to sacrifice does not go beyond the bare instinct of self-preservation of the individual" (MK 414). Hence, the Jew has no "culture-creating energy whatsoever" (MK 418) and "was never in possession of a culture of his own" (MK 413). This Hitler linked to a biomedical vision: they are not only uncreative but live as parasites "in the body of other peoples" (MK 419). The body in which they appear will sooner or later die (MK 420).

In this characterization he echoed others who had described Jews as cancerous tumors (Wilhelm Marr), as bacteria, or as trichina endoparasites (Paul de Lagarde). For Hitler they were also bloodsuckers, vampires, bacilli, germs, vermin. Eventually they became viruses. "The discovery of the Jewish virus," he said in a "Table Talk" in 1942, "is one of the greatest revolutions that have taken place in the world. The battle in which we are engaged today is of the same sort as the battle waged, during the last century, by Pasteur and Koch. How many diseases have their origin in the Jewish virus. . . . We shall regain our health only by eliminating the Jew" (Hitler 1953, 269). In this quasi-medical discourse, Jews are portrayed not as people—not even inferior people—but as dangerous microorganismic carriers of disease. Hitler's intellectual adjutant Alfred Rosenberg saw Jews as "entering the open wounds of society" (in Bein 1965, 136). They kill their host through the power of their intellect and through sexual seduction. The key to the decomposing power of their intellect, Hitler wrote, lies in their rejection of "the aristocratic principle in nature . . . the eternal principle of force and strength. . . . [This] denies the value of the individual in man, disputes the meaning of nationality and race, depriving mankind of the assumption for its existence and culture. As the basis of the universe it would lead up to the end of all order conceivable to man" (MK 83–84).

In their definitions of the Volksgemeinschaft, communitarians and elitists agreed that a line must be drawn between insiders— those sharing a common essence based on race—and outsiders, who should be denied access to that Volkish essence and the honors it bestowed. They also agreed that the closed circle of Volkhood must be defended against racial pollution (*Rassenschande*). For the communitarians, however, racial comrades in the Volk-community constituted equals in "social honor," while the elitists saw the Volk as differentiated by gradations of racial purity and creativity and envisaged allocating social rewards unequally in terms of purity or mixture.

Yet Hitler added a further qualification for Volkhood: that all aspirants to elite positions demonstrate their abilities in a struggle for survival. All would have to prove themselves "Aryans" by descent in order to belong to the community, while advancement in position or rank would depend on the ability to demonstrate will, energy, and dedication in the service of racial purity within an arena of competition. Rank was thus not only ascribed; it had to be achieved through displays of will and hardness.

Therefore, what Germans needed was a state that could guide the Volk toward its destiny. The state was not to be an end in itself but "a means to an end" (MK 594), which is "the preservation of those racial primary elements which, supplying culture, create the beauty and dignity of a higher humanity" (MK 595). The goal of the state is to purify the race; it had to put an end to hybridization and race mixture and to multiply the culture-creating Aryan-Nordic component of the German people. Throughout history the unity of the German people has been undermined by "the influx of foreign blood" (MK 597), and this "blood-poisoning . . . led not only to a decomposition of our blood but also of our soul" (MK 598). As a result the Germans lack "the sure herd instinct which is rooted in the unity of the blood." Had they possessed that sure instinct, Germany would now be the mistress of the globe. The new German state would strengthen the Volk through racial purification and by mobilizing the people for war, enabling it to struggle for "the victory of the best and the strongest in this world" (MK 396).

THE STATE AS GUARDIAN OF RACIAL HEALTH

Hitler envisaged a number of strategies to strengthen Germany demographically and move it closer to the Aryan ideal. One was to turn women away from their pursuit of equality and back to their proper role as mothers, to make them once more "the priestesses of the family and nation."[6] For Hitler, "the goal of female education has invariably to be the future mother" (MK 621), and "the programme of our National Socialist women's movement really only contains one single point and that point is: the child" (in Fest 1970, 268–69). Abortion was made punishable with two years' imprisonment in peacetime; with the advent of war the penalty was execution. Motherhood and large families were rewarded with special exemptions, privileges, and honors. Women received special instruction in caring for children, and after 1935 the right to marry required prior certification by local health authorities.

If intense pronatalism was one strategy to create a superior race, eugenics was another. Enforced sterilization and euthanasia would eliminate "life unworthy of being lived." In making such a program a function of the state the National Socialists were in fact implementing measures then widely approved of by biomedical professionals. There were at the time eugenicists on the Left as well as the Right, and ideas were exchanged between German eugenicists and those in Britain and the United States (Proctor 1988b; Kühl 1994). What remains unique to Germany was the intensive enlistment of the medical establishment in the cause of racial hygiene and the significant role played by German physical anthropologists in that cause.

In pursuit of eugenic goals, an estimated 320,000 people were sterilized between 1934 and the beginning of the war in 1939 (Burleigh and Wippermann 1991, 253). Since the NS definition of hereditary defects covered not only genetically determined illness but also racial traits that were deemed undesirable, a 1933 law for the Prevention of Genetically Diseased Offspring was applied in 1937 to sterilize some 500 offspring of black French occupation troops and German women, in a joint operation of the genetic health court and the Gestapo (Proctor 1988a, 112–14). Empowered by a "top secret" decree, a group of physicians and managers selected and killed at least 5,000–6,000 children between 1938 and 1941 (Burleigh 1994, 111; Friedlander 1995, 61). After the defeat of Poland in 1939, SS units executed large numbers of hospital patients in the conquered country (Burleigh 1994, 130–32), while within the Reich the euthanasia team T4 in 1940–1941 did away with more than 70,000 handicapped adult hospital patients by gassing them with carbon monoxide (Burleigh 1994, 160; Friedlander 1995, 110). In 1941, the SS and T4 together gassed between 15,000 and 20,000 "ballast existences" of concentration-camp victims (Burleigh 1994, 220). When the German leadership moved toward a "final solution" of the Jewish problem after 1941, it drew on the expertise and personnel of the T4 program to set up and operate extermination centers in Poland and Istria.

A third strategy for creating racial utopia was to intensify the racial selection of the SS. "We want to create an upper class for Germany, selected constantly over the centuries," announced Himmler (in

Wegner 1985, 567, fn. 7). To this end, SS officers were required to certify their Aryan descent back to 1750 and SS enlisted men to 1800, while ordinary Germans had to demonstrate Aryan descent only back to their grandparental generation. SS candidates were evaluated by physical appearance and racial affiliation. Only three categories were on the approved list: pure Nordics, men predominantly Nordic or Phalic, and those exhibiting a harmonic Nordic-Phalic mix with light Alpine, Dinaric, or Mediterranean admixtures. In the Engagement and Marriage Order for the SS of 1931, Himmler gained the right to inspect potential marriage partners of SS personnel, to ensure their racial correctness.

The state was thus envisaged neither as an arbiter of diverse interests, as under liberalism, nor as the executive of a class, as in communism. It was not even understood as an organization to ensure the popular welfare, as under one or another variety of populism. Instead it was defined, to a large extent, as an instrument to further racial purification and hygiene.

STRENGTHENING THE SOCIAL BODY

NS ideology was conveyed not only through rhetoric but also through dramatic displays of warlike prowess. These symbolically transformed individual participants into organic components of the collective, armed and armored Volkish body (*Volkskörper*). "In my *Ordensburgen* [castles of the Teutonic Order]," Hitler said, "a youth will grow up before which the world will shrink back. A violently active, dominating, intrepid, brutal youth—that is what I am after" (in Rauschning 1940, 252).

To that end, training was necessary to produce "absolutely healthy bodies. Of secondary importance is the training of the mental abilities. But here again first of all the development of the character, especially the promotion of will power and determination" (MK 613). Once so formed, the individual would pass into the school of the army (MK 620). To Hitler, this role of the army was the achievement of Prussia: "Precisely the German nation, super-individualistically disintegrated because of its jumbled blood, regained from discipline through the Prussian army organism, at least in part, the capacity for organization which it had long missed. What is aboriginally present in other nations as a result of their herd instinct, we artificially required for our national community, at least partially, through the process of military training" (MK 942). Prussian military discipline was not an end in itself; it was a strategy for shaping men-to-be.

Klaus Theweleit characterized such military training as the birth process of "a true child of the drill-machine, created without help of a woman, parentless" (1989, 2: 160), in analogy to what anthropologists have described as the "making-of-man cult," a ritual rebirth of men without the intervention of women. In Theweleit's analysis this man, reborn as warrior, becomes the model of the ideal adult male. The military organization set in motion by Prussia becomes a surrogate mother for the whole nation, and marching in massed array and in close-order drill serves as a physical metaphor that both embodies and canalizes power. Military mobilization transcends all social conflicts and schisms. Thus war, as Geyer says, becomes "an allegory for the nation" (1992, 76).

NS texts and rituals exalt the qualities that will turn boys into soldiers and soldiers into German men. The exemplar of these qualities was the disciplined, bounded, and armored male self. Unsoldierly behavior was defined as emotional, feminine, and weak, and it had to be avoided. The warrior who emerged from this ordering of body and mind had to be ready to engage in violence. His deeds and sufferings were portrayed in representations of the Time of Struggle (*Kampfzeit*), when NS storm troops fought in street battles and assembly halls, as well as in an extensive literature glorifying war. Finally, the battle-ready soldier-male was called upon to join the military and paramilitary displays of massed power, such as the party rallies depicted in Leni Riefenstahl's film, "The Triumph of the Will" (1934). As a fighter for the Reich, he became a "machine-component" of a "totality-machine" (Theweleit 1989, 2: 153), embodied in the heavily muscled, naked men of NS sculpture, of whom George Mosse said that they "look like gods, to be worshipped but neither desired nor loved" (1985, 172).

Warlike conduct was not confined to the military domain; its models of behavior were diffused well beyond the barracks and the parade ground, to shape the ways people were expected to comport themselves. The diffusion of the warrior habitus undermined primary groups and civic associations, while constant ideological exhortation and surveillance invaded relationships among friends and neighbors, between men and women, and between old and young. This curtailed the autonomy of private domains and opened up ever more social spaces to ideological scrutiny, at the same time exacerbating tensions between party activists and more passive citizens. It must be remembered that this revalorization of human relationships took place within a structure of coercion. Conflict could spawn denunciation to the agents of state security. Thus, enthusiasm for the new order was combined with fear, as expressed in the parody of the children's prayer: "Lieber Herrgott, mach mich stumm, dass ich nicht nach Dachau kumm" ("Dear Lord, strike me dumb, so to Dachau I don't come"). It is no accident that the most prevalent popular forms of resistance were not political but consisted rather of nonconformist jazz and swing sessions and the adoption of a "sleazy life" that countered the ideal of military comportment (Peukert 1987, 165–69).

The Jews

Aryanism would save the world, but that goal was contested by an implacable enemy, the main cause of entropy: the Jews. Anti-Judaism had, of course, a long history in Christian Europe, where the Jews had persisted through the ages as the living contradiction of Christianity, at once "the venerable fathers of Christendom and its hateful, execrable detractors" (Bauman 1989, 37). The Jews were accused of killing Christ, refusing to accept his divinity, rejecting conversion, desecrating the host, and ritually slaughtering Christian children. They were also charged with bringing disease and pestilence by poisoning wells and by association with demonic forces. When excluded from other occupations they fell back on lending money at interest, and they were accused of advancing credit to Christians at exorbitant rates. There were claims that the Talmud contained specific instructions on how to deceive Christians, even on how to murder them. To isolate the Jews from the rest of society, they were segregated in residential ghettos and marked by special dress. Both public law and rabbinical interdiction prohibited their eating with and marrying non-Jews.

In France, these restrictions were dismantled in the wake of the French Revolution. In 1791 the National Assembly opened the doors to emancipation of Jews, declaring them to be French citizens legally and socially equal to other Frenchmen. Napoleon declared freedom of worship, abolished ecclesiastical and feudal property, issued laws of private property and partible inheritance for all citizens, and established institutions of secular public education. He dismantled the ghettos and released their inhabitants into the general life of society. In the Germanies, however, emancipation "became a process rather than an event" (Gay 1992, 127). There, the issue of making the Jews into citizens had to be fought out separately in each of the three hundred or so distinctive domains. The process gained momentum when the Napoleonic armies defeated Prussia and granted Jews equal citizenship in the Confederation of the Rhine. Spurred by that example, the liberal Prussian leaders, who hoped to counter the French through reforms instituted "from above," in 1812 proclaimed equal rights of citizenship for Jews, allowing them to serve in the army and to move, buy land, and marry without restrictions. However, emancipation then proceeded fitfully, against local and regional opposition, as various German states proclaimed or rescinded Jewish citizenship rights, until the Second Reich extended national citizenship to Jews in 1871. Unsurprisingly the Jews were soon accused of smuggling into Germany the "pestilential Gallic spirit," while their newly gained mobility became evidence that the old social order had collapsed and given way to social chaos.

During most of the medieval period, Jews were barred from owning and working land and from the guild-operated handicraft economy. Many turned to commerce and moneylending and acquired skills of using money as a source of credit and investment. Like middlemen groups elsewhere, such as the Chinese in Southeast Asia (Zenner 1991), they were then readily associated with the dissolution of old social ties. Moreover, as money took on the form of capital and became increasingly central to social life, the Jews could be seen as quintessentially associated with capitalism and its discontents. They could be connected with the vagaries of the market and condemned for aiding governments—both German and foreign—in the execution of economic policies. They were charged with lacking roots in local traditions and locally grounded forms of thought. Seen as dissolving all intimate, particularistic sentiments into universalistic abstractions, they were identified as "elements of decomposition."[7] If they joined socialist movements and became critics of existing society, they could be viewed as agents of social dissolution; if they spoke on behalf of peace instead of war, they could be attacked for cowardice, insufficient patriotism, and treasonable intentions against the defenders of traditional right and might.

These characterizations, assembled from diverse temporal and spatial contexts, were brought together around a central, all-encompassing metaphor of the eternal demonic, satanic, wandering, mercantile, universalizing, analytical Jew. Once unified, the metaphor could furnish metonymic connections to any and all tangible conditions, and it gained ground as the Germanies were forced to reorder their societies. By the 1870s—when the new Reich extended national citizenship to Jews—the metaphor provided the burgeoning anti-Semitic movements with a common denominator.

As these movements spread and became politically significant, this metaphor was extended to embrace the imagery of an active Jewish world conspiracy. That notion was not originally German. It was launched among French opponents of the French Revolution, who interpreted the call for equality and secularism as part of a Jewish-led conspiracy that used the secretive organizations of freemasonry to attain world power. The imagery of a Jewish conspiracy was then expanded and further transformed—first in France and then in Russia— by assorted seekers after occult knowledge, many of whom were also opposed to the Enlightenment appeal to Reason. At the beginning of the twentieth century, French and Russian anti-Semites joined in forging a supposed plan by Jewish conspirators to destabilize and rule the world, the *Protocols of the Elders of Zion* (Webb 1976; Cohn 1996). Brought to Germany by exiles fleeing the Russian Revolution (among them the later NS leader Alfred Rosenberg), this forgery became a strategic instrument of the Volkish and nationalist movement. Hitler acknowledged it as demonstrating "with a truly horrifying certainty, the nature and the activity of the Jewish people" and as exposing them "in their inner connection as well as in their ultimate final aims" (MK 424).[8] When the National Socialists attained power, the book became standard reading in the schools.

THE JUDEOCIDE

The first year following the NS seizure of power, 1933–1934, witnessed numerous acts of overt violence against Jews, in many cases authorized by the regime. For some years after that, however, overt attacks in public diminished. During this period of apparent quietude, the regime routinized its control by sequestering detainees in its concentration camps and relying on bureaucratic means to re-order relations between Jews and other Germans through new laws and anti-Jewish economic controls.

Despite the restraints on shows of anti-Jewish violence, Jews were gradually separated from the rest of society, first through boycotts of Jewish stores, withdrawal of citizenship, interdictions on intercourse with gentiles, and the setting up of "honor courts" to punish trans-gressors. There followed other measures abrogating the property rights and employment contracts of Jews, purging them from civil and public service, limiting their use of public facilities, and requir-ing them to alienate their belongings to the state. Then, their pass-ports were stamped with a "J," while the name "Isaac" was made mandatory for Jewish men and "Sarah" for women, thus depriving the bearers of their individuality.

Intense propaganda through the media and schools further in-creased the social distance between Jews and others by constant rep-resentation of the Jew as an "antirace." Julius Streicher's illustrated newspaper Der Stürmer (The Stormer)—featuring anti-Semitic ar-ticles, cartoons, and stories of ritual murders and rapes, together with columns devoted to personal denunciations—achieved a circulation of a million and became daily classroom reading in the schools. Jews were spoken of as organisms of disease, evoking fears of infection and pollution—fears both exacerbated and masked by references to "racial hygiene." If Jews were the source of all social and psychologi-cal "dirt" in society, then their separation and destruction could also be seen as a cleansing of the social body. Dirt, as Mary Douglas has pointed out, is "matter out of place," and as such contravenes rules of proper order (1966, 35). If Jews are defined as "cosmic dirt," then proper hygiene demands their extirpation. Some of the same moti-vations underwrote the NS persecution and attempted destruction of the Roma and Sinti ("Gypsies") as rootless, asocial, work-shy crim-inals (Burleigh and Wippermann 1991, chap. 5).

These developments benefited people who occupied the profes-sional and civil-service positions vacated by Jews, as well as those who profited from the enforced "Aryanization" of real estate, busi-

nesses, bank accounts, and personal property. They also made it easier to blame Jews for all social tensions, including those generated by
the regime itself. The National Socialists did little to improve working conditions for labor, to equalize pay differentials among economic sectors, or to ease invidious distinctions of social class, despite
the communitarian promises. Their aggressive foreign policy further
rattled nerves with continuous threats of war. Painting the Jews as
subhuman disease bearers, actively fomenting international trouble,
could thus find easy resonance.

Finally, one must not underestimate the ability of the regime to
monopolize public discourse, direct party members to exercise surveillance over others, and subject people to bodily harm through denunciation to the security apparatus. It would appear, however, that
the NS regime had little need to resort to outright force, and violence. Even the dreaded Gestapo remained numerically small and recruited its personnel primarily among local career policemen, not
from the SA or the SS (Gellately 1993, 45). The regime could rely, to
a remarkable degree, on the willingness of ordinary people to de-
nounce each other, "to the point where the flood of information
threatened to incapacitate the system" (p. 49). Informers were especially eager to report real and imaginary breaches in racial policy.
The guiding motivation may have been less ideological than hope
for one's own advancement, liberally laced with fear.

Some German Jews imagined they would be shielded by a collective social sense of responsibility, which did protect Jews in several
other countries of Europe. In Germany, however, any potential organized support vanished with the collapse of the parties of the Left
(Jacobs 1989). Thereafter, there were occasional interventions on behalf of Jews and individual acts of kindness, but no concerted effort
to stem the trend. Many people protested the boycott of Jewish busi-
nesses in the wake of the NS takeover in 1933, as well as the destruction of synagogues and Jewish stores and the beating of Jews by mobs
during the *Kristallnacht* of November 1938 (Kershaw 1983, 267–71;
1989, 234). That event, unleashed by Security Police Chief Heydrich
and Propaganda Minister Göbbels ostensibly to avenge the murder
of a German diplomat in Paris by a young Jew, marked the resump-
tion of open violence against Jews. The arson and rioting were quickly
called off, in response to criticism from abroad and from people in

the affected communities (these perhaps more out of distaste for the mob violence and the disruption it occasioned than concern for the victims). Only three days later, however, new bureaucratic decrees were issued excluding Jews from German economic life and forcing them to sell their assets to the state. In April 1939 the first steps were taken to segregate Jews residentially in specific areas of towns decided upon by local authorities. On September 1, 1941, they were compelled to wear the yellow "Jewish star" in public.

Deportations of Jews from the Old Reich and incorporated Austria began sporadically after the blitzkrieg against Poland in September 1939, and they gradually encompassed Jews throughout Western and Eastern Europe in ever-increasing numbers. In October 1939 Gestapo Chief Müller authorized Adolf Eichmann to deport Jews from Upper Silesia to Poland, suggesting that this would "serve first of all to collect experiences, in order . . . to be able to carry out evacuations of much greater numbers" (in Browning 1992, 9). After running two experimental trains of deportees, Eichmann set to work on plans for "a comprehensive deportation program" (p. 10). Massive transport of people from western to eastern Poland, Jews and Poles, began at this time. Between March 1940 and the beginning of 1942, the efforts to move large numbers of people were put on hold and replaced by an improvised policy of setting up Jewish ghettos and sealing them against contact with the outside world. Long-term plans for vast population movements and resettlement were, however, being made. In November 1939 Himmler's Racial Political Office prepared a memorandum on "The Treatment of the Population of Former Polish Territories according to a Racial-Political Viewpoint." It sketched out how 23 million relocated "ethnic mush" could be dumped in the German-run General Government of the Occupied Polish Areas (p. 16). At that time, the top leadership was still discussing the possibility of shipping all European Jews to Madagascar, but this project proved stillborn when the British refused to acknowledge defeat after Dunkirk.

Killing of Jews on a large scale began with the invasion of Russia in June 1941. The ill-famed mobile *Einsatzgruppen* followed in the wake of the German armies, to kill Jewish men, women, and children by the thousands. The orders were probably issued before the invasion (Goldhagen 1996, 519). In the first six months of Operation

Barbarossa, these special troops massacred between 500,000 and 750,000 Jews (Mayer 1988, 274; Noakes and Pridham 1995, 1102) by shooting them with small arms.

Such "handicraft methods" of killing were augmented by the construction of "industrialized" extermination centers, and gassing large numbers of people began at Chelmno in December 1941. The Judeocide has been largely identified with extermination in these factories of death. Recently, however, Daniel Goldhagen (1996) has drawn emphatic attention to the massive killing operations outside these "industrialized centers," carried out by German military police, guards in forced-labor camps, and troops supervising the forced marches of inmates from camps and killing centers back to Germany ahead of the Soviet advance. These forced marches alone accounted for 250,000–375,000 deaths (Goldhagen 1996, 330). The extermination rates in these decentralized operations did not lag far behind those of the mass killing centers. "Handicraft" killing also involved many more participants than have been acknowledged heretofore. Goldhagen points out that the Germans continued to shoot Jews en masse throughout the war and that "it is not at all obvious that gassing was a more 'efficient' means of slaughtering Jews than shooting was" (p. 521).

Nevertheless, the NS leadership may have decided that wholly new methods were needed to deal with the large Jewish population they encountered in the East, methods that could shorten the intervals between killings while enlarging their scale, without depleting their diminishing military manpower. The SS heads also feared that the killings would overtax the psychological capacities of the troops. As Goldhagen says, they searched "for a method that would ease the psychological burden of killing for the Germans" (1996, 157). Industrial killing, moreover, facilitated the disposal of bodies and—one might add—the industrial "harvesting" of body products, clothing, and jewelry that attended it. This rationale has recently gained greater credibility through revelations that the NS regime had a special interest in augmenting its gold reserves to cover its expenditures for the war. Furthermore, the construction of death factories allowed "the Germans to conduct the killings out of sight of the unwanted onlookers" (p. 157). This would accord with Himmler's definition of this murderous task as furnishing "a glorious page in our history and one that has never been written and can never be written" (*ein niemals geschriebenes und niemals zu schreibendes Ruhmesblatt*) (in Noakes and Pridham 1995, 1199).

Whatever the reasons, "industrial" methods were adopted to kill and dispose of large numbers of people. These methods built upon the experiences of the NS euthanasia programs. By late 1940 the specialists of the T4 team (who had previously gassed only children), and units of the SS acting separately, began to gas adults in mental asylums in Germany and Poland. By April 1941, T4 had intensified its collaboration with the SS to gas between 15,000 and 20,000 "asocial prisoners," together with felons, Jews, and political prisoners drawn from German concentration camps (Burleigh 1994, 220; Friedlander 1995, 150). It was a harbinger of things to come.

When Himmler witnessed the shooting of one hundred prisoners at Minsk in August 1941, he ordered his staff to find less brutalizing methods. After blowing up mental patients with explosives, they gassed 10,000 mental patients by using the exhaust of a truck. Beginning in December 1941 gas vans were used, under SS auspices, to kill 145,000 people at Chelmno (Burleigh 1994, 132). According to the head of T4, by 1941 "it was an 'open secret' that Germany's rulers intended to exterminate the whole Jewish population of Germany and the occupied territories" (in Burleigh 1994, 231, 332). In the fall of that year another annihilation complex was mounted at Auschwitz in eastern Poland. First laid out in 1940 as a prisoner-of-war camp for about 10,000 inmates, it was expanded to employ increasing numbers of prisoners as industrial labor. By midsummer 1941, gassing began with the killing of sick or resistant non-Jewish Polish and Soviet prisoners. On September 3, 1941, Deputy Commander Fritzsch used the insecticide Zyklon B to gas 600 Soviet prisoners of war and 250 tubercular patients, thereby hitting on a suitable method for extermination of the ever-larger arrivals of Jewish deportees. Auschwitz became the largest of the extermination centers, though the numbers actually killed there remain uncertain; Eichmann has said that 2.5 million people were killed outright in Auschwitz, while another 500,000 died of starvation or disease (Friedrich 1994, viii–ix). In December 1941 the T4 specialists also set up gassing facilities at Belzec, Sobibor, and Treblinka, and eventually more than 1.5 million people were killed at these three centers (Burleigh 1994, 233).

SEEKING EXPLANATION

Attempts to explain this frenzy of brutality and killing have taken a number of forms, many of them understandably addressed to the question of who could be held responsible for initiating and executing the decisions. Posing that kind of question has yielded substantial knowledge about the identity and intentions of individual participants, as well as about means they employed, but such information does not yet address the larger question of what rendered such a genocidal project possible at all. That question requires a grasp of the conditions within which intentions and the choice of means arise and develop. It is necessary to distinguish between general and proximate conditions, always with the aim of visualizing both levels in their mutual connection.

The search for general conditions has often begun by asking how this could have happened at all within "modern civilization." Posing the question that way usually assumes that "modernity" means progress in the rule of reason and the belief that rationality will liberate humankind from ignorance and brutality. There have been critics of this perspective, of course, from the conservative Right, with its traditional distrust of reason, and from the Left, who came to fear the use of rationality in domination (Horkheimer and Adorno 1972). The sociologist Zygmunt Bauman has built on these critiques to ask what in "modernity" specifically might underwrite so massive a genocidal project (1989). He points to such features as the extensive division of labor in society, which separates people working in different domains; the awesome development of technology; the growth of large and impersonal bureaucracies, which can produce cumulative results without ever having to inquire into the reasons for what is being done; and the triumphant growth of science and the rational modes of thought associated with it. All these features were implicated, he argues, in the way the NS regime became established and then erupted into violence on a continental scale. This complex of features "was not the Holocaust's sufficient condition; it was, however, most certainly its necessary condition. . . . It was the rational world of modern civilization that made the Holocaust thinkable" (Bauman 1989, 13).

Other discussions dovetail with Bauman's analysis. Omer Bartov has stressed the human implications of "industrial killing" in World

War I, suggesting that "modern war provides the occasion and the tools, the manpower and the organization, the mentality and the imagery necessary for the perpetration of genocide" (1996, 50). The wars of colonization and imperialist expansion fought by Europeans against native populations may have had a similar effect. These wars produced ideologies promising to "uplift" the colonized, but also calls to "exterminate the brutes." Germany was a latecomer in the competition for colonies overseas, but it grafted imperialist projects for seizure of Lebensraum upon older traditions of conquest and settlement in the Slavic East (Smith 1986, 145–52). These projects came to the fore during World War I and gained a new life through the sanguinary operations of the Freikorps afterward. The invasion of the Soviet Union took up these earlier efforts, reinforced by an ideological vision of triumph of the Germanic master race (*Herren-rasse*) over the "subhuman" Slavs.

If anti-Semitism is posed as a general condition for the Judeocide, it is important to remember that, like all general and proximate conditions, it developed and changed over time. A purely synchronic analysis would risk essentializing the set of relations it proposed as significant. It would therefore be an error to interpret the Judeocide as simply another repetition of the same anti-Semitism that has "always" characterized relations between Jews and non-Jews in Germany as elsewhere.

Bauman has made an interesting effort to show why this approach would fall short (1989, 64–65). He argues that we need to distinguish among various responses to "strangers in our midst": fear and resentment of what is different ("heterophobia"); efforts to draw boundaries between the we-group and those thought to encroach upon it ("contestant enmity"); and the outright removal of people in the offending category (which he labels "racism"). These categories will shade into each other in any particular case, and the term "racism" may be inapt. Yet Bauman's typology has the merit of seeing heterophobia, separation, removal, and annihilation as possible phases in a social process of escalation and thus raises also the question of how to account for the shifting of social gears from one level to the next.

In the Germanies heterophobia of Jews was certainly ancient and widespread, and contestant enmity was managed by segregating Jews as a pariah people within the confines of the ghettos. The rise of explicitly anti-Semitic movements in the 1870s, however, brought on a qualitative change in relations between non-Jews and Jews, because the inimical contest was now deployed in the context of a mass market of political options in which mobilized groups and parties competed for control of the political terrain. In this context anti-Semitism became politically effective only when it forged alliances with other interest groups on different grounds. Thus, in 1907, the "Ariosophist" and editor of a "Library for the Blond-Haired and Male Supremacists" Adolf Lanz (who called himself Jörg Lanz von Liebenfels) declared that being "purely anti-Semitic" was not enough: anti-Semitism had to develop a positive side in the vision of the unified Volksgemeinschaft of people and race.

Just as depictions of anti-Semitism have to be tied to the contexts in which it made its appearance and became politically salient, so also one must not assume that it had the same form and degree of intensity throughout a given group. Many Germans drew a distinction between individual Jews and Jews in general, as Himmler well understood when he addressed the SS Group Leaders in 1943: "'The Jewish people are to be exterminated.' . . . And then they come along, the eighty million worthy Germans, and each one of them produces his decent Jew. It's clear the others are swine, but this one is a fine Jew" (in Noakes and Pridham 1995, 1199). Even within the NS leadership some were more passionately Judeophobic than others. Only one-quarter of the 581 "early" National Socialists who wrote autobiographies for sociologist Theodore Abel evidenced a virulent anti-Semitism; among the rest the intensity varied greatly, both in absolute terms and relative to other concerns (Abel 1938; Merkl 1975, 499). Rainer Baum may have been close to the mark when he concluded that for many, perhaps most, the Judeocide was "a sideshow, something that you did not bother about while engaged in the big show, securing a place for yourself in the wonderland of the New Order in Europe" (1981, 9).

Where Bauman spoke to the general conditions that might underlie the Judeocide, the social psychologist Herbert Kelman tried to identify the proximate conditions required to remove the customary restraints on open violence against individuals and groups (1973). He proposed three such conditions. The first is the authorization of such violence by legally entitled superior authorities. This condition was put in place through the encouragement of violence by the NS state and the predatory competition it sponsored. The second condition is the development and perfection of a bureaucracy able to deploy violence "by the book." As we have seen, a technology and bureaucracy of violence against Jews and others was increasingly elaborated, especially after 1939. Raul Hilberg lists twenty-seven different institutions and organizations involved in carrying out the process of destruction (1992, 21–24).

Kelman's third condition for the unleashing of violence, once authorized and routinized, is that the victims be *dehumanized*. This condition was met through the exercise of "cold" bureaucratic violence coupled with rabid propaganda. As long as Germans and Jews still lived under conditions of heterophobia or contestant enmity, members of the Volk might conceivably still experience a momentary human identification with their opposite "others." Once such others are defined as disease organisms or agents of universal entropy, the imagery of evil becomes abstract and powerful enough to justify not merely severance but destruction.

THE ORCHESTRATION OF BRUTALITY

No discussion of the Judeocide would be complete without reference to its extraordinary cruelty. As Goldhagen has stressed (1996), accounts of the mass killings of Jews tend to represent most of the perpetrators as either neutral or reluctant operators of an impersonal killing machine that produced dead bodies the way an assembly line produces packaged products. Those who enjoyed showing off their power, and the "scientists" who experimented on live humans, are then explained either as exceptional sadists or as mental Svengalis who could separate the sensitive, domestic part of their selves from their murderous egos through "doubling." What these explanations miss is the extreme degree of routine lethal violence against women, children, and men.

There can be no doubt that some people found Jew-baiting pleasurable and exciting. Certainly the ways in which the regime invited and rewarded acts of institutional violence against political opponents, as well as Jews, changed what Norbert Elias called the balance between self-constraint and constraint by others. Warriors trained to be hard and pitiless took pride in directing their passions—disciplined within—against designated targets. Turning all men into soldiers, as well as demanding that women serve as handmaidens of warrior masculinity, reinforced the repression of pity, lest one appear weak to oneself or to others, while self-esteem could be enhanced by multiplying the suffering of enemies, especially those defined as "subhumans." Since ideology furnished ready-made stereotypes accounting for why things are the way they are—which were rendered immune to critical discussion—the would-be warrior could concentrate on how things were done rather than ask why, and garner recognition for his heroism.

A small-group experiment set up to simulate a prison has shown how quickly ordinary, self-controlled people can turn to destructive and humiliating behavior against stigmatized others (Haney, Banks, and Zimbardo 1973). The sociologist Philip Zimbardo divided a group of male American student volunteers randomly into prisoners, dressed in ridiculous gowns and caps, and prison guards in uniforms and dark glasses. The prisoners were then subjected to humiliating and undignified regulations. In ways quite unforeseen, these conditions gave rise to a cumulative cycle of behaviors, with the prison guards devising ever more degrading acts while the prisoners responded with acts of self-humiliation. The experiment had to be discontinued before it got out of hand, but it suggests that social conditions more than individual motivations drive behavior under such circumstances. Such sequences of behavior went on uninterruptedly as the German regime carried out its program of mass homicide in the conquered lands to the east. In this escalation of human misery NS ideology furnished ready-made formulas to define the problem to be solved and to select ways to solve it.

As the Soviet invasion proceeded, breaches of combat discipline within the German units came to be dealt with more severely, often by execution. At the same time, official orders to the troops virtually effaced the distinction between enemy soldiers and civilian populations. The fighting units were now expected to destroy enemy forces and civilians together with the habitat that supported them. Required to live off the resources of the land, the German military routinely plundered the population to obtain supplies, and unau-

thorized crimes of depredation and murder were increasingly toler-
ated. Legal and moral constraints were further abrogated when the
German armies on the eastern front experienced massive failures of
strategy, organization, and equipment in their battles against an indomitable enemy in an unconquerable landscape.

Jew-baiting often took on carnivalesque dimensions, not in
Bakhtin's sense of carnival as a means of social protest but rather as
shows of playful aggression directed against "outsiders." The public
mistreatment of Jews—especially of old, traditionalizing Jews who
were harassed, degraded, and besmirched in public "rituals of degradation" to the accompaniment of general merriment—recollects the
treatment of animals that were goaded and beaten in the village fairs
of earlier times. But in the turn to genocide, such baiting of Jews—
stripping them naked and making them dance, for example—was
only prelude to the "final solution," obliteration of the victim
altogether.

It would be difficult to explain the Judeocide in the terms of any
rational economy of peace or war. Prior to implementation of the
"final solution," there were "productionists" who worked to make
the ghettos self-sustaining; these efforts increased production and
generated a demand for Jewish labor, but they were terminated by
orders from the top (Browning 1992, 65–76). Similarly, requests to retain skilled Jews in strategic sectors of the economy were denied since
"economic considerations are to be regarded as fundamentally irrelevant to the settlement of the problem."[9] The employment of Jews
in labor camps was systematically rendered unproductive through
maltreatment and disease, and they were not even mobilized as helot
labor, as were the 7 million Polish, French, and Russian forced laborers. The massive effort to transport Jews to killing centers also interfered with military logistics in the midst of a hard-fought war.

The Spanish Inquisition, in its day, had committed resistant Jews
to the flames in a program to convert the infidels and save souls; but
this was not a motivation in the German case. There was no impulse
to assimilate the Jews or to make an example of them in some ritual
exhibition. They were not required to fill a sacrificial role in any project of reciprocity with or offering to a supernatural; they were not
treated as scapegoats to carry off the collective sins of a human community, as René Girard has argued (1977). The goal was to extirpate

the Jews altogether, stripping them of their personal identity and dignity in the process. They were made to vanish from the earth, their relics consigned to special museums, such as the Museum of a Vanished Race set up by the German occupiers in Prague.

Expansion to the East

In *Mein Kampf* Hitler had announced his aim to destroy the Soviet Union militarily and expand Germany's Lebensraum into Eastern Europe. This goal, always his "great and real task" (in Hillgruber 1981, 79), was no secret, but there is reason to think that he envisaged this conquest in terms of "distinct, separately timed 'lightning wars' against one enemy at a time without bringing on a world war" (p. 62). The initial steps toward conquest of the East—the sequential occupations of Austria, then of Czechoslovakia's Sudeten region, and finally the takeover and dismemberment of the Czechoslovak Republic—combined diplomacy, threats of military power, and sponsorship of internal subversion. Hitler planned for localized shooting wars to commence in 1940 and projected the conquest of Russia for 1943–1945. Contrary to his expectation, however, his invasion of Poland in September 1939 triggered French and British intervention and unleashed a general war. At that time, German raw-material supplies were budgeted only for a short war of nine to twelve months (p. 63). Hitler's strategy was then threefold: to sign a temporary pact with the Soviet Union to divide Poland and thereby secure his rear; to break the power of France; and then to persuade the British to accept German domination of the Continent while they continued to rule the seas. He conquered France in mid-1940 and drove British forces back to their island base. Though Britain would not accede to his demands, he now felt free to engage the Soviet Union.

This undertaking was to be another lightning war of nine to seventeen weeks. This time frame would suffice to bring the Soviet armies to heel, because they were thought incapable of calling up the reserves at such short notice and transporting them to the front. Thus, "they will quickly succumb to the superiority of German troops and leadership" (in Hillgruber 1981, 80). This appraisal was shared by Göring, who had been put in charge of economic planning for the to-be-conquered areas. Göring envisaged no problem in laying hold of Soviet economic resources and thought that the whole Bolshevik state would collapse as soon as German troops marched into Russia (Rich 1992, 215).

BARBAROSSA

Operation Barbarossa began on June 22, 1941. The Germans committed 153 divisions, more than 3 million men, retaining only 385,000 troops in reserve in the expectation of a short war (Noakes and Pridham 1995, 817). That expectation was not met. In December the German forces were halted before the gates of Moscow. By early 1942, on the testimony of General Alfred Jodl, Hitler knew that "victory was no longer attainable," and he ruminated: "If the German people are not prepared to stand up for their own preservation, fine. Then they should perish" (Hildebrand 1973, 96). The German advance resumed, until by October it controlled most of Stalingrad, but a month later the Soviet counteroffensive broke the siege and destroyed the encircled German army. A further German attempt in mid-1943 to win back the initiative by storming Kursk ended in failure.

The considerable successes of the Wehrmacht, first in Poland and then in Norway and on the Western Front, was due to "an innovative and highly efficient employment of its limited resources" (Bartov 1992, 12). However, the German army never recovered from the failure of the initial blitzkrieg against the Soviet Union. The resources supplied to the war effort rose steadily from 1940 to 1944 (Hayes 1993, 197), but the production of promised "wonder weapons"—the V–1 and V–2 rockets—came too late to reverse the slide toward defeat. Yet surprisingly, the Reich did not move toward "total war," the complete mobilization of resources for military ends, until after the abortive plot to kill the Führer in July 1944. Then Hitler appointed Göbbels to conduct this last-ditch effort.

As a result of the botched winter campaign in Russia, the ensuing battles on the Russian front were marked by an ever-widening gap in resources and technology between the Red Army and the Wehrmacht. Bartov has characterized the outcome as an experience "of profound demodernization, of a return to the trench warfare of the Great War made worse by the enemy's growing technological capacity" (1992, 16). In his opinion, this military reversal greatly intensified the role of ideology as the missing "wonder weapon" that would compensate for the poor preparation for the Russian campaign. Indeed, NS ideology furnished much of the social and psychological fuel that sustained the ever more nightmarish battles on the Eastern Front. As conditions for the Wehrmacht worsened, the German soldiers increasingly took recourse to that ideology to explain their situation and harden their morale. Yet it had been precisely this ideology that had led them into the disaster. It now sealed their fate by offering them the false solace of a distorted reality.

TOWARD A GREATER REICH IN THE EAST

The basic premises for the war against the Soviet Union had been spelled out in *Mein Kampf.* If a people want to be strong, it has to multiply and occupy land to sustain its numbers. Since land is limited, people will have to fight for it, the victory going to the strongest, "according to the law of the natural order of energy" (MK 175). For Germany, "if we talk about new soil and territory in Europe today, we can think primarily only of Russia and its vassal border states" (MK 950–51).

Some of these themes had been influential in German policymaking circles during World War I. The last emperor, Wilhelm II, had spoken about an eternal struggle of Teutons against Gauls and Slavs. Among the German court elite, discussion of war aims in the East emphasized the creation of a pro-German Poland to act as a buffer between Germany and Russia and then the formation of a "Frontier Strip" to divide Poland and Germany. As the war proceeded, these goals expanded to include "wider frontiers" for the German people by incorporating Estonia, Latvia, parts of Lithuania, and the Ukraine. These territorial claims were accompanied by demands that Poles and Jews be expelled from Prussia and the Strip and replaced by Germans drawn either from within the Reich or from other areas of German settlement in Eastern Europe. Plans were also laid to Germanize the Estonian and Latvian populations (Fischer 1967, 113–17, 162–73, 273–79, 456–72).

These ideas were still alive when Hitler made his first bid for leadership in the Weimar Republic, but he added to them a raciological evaluation of Slavdom. As he saw it, Slavs were incapable of developing a state structure on their own; "the organization of a Russian state structure was not the result of Russian Slavdom's State-political capacity, but rather a wonderful example of the State-building activity of the German element in an inferior race" (MK 951). For him the "German element" had been the Russian aristocracy, but in the Revolution of 1917, this noble group had been replaced by the Jews. Some of these ideas may have come from Hitler's reading the British Germanophile H. S. Chamberlain, who characterized Russia as a manifestation of racial chaos, others from the postwar White Russian and Baltic émigrés in Munich, among them Alfred Rosenberg. Rosenberg drew heavily on Chamberlain, as well as on the German Balt Victor Hehn (1857–1873), who offered a veritable "theory of Russophobia" (Laqueur 1971, 357) that strongly influenced German policymaking circles under Wilhelm II. To the notion that Russia represented "racial chaos" unified only by an absolutist state, Hitler added the crucial idea that this state had now been taken over by Jewry. Yet "Jewry itself is not an organizing element, but a ferment of decomposition," as well as "criminal," "the scum of humanity," savagely bloodthirsty, combining "a rare mixture of bestial horror with an inconceivable gift of lying" (MK 952, 959). Cutting off this "Jewish-Bolshevik head" would deprive the Slav peoples of leadership and return "the Slavic masses to their natural state of slavery" (in Nolte 1969, 451).

These ideological premises throw light on both the motivations for the NS onslaught against the Soviet Union and the mode of its execution. Operation Barbarossa was marked by two salient features. One was the poor logistic and strategic planning (see Leach 1973), which not only ignored limitations of space and time but also severely underestimated the military and political capabilities of an enemy they had defined as "subhuman." The second was the extreme brutality of the military operation. Hitler characterized the Russian campaign as no ordinary war but as a life-and-death struggle between two races, Germans and Slavs, and between two ideologies, National Socialism and the Jewish Bolshevik threat to civilization.[10] Thus, this war could only be fought by setting aside outdated concepts of chivalry in combat, together with the usual laws of war: the Bolshevik-

Jewish intelligentsia and the Communist leadership cadre were not to be treated humanly but to be wiped out.

Three directives in 1941 formulated how these goals were to be accomplished. The so-called Barbarossa Directive of May 13 removed restrictions on retaliation by German troops against "criminal attacks" by Soviet civilians. The Commissar Order of June 6 ordered troops to execute Red Army commissars upon capture, an order that was repeated numerous times by lower-level commanders and usually acted upon (Bartov 1992, 129–32). The third directive, dated July 17, allowed Reinhold Heydrich, the head of State Security, to send SS "dispositional units" to comb through Soviet prisoner-of-war camps and remove "political criminals and other disreputable elements," to include "all important functionaries of the state and the party, in particular professional revolutionaries . . . all former commissars in the Red Army . . . the leading personalities . . . of the state bureaucracy . . . ; and the Soviet intelligentsia, all Jews . . . all persons proven to be agitators or fanatical Communists and racially intolerable elements" (in Mayer 1988, 252). These elements were to receive "special treatment," but "executions [were] not to be carried out in or near prison camps" (in Mayer 1988, 252). "Several hundred thousand prisoners became victims of the ensuing selections, which continued to the end of the war" (Streit 1990, 147).[11]

Other Red Army prisoners were subjected to unusually harsh treatment and deprivation. The use of firearms against prisoners was not only permitted, but approved in this conflict waged for "the destruction of a world view" (Streit 1990, 146). Many Soviet prisoners perished through overwork and disease, or through the intentional denial to them of the basic provisions for survival. Of the 5.7 million Red Army soldiers taken prisoner, 57 percent died in prison camps. In comparison, of 3.25 million German soldiers captured by Soviet forces, 36 percent died in captivity (Streit 1990, 142).

ORGANIZING THE EAST

Had Barbarossa succeeded, the Reich had plans for the East. In 1939 conquered Poland had been split between a northern and western region, slated to become parts of the German Reich proper, and a central region, to be demarcated as the General Government. Eastern Poland was turned over to the Soviet Union until Barbarossa. The districts to be incorporated into the Reich were to be wholly Germanized, primarily through the settlement of some 600,000 Ethnic Germans from elsewhere in Eastern Europe. This project to resettle Germans in the Reich and transform them into military peasants (*Wehrbauern*) to guard the eastern frontiers had been announced in *Mein Kampf*, and it was also one of Himmler's pet projects.

The aim of resettlement of the Ethnic Germans in areas forcibly vacated by Poles, Jews, and Gypsies was combined by Himmler with other goals, laid out in a secret memorandum on "The Treatment of Racial Aliens in the East" of May 25, 1940 (Krausnick 1957). This document specified the intent to select Polish children "racially above reproach" and "recognized to be of our blood," send them to school in the Reich, and eventually settle them there permanently. The rest of the population in the Central Government, "composed of the remaining inferior population supplemented by those deported from the eastern provinces . . . will consist of laborers without leaders, and will furnish Germany annually with migrant workers and labor for special tasks (roads, quarries, construction of buildings)" (in Milton 1990, 151–52).

Actual plans for regrouping the peoples under German control in the East had not yet been prepared at the time of the invasion of Poland in 1939, and they crystallized only as events unfolded (Browning 1992, 8). To make room for the new Ethnic German settlers, about a million people—Poles, Jews, and Gypsies—were expelled from western Poland and moved eastward, Poles into the area of the General Government and Jews to its extreme eastern frontiers with the Soviet Union. However, the project of redeploying hundreds of thousands, even millions, of people soon ran up against limitations of available transport and economic support for both settlers and deportees. At the same time, the German governors of the newly acquired territories began to protest the large-scale dumping of poor and miserable people into their satrapies. Finally, military preparations for the impending invasion of the Soviet Union placed wholesale relocations on hold.

As the invasion advanced, settlement zones behind the lines passed into German hands, and the occupied territories to the rear of the military zone were placed under a specially created Reich Ministry (the *Ostministerium*) under Alfred Rosenberg, Hitler's "specialist" in Eastern European affairs. This administration, however, lacked control over competing power blocs—Himmler's security apparatus, Göring's economic staff, the military machine of the Wehrmacht, and the German commanders of occupied districts. Reich commissars supposedly subordinate to Rosenberg soon turned their jurisdictions into satrapies of their own, leading Göbbels to dub the Ostministerium the *Chaost-Ministerium* and its head "a monarch with neither country nor subjects" (in Fest 1970, 173).

Flushed with the news of initial successes, on July 16, 1941, Hitler announced that the Crimea, Galicia, the Baltic, the Volga German settlements, and Baku would all become parts of the German Reich. Out of the newly won territories he intended to create "a Garden of Eden." "All necessary measures—shootings, resettlement, etc." would be utilized. Luckily, he said, the Russian order for partisan warfare "gives us the opportunity to exterminate anyone who is hostile to us" (in Browning 1992, 105–6).

Göring, as czar of the economy, had already acquainted senior economic officials with his plans for how to exploit the resources that would come into their grasp with the conquest of the Soviet Union. He overrode all doubts, arguing that the war would prove short and decisive and that it would allow "the immediate and maximum exploitation of the occupied territory to the benefit of Germany." Emphasis would be placed on the extraction of foodstuffs and oil, as well as the maintenance of transport, but any reconstruction would be undertaken only where justified by significant increases in yield. It was thought to be acceptable that "tens of millions of people will undoubtedly die of starvation, if we take what we need from the country" (in Noakes and Pridham 1995, 901).

At best this was a strategy of plunder; at worst, one of utter devastation. It also contrasted markedly with earlier efforts, in 1939–1940, by several government agencies to organize an integrated Europewide economic sphere under German leadership (Noakes and Pridham 1995, 884–98). Increasingly, however, the German regime concentrated on "policies which would produce the most immediate benefits in terms of the German war effort, in other words on extracting the maximum resources from the occupied territories"

(p. 898). As Timothy Mason noted, procurement of resources for the war effort became the goal of war itself; means and ends of war "collapsed into each other." This also accounted, he argued, for the unwillingness of the regime to put an end to the war (1993, 180).

In 1941, Himmler's "planning intelligentsia" worked on a master plan for the East, the so-called Plan Ost, which was issued on April 27, 1942 (Heiber 1958; Madajczyk 1962). This document explicated NS goals for the resettlement and political reshuffling of the East. It evaluated in raciological terms the utility of the various ethnic-racial populations conquered and to be conquered. All Jews and Gypsies were to be eliminated, together with a quarter of the Russians. Thirty-one million inhabitants of Poland and the western Soviet Union were to be moved either to the General Government or to Siberia; 14 million of these were slated for eventual Germanization, while the rest were to serve the incoming Ethnic German settlers from Eastern Europe and the South Tyrol. The General Government was to become a "gigantic Polish work camp," populated by a "reservoir of manpower for unskilled labor" (Himmler, in Ackermann 1970, 216). A document issued at the same time by the colonization division of the Ostministerium raised the number of people slated for removal to about 50 million but suggested that it was not enough to think in demographic and ethnic terms alone. It was important "to destroy the Russians as a people, separate and alienate them. It is essential that the majority of the people remaining on Russian territory be of a primitive, semi-European type" (in Kumanev 1990, 131).

If Slavs were to serve the Germans, they would not need higher education. As Himmler put it: "We have no need to bring culture to these people. It is sufficient (1) when the children learn the traffic signs in school so that they do not run into our automobiles, (2) when they learn the multiplication table up to 25 and can count that far, and (3) when they learn to write their own names. Anything more is unnecessary" (in Ackermann 1970, 220). Hitler's private secretary, Martin Borman, stated in an official memorandum that "the Slavs are to work for us. In so far as we don't need them, they may die. Therefore compulsory vaccination and German health services are superfluous. The fertility of the Slavs is undesirable." (in Hunczak 1990, 118).

In defining the project to reorder people and societies in the East according to a raciology, German Volkish thought and NS ideology encountered a logical difficulty in trying to explain why Slavs, technically Aryan, had never engaged in state building, having imported the perquisites of a higher humanity from abroad. Perhaps this was due to the Mongol element in their racial makeup. The Slavs, moreover, had allowed themselves to be conquered by the Jews; it was impossible for "the Russians alone to shake off the yoke of the Jews through their own strength" (MK, 52). Barbarossa would thus return the world to its natural state, ensure the victory of the Reich over the forces of dissolution, and return the Slavs to their proper station as serfs and laborers for the Teutonic world order.

A consequence of this understanding of the eastern lands was that it quickly led to grouping together all the occupants of these territories as "subhuman." This had always been Hitler's position, and it came to be shared by Himmler and other top aides. Not only would the Judeo-Bolshevik elite have to be physically eliminated, but the entire remaining population was destined to become a dependent labor pool. No account would be taken of whether they favored Soviet or German rule or of the possibility of organizing them into client states that might support Greater Germany in exchange for a measure of autonomy. "As for the ridiculous hundred million Slavs," Hitler is quoted as saying, "we will mold the best of them to the shape that suits us, and we will isolate the rest of them in their own pigsties; and anyone who talks about respecting the local inhabitants and civilizing them goes straight off into a concentration camp" (in Baird 1974, 158).

By adopting this view, the Reich not only failed to enlist on its side Slavic populations with a long history of dissidence against the Soviet Union but actually drove them into supporting Soviet partisan resistance. The Hitler-Himmler perspective prevailed, even though alternative approaches to the "eastern question" were put forward by others in both the party and army. Rosenberg argued for a series of anti-Russian buffer states to be established under the protection of the Reich, in order to isolate the Great Russians, while some spoke for creating an anti-Bolshevik Russian state (Dallin 1957, 43–56). Arguments were made for an alternative policy that would not drive the native population into partisan resistance, including the recruitment of Russian troops into the Wehrmacht—efforts had already begun informally. In early 1943, Göbbels issued decrees reversing stated policy, asking that help from Slavs be welcomed to ensure final victory and that care be taken in discussing Eastern national groups in official publications (Baird 1974, 147–65).

Official policy and ideology were not, however, easily reversed. In 1942 the SS Central Office, on Himmler's behalf, published a wildly racist comic book entitled *Der Untermensch* (The Subhuman) portraying humanlike creatures that had crawled out of a primordial swamp and had been recruited by the Jews to be put to murdering people. Göbbels thought the pamphlet was ill-advised, since reports showed that it displeased not only Russians but also German soldiers who had learned to respect the skills and equipment of the Red Army. Despite efforts by Göbbels to have it withdrawn, it was never removed from circulation.

Discussion

In the cases previously described, we saw that Kwakiutl ideology carried forward older cultural understandings to strengthen the chiefship against the challenges of new times, while Tenochca ideology sacralized state making by an upstart elite and provided the rationale for war and political expansion. The National Socialist ideology developed in a different structural context—that of a twentieth-century industrialized nation-state in modern Europe, a region characterized by diverse national histories and wide-ranging flows of different ideas. The greater complexity of the NS case material, however, is also due to the abundance of detailed historical information. This information allows us not only to see ideology in its functional connections with particular hierarchical social orders but also to grasp the relationship between ideology and structures of power, as both were made and unmade in one of the most fateful episodes in recent history. The ideology of National Socialism that guided the Third Reich, which was largely systematized in Hitler's *Mein Kampf*, was not a "reflection" of existing social realities. It was a medley of propositions developed during the nineteenth century, and even before, out of diverse social and economic arrangements.

This conceptual amalgam was used by the National Socialists to underwrite a project for political domination and expansion that had to be imposed and maintained by force as well as persuasion and that was only partially achieved.

As in the first two cases, I have argued that the nexus between ideas and power must be located in processes that unfold in space and time. The events that surrounded the NS seizure of power were triggered by the German defeat in World War I and by the economic and political dislocations that followed, but the general conditions from which these immediate causes sprang have their origins in a longer course of German history. I emphasized that two sets of circumstances in that history had recurrent consequences. One was the persistence of local particularisms, supported by the fragmentation of the Germanies into multiple political bodies and entities. These polities not only strove to encompass the loyalties of their subjects but they long enforced local bodies of law and distinctive religious affiliations. The multiplication of local arrangements worked against political unification, created obstacles to economic interchange within the Germanies and with the rest of Europe, and curtailed German participation in the transoceanic expansion that founded the empires of other European nations.

The second set of circumstances underlined was the proliferation of social distinctions and their counterparts in status honor. Variable by locality, region, and political entity, these distinctions of ascriptive social honor set off aristocrats and commoners, as well as members of despised occupations "outside the categories of social honor" altogether, and numerous subcategories of each. Such codes also separated Christians and Jews. In all cases, these social ascriptions defined as well the economic and political abilities and disabilities of each category. Produced within the narrow orbits of multiple principalities, the distinctions worked to confine the inhabitants within the limits of these domains, while ordinances governing social disparities multiplied all across the German lands.

These circumstances not only had consequences for the organization of society and polity, but at the same time they gave rise to tendencies to modify or even undo them. Further pressures were generated in response to ideas introduced from outside the Germanies. Most significant were the reactions to France and the French

Revolution. The France of the seventeenth and eighteenth centuries impressed people in the Germanies by its political unity around a stellar royal court, located in a capital city. The comportment and ideas elaborated in Paris and centered on its royal establishment became the cynosure of German princes and aristocrats, who copied French political, artistic, and intellectual styles. Many of the effervescent new ideas produced by the French Enlightenment found resonance in the Germanies, and even critiques of the political order often received a sympathetic hearing. Yet when the French Revolution decapitated the aristocracy and its armies crossed into the German lands to implement the program of liberty, equality, and fraternity, the efforts to impose a universal order under French hegemony were a direct challenge to German political parochialism and codes of social honor.

The reaction in the Germanies against this imposition transformed ideas about national identity into anti-French and anti-foreign nationalism. It built on French Enlightenment notions of the moral and collective body of "the people" but offered a vision of shared cultural identity in the German Volk in place of a project of political unification. This vision fortified hopes for a Reich of all the Germans, but it spelled out no practical politics to turn that dream into reality. Politicians assented to reforms "from above," on the Prussian model, but failed in various efforts to install a liberal and democratic federalism, inspired by French or English thought. There were also some attempts to modify the ascribed social hierarchies, but these were altered more directly and more brutally by the forces of capitalist transformation than by changes of policy and law. The resulting pressures produced reactions particularly against Jews, who were increasingly identified with the destabilization of customary hierarchies through their legal emancipation in some regions and their visibility in monetary transactions. As local and regional exponents of liberal and democratic ideas increasingly lost influence, Bismarck was able to consolidate a strongly militaristic and bureaucratic Second Reich under Prussian aegis in 1871. This Reich came to an end with the German defeat in World War I and the abdication in 1918 of the last Hohenzollern emperor in favor of a republic and a new constitution drafted at Weimar.

With the benefit of hindsight, one can see that ideas which would play strategic roles in power struggles after World War I had already emerged in the preceding, contradiction-ridden century. One was the concept of the Germans as a Volk, characterized by a common cultural soul but not yet including all Germans within an encompassing Reich. Another was the conception of society as an ordered hierarchy of distinctions, an idea that was increasingly challenged by the all-too-real social and economic changes flowing from capitalist expansion. These changes produced new social categories and groups and rearranged relations among the classes. They diminished the power and prestige of an aristocracy based on control of titles and lands in favor of moneyed wealth; impoverished many small merchants, artisans, and peasants; and multiplied the proletariat. As shown in the spread of the dueling complex, the titled nobility and the merely rich developed common forms of crypto-aristocratic sociability. At the bottom of the social hierarchy the workers, excluded altogether from the circle of social honor, formed their own class-based organizations with distinctive social and cultural patterns of associational life and forged strong connections with the parties of the Left. At the turn of the century, intellectuals like Möller van der Bruck, Spengler, and Weber spoke for a strategy whereby Germany would integrate the working class through an alliance of industrial and military elites with nationalist labor leaders, who could draw the proletariat away from international socialism.

The development of political anti-Semitism toward the end of the century laid further groundwork for what was to come. Increasingly, anti-Semites formulated distinctions between the Volk and the Jews not on religious or social lines but in terms of raciological science, representing Jews both as *artfremd*—different in body as well as spirit from the "Aryan" host population—and as collectively responsible for all the problems of the Germans since time immemorial. Arguably, this mode of discourse available to all the Germans—divided by regional distinctiveness, political affiliation, and religion—underlined common bonds in the midst of counterfactual economic realities and class relations.

The loss of World War I, and the economic, social, and political convulsions of the weak republic that followed, led to the rise of National Socialism. Upon its seizure of power in 1933, the movement succeeded in dissolving Parliament and dismantling the legal and constitutional guarantees developed by the Weimar Republic. It put an end to political parties, destroyed the autonomous organizations of the working class, and placed labor under the control of the state. By using force to eliminate independent labor politics, the new regime "solved" the problem of labor participation in national governance. The new government also abrogated limits to rearmament and embarked on a program of rearming the nation and preparing it for war. It maintained most government bureaucracies, together with their Prussian traditions, but complemented them with a multiplicity of parallel institutions and organizations specifically tied to the NS party. Ultimate decision-making power was in the hands of the Führer, but the actual implementation of his policies was hammered out through competition and accommodation among power blocs—coalitions of elite groups variously drawn from industry, government, army, and party. At the same time, widening opportunities for employment and political careers enhanced social mobility for many.

As part and parcel of this project of installing NS power, Hitler and his collaborators forged an ideology out of the fragmented ideas that had gained currency before World War I. Like the protagonists of other revitalization movements, they represented National Socialism as a heroic effort to restore a world "turned upside down" to health and vitality. Drawing together many of the kindred themes familiar from the past, Hitler added a novel twist with his particular conception of the Volksgemeinschaft.

This community of the Volk would not be confined to the territory of the Second Reich but would embrace Germans everywhere. It would not be the society ruled over by traditional elites advocated by the conservatives but would include plebeians and aristocrats alike and draw on the capacities of all strata. Furthermore, while many understood the Volk-community as a people organized to furnish material and spiritual support, for Hitler it was a project to create a cultural-political entity able to compete and emerge victorious in the relentless struggle for dominance. This view was grounded in a cosmology that saw the world as a scenario of strife in which the strong were rewarded and the weak destroyed. Germany had lost the last war because it had grown weak; to rebuild its strength it was first necessary to make war on weakness. Ultimately that weakness was

due to undermining of the hereditary endowment that had en-
nobled the Aryans in the Golden Age before race mixture. Making
war on weakness would require that the Volksgemeinschaft not subordinate itself to the state, as envisaged in conservative thought, but
employ the state as an instrument—a warrior sword—to restore racial purity, strength, and will.

Making war on Germany's weakness meant first destroying the
enemies within—socialists, communists, Jews, and Gypsies. There
could, however, be no end to internal war, since Germany had allowed its primordial Aryan substance to be polluted. Hence there
was need for a state that would purify the desirable biological strains
through eugenics and racial selection. The state would also repair the
weakened moral fiber of the people by hardening it in military training patterned on the experience of the Prussian army. Yet these measures of military socialization were only means to create a nation-at-
arms, imbued by its Führer and his paladins with the fanatical will to
reverse past defeats and start once more on a road to conquest that
would lead to the fantasized Aryan Reich.

This ideology thus implied a program of endless control, training,
and vigilance to develop the master race that would dominate in the
cosmic struggle. In this struggle, the ultimate enemy was represented
by the Jew. Where the Aryans were called to be powerful masters, able
to command inferior people to construct culture, egalitarian and
parasitic Jewry represented their antithesis. It was necessary to defeat
these demons: first through the destruction of Jewry everywhere,
and second, through victory over Judeo-Bolshevism, the tyranny
over Slavdom supposedly instituted by the Revolution of 1917. Once
the Jews were gone and the Slavic East freed from their grip, nature
would be restored to its proper course, and the Germanic victors
would be able to build upon Slavic labor the "Holy Teutonic Reich
of the German Nation."

War, however, would never end. If war made possible more abundant life, the defense and expansion of that life would necessitate
further war. The struggle would require, generation after generation, the natural selection of new candidates for mastery, possessed
of the will to dominate and legitimizing their claims to rulership
through waging war. If nature required an endless life-and-death
struggle, such a vision left no room for any human goals that might

look beyond the struggle and strive to transcend it. Thus, the ideology was in the grip of a vicious circle requiring the obsessive repetition of the death-dealing struggle that had allowed the life-carrying group to prevail in the first place.

This ideology, however, could not be fully realized, because it misrepresented the operational environment in which it was put to work. It may have motivated many Germans to vote for the National Socialists, but never in numbers large enough to win an uncoerced election. The movement did not come to power electorally, only through the manipulations of a conservative clique, and it always required the use of force and violence to maintain its grip on society. It never set up a unitary Führer-state but produced instead a duplication of party organizations and government institutions and dispersed state power among competing and shifting coalitions of power holders. These arrangements served many interest groups in the context of an ever-expanding war effort, but they gave rise to serious tensions that might have erupted even if the war had been won.

The regime was able to rearm and to occupy Austria and Czechoslovakia without opposition, and it proved victorious in lightning strikes against a militarily weak Poland and a defeatist France. Meeting only sporadic resistance, it was largely unhindered in carrying out the Judeocide, but it also paid an economic and military price in assigning energies and resources to this ideological task. It misjudged on wholly ideological grounds the fighting will and capacity of the Western allies, and even more so that of the Soviet Union, against which it opened an all-out war in 1941. On April 30, 1945, Hitler shot himself in his underground headquarters; the next day the despised Soviet soldiers raised their flag over the gutted Reichstag building in Berlin.

Despite the bloody demise of National Socialism, there are disquieting signs that the "syndrome" of features that characterized it has survived. One reason for thinking so is that many nations and nation-states of the world are no more secure today than in the past. They are, if anything, weaker now than before World War II, with a weakness that bears some resemblance to the condition of Germany after its defeat in 1918. The rapid diffusion of international finance and commerce has strengthened industrial corporations and business organizations in their dealings with host governments. Governments are further destabilized by the growth of autonomous military-industrial cartels and commercial consortia that often find allies in government agencies and by a lack of coordination among the agencies themselves. In turn, controls exercised by such governments over their own societies and economies are frequently called into question by movements for regional autonomy and ethnic separateness. Such movements require ideologies that can define rights to membership, construct justificatory ontogenies for their cadres, and lay down criteria for denying participation and benefits to groups deemed unwelcome, unworthy, or deleterious.

Everywhere the exercise of public power is being challenged by rising claims for privatization, not only of property and service provision but also of means of violence. In many areas, armies are attempting to expand their economic and political influence, while paramilitary formations, private armies, and security forces proliferate. Not infrequently, such groups enter into connections with "mafias," able to employ extralegal force in operations that can range from supplying the drug trade to clearing people off land to make it available for alternative uses. All such violence-prone situations favor the emergence of armed entrepreneurs who attract followers and build group solidarity through quasi-military styles of cohesion, preparedness, and discipline. For such groups, the National Socialist syndrome continues to furnish a ready prototype of ideas and modes of action, to be copied wholesale or varied according to circumstance.

6

Coda

The three cases presented in this book revealed societies under increasing stress, facing a multiplicity of tensions posed by ecological, social, political, or psychological crises. In each case the response entailed the development of an ideology that Kroeber would have characterized as an "extreme expression." These ideologies, carried forward by elites, were fashioned out of preexisting cultural materials, but they are not to be understood as disembodied cultural schemata. They addressed the very character of power in society, specifically the power that structured the differentiation, mobilization, and deployment of social labor, and they rooted that power in the nature of the cosmos.

Kwakiutl society confronted the encroachment of a novel political-economic order that put relations of status and precedence under severe strain. The Tenochca wrestled with the great changes brought about by their rapid rise from a mercenary warrior band to control of a regional empire. National Socialist Germany emerged from the shambles of a lost war and the transvaluation of social relations wrought by political change and economic crisis. In the three instances, such challenges played a part in mobilizing groups for action. They also provided contexts and opportunities that propelled some social groups and segments to the fore while weakening and demobilizing others. Each of the cases showed culture being made and unmade (in Richard Fox's terms) as people engaged each other in diverse social, economic, and political arenas. Old ideas were re-phrased to fit different circumstances, and new ideas were presented as age-old truths. Culture is constructed in such encounters, but these are staged, prosecuted, and resolved through the exercise of power.

Structural Power and Ideology

Distinctive as these three cases are, they are yet ame-nable to an analysis that stresses how ideas intertwine with power around the pivotal relationships that govern social labor. In each case, that structural power engendered ideas that set up basic distinctions between the organizers of social labor and those so organized, be-tween those who could direct and initiate action to others and those who had to respond to these directives. The dominant mode of mo-bilizing social labor set the terms of structural power that allocated people to positions in society; the ideas that came to surround these terms furnished propositions about the differential qualifications or disqualifications of persons and groups and about the rationales underlying them.

Kwakiutl society before the advent of the Europeans and into the middle of the nineteenth century was dominated by what I have called the kin-ordered mode of mobilizing social labor (Wolf 1982, 88–99). By this term I mean not that the mode was based on kin-ship as such but that it employed metaphors of kinship to model so-cial relations. Kwakiutl society was divided into numayms, or houses, each headed and directed by a line of chiefs. Other members of the numaym occupied statuses defined by their genealogical distance from this line: closer kin were nobles, more distant kin commoners. The numayms also included unrelated commoners, who accepted temporary terms of service, and slaves, who were property obtained from elsewhere through war or trade. While chiefs engaged in hunt-ing and fishing, they were mainly organizers of ritual and political events; all others in the numaym sustained it with their labor.

Chiefship and its powers were surrounded by a cosmological ra-tionale which stipulated that the chiefs reenact the animal ancestor of the line and wield the privileges bestowed by him. Each time such a privilege was assumed, a redistributive event organized by the chief "fastened on" the name obtained and transferred vital forces to invited guests. Chiefs were also held responsible for maintaining the appropriate relations between humans and animals, and aspirants to the chiefship underwent an initiatory experience that enabled them to mediate on issues of life and death between spirits and the living.

Toward the end of the century, Kwakiutl society in general and the chiefs in particular confronted the increasing pressures of advancing capitalism. That new mode multiplied sources of wealth and diminished the chiefly grip on resources and labor. Simultaneously, epidemics reduced the number of legitimate heirs to chiefly titles, while the beneficiaries of new wealth obtained through the market could employ it to advance claims to positions. The resulting struggle produced a change in the nature of distributional events, from reenactments of primordial and reciprocal transfers of wealth and vital forces among constituted chiefs and their numayms to an ever more inflationary competition for privileges, precedence, and followings among both legitimate and newly rich aspirants to titles.

Aztec, or Tenochca, society was dominated by what I have characterized as a tributary mode of mobilizing social labor (1982, 79–88), in which a hereditary class of commoners sustained through their tribute a hereditary class of nobles. The lines of distinction between commoners and nobles came to be reinforced by sumptuary laws, although selected commoners could obtain certain noble privileges in recognition of unusual military prowess. Commoners and nobles were further distinguished from slaves, who were defined as such by criteria of social failure or transgression against the social order.

In the first quarter of the fifteenth century, this social ensemble fell into the hands of a military faction, which carried forward the Tenochca expansion and political consolidation. This group of leaders surrounded their newly gained power with the aura of an ambitious ideological program. Devising new versions of myth-histories and backing them with the construction of monumental art, the newcomers depicted themselves as heirs of ancient polities, as special devotees and beneficiaries of their god of conquest and plunder, and as executives of an "exemplary center" of the universe. After Motecuzoma I came to power in 1440, the process of sacralization of the ruler advanced apace, and the tlatoani became responsible for sustaining time and the sun within the new Tenochca epoch. Yet the new rulers could never be wholly certain of their claim to represent the true incumbents of Toltec rulership, and they remained ever anxious that their Fifth Sun might come to a sudden fiery end. Thus, political and economic policy combined with existential doubt to feed an ideology of world renewal, in which a salient role fell to human sacrifice.

Different as these cases may be, they exhibit a number of similarities. Kwakiutl chiefs and Tenochca royals both claimed rights to rule by ascribing their roles to the cosmological order of the world in general, and within that order to special links with the supernatural that set them off from the rest of humankind. In both instances the propositions that defined the cosmic order in these terms were probably produced during a long prior history. In the Tenochca case, we know that they derived from various Mesoamerican traditions in which intellectual specialists had the function of defining the special characteristics of elites and offering ideological rationales for rulership. These ideas were certainly long familiar to the populations concerned, thus furnishing a matrix of expectations into which the specific, ideologized myth-histories of the Tenochca could be inserted. In both the Kwakiutl and Tenochca examples, too, the larger cosmological orders were depicted as trophic hierarchies in which gods and spirits, humans, and animals and plants fed upon one another and in which the ruling elite was accorded a special role in managing the cosmic arrangements of predation and commensality.

In both cases ideology making relied heavily on the skills of rhetoric and oratory. Among the Kwakiutl the relevant cosmological and ideological texts were recited publicly by chiefs and members of their lineages holding appropriate rights, thus granting the stratum of title-holders a near-monopoly over the messages and channels of ideological communication. These oratorical acts did more than reiterate rights to privileges; in stressing the ontogeny of these privileges they placed the chiefs within a cosmology of the Kwakiutl world as a whole and fortified their possession of a distinctive "truth."

Oratory had a similar truth-defining role among the Tenochca. Scribes and other specialists propounded cosmological propositions and myth-histories with the aid of politically approved pictorial records. The king—"the speaker"—also delivered major hortatory orations in which he upheld the virtuous and castigated the evil and negligent. These moralizing discourses did not merely advertise norms of proper conduct, but they projected the hegemonic values that governed a whole cultural world; and the myth-histories were not so much narratives of actual events as allegorical accounts of the Tenochca past that enshrined a teleology for the future. Such discourses and narratives, coupled with ritual performances and with the symbolic emblems drawn from them, projected an "imagined" world in which the holders and wielders of power were assigned a strategic position.

The travails of the imagination in the service of power is even more evident in the case of National Socialist Germany. Prelude to that phenomenon was a century in which the Germanies underwent a convulsive transition from local artisanry to industrial capitalism and an abrupt political unification whereby multiple, socially distinctive local and regional entities were brought under the aegis of a militaristic and bureaucratic Prussia. The resulting dissonances incubated utopian aspirations for a spiritually and culturally unified Volk, aspirations that were further exacerbated by defeat in World War I, as well as by the economic and political dislocations under the republic that followed. National Socialist ideology drew many themes from this cumulation of turmoils, such as the concept of the people as the source of ultimate sovereignty, which was borrowed from the armamentarium of the French Revolution, notions of a plebeian and nationalist populism, and ideas that identified the advocates of equality, pacifism, utilitarianism, and internationalism with Germany's enemies within and without.

Although it called itself "socialist," the new regime did not alter the capitalist relations that had guided the country's mobilization of social labor throughout its forward thrust into industrial capitalism after the mid-nineteenth century (see Wolf 1982, 77–79). It abolished Parliament, broke the political and social power of labor organizations, and curtailed the free movement of workers. While maintaining the basic order of capitalist relations in the workings of the economy, the National Socialists subjected it to their "primacy of politics." Decisions regarding labor were now to be negotiated among power blocs, in which representatives of the Führer played strategic roles. At the same time, ideology was unleashed to rearm the national "will" and build an industrial machine for war.

As among the Kwakiutl and Tenochca, the ideology formulated to justify rulership built on a cosmology. It envisioned the world as Nature, a scenario in which human groups, subject to the same forces that operated in animal and plant communities, were ranged against one another in constant struggle. When this vision was combined with the "scientific" view that human types or "races" had distinct natural origins and different inborn potentialities, history could be reconceptualized as a struggle in Nature for predominance of the Aryan race. There was, however, no certainty that victory would always go to the fittest, who could be defeated by misfits through conspiracy and deceit. The ideology thus added another element. Drawing on old German lore as well as notions imported from abroad, it built into its myth-history a terrifying force of entropy and disintegration, identifiable as the Jew.

Victory therefore required a counterforce to destroy this demonic organism: the National Socialist party and movement led by the Führer. This would institute a new Volksgemeinschaft dedicated to "warding off the Jews" and purifying its blood through racial selection. Cleansing itself of any taints of biological and psychological weakness, it would become indomitable in the pursuit of war. National Socialist propaganda fused its ideological rhetoric with displays of warlike emblems and with shows of physical violence in mass rallies, marches, street fights, and beer-hall brawls. Collective violence, with its exhortations to soldierly masculinity and habitus, further knit together participants and prospective recruits. National Socialist ideology and "propaganda of the deed" fueled the cataclysmic project of conquest and destruction that was to follow.

These three cases serve as entry points into a discussion of ideology, but as historical manifestations they remain incommensurate. They do not conform to a common social type; nor do they furnish a sample of a range of ideologies characterized by a common denominator. In each instance, the regnant ideology had its roots in a distinctive prior cultural history. Moreover, the use of ideology in the three societies had profoundly different effects in the operational world.

In the Kwakiutl case a chiefly elite, defending itself against destabilizing forces, compensated through ritual and displays of art and performance for its loss of effective power. This greatly intensified the politics of renown, fought out through metaphors of antagonism, precedence, dominance, and war. These verbal and emblematic displays, however, were not matched by acts of warlike violence. In the Aztec case a faction of the noble class wove accounts of its ascendancy and ostensible mission into an already existing cosmology. That mission granted them dominance, which in turn entailed the obligation to sustain the gods through sacrifice. Tenochca rulership made possible an archaeologically measurable gain in horticultural intensification and widening markets, together with a marked rise in social and political complexity and control. These developments were predicated upon the working out of an ideology that made productivity and renewal dependent upon ritualized "transformative" violence.

National Socialist Germany sought to undo and avenge past defeats through concentrated ideological rearmament in the pursuit of war and conquest. Internally, society was to be recast around hierarchically organized bodies of warlike men, and the agents of national weakness were to be extirpated. Wars waged abroad were to underwrite extensive projects of domination and to reduce stipulated populations to helots. In the process, both internal mobilization and external war gained a self-reinforcing genocidal momentum that brutalized and murdered people by the millions and ended only with the collapse of the German war machine.

In the three cases ideology helped orient society to act within the field of its operations, yet it did so in different ways and within different structural contexts. The three ideologies differed in cultural form and logic, and formulated rationales for action within the distinctive circumstances of each. Most significantly, they were variable in their effects. Thus, specification of ideologies in cultural terms can only be a part of our task. We must also know how these cultural forms engage with the material resources and organizational arrangements of the world they try to affect or transform.

The Problem of Cosmology

In all three cases, the power of the controllers of social labor over those made subject to these controls was formulated as cosmological imperatives, which at once required the exercise of power and supported its execution. Power was thus made to depend not merely on "production" (the active interchange of humans with nature) and on "society" (the normatively governed interactions among humans) but also on relationships with imaginary elements and beings projected beyond tangible experience into metaphysical worlds.

This thrust into metaphysics is not easily accommodated by anthropological efforts to explain human doings as practical ways of obtaining practical results. This is so despite the fact that the transactions of people with imaginary beings are both observable and describable, in that people engage in behaviors they then talk about. We have sought not so much to engage the imaginary as to explain it away, reducing "the output of minds" to seemingly more basic substrates.

One way of explaining ideas has been to see them as outcomes of productive activity or social action; another way has been to treat them as epiphenomena of ecological processes. A more elaborate phrasing has been to link systems of ideas used to classify aspects of the world to patterns of social and political organization, either as direct effects of social arrangements or as related to them in a functional fit. Explaining these imaginings as variables in ecological or social systems can indeed elucidate their functions, but it does not speak either to how ecology and society are articulated with imaginary entities or to the characteristics of the imaginings themselves.

Alternatively, imaginary beings and relationships could be ascribed to the firing of neurons in the human nervous system and thus collapsed into the psychophysics of the brain. Even Claude Lévi-Strauss, often thought of as the quintessential idealist, locates the faculty of human minds for sorting phenomena through "binary opposition" in the brain (1962, 130, 263–64), thus anchoring the distinction between making and imagining things in the biophysically constituted mind. That creatural organ receives inputs from nature, yet grinds out and permutates distinctions that are not found in nature but are "cultural." It is indeed conceivable that common neuropsychological structures underlie concept formation in all humans, but we do not yet understand how such proclivities lead to concepts and lead from particular concepts to ideas that explicate what the world is about. Such studies as Lévi-Strauss's "Mythologiques" and Eva Hunt's analysis of a Mesoamerican hummingbird myth show how complex combinatory sets of ideas can become. They also show how useful structuralist methods can be in laying out the relevant categories and classifications and in elucidating how these combine to generate veritable "memory-palaces" of knowledge. Yet such architectural organization constitutes only one aspect of that knowledge; an equally important aspect bears on the question of what all this activity is *about*—a question not about structure but about content.

This issue was addressed in the work of the French linguist and Sanskritist Émile Benveniste (1971). Benveniste insisted that a semiotics of signs, focused on how significance was created by distinguishing the features of signs from each other, was not the same thing as a semantics of the sentence. While a semiotics of signs makes use of entities—phonemes, morphemes, syntactic forms—within linguistic systems, a semantics of sentences allows a linguistic system to refer to a state of affairs outside language. It affirms that something is the case about the world, and therefore it possesses a referent. This point, missing in Lévi-Strauss's structuralism, raises questions about what these complex constructions of cultural signs point to, what they entail, what kind of world they envisage, and who is setting up these valuations for whom and under what circumstances.

Some of these referents will be imaginary, but one can adopt a naturalistic perspective and note that human beings do in fact imagine phantasmagoric beings of all kinds, from the wild dzonokwa woman of the Kwakiutl woods to aliens from outer space. Humans also maintain vast storehouses of objects to which they ascribe imaginary powers—slivers of the holy cross, prayer wheels, teeth of Buddha. If these imagined beings and objects do not respond to criteria of verification or falsification, they are nevertheless real in their consequences, and both the terms in which they are formulated and their consequences are amenable to inquiry. Thus, the French historian Georges Duby (1980) studied the imaginary medieval European tripartite division of society and cosmos into warriors, priests, and peasants and demonstrated how this model was manipulated differently by different classes over time. Similarly, the preceding chapters have depicted the role played by imaginary worlds in social struggles and transformations. Combining a historical perspective with social and cultural analysis of who is talking about what to whom allows us to take discourse seriously, at the same time going beyond the supposition that discourse is only a matter of literary form and genre. Discourse has its reasons; it also has consequences.

The ideologies in the three cases envision and project such imaginary worlds. Each one centers upon key predicates, axiomatic conditions asserted to be true of that world. The Kwakiutl assigned transhuman values to certain kinds of objects and made their distribution and exchange a major theme of their lives. Circulation of these objects was understood to govern the exchanges of vital powers between humans and animals, and among groups of humans. Privileges and agency in circulating the objects were assigned to chiefs and their heirs; these privileges entailed the obligation to enact the "strict law that bids us dance" (Masco 1995, 41). The Tenochca imagined that they owed life to the gods and that war and sacrifice were necessary to requite the debts thus incurred. Tenochca royals and nobility were accorded the functions of carrying on sacred war and of immolating chosen victims to feed the gods and maintain the cyclical rhythms of the world. For the National Socialists, the struggle for survival through war was the raison d'être of existence. To fight that war required strength, which demanded that the people foster and conserve the hereditary endowment of their Aryan forebears. Therefore, the Führer, his party cadres, and his soldiers saw themselves as carrying out the law of nature: to harden the nation and to destroy the Jew, the primordial source of its debility.

It is often productive to deal with such foundational ideas in terms of their functions in society. They can be shown to legitimate and justify forms of rulership. They proclaim ideals to follow, define standards of reward, and exalt those able to live up to them. They announce that acting in ideal ways will enhance virtue and allow claimants to virtue to assert that they have lived up to the ideals. They underwrite and fortify the motivations of the ruling cadre. At the same time, these functions anchor rulership in a cultural structure of imaginings, which is characterized by forms that are not directly explicable in functionalist terms. These imaginings postulate cosmologies; cosmologies, in turn, articulate with ideologies that assign to the wielders of power the role of mediators or executors on behalf of larger cosmic forces and grant them "natural" rights to dominate society as delegates of the cosmic order. Representing that order, these cosmic delegates also enact it in their own lives.

Indeed, the functionalist program in the history of anthropology was never meant to engage such imaginings. It was itself a reaction against an older anthropology, best represented by James Frazer. That prefunctionalist anthropology interpreted magic and rituals as efforts to enhance reproduction and fertility, efforts supposedly based on the faulty premises of "associative thinking," said to be still characteristic of Primitive Man. Unfortunately, this Frazerian anthropology still resonates for all the wrong reasons in present-day literary studies and in efforts to visualize the mental life of Early Man. Properly, the functionalists wanted no part of such evolutionary reconstructions, which for them were doubly "metaphysical": in imagining a past Age of Magic and in tracing magic and ritual to primitive forms of thought. We would not want to return to such questionable notions about the evolution of mind, but we can reread this work as attempts to lay out and explicate recurrent schemata of human imaginings. What these predecessors saw as modes of primitive thought, we can reinterpret as the beginnings of a comparative phenomenology of human dealings with the world. We are also in a better position than were they to connect these schemata with social practices and the exercise of power. In that sense we may welcome the recent renewed interest in half-forgotten figures like James Frazer, Arthur Hocart, Robert Hertz, and Arnold Van Gennep, not because they can help us resurrect an earlier humanity but because they engaged the human capacity to construct imaginary worlds.

Taking a different perspective on foundational ideas, Roy Rappaport has described them as "ultimate sacred propositions," which have special properties (1979). Following the historian R. G. Collingwood, who argued that knowledge was grounded in "absolute presuppositions" that could neither be verified nor falsified (1940), Rappaport added that they are "cryptic," "ambiguous," and even "without sense." Precisely because of these qualities, moreover, they can be sacralized and made to underwrite the "understandings in accordance to which people conduct their lives" (Rappaport 1979, 119). Such propositions define the nature of entities and beings in the world (spirits, ancestors, gods) and set up rules for human behavior toward them. Paradoxically, "the unfalsifiable yields the unquestionable, which transforms the dubious, the arbitrary and the conventional into the correct, the necessary, and the natural" (p. 217).

This paradox is provocative, but it raises further questions. As an ecological anthropologist, Rappaport had a special interest in how living systems become adaptive and persist as adaptations. Searching out what makes structures adaptive, he argued that it is precisely the meaninglessness of ultimate sacred propositions that contributes most powerfully to homeostasis and adaptive persistence. For me, however, Rappaport's paradox suggests a different possibility: that the structural power at work in human systems can embed itself in such ineffable and cryptic suppositions and draw on them to sanctify and defend its rule. Hence, it will also come to depend on them.

It seems to me unlikely that ultimate sacred propositions remain in place by virtue of their own ineffable qualities. It is more probable that their very ambiguity will invite challenges and threaten destabilization, unless they can be made secure through adequate means of domination. Such means usually combine outright force with hegemonic powers of persuasion. Since basic propositions can be "ultimate" both in a temporal and logical sense, power is enhanced by rooting it in primordial cosmological arrangements. In the cases examined, a great part of the work of ideology is to confound origins and logical implications: to locate prototypical happenings at the beginning of the world and then make them into fundamental premises to which all thought and discourse should be referred. Sacralizing the basic suppositions by ascribing them to transhuman forces, in turn, imparts to their spokesmen a special aura of authority and enhances the efficacy of their words and ritual performance. In analogy with Austin's analysis of "how things are done with words" (1962), one might speak of such discourses and performances as "perlocutionary" or "performative," producing perlocutionary and performative truths.

Culture and Power

We return now to a consideration of culture and of the way power is implicated in cultural ideas. I have characterized the beginnings of anthropology as part of a wider orchestration of claims against the Enlightenment vision of the rule of universal reason. These diverse counterclaims were incorporated into a concept of culture that emphasized the particularities of different peoples, each with its separate history and language and with distinctive qualities of mind that shaped its authentic being. The outcome was a long and contentious discourse between universalizers and particularists, and the opposition of universalist claims and particularistic counterclaims marked anthropology thereafter, whatever its current paradigms. Anthropologists became more tentative in making generalizations and critical of any "self-evident truths." Whatever might be said to be true of humans everywhere and at all times had to be demonstrated rather than assumed. It became important to hold up any assertion about a panhuman psychology, sociology, economics, or history against the great variety of human conditions uncovered in anthropological fieldwork, to challenge overenthusiastic generalizers at every turn.

Yet we can see now that the counterposition of "civilization" based on Reason as a hallmark of all mankind and culture as the property of particular peoples in particular times and places poses a false opposition. If the party of civilization and Reason speaks for humanity in general, as often as not that language is part of the cultural politics of a stratum hoping to break down barriers to social and political advancement or seeking to open markets and render them more inclusive. The first advocates of such claims to represent universal humanity came out of the bourgeoisie—the Third Estate, between aristocrats and peasants—a stratum that expanded rapidly as European populations grew and became urbanized, as markets spread, and as professional positions multiplied in private and government sectors. In the eighteenth century the bourgeoisie "began to make demands and formulate ideals appropriate to their talents, ambitions, efficiency, and competitive individualism—ideals formulated in the language of 'humanity' and 'human rights'" (Solomon 1979, 8). This language allowed its users to advocate their own interests, while fortifying them with a moral righteousness about their proclaimed "self-evident truths." They also spun out numerous proposals that promised the True, Good, and Beautiful if only their principles were adopted, generating at the same time a utopian vision of the West as the standard-bearer of human progress. A distinctive place in that utopia was granted to those who at any time claimed to represent the party of "progress" and to speak for a universal order based on Reason and rational governance by the sovereign state. Yet this utopia entailed also a place for its opposite—what Michel-Rolph Trouillot has called "the savage slot" (1991)—the state of Nature outside the governance of Reason.

Against such rhetoric and the claims and cosmological visions implied in it, the opponents of the expanding Third Estate invoked ancient custom and rights, authenticity, hallowed truth, tradition, and faith. In their hands "folklore" and "custom" became "culture," meaning not just another set of practices and discourses but an organic whole imbued by a common spirit. This formulation allowed its proponents to become spokesmen for that organic and spiritual unity and to challenge those at home and abroad who advocated universal progress and free advancement. In the process they made themselves defenders of culture against the onslaught of civilization, denying to the universalizers anything like culture of their own. The universalizers, in turn, wished to dissociate themselves from an outdated and nonprogressive "culture" and adopted instead styles of dress and comportment, educational innovations, reading habits, and other patterns of behavior and thought represented as in the realm of universal Reason.

Clearly this politically argumentative version of culture cannot serve our comparative anthropology, and if we want to continue to use the concept we must transform it. There are indeed good reasons for keeping a notion like culture, precisely because it refers to a level of human practices and discourses covered neither by progressive universalism nor by retrograde parochialism.

There are anthropologists who would prefer to jettison the idea of culture entirely. If humans are biological creatures, animals like other animals, they argue, we should be able to understand and analyze them the way we do other animal species. This perspective has been used, for instance, in studies of ecosystems that define the energy exchanges or competition of human populations, anchored in their ecological niches, with other organisms in the same operational environment. Such approaches may be enlightening, if only because they remind us of the extent to which humans share a habitat with other kinds of creatures, whether bacteria, rodents, or our barnyard friends. Yet reduction to biology or ecology misses the key dimension that distinguishes human adaptations (and human troubles) from those of other animals—the ability to generate regular forms of behavior by making and manipulating signs that allow people to imagine the worlds they thus create.

Humans share some of the capacities that underlie this ability with other animals, such as our chimpanzee and bonobo cousins, but its full human orchestration is far more complex and powerful than theirs. It allows us to model experience in the mind, thus freeing us of much of the travail of trial and error. We can set up generalizing concepts and abstract types in our minds to explore alternative courses of behaving. At the same time, however, this capacity for abstraction is part of our ability to name and invoke both physically proximate objects and conceptually intangible entities. That quintessential human capability is double-edged. It allows us to map the world and plan our engagements with it, but it also enables us to construct figments in our minds. We gain greater control of our operational environment, but we also increase the risk of having to deal with imaginary entities that can inflame our passions or scare us out of our wits.

Furthermore, we need a concept like "culture" because we still lack a convincing way to understand how the human mind can produce such great socially patterned variability in "minding." Psychobiological inquiries have substantially enlarged our understanding of human nervous systems, but they have not yet achieved a consensus on how nervous systems manage perception, cognition, and language, even less on how they permit such a luxuriant variability of responses both on the collective and on the individual level. This capacity to vary thought and behavior is at the root of the human ability to bring forth new cultural forms and to speak of things never spoken of before; it underwrites human self-organization and creativity. Specifically, we are still unable to account psychobiologically either for metaphors and metonyms or for the ability—crucial to culture—to draw together different systems of thought and action by extending and multiplying sign-dependent connotations across different domains.

The concept of culture remains serviceable as we move from thinking about what is generically human to the specific practices and understandings that people devise and deploy to deal with their circumstances. It is precisely the shapeless, all-encompassing quality of the concept that allows us to draw together—synoptically and synthetically—material relations to the world, societal organization, and configurations of ideas. Using "culture," therefore, we can bring together what might otherwise be kept separate. People act materially upon the world and produce changes in it; these changes then affect their ability to act in the future. At the same time, they make and use signs that guide their actions upon the world and upon each other. In the process they deploy labor and understandings and cope with power that both directs that labor and informs those understandings. Then, when action changes both the world and people's relationships to one another, they must reappraise the relations of power and the propositions that their signs have made possible. These activities can be separated out analytically; but in enacting real life people engage and activate bodies and minds as whole persons. If we want to understand how humans seek stability or organize themselves to manage change, we need a concept that allows us to capture patterned social flow in its multiple interdependent dimensions and to assess how idea-dependent power steers these flows over time. "Culture" is such a concept.

Yet to this end, we must both make culture more flexible and open-ended and connect it with power. Efforts to strip culture of the attributes of totality and homogeneity have been under way in anthropology for some decades, as have efforts to make more of its distributive character—namely, the variation of cultural phenomena among genders and generations, status groups and classes—and to understand how this variation is coordinated. Anthropology is also rich in studies that demonstrate what Robert Lowie called "generalizations of limited validity" (1948, 53), showing how people organize themselves for different kinds of work, engage in reciprocity and exchange, or employ techniques to call up the spirits; and such studies invite the question of how patterned behavior in one domain bears upon that in another. Once heterogeneity and variation are recognized, along with the awareness that the entities described in those terms are likely to intertwine in wider fields of involvement, the question appropriately becomes who and what holds it together—in Anthony Wallace's terms, how that diversity is organized (1970,

23–24). Immediately, then, we must ask who and what is organized, by what kinds of imperatives, on what level. If organization has no central core—no motivating Hegelian spirit, no economy "in the last instance," or Mother Nature in the guise of the environment—how are we to understand the manner in which organizing imperatives are orchestrated?

I believe that we can approach these questions by bringing together a concept of culture with structural power. By calling attention to the nexus that defines and governs the deployment of social labor, the notion of structural power points to how people are drawn into articulation within the social ensemble. That needs to be addressed before further questions can be asked about specific forms of tactical power used by individuals and groups to gain resources or advantages over others. I have also argued that a concept of structural power leads to the issue of how the distinctions that segment a population are rendered manifest. The case material suggests that these distinctions are defined and anchored in specific cosmologies that represent them as attributes of the order of things, in both the temporal and the logical sense. Aspects of cosmology are further extended and elaborated into ideologies that explain and justify the aspirations of particular claimants to power over society.

What makes people receptive to such power-laden ideas? It is sometimes assumed that humans act to maximize the complexity and orderliness of their experience (Wallace 1970, 169), but this generalization needs to be treated with caution. The readiness of many people to live with contradictions, as well as the proclivity of most to pay little heed to internal cognitive coherence, suggests that the installation of a vision of cosmic order is more likely to be an imperative for those trying to organize power than the reflection of a general striving for cognitive consistency. This becomes all the more likely when we recall Rappaport's characterization of ultimate sacred propositions as ambiguous, mystifying, and cryptic and when we remember that what is at stake in the establishment of a cosmology is the propagation of "perlocutionary truths" that do not maximize the organization of minds so much as move them in a certain direction.

Cosmologies and ideologies do, however, exhibit an ability to connect questions of power with the existential concerns of everyday life. The ideologies in all three cases focused explicitly on matters of life and death, and they imparted to the holders of structural power a superhuman aura of involvement with them. The wielders of power assumed the guise of extraordinary beings whose intimacy with the sources of vitality enabled them to marshal the forces of growth and destruction that govern society. The issues posed by ideology have had too little attention in anthropology since the advent of functionalism and structuralism. Yet they deal with what a society or culture is *about*. At this millennial transition, the human capacity to envision imaginary worlds seems to be shifting into high gear. For anthropologists and others, greater concern with how ideas and power converge seems eminently warranted.

Notes

Notes to Chapter 3

1. Among the studies attempting to historicize the Kwakiutl that I have benefited from are: Joyce Wike on "The Effect of the Maritime Fur Trade on Northwest Coast Society," an innovative 1947 doctoral thesis; Helen Codere on changes in Kwakiutl potlatching and warfare from 1792 to 1930 (1950, 1961); Vernon Kobrinsky on the changes in Kwakiutl culture as evidence of class struggle (1975); Rolf Knight's account of native Indian labor in British Columbia, 1858–1930 (1978); and Joseph Masco's examination of the effects of the European colonial dynamic on Kwakiutl social organization, ritual, and cosmology (1995). In discussing cosmology I have drawn on the work of Irving Goldman (1975), Stanley Walens (1981), and the linguistically informed study of Kwakiutl "myth-history" by Judith Berman (1991). Michael E. Harkin (1990, 1996, 1997) has explored the culture of the Heiltsuk, neighbors of the Kwawaka'wakw to the north and a significant source of the Kwakiutl cultural repertoire.

2. The figure is based on a 1983 census covering the fifteen bands, including residents on and off the reserves (Webster 1990, 387).

3. I use the term "myth-history" to refer to cultural texts that combine narratives of how the foundations of human existence were laid down and reaffirmed with accounts of the flow of events in the lives of individual and groups. The Kwakiutl called such texts *nuyam,* usually translated as "myth, history" (Berman 1991, 117). Emiko Ohnuki-Tierney used "myth-history" for accounts written at the behest of the seventh-century Japanese emperor to establish his divine origin and the introduction of rice by his ancestral goddess (1993). I adopt the term for more general application.

4. Berman (1991, 62) uses *namimut* (sing.), *natlanamimut* (pl.); Gold-

man (1975) employs *numema;* Rohner and Rohner (1970), who worked on Gilford Island, use *numina* (sing.), *numinot* (pl.). Since Boas's terminology is widely reproduced in the extant literature, I will follow Wilson Duff (1964), who used *numaym* (sing.) and anglicized the plural as *numayms*.

5. Oddly, while George Hunt had recorded the special term *naenxwa* for "mask" and translated it as "animal skin coverings," Boas rendered it simply as "blankets" (Goldman 1975, 125).

6. This discussion owes much to Goldman (1975) and Walens (1981). In referring to "vital forces," however, I sidestep the problems posed by their use of the term "souls," in part because Boas states that "it is nowhere said that the soul is life" (1966, 169). I note that Raymond Lenoir (1924) recognized a common supernatural referent in Kwakiutl marriages, war making, and potlatches and called it "social mana." This accentuates the common symbolic operator in these phenomena but draws an analogy to a Polynesian concept that has been contested in its own right. I thus follow Goldman when he says that "we see properties rather as one expression of vital force moving in concert with names, crests, and powers, which represent still another set of vital forces" (1975, 126).

Notes to Chapter 4

1. Sahagún's Mexican encyclopedia, generally known as the *Historia general*, went through several stages of writing, embodied successively in the *Primeros memoriales* (abbreviated here as PM), the *Madrid Codices* (MC), and the *Florentine Codex* (FC). These manuscripts differ somewhat in content, in the Nahuatl texts, and in the Spanish translations that correspond to them. The availability of the Nahuatl texts provided by Sahagún's informants offers an important check on the Spanish versions. Translations differ in the extent to which they take account of the polysynthetic character of Nahuatl and of its abundant use of metaphors and parallelisms. I have drawn primarily on the translation of the Florentine Codex by Arthur J. O. Anderson and Charles Dibble, indicated by the date of publication (1950–1969) and the number of the Book in the Codex; page references correspond to this edition. I have also occasionally referred to translations by Miguel León-Portilla, Leonhard Schultze-Jena, and Theda Sullivan, who were especially attentive to Nahuatl metaphors.

2. Since I became involved in Mesoamerican studies in 1951, my sources for this case have grown to be far more extensive than I can list. I refer here to the works and influences that have especially guided my thinking in connection with the present project.

I was fortunate to find my way into this field when ecological and political-economic perspectives were transforming Mexican archaeology and ethnology. My education during this time owes a great deal to Pedro Armillas, Pedro Carrasco, Angel Palerm, and William Sanders. The book by

Sanders and Price, *Mesoamerica* (1968), remains a milestone for me. The volumes edited by Pedro Carrasco and Johanna Broda on social stratification in Mesoamerica (1976) and on economics, politics, and ideology (1978); Ross Hassig's studies of trade and tribute (1985) and war (1988); and Brigitte Boehm de Lameiras's work on pre-Hispanic state formation (1986) have proved particularly valuable.

Eva Hunt's *The Transformation of the Hummingbird* (1977) and Gary Gossen's collection of essays on Mesoamerican ideas (1986) made me aware of the insights available through native sources and Nahuatl studies. A landmark study using Nahuatl is Louise M. Burkhart's analysis of Nahua-Christian moral dialogue, *The Slippery Earth* (1989). In approaching Aztec ideology I learned much from Alfredo López Austin (especially 1980, 1989, 1990), Mario Erdheim's *Prestige und Kulturwandel* (1973), and Rudolf van Zantwijk's *The Aztec Arrangement* (1985). The excavations of the Great Temple of Tenochtitlan under the direction of Eduardo Matos Moctezuma have yielded a wealth of archaeologically based information and interpretation, including *The Aztec Templo Mayor,* edited by Elizabeth Hill Boone (1987) and the book by Johanna Broda, Davíd Carrasco, and Eduardo Matos Moctezuma, *The Great Temple of Tenochtitlan* (1987). That work has drawn on art historians such as Cecelia Klein (in Boone 1987) and Emily Umberger (1987, 1996). I have also benefited from reading Kay Almere Read on Mexica-Tenochca concepts of time and sacrifice (1991).

3. In the extant painted codices, as well as in Nahuatl and Spanish annals, the Tenochca at this time in history are often represented as "Chichimecs," primordial hunters and gatherers, who lived in caves, dressed in animal skins, made use of the bow and arrow, and cooked up snakes for supper over open fires. There has been a general temptation to take this depiction literally. The ancestors of the Tenochca, like other Nahua-speaking groups, may indeed have been mobile food gatherers and desert cultivators when they appeared on the northern frontiers of Mesoamerica, but their representations in myth-histories are often metaphorical and do not portray empirical reality. Nahua-speaking Mesoamericans used the term "Chichimec" to designate populations of quite varied cultural and linguistic backgrounds living in the northern frontier zones of the area. These groups shared only the negative attribute of having not yet become acculturated to the patterns of life in the "Toltec" city-states, much as Greeks called "barbarian" any group that did not speak Greek and was not fully used to the urban lifeways of Mediterranean civilization. Actually, Chichimec groups exhibited a wide range of accommodations to Toltec institutions, ranging from near-complete symbiosis to refusals to acculturate or integrate.

This contrast between "Toltecs" and "Chichimecs" gave rise to further metaphorical connotations that varied contextually. Myth may have used the metaphor of alternation between night and day to depict the arrival of the Tenochca on the stage of history as a phase of political change, from the glories of the sun-imbued Toltec polity through the darkness of Toltec disintegration to the renewed rise of the sun under Tenochca hegemony (Grau-lich 1981a, 1981b, 1983, 1984). Chichimec-hood was sometimes stressed proudly as evidence of connection with primordial energies or warrior de-scent and at other times used negatively to depict defeated enemies, with the victors underlining their claims to rulership by donning Toltec apparel and attributes. Appearing in Toltec garb signified victory and domination; wearing "Chichimec" garments woven from maguey fiber denoted defeat and humiliation. Identification as Toltec could also serve to draw a distinc-tion between the landowning and governing class of nobles and the Chichimecs, this time identified with the subject population of commoners (Umberger 1996, 101–6). Such metaphoric use of the terms also appears in postconquest documents of the sixteenth century from Nahuatl-speaking towns in Central Mexico. These documents conflate the time before the conquest and before Christianity with the Chichimec "original general nonsedentary stage of existence" and associate postconquest times with sedentism, rule by the Spanish king, and Catholic conversion (Lockhart 1982, 381–82). In the seventeenth-century Nahuatl texts of Hernando Ruíz de Alarcón's *Treatise on Heathen Superstitions* "the word *Chichimec* is a metaphor for any of several dangerous or harmful things" (1984, 222).

4. This document, written in both Nahuatl and Spanish, is entitled *Coloquios y Doctrina Christiana*. It was long thought to be lost until it was recovered from the Vatican archives in 1927 (Lehman 1949). The book pre-sents in dialogue form the discussions held shortly after the Spanish con-quest between the high priests of Tenochtitlan and the twelve Franciscan friars first sent to convert the natives. Presenting the opposing views on the nature of religion held by the contending parties, it ostensibly offers the foundational rationales of the Tenochca interlocutors in their own words. However, the textual base of the document apparently consisted of notes written in Spanish by Sahagún in 1525 or 1526, with the full and elaborated text now extant apparently not composed until some thirty-five years later, in the 1560s. The Spanish text may well have been written by Sahagún him-self; the Nahuatl text, rendered in classical literary Nahuatl, was, as Sahagún writes, composed with the assistance of "four very adept elders instructed in their language and in all their antiquities" (in Dibble 1974, 229). Editor-ial work may also have shaped the document to enhance its dramatic ap-peal; the historian James Lockhart has appropriately said that it puts "one in mind of the Nahuatl religious plays intended for performance before an audience" (1992, 205). Thus, the text may offer a key, perhaps an important one, to clarifying the understandings that motivated this way of life; but it is a key to be used with caution. (See also Mignolo 1995, 96–122.)

5. The term *ixiptla* presents problems of translation and also of recon-ceptualization. It is composed of two morphemes, *ixtli* and *xip*. In Nahuatl *ixtli* means "face, surface" and, by extension, also the "eye" (Karttunen 1992, 121). *Xip* is an element in many compounds and stands for "peeling, shaving, flaying"; *xipehua* is a transitive verb that means "to flay, peel, hull

something"; *xipetzoa* is "to strip, to take off clothing"; *xipintli* is the male foreskin. Sahagún translates *ixiptla* as "representative"; Molina has *ixiptlayotia,* "to stand in for someone," and also "to make something in one's image." Such a "representative" or "stand-in" did not always have to be human. People formed images of the gods out of amaranth dough (Sahagún 1950–1969, 1: 22), shaped as mountains with gourd-seed teeth and black-bean eyes, and ate them ceremonially; or a day-sign could be represented by an ixiptla, an image named after it that could receive offerings (Clendinnen 1991, 251). Nor did all human ixiptlas die a sacrificial death. The high priests who impersonated gods at Tlacaxipeualiztli, the Flaying of Men, were called *ixiptlas,* "impersonators, the proxies, the lieutenants, the delegates of the gods." The term was also applied to a king's son when his father died or to royal emissaries (Sullivan 1994, 209).

6. Johanna Broda believes that Durán's figure on captives sacrificed in 1487 "is not a real number but denotes the expression of an unlimited quantity according to the vigesimal system" (1987b, 66). Zantwijk thinks that it represents either the error of a scribe or a form of Tenochca exaggeration (1988, 12–13). The Codex Telleriano Remensis puts the number at 20,000; the Codex Mexicanus, at 320. Tezozómoc puts the number of skulls placed in the skull rack (*tzompantli*) during the entire period from the mid-fourteenth century to 1520 at 62,000. There were, however, several skulls racks in the city, and after Ahuizotl's dedicatory ceremonies prisoners were still being sacrificed at the temple for foreign gods and in the armories (Durán and Sahagún, in Hassig 1988, 121).

Notes to Chapter 5

1. On Mühlmann's political course, see Hauschild 1987.

2. This point came clear to me from reading the German refugee anthropologist Paul Kosok's *Modern Germany: A Study of Conflicting Loyalties* (1933); Mack Walker's *German Home Towns* (1971); and Norbert Elias's *Studien über die Deutschen* (1989). Any inquiry into the history of ideas and ideology in Germany must also draw on George L. Mosse's work on the development of political symbolism in Germany (1975, 1981), as well as Fritz Stern's account of the making of Germanic ideology (1974).

3. Several reassessments of knowledge about the Reich have been useful to me, including Ayçoberry (1981), Hiden and Farquharson (1983), Maier (1988), Kershaw (1989), and Childers and Caplan (1993). Among the growing body of writings on the destruction of European Jewry I found most helpful *The Holocaust in History* by the Canadian historian Michael Marrus (1987), as well as Omer Bartov's *Murder in Our Midst* (1996). The ethical considerations surrounding the mass killings unleashed by Germany's eruption into Eastern Europe have been addressed by Haas (1988) and Langer (1995).

4. Paradoxically, this model of a war economy had been pioneered and carried through by Walter Rathenau, the "Jewish swine" assassinated in 1921 by right-wingers who thought he was one of the elders directing the Jewish conspiracy to control the world (Cohn 1996, 161). Even more paradoxically, it also served as a model for a centralized *Planwirtschaft* for socialists in both Germany and Russia and influenced the development of Soviet planning (Smolinski 1967).

5. Letter to then Colonel Walther von Reichenau, December 4, 1932, quoted in Noakes and Pridham 1995, 622.

6. The quotation is from Reichsführer for Women Scholtz-Klink (in Fest 1970, 268).

7. The German verb for "decomposing," *zersetzen,* was extended from earlier usages in mining and chemistry to describe the supposed proclivity of Jews to decompose everything that was heartfelt and holy to people, to kill authentic emotions by decomposing them through analysis (Schäfer 1962).

8. Hermann Rauschning, until his resignation NS President of the Senate in Danzig, told Hitler that the *Protocols* were a forgery and reports that Hitler "did not care two straws, he said, whether the story was historically true. If it was not, its intrinsic truth was all the more convincing to him" (Rauschning 1940, 238). The Volkish parliamentarian, and later National Socialist, Count Ernst zu Reventlow admitted in 1940 that he thought the document was "a pretty clumsy hoax" but "called it genuine, because this seemed to me to answer the purpose best at that time" (in Cohn 1996, 155).

9. Otto Bräutigam, head of the political department of the Ostministerium, December 18, 1941 (in Noakes and Pridham 1995, 1097–98).

10. German Chief of Staff (1938–1942) Franz Halder, war diary entry for March 30, 1941 (1962–1964, 2: 336–37).

11. This project to decapitate the Soviet elite had a precedent in the execution of 16,000–20,000 Poles following the invasion of Poland. These measures had been planned before the onset of war with the intention of annihilating the Polish elite (Browning 1993, 213, 227–28).

References

General

Aarsleff, Hans. 1974. "The Tradition of Condillac: The Problem of the Origin of Language in the Eighteenth Century and the Debate in the Berlin Academy before Herder," in Dell Hymes, ed., Studies in the History of Linguistics: Traditions and Paradigms, 93–156. Bloomington: Indiana University Press.

———. 1982. From Locke to Saussure: Essays on the Study of Language and Intellectual History. Minneapolis: University of Minnesota Press.

Allen, N. J. 1985. "The Category of the Person: A Rereading of Mauss's Last Essay," in Michael Carrithers, Steven Collins, and Steven Lukes, eds., The Category of the Person: Anthropology, Philosophy, History, 26–45. Cambridge: Cambridge University Press.

Althusser, Louis. 1971. Lenin and Philosophy and Other Essays. London: New Left Books.

Althusser, Louis, and Étienne Balibar. 1970. Reading Capital. New York: Pantheon Books.

Arato, Andrew. 1978. "Introduction," in Andrew Arato and Eike Gebhardt, eds., The Essential Frankfurt School Reader, pt. 2: 185–219. New York: Urizen Books.

Aswad, Barbara C. 1970. "Social and Ecological Aspects in the Formation of Islam," in Louise E. Sweet, ed., Peoples and Cultures of the Middle East, 1: 53–73. Garden City, N.Y.: Natural History Press.

Austin, J. L. 1962. How to Do Things with Words. Oxford: Oxford University Press.

———. 1976. How to Do Things with Words, 2d ed., edited by J. O. Urmson and Marisa Shisá. Oxford: Oxford University Press.

Balibar, Étienne. 1988. "The Vacillation of Ideology," in Cary Nelson and Lawrence Grossberg, eds., Marxism and the Interpretation of Culture, 159–209. Urbana: University of Illinois Press.

Barth, Hans. 1974. Wahrheit und Ideologie. Frankfurt on the Main: Suhrkamp.

Bell, Catherine. 1992. Ritual Theory, Ritual Practice. New York and Oxford: Oxford University Press.

Benedict, Ruth. 1934. Patterns of Culture. New York: Mentor Books.

Benveniste, Émile. 1971. Problems in General Linguistics, translated by Mary Elizabeth Meek. Miami Linguistics Series 8. Coral Gables, Fla.: University of Miami Press.

Berlin, Isaiah. 1982. Against the Current: Essays in the History of Ideas. London: Penguin Books.

———. 1990. "Joseph de Maistre and the Origins of Fascism," New York Review of Books 37 (14): 57–64.

Bloch, Ernst. 1962 [1935]. Erbschaft dieser Zeit. Frankfurt: Suhrkamp.

Bloch, Maurice. 1974. "Symbols, Song, Dance and Features of Articulation," European Journal of Sociology 15: 55–81.

———. 1977. "The Past and the Present in the Present," Man 12: 278–92.

Bonte, Pierre. 1981. "Marxist Anthropology and Anthropological Analysis: The Study of Nomadic Pastoralist Societies," in Joel S. Kahn and Josep R. Llobera, eds., The Anthropology of Pre-Capitalist Societies, 22–56. Atlantic Highlands, N.J.: Humanities Press.

Bottomore, Tom. 1983. "Class," in Tom Bottomore, ed., A Dictionary of Marxist Thought, 74–78. Cambridge, Mass.: Harvard University Press.

Bourdieu, Pierre. 1989. La noblesse d'état: Grands corps et grands écoles. Paris: Éditions de Minuit.

Bourdieu, Pierre, and Loïc J. D. Wacquant. 1992. An Invitation to Reflexive Sociology. Chicago: University of Chicago Press.

Bramson, Leon. 1961. The Political Context of Sociology. Princeton, N.J.: Princeton University Press.

Bunzl, Matti. 1996. "Franz Boas and the Humboldtian Tradition: From Volksgeist and Nationalcharakter to an Anthropological Concept of Culture," in George W. Stocking Jr., ed., Volksgeist as Method and Ethic: Essays on Boasian Ethnography and the German Anthropological Tradition, 17–78. History of Anthropology 8. Madison: University of Wisconsin Press.

Chomsky, Noam. 1964. "Current Issues in Linguistic Theory," in Jerrold J. Katz and Jerry A. Fodor, eds., The Structure of Language, 50–118. Englewood Cliffs, N.J.: Prentice Hall.

Collingwood, R. G. 1940. An Essay on Metaphysics. London: Oxford University Press.

Corrigan, Philip, and Derek Sayer. 1985. The Great Arch: English State Formation as Cultural Revolution. Oxford: Basil Blackwell.

Craig, Gordon A. 1971. "Delbrück: The Military Historian," in Edward Mead Earle, ed., Makers of Modern Strategy, 260–83. Princeton, N.J.: Princeton University Press.

Culler, Jonathan. 1977. Ferdinand de Saussure. Harmondsworth, England: Penguin Books.

De Brosses, Charles. 1760. Du culte des Dieux fétiches ou parallèle de l'ancienne religion de l'Egypte avec la religion de la Nigritie. Paris.

Destutt de Tracy, Antoine. 1824–1826. Éléments d'ideologie. 5 vols. Paris.

Dostal, Walter. 1991. "Mecca before the Time of the Prophet—Attempt of an Anthropological Interpretation," Der Islam 2: 193–231.

Duby, Georges. 1980. The Three Orders: Feudal Society Imagined. Chicago: University of Chicago Press.

Dumont, Louis. 1970. Homo Hierarchicus: An Essay on the Caste System. Chicago: University of Chicago Press.

———. 1986. Essays on Individualism: Modern Ideology in Anthropological Perspective. Chicago: University of Chicago Press.

Durkheim, Émile. 1947 [1915]. The Elementary Forms of the Religious Life: A Study in Religious Sociology. Glencoe, Ill.: Free Press.

Eagleton, Terry. 1991. Ideology: An Introduction. London and New York: Verso.

Eco, Umberto. 1976. A Theory of Semiotics. Bloomington: Indiana University Press.

Eickelman, Dale F. 1967. "Musaylima: An Approach to the Social Anthropology of Seventh Century Arabia," Journal of Economic and Social History of the Orient 2, pt. 1: 2–25.

Elias, Norbert. 1971. Was ist Soziologie? Munich: Juventa Verlag.

Ellen, Roy. 1988. "Fetishism," Man 23: 213–35.

Engels, Frederick. 1971 [1845]. The Condition of the Working Class in England, translated and edited by W. O. Henderson and W. H. Chaloner. Oxford: Basil Blackwell.

———. 1972 [1876]. The Origin of the Family, Private Property and the State, edited by Eleanor Burke Leacock. New York: International Publishers.

Fernandez, James W. 1965. "Symbolic Consensus in a Fang Reformative Cult," American Anthropologist 67: 902–29.

Festinger, Leon. 1957. A Theory of Cognitive Dissonance. Evanston, Ill.: Row, Peterson.

Firth, J. R. 1964. "Ethnographic Analysis and Language with Reference to Malinowski's Views," in Raymond Firth, ed., Man and Culture: An Evaluation of the Work of Bronislaw Malinowski, 93–118. New York and Evanston, Ill.: Harper Torchbooks.

Foucault, Michel. 1977. Discipline and Punish. New York: Pantheon Books.

———. 1984. "The Subject and Power," in Brian Wallis, ed., Art after Modernism: Rethinking Representation, 417–32. New York: New Museum of Contemporary Art.

Fox, Richard G. 1985. Lions of the Punjab: Culture in the Making. Berkeley and Los Angeles: University of California Press.

———. 1989. Gandhian Utopia: Experiments with Culture. Boston: Beacon Press.

Friedman, Jonathan. 1979. System, Structure and Contradiction: The Evolution of "Asiatic" Social Formations. Social Studies in Oceania and South East Asia 2. Copenhagen: National Museum of Denmark.

Geertz, Clifford. 1960. The Religion of Java. Glencoe, Ill.: Free Press.

———. 1973. The Interpretation of Culture: Selected Essays. New York: Basic Books.

Gellner, Ernest. 1988. Plough, Sword and Book: The Structure of Human History. London: Collins Harvill.

Gerth, H. H., and C. Wright Mills. 1946. From Max Weber: Essays in Sociology. New York: Oxford University Press.

Giddens, Anthony. 1972. Politics and Sociology in the Thought of Max Weber. London: Macmillan.

Godelier, Maurice. 1970. "Préface," Centre d'Études et de Recherches Marxistes, Sur les sociétés precapitalistes, 13–142. Paris: Éditions Sociales.

———. 1977. Perspectives in Marxist Anthropology. Cambridge Studies in Social Anthropology. London: Cambridge University Press.

Guthrie, Stewart E. 1993. Faces in the Clouds: A New Theory of Religion. New York and Oxford: Oxford University Press.

Hall, Stuart. 1978. "The Hinterland of Science: Ideology and 'The Sociology of Knowledge,'" in On Ideology, 9–32. Centre for Contemporary Cultural Studies. London: Hutchinson.

Harris, Marvin. 1979. Cultural Materialism: The Struggle for a Science of Culture. New York: Random House.

Hawkes, Terence. 1977. Structuralism and Semiotics. Berkeley and Los Angeles: University of California Press.

Herskovits, Melville J. 1940. Economic Anthropology. New York: Norton.

Hobsbawm, Eric J. 1962. The Age of Revolution: Europe, 1789–1848, London: Weidenfeld and Nicolson.

Hughes, H. Stuart. 1961. Consciousness and Society: The Reorientation of European Social Thought, 1890–1930. New York: Vintage Books.

Hunt, Eva. 1977. The Transformation of the Hummingbird: Cultural Roots of a Zinacanteco Poem. Ithaca, N.Y.: Cornell University Press.

Kalberg, Stephen. 1994. Max Weber's Comparative-Historical Sociology. Chicago: University of Chicago Press.

Kapferer, Bruce. 1988. Legends of People, Myths of State: Violence, Intolerance, and Political Culture in Sri Lanka and Australia. Washington, D.C.: Smithsonian Institution Press.

Kluckhohn, Clyde, and Olaf Prufer. 1959. "Influence during the Formative Years," in Walter Goldschmidt, ed., The Anthropology of Franz Boas:

Essays on the Centennial of His Birth, 4–28. American Anthropological Association Memoir 89. Menasha. Wis.: American Anthropological Association.

Kroeber, Alfred L. 1947. Cultural and Natural Areas of North America. University of California Publications in American Archaeology and Ethnology 38. Berkeley and Los Angeles: University of California Press.

———. 1952. The Nature of Culture. Chicago: University of Chicago Press.

———. 1955. "On Human Nature," Southwestern Journal of Anthropology 11: 195–204.

———. 1962. A Roster of Civilizations and Culture. Chicago: Aldine Press.

———, ed. 1953. Anthropology Today. Chicago: University of Chicago Press.

Kroeber, Alfred L., and Clyde Kluckhohn. 1952. Culture: A Critical Review of Concepts and Definitions. Papers of the Peabody Museum of American Archaeology and Ethnology 47 (1). Cambridge, Mass.: Peabody Museum, Harvard University.

Kroeber, Alfred L., and Talcott Parsons. 1958. "The Concept of Culture and of Social Systems," American Sociological Review 23: 582–83.

Kurtz, Donald V. 1996. "Hegemony and Anthropology: Gramsci, Exegeses, Reinterpretations," Critique of Anthropology 16: 103–35.

Larrain, Jorge. 1979. The Concept of Ideology. London: Hutchinson.

Lavandera, Beatriz R. 1988. "The Study of Language in Its Socio-Cultural Context," in Frederick J. Newmeyer, ed., Linguistics: The Cambridge Survey, vol. 4, The Socio-Cultural Context, 1–13. Cambridge: Cambridge University Press.

Lévi-Strauss, Claude. 1962. Le Totémisme aujourd'hui. Paris: Presses Universitaires de France.

———. 1964–1971. Mythologiques I–IV. Paris: Plon.

Lindstrom, Lamont. 1990. Knowledge and Power in a South Pacific Society. Washington, D.C.: Smithsonian Institution Press.

Lo Piparo, Franco. 1979. Lingua Intelletuali Egemonia in Gramsci. Rome and Bari, Italy: Laterza.

Lowie, Robert H. 1948. Social Organization. New York: Rinehart.

Lukács, Georg [Gyorgy]. 1971 [1922]. History and Class Consciousness, translated by Rodney Livingstone. London: Merlin Press.

Mannheim, Karl. 1936 [1929]. Ideology and Utopia: An Introduction to the Sociology of Knowledge. New York: Harvest Books.

———. 1953 [1927]. "Conservative Thought," in Karl Mannheim, Essays on Sociology and Social Psychology, edited by Paul Kecskemiti, 77–164. New York: Oxford University Press.

Marx, Karl. 1923 [1867]. Das Kapital: Kritik der politischen Ökonomie, vol. 1, edited by Karl Kautsky. Berlin: J. H. W. Dietz Nachf.

————. 1963 [1869]. The 18th Brumaire of Louis Napoleon. New York: International Publishers.

————. 1976 [1867]. Capital, vol. 1, translated by Ben Fowkes. New York: Vintage Books.

Marx, Karl, and Friedrich [Frederick] Engels. 1976 [1845–1846]. The German Ideology. Collected Works, vol. 5. New York: International Publishers.

Masco, Joseph. 1995. "'It Is a Strict Law That Bids Us Dance': Cosmologies, Colonialism, Death, and Ritual Authority in the Kwakwaka'wakw Potlatch, 1849 to 1922," Comparative Studies in Society and History 37: 41–75.

Mauss, Marcel. 1954 [1925]. The Gift: Forms and Functions of Exchange in Archaic Societies. Glencoe, Ill.: Free Press.

Mead, Margaret. 1959. An Anthropologist at Work: Writings of Ruth Benedict. Boston: Houghton Mifflin.

Ollman, Bertell. 1976. Alienation: Marx's Conception of Man in Capitalist Society, 2d ed. Cambridge: Cambridge University Press.

Ortner, Sherry B. 1989. High Religion: A Cultural and Political History of Sherpa Buddhism. Princeton, N.J.: Princeton University Press.

————. 1990. "Patterns of History: Cultural Schemas in the Foundings of Sherpa Religious Institutions," in Emiko Ohnuki-Tierney, ed., Culture through Time: Anthropological Approaches, 57–93. Stanford, Calif.: Stanford University Press.

Osgood, Cornelius. 1940. Ingalik Material Culture. Yale University Publications in Anthropology 22. New Haven, Conn.: Yale University Press.

Parmentier, Richard J. 1994. Signs in Society: Studies in Semiotic Anthropology. Bloomington and Indianapolis: Indiana University Press.

Peirce, Charles Sanders. 1955 [1893–1910]. Philosophical Writings of Peirce, edited by J. Buchler. New York: Dover.

Petersen, Glenn. 1995. "Reclaiming Rousseau: The Government of Poland's Relevance for Modern Anthropology," Dialectical Anthropology 20: 247–83.

Popper, Karl R., and John C. Eccles. 1983. The Self and Its Brain: An Argument for Interactionism. London: Routledge.

Quine, W. V. 1987. Quiddities: An Intermittently Philosophical Dictionary. Cambridge, Mass.: Belknap Press, Harvard University Press.

Rappaport, Roy A. 1971. "Nature, Culture and Ecological Anthropology," in Harry L. Shapiro, ed., Man, Culture and Society, 237–67. London: Oxford University Press.

————. 1979. Ecology, Meaning, and Religion. Richmond, Calif.: North Atlantic Books.

Rebel, Hermann. 1991. "Reimagining the Oikos: Austrian Cameralism in Its Social Formation," in Jay O'Brien and William Roseberry, eds., Golden Ages, Dark Ages: Imagining the Past in Anthropology and

History, 48–80. Berkeley and Los Angeles: University of California Press.

Redfield, Robert. 1953. "Relations of Anthropology to the Social Sciences and to the Humanities," in Alfred L. Kroeber, ed., Anthropology Today, 728–38. Chicago: University of Chicago Press.

Ringer, Fritz. 1969. The Decline of the German Mandarins. Cambridge, Mass.: Harvard University Press.

Ruesch, Jurgen, and Gregory Bateson. 1951. Communication: The Social Matrix of Psychiatry. New York: Norton.

Sahlins, Marshall D. 1976. Culture and Practical Reason. Chicago: University of Chicago Press.

———. 1977. "The State of the Art in Social/Cultural Anthropology: The Search for an Object," in Anthony F. C. Wallace, ed., Perspectives on Anthropology 1976, 14–32. American Anthropological Association Special Publication 10. Washington, D.C.: American Anthropological Association.

———. 1995. Historical Metaphors and Mythical Realities: Structure in the Early History of the Sandwich Islands Kingdom. Association for Social Anthropology of Oceania Publication 1. Ann Arbor: University of Michigan Press.

Saussure, Ferdinand de. 1983 [1916]. Course in General Linguistics, translated and annotated by Roy Harris. London: Duckworth.

Sayer, Derek. 1991. Capitalism and Modernity: An Excursus on Marx and Weber. London and New York: Routledge.

———, ed. 1989. Readings from Karl Marx. London and New York: Routledge.

Sewell, William. 1980. Work and Revolution in France: The Language of Labor from the Old Regime to 1848. New York: Cambridge University Press.

Solomon, Robert C. 1979. History and Human Nature: A Philosophical Review of European Philosophy and Culture, 1750–1850. Lanham, Md.: University Press of America.

Stocking Jr., George W. 1968. Race, Culture, and Evolution: Essays in the History of Anthropology. New York: Free Press–Macmillan.

Thompson, Edward P. 1966. The Making of the English Working Class. New York: Vintage Books.

Thompson, John B. 1984. Studies in the Theory of Ideology. Berkeley and Los Angeles: University of California Press.

Till, Nicholas. 1993. Mozart and the Enlightenment: Truth, Virtue and Beauty in Mozart's Operas. New York and London: Norton.

Trouillot, Michel-Rolph. 1991. "Anthropology and the Savage Slot: The Poetics and Politics of Otherness," in Richard G. Fox, ed., Recapturing Anthropology: Working in the Present, 17–44. Santa Fe, N.Mex.: School of American Research Press.

Turner, Bryan S. 1981. For Weber: Essays in the Sociology of Fate. London: Routledge and Kegan Paul.

———. 1988. Review of José Antonio Maravall, *Culture of the Baroque: Analysis of a Historical Structure,* Theory, Culture and Society 5: 173–75.

Valeri, Valerio. 1990. "Constitutive History: Genealogy and Narrative in the Legitimation of Hawaiian Kingship," in Emiko Ohnuki-Tierney, ed., Culture through Time: Anthropological Approaches, 154–92. Stanford, Calif.: Stanford University Press.

Verburg, Pieter A. 1974. "Vicissitudes of Paradigms," in Dell Hymes, ed., Studies in the History of Linguistics: Traditions and Paradigms, 191–230. Bloomington: Indiana University Press.

Verdery, Katherine. 1991. "Theorizing Socialism: A Prologue to the 'Transition,'" American Ethnologist 18: 419–39.

Vološinov, Valentin N. 1986 [1929]. Marxism and the Philosophy of Language. Cambridge, Mass.: Harvard University Press.

Wallace, Anthony F. C. 1970. Culture and Personality, 2d ed. New York: Random House.

Weber, Max. 1920. Gesammelte Aufsätze zur Religionssoziologie, vol. 1, 1–206. Tübingen: Mohr.

———. 1930 [1920]. The Protestant Ethic and the Spirit of Capitalism, translated by Talcott Parsons. New York: Scribner's.

———. 1968 [1921]. Economy and Society, edited by Guenther Roth and Claus Wittich. New York: Bedminster.

Whitman, James. 1984. "From Philology to Anthropology in Mid-Nineteenth Century Germany," in George W. Stocking Jr., ed., Functionalism Historicized: Essays on British Anthropology, 214–29. History of Anthropology 2. Madison: University of Wisconsin Press.

Williams, Raymond. 1959. Culture and Society, 1780–1950. Garden City, N.Y.: Anchor Books.

Wolf, Eric R. 1951. "The Social Organization of Mecca and the Origins of Islam," Southwestern Journal of Anthropology 7: 329–56.

———. 1953. "La formación de la nación," Ciencias Sociales 4: 50–62, 98–111, 146–71.

———. 1959a. Sons of the Shaking Earth. Chicago: University of Chicago Press.

———. 1959b. "The Virgin of Guadalupe," Journal of American Folklore 71: 34–39.

———. 1969. "Society and Symbols in Latin Europe and the Islamic Near East," Anthropological Quarterly 42: 287–301.

———. 1982. Europe and the People Without History. Berkeley and Los Angeles: University of California Press.

———. 1990. "Distinguished Lecture: Facing Power—Old Insights, New Questions," American Anthropologist 92: 586–96.

Yengoyan, Aram A. 1977. Review of N. Volosinov, *Marxism and the Philosophy of Language,* American Anthropologist 79: 700–701.

The Kwakiutl

Adams, John W. 1973. The Gitskan Potlatch: Population Flux, Resource Ownership and Reciprocity. Toronto: Holt, Rinehart, and Winston.

———. 1981. "Recent Ethnology of the Northwest Coast," Annual Review of Anthropology 10: 361–93.

Ames, Kenneth M. 1994. "The Northwest Coast: Complex Hunter-Gatherers, Ecology, and Social Evolution," Annual Review of Anthropology 23: 209–29.

Barnett, Homer G. 1955. The Coast Salish of British Columbia. Studies in Anthropology Monograph 4. Eugene: University of Oregon Press.

Barnouw, Victor. 1980. "Ruth Benedict," American Scholar 49: 504–9.

Bataille, Georges. 1967. La Part Maudite précédé de La Notion de Dépense. Paris: Les Éditions de Minuit.

Bateson, Gregory. 1972. Steps to an Ecology of Mind. New York: Ballantine Books.

Bell, Catherine. 1992. Ritual Theory, Ritual Practice. New York and Oxford: Oxford University Press.

Benedict, Ruth. 1934. Patterns of Culture. New York: Mentor Books.

Benjamin, Walter. 1969 [1936]. "The Work of Art in the Age of Mechanical Reproduction," in Hannah Arendt, ed., Illuminations, 217–51. New York: Schocken Books.

Berman, Judith. 1991. "The Seals' Sleeping Cave: The Interpretation of Boas' Kwakwala Texts." Ph.D. diss., University of Pennsylvania.

Bloch, Maurice. 1974. "Symbols, Song, Dance and Features of Articulation," European Journal of Sociology 15: 55–81.

———. 1984. Prey into Hunter: The Politics of Religious Experience. The Lewis Henry Morgan Lectures 1984, University of Rochester. Cambridge: Cambridge University Press.

Boas, Franz. 1897. The Social Organization and Secret Societies of the Kwakiutl, Report for 1895: 311–738. Washington, D.C.: United States National Museum.

———. 1921. Ethnology of the Kwakiutl: Based on Data Collected by George Hunt, Bureau of American Ethnology, 35th Annual Report, pts. 1 and 2, 1913–1914. Washington, D.C.: Government Printing Office.

———. 1925. Contributions to the Ethnology of the Kwakiutl. Columbia University Contributions to Anthropology 3. New York: Columbia University Press.

———. 1935. Kwakiutl Culture as Reflected in Mythology. American Folklore Society Memoir 28. New York: G. E. Stechert.

———. 1940a [1896]. "The Growth of the Secret Societies of the Kwakiutl," in Franz Boas, Race, Language and Culture, 379–83. New York: Free Press.

———. 1940b [1920]. "The Social Organization of the Kwakiutl," in Franz Boas, Race, Language and Culture, 356–69. New York: Free Press.

———. 1940c [1924]. "The Social Organization of the Tribes of the North Pacific Coast," in Franz Boas, Race, Language and Culture, 370–78. New York: Free Press.

———. 1940d [1927]. "Religious Terminology of the Kwakiutl," in Franz Boas, Race, Language and Culture, 612–18. New York: Free Press.

———. 1940e [1929]. "Metaphorical Expressions of the Kwakiutl," in Franz Boas, Race, Language and Culture, 232–39. New York: Free Press.

———. 1940f [1933]. Review of G. W. Lochner, *The Serpent in Kwakiutl Religion: A Study in Primitive Culture,* in Franz Boas, Race, Language and Culture, 446–50. New York: Free Press.

———. 1966. Kwakiutl Ethnography, edited by Helen Codere. Chicago: University of Chicago Press.

Bölscher, Marianne. 1982. The Potlatch in Anthropological Literature: A Re-Evaluation of Certain Ethnographic Data and Theoretical Approaches. Abhandlungen der Völkerkundlichen Arbeitsgemeinschaft, Heft 34. Nortorf, Germany: Völkerkundliche Arbeitsgemeinschaft.

Boyd, Robert T. 1990. "Demographic History, 1774–1874," in Wayne Suttles, ed., Handbook of North American Indians 7: Northwest Coast, 135–48. Washington, D.C.: Smithsonian Institution.

Cannizzo, Jeanne. 1983. "George Hunt and the Invention of Kwakiutl Culture," Canadian Review of Sociology and Anthropology 20: 44–58.

Codere, Helen. 1950. Fighting with Property: A Study of Kwakiutl Potlatching and Warfare 1792–1930. Monograph 18. New York: American Ethnological Society.

———. 1956. "The Amiable Side of Kwakiutl Life: The Potlatch and the Play Potlatch," American Anthropologist 58: 334–51.

———. 1961. "Kwakiutl," in Edward H. Spicer, ed., Perspectives in American Indian Culture Change, 431–516. Chicago: University of Chicago Press.

Cole, Douglas. 1985. Captured Heritage: The Scrambles for Northwest Coast Artifacts. Seattle: University of Washington Press.

———. 1991. "The History of the Kwakiutl Potlatch," in Aldona Jonaitis, ed., Chiefly Feasts: The Enduring Kwakiutl Potlatch, 135–68. New York: American Museum of Natural History; Seattle: University of Washington Press.

Cole, Douglas, and Ira Chaikin. 1990. An Iron Hand upon the People: The Law against the Potlatch on the Northwest Coast. Seattle: University of Washington Press; Vancouver and Toronto: Douglas and McIntyre.

Crapanzano, Vincent. 1995. "The Moment of Prestidigitation: Magic and Illusion in Marcel Mauss," in Ronald Bush and Donald Barkan, eds.,

Prehistories of the Future: The Primitivist Project and the Culture of Modernism, 95–113. Stanford, Calif.: Stanford University Press.

Donald, Leland. 1990. "Liberty, Equality, Fraternity: Was the Indian Really Egalitarian?," in James A. Clifton, ed., The Invented Indian: Cultural Fictions and Government Policies, 145–67. New Brunswick, N.J.: Transaction Publishers.

Donald, Leland, and Donald Mitchell. 1975. "Some Correlates of Local Group Rank among the Southern Kwakiutl," Ethnology 14: 325–46.

Drucker, Philip. 1951. The Northern and Central Nootkan Tribes. Bulletin 44. Washington, D.C.: Bureau of American Ethnology.

———. 1963. Indians of the Northwest Coast, Garden City, N.Y.: Natural History Press.

Drucker, Philip, and Robert F. Heizer. 1967. To Make My Name Great: A Reexamination of the Southern Kwakiutl Potlatch. Berkeley: University of California Press.

Duff, Wilson. 1964. The Indian History of British Columbia. Anthropology Memoir 4. Victoria, B.C.: Provincial Museum.

Ferguson, Brian F. 1983. "Warfare and Redistributive Exchange on the Northwest Coast," in Elizabeth Tooker, ed., The Development of Political Organization in Native North America. 1979 Proceedings of the American Ethnological Society, 133–47. Washington, D.C.: American Ethnological Society.

———. 1984. "A Reexamination of the Causes of Northwest Coast Warfare," in Brian F. Ferguson, ed., Warfare, Culture, and Environment, 267–328. Orlando, Fla.: Academic Press.

Fisher, Robin. 1977. Contact and Conflict: Indian-European Relations in British Columbia, 1774–1890, Vancouver: University of British Columbia Press.

Ford, Clellan S. 1941. Smoke from Their Fires. Hamden, Conn.: Archon.

Galois, Robert. 1994. Kwakwaka'wakw Settlements, 1775–1920: A Geographical Analysis and Gazetteer. Vancouver: UBC Press; Seattle: University of Washington Press.

Goldman, Irving. 1975. The Mouth of Heaven: An Introduction to Kwakiutl Religious Thought. New York: John Wiley and Sons.

Harkin, Michael E. 1990. "Mortuary Practices and the Category of the Person among the Heiltsuk," Arctic Anthropology 27: 87–108.

———. 1996. "Carnival and Authority: Heiltsuk Cultural Models of Power," Ethos 24: 281–313.

———. 1997. The Heiltsuks: Dialogues of Culture and History on the Northwest Coast. Lincoln: University of Nebraska Press.

Harris, Marvin. 1968. The Rise of Anthropological Theory: A History of Theories of Culture. New York: Thomas Crowell.

Jonaitis, Aldona, ed. 1991. Chiefly Feasts: The Enduring Kwakiutl Potlatch. New York: American Museum of Natural History; Seattle: University of Washington Press.

Jorgensen, Joseph G. 1980. Western Indians: Comparative Environments, Languages, and Cultures of 172 Western American Indian Tribes. San Francisco: W. H. Freeman.

Keithahn, Edward I. 1963. Monuments in Cedar: The Authentic Study of the Totem Pole. Seattle: Superior Publishing.

Knight, Rolf. 1978. Indians at Work: An Informal History of Native Indian Labour in British Columbia, 1858–1930. Vancouver, B.C.: New Star Books.

Kobrinsky, Vernon. 1975. "Dynamics of the Fort Rupert Class Struggle: Fighting with Property Vertically Revisited," in V. Serl and H. Taylor, eds., Papers in Honor of Harry Hawthorn, 32–59. Bellingham: Western Washington State College.

———. 1979. "The Mouth of Heaven: The Dialectical Allegories of the Kwakiutl Indians," Dialectical Anthropology 4: 163–77.

Kroeber, Alfred L. 1947. Cultural and Natural Areas of Native North America. University of California Publications in American Archaeology and Ethnology 38. Berkeley: University of California Press.

Legros, Dominique. 1982. "Réflexions sur l'origine des inégalités sociales à partir du cas des Athapaskan tutchone," Culture 2: 65–84.

Lenoir, Raymond. 1924. "Sur l'institution du potlatch," Revue Philosophique de la France et de l'Étranger 97: 233–67.

Lévi-Strauss, Claude. 1979. "L'Organisation sociale des Kwakiutl," in Claude Lévi-Strauss, La Voie des masques, 164–92. Paris: Librairie Plon.

Masco, Joseph. 1995. "'It Is a Strict Law That Bids Us Dance': Cosmologies, Colonialism, Death, and Ritual Authority in the Kwakwaka'wakw Potlatch, 1849 to 1922," Comparative Studies in Society and History 37: 41–75.

Mauss, Marcel. 1954 [1925]. The Gift: Forms and Functions of Exchange in Archaic Societies. Glencoe, Ill.: Free Press.

Mauzé, Marie. 1986. "Boas, les Kwagul et le potlatch: Élements pour une reévaluation," Homme 26: 21–53.

McDonald, James A. 1994. "Social Change and the Creation of Underdevelopment: A Northwest Case," American Ethnologist 21: 152–75.

Mitchell, Donald. 1984. "Predatory Warfare, Social Status, and the North Pacific Slave Trade," Ethnology 23: 39–48.

Oberg, Kalervo. 1937. "The Social Economy of the Tlingit." Ph.D. diss., University of Chicago.

Ohnuki-Tierney, Emiko. 1993. Rice as Self: Japanese Identity through Time. Princeton, N.J.: Princeton University Press.

Orans, Martin. 1975. "Domesticating the Functional Dragon: An Analysis of Piddocke's Potlatch," American Anthropologist 77: 312–28.

Piddocke, Stuart. 1965. "The Potlatch System of the Southern Kwakiutl: A

New Perspective," Southwestern Journal of Anthropology 21: 244–64.

Ray, Verne F. 1955. Review of Melville J. Herskovits, *Franz Boas,* American Anthropologist 57: 139–40.

Reid, Susan K. 1973. "Fondements de la pensée Kwakiutl," Recherches Amérindiennes au Quebec 3: 117–25.

———. 1979. "The Kwakiutl Man Eater," Anthropologica (Ottawa) n.s. 21: 247–75.

Rohner, Ronald P., and Evelyn C. Rohner. 1970. The Kwakiutl Indians of British Columbia. New York: Holt, Rinehart, and Winston.

Rosman, Abraham, and Paula G. Rubel. 1971. Feasting with Mine Enemies: Rank and Exchange among Northwest Coast Societies. New York: Columbia University Press.

———. 1986. "The Evolution of Central Northwest Coast Societies," Journal of Anthropological Research 42: 557–72.

———. 1990. "Structural Patterning in Kwakiutl Art and Ritual," Man, n.s., 25: 620–40.

Rubel, Paula G., and Abraham Rosman. 1983. "The Evolution of Exchange Structures and Ranking: Some Northwest Coast and Athapaskan Examples," Journal of Anthropological Research 39: 1–25.

Sahlins, Marshall D. 1972. Stone Age Economics. Chicago: Aldine-Atherton.

Shore, Bradd. 1989. "Totem as Practically Reason: Food for Thought," Dialectical Anthropology 14: 177–95.

Snyder, Sally. 1975. "Quest for the Sacred in Northern Puget Sound: An Interpretation of the Potlatch," Ethnology 14: 149–61.

Spradley, James P., and James Sewid. 1972. Guests Never Leave Hungry: The Autobiography of James Sewid, a Kwakiutl Indian. Montreal: McGill-Queens University Press.

Suttles, Wayne. 1958. "Private Knowledge, Morality, and Social Change among the Coast Salish," American Anthropologist 60: 497–507.

———. 1960. "Affinal Ties, Subsistence, and Prestige among the Coast Salish," American Anthropologist 62: 296–305.

———. 1962. "Variation in Habitat and Culture in the Northwest Coast," Akten des 34. Internationalen Amerikanisten-Kongresses, 522–37. Horn-Vienna: Austria Verlag Ferdinand Berger.

———. 1968. "Coping with Abundance: Subsistence on the Northwest Coast," in Richard B. Lee and Irven DeVore, eds., Man the Hunter, 56–69. Chicago: Aldine.

———. 1991. "Streams of Property, Armor of Wealth: The Traditional Kwakiutl Potlatch," in Aldona Jonaitis, ed., Chiefly Feasts: The Enduring Kwakiutl Potlatch, 71–133. New York: American Museum of Natural History; Seattle: University of Washington Press.

Veblen, Thorstein. 1899. The Theory of the Leisure Class. New York: Macmillan.

Walens, Stanley. 1981. Feasting with Cannibals: An Essay on Kwakiutl Cosmology. Princeton, N.J.: Princeton University Press.

Webster, Gloria Cranmer. 1990. "Kwakiutl since 1980," in Wayne Suttles, ed., Handbook of North American Indians 7: Northwest Coast, 387–90. Washington, D.C.: Smithsonian Institution Press.

———. 1991. "The Contemporary Potlatch," in Aldona Jonaitis, ed., Chiefly Feasts: The Enduring Kwakiutl Potlatch, 227–48. New York: American Museum of Natural History; Seattle: University of Washington Press.

White, Leslie A. 1963. The Ethnography and Ethnology of Franz Boas. Texas Memorial Museum Bulletin 6. Austin: Texas Memorial Museum, University of Texas.

Widerspach-Thor, Martine de. 1981. "The Equation of Copper," in Donald N. Abbott, ed., The World Is as Sharp as a Knife: Anthology in Honor of Wilson Duff, 157–74. Victoria: British Columbia Provincial Museum.

Wike, Joyce. 1947. "The Effect of the Maritime Fur Trade on Northwest Coast Society." Ph.D. diss., Columbia University.

———. 1952. "The Role of the Dead in Northwest Coast Culture," in Sol Tax, ed., Indian Tribes of Aboriginal America: Selected Papers of the Twenty-Ninth International Congress of Americanists 3: 97–103. Chicago: University of Chicago Press.

———. 1957. "More Puzzles on the Northwest Coast," American Anthropologist 59: 301–17.

———. 1984. "A Reevaluation of Northwest Coast Cannibalism," in Jay Miller and Carol M. Eastman, eds., The Tsimshian and Their Neighbors of the North Pacific Coast, 239–54. Seattle: University of Washington Press.

Woodburn, James. 1982. "Social Dimensions of Death in Four African Hunting and Gathering Societies," in Maurice Bloch and Jonathan Parry, eds., Death and the Regeneration of Life, 187–210. Cambridge: Cambridge University Press.

The Aztecs

Acosta Saignes, Miguel. 1945. Los pochteca: Ubicación de los mercaderes en la estructura social tenochca. Acta Antropológica (Mexico) 1, no. 1.

Adams, Robert M. 1966. The Evolution of Urban Society. Chicago: Aldine.

Alba, Carlos H. 1949. Estudio comparado entre el derecho azteca y el derecho positivo mexicano. Ediciones Especiales 3. Mexico City: Instituto Indigenista Interamericano.

Arens, William. 1979. The Man-Eating Myth: Anthropology and Anthropophagy. Oxford: Oxford University Press.

Aveni, Anthony F. 1991. "Mapping the Ritual Landscape: Debt Payment to Tlaloc during the Month of Atlcahualo," in Davíd Carrasco, ed., To Change Place: Aztec Ceremonial Landscape, 58–73. Niwot: University Press of Colorado.

Baird, Ellen T. 1989. "Stars and Wars at Cacaxtla," in Richard A. Diehl and Janet Catherine Berlo, eds., Mesoamerica after the Decline of Teotihuacan, A.D. 700–900, 105–22. Washington, D.C.: Dumbarton Oaks Research Library and Collection.

Berdan, Frances F. 1996. "The Tributary Provinces," in Frances F. Berdan and others, Aztec Imperial Strategies, 115–35. Washington, D.C.: Dumbarton Oaks Research Library and Collection.

Berdan, Frances F., and Michael E. Smith. 1996. "Imperial Strategies and Core-Periphery Relations," in Frances F. Berdan and others, Aztec Imperial Strategies, 209–17. Washington, D.C.: Dumbarton Oaks Research Library and Collection.

Berrin, Kathleen, ed. 1988. Feathered Serpents and Flowering Trees: Reconstructing the Murals of Teotihuacan. San Francisco: Fine Arts Museum of San Francisco.

Blanton, Richard E. 1996. "A Consideration of Causality in the Growth of Empire: A Comparative Perspective," in Frances F. Berdan and others, Aztec Imperial Strategies, 219–25. Washington, D.C.: Dumbarton Oaks Library and Collection.

Boehm de Lameiras, Brigitte. 1986. Formación del estado en el México prehispánico. Zamora, Mexico: Colegio de Michoacán.

Boone, Elizabeth Hill, ed. 1987. The Aztec Templo Mayor: A Symposium at Dumbarton Oaks, 8th and 9th October 1983. Washington, D.C.: Dumbarton Oaks Research Library and Collection.

Broda, Johanna. 1976. "Los estamentos en el ceremonial mexica," in Pedro Carrasco, Johanna Broda, and others, Estratificación social en la Mesoamérica prehispánica, 37–77. Mexico City: Centro de Investigaciones Superiores, Instituto Nacional de Antropología e Historia.

———. 1978. "Relaciones políticas ritualizadas: El ritual como expresión de una ideología," in Pedro Carrasco and Johanna Broda, eds., Economía política e ideología en el México prehispánico, 219–55. Centro de Investigaciones Superiores, Instituto Nacional de Antropología e Historia, SEP INAH. Mexico City: Editorial Nueva Imagen.

———. 1982. "Astronomy, Cosmovisión, and Ideology in Pre-Hispanic Mesoamérica," in Anthony F. Aveni and Gary Urton, eds., Ethnoastronomy and Archaeoastronomy in the American Tropics, 81–110. Annals of the New York Academy of Sciences 385. New York: New York Academy of Sciences.

———. 1987a. "The Provenience of the Offerings: Tribute and Cosmovisión," in Elizabeth Hill Boone, ed., The Aztec Templo Mayor: A Symposium at Dumbarton Oaks, 8th and 9th October 1983, 211–56. Washington, D.C.: Dumbarton Oaks Research Library and Collection.

————. 1987b. "Templo Mayor as Ritual Space," in Johanna Broda, Davíd Carrasco, and Eduardo Matos Moctezuma, The Great Temple of Tenochtitlan: Center and Periphery in the Aztec World, 61–123. Berkeley and Los Angeles: University of California Press.

Broda, Johanna, Davíd Carrasco, and Eduardo Matos Moctezuma. 1987. The Great Temple of Tenochtitlan: Center and Periphery in the Aztec World. Berkeley and Los Angeles: University of California Press.

Brotherston, Gordon. 1974. "Huitzilopochtli and What Was Made of Him," in Norman Hammond, ed., Mesoamerican Archaeology: New Approaches, 155–66. Austin: University of Texas Press.

Brundage, Burr Cartwright. 1979. The Fifth Sun: Aztec Gods, Aztec World. Austin: University of Texas Press.

————. 1985. The Jade Steps: A Ritual Life of the Aztecs. Salt Lake City: University of Utah Press.

Burkhart, Louise M. 1989. The Slippery Earth: Nahua-Christian Dialogue in Sixteenth-Century Mexico. Tucson: University of Arizona Press.

Cabrera, Rubén, George Cowgill, Saburo Sugiyama, and Carlos Serrano. 1989. "El Proyecto Templo de Quetzalcoatl," Arqueología, no. 5: 51–79. Mexico City: INAH.

Calnek, Edward E. 1972a. "The Organization of Urban Food Supply Systems: The Case of Tenochtitlan," Atti del XL Congresso Internazionale degli Americanisti, Rome and Genoa, 4: 97. Genoa: Tilgher.

————. 1972b. "Settlement Pattern and Chinampa Agriculture in Tenochtitlan," American Antiquity 37: 104–15.

————. 1974. "The Sahagún Texts as a Source of Sociological Information," in Munro Edmonson, ed., Sixteenth-Century Mexico: The Work of Sahagún, 189–204. Albuquerque: University of New Mexico Press.

————. 1976. "The Internal Structure of Tenochtitlan," in Eric R. Wolf, ed., The Valley of Mexico: Studies in Pre-Hispanic Ecology and Society, 287–302. Albuquerque: University of New Mexico Press.

————. 1978. "The City-State in the Basin of Mexico: Late Pre-Hispanic Period," in Richard P. Schaedel, J. E. Hardoy, and N. Scott Kinzer, eds., Urbanization in the Americas from Its Beginnings to the Present, 463–70. The Hague: Mouton.

————. 1982. "Patterns of Empire Formation in the Valley of Mexico: Late Prehispanic Period," in George A. Collier, Renato I. Rosaldo, and John D. Wirth, eds., The Inca and Aztec States, 1400–1800: Anthropology and History, 43–62. Stanford, Calif.: Stanford University Press.

Carrasco, Davíd. 1982. Quetzalcoatl and the Irony of Empire: Myths and Prophecies in the Aztec Tradition. Chicago: University of Chicago Press.

————. 1987. "Myth, Cosmic Terror, and the Templo Mayor," in Johanna Broda, Davíd Carrasco, and Eduardo Matos Moctezuma, The Great Temple of Tenochtitlan: Center and Periphery in the Aztec World, 124–62. Berkeley and Los Angeles: University of California Press.

Carrasco, Pedro. 1976. "La sociedad mexicana antes de la conquista," in Daniel Cosío Villegas, ed., Historia general de México, 1: 165–288. Mexico City: Colegio de México.

———. 1978. "La economía del México prehispánico," in Pedro Carrasco and Johanna Broda, eds., Economía política e ideología en el México prehispánico, 15–76. Centro de Investigaciones Superiores, Instituto Nacional de Antropología e Historia, SEP INAH. Mexico City: Editorial Nueva Imagen.

———. 1984. "Royal Marriages in Ancient Mexico," in Herbert R. Harvey and Hanns J. Prem, eds., Explorations in Ethnohistory: Indians of Central Mexico in the Sixteenth Century, 41–81. Albuquerque: University of New Mexico Press.

Carrasco, Pedro, and Johanna Broda, eds. 1978. Economía política e ideología en el México prehispánico. Centro de Investigaciones Superiores, Instituto Nacional de Antropología e Historia, SEP INAH. Mexico City: Editorial Nueva Imagen.

Carrasco, Pedro, Johanna Broda, and others. 1976. Estratificación social en la Mesoamérica prehispánica. Centro de Investigaciones Superiores, Instituto Nacional de Antropología e Historia. Mexico City: SEP INAH.

Clendinnen, Inga. 1991. Aztecs: An Interpretation. Cambridge: Cambridge University Press.

Davies, Nigel. 1980. The Aztecs: A History. Norman: University of Oklahoma Press.

De Heusch, Luc. 1985. Sacrifice in Africa: A Structuralist Approach. Bloomington: Indiana University Press.

Dibble, Charles. 1974. "The Nahuatlization of Christianity," in Munro Edmonson, ed., Sixteenth-Century Mexico: The Work of Sahagún, 225–33. Albuquerque: University of New Mexico Press.

Durán, Fray Diego. 1964 [1581]. The Aztecs: The History of the Indies of New Spain, translated by Doris Heyden and Fernando Horcasitas. New York: Orion Press.

———. 1967 [1581]. Historia de las Indias de Nueva España e Islas de Tierra Firme, 2 vols. and atlas, edited by Angel María Garibay K. Mexico City: Editorial Porrúa.

———. 1971 [1570, 1579]. The Book of the Gods and the Ancient Calendar, translated by Fernando Horcasitas and Doris Heyden. Norman: University of Oklahoma Press.

———. 1984 [1581]. Historia de las Indias de Nueva España e islas de tierra firme, 2 vols., edited by Angel María Garibay K., 2d ed. Mexico City: Editorial Porrúa.

Duverger, Christian. 1983. La flor letal: Economía del sacrificio azteca. Mexico City: Fondo de Cultura Económica.

Edmonson, Munro, ed. 1974. Sixteenth-Century Mexico: The Work of Sahagún. Albuquerque: University of New Mexico Press.

Elzey, Wayne. 1976. "The Nahua Myth of the Suns: History and Cosmology in Pre-Hispanic Mexican Religion," Numen 23: 114–35.

Erdheim, Mario. 1973. Prestige und Kulturwandel: Eine Studie zum Verhältnis subjektiver und objektiver Faktoren des kulturellen Wandels zur Klassengesellschaft bei den Azteken. Kultur-anthropologische Studien zur Geschichte 2. Wiesbaden: Focus-Verlag.

———. 1978. "Transformaciones de la ideología mexica en realidad social," in Pedro Carrasco and Johanna Broda, eds., Economía política e ideología en el México prehispánico, 193–220. Centro de Investigaciones Superiores, Instituto Nacional de Antropología e Historia, SEP INAH. Mexico City: Editorial Nueva Imagen.

Feeley-Harnik, Gillian. 1985. "Issues in Divine Kingship," Annual Review of Anthropology 14: 273–313.

Florescano, Enrique. 1995. El mito de Quetzalcóatl. Mexico City: Fondo de Cultura Económica.

Furst, Jill Leslie. 1995. The Natural History of the Soul in Ancient Mexico. New Haven, Conn.: Yale University Press.

Gardner, Brant. 1986. "Reconstructing the Ethnohistory of Myth: A Structural Study of the Aztec 'Legend of the Suns'," in Gary H. Gossen, ed., Symbol and Meaning beyond the Closed Community: Essays in Mesoamerican Ideas, 19–34. Albany: Institute for Mesoamerican Studies, State University of New York.

Garn, Stanley M. 1979. "The Noneconomic Nature of Eating People," American Anthropologist 81: 902–3.

González de Lesur, Yolotl. 1966. "El dios Huitzilopochtli en la peregrinación mexica de Aztlan a Tula," Anales, Instituto de Antropología e Historia 19: 175–90.

González Torres, Yolotl. 1985. El sacrificio humano entre los Mexicas. Instituto Nacional de Antropología e Historia. Mexico City: Fondo de Cultura Económica.

Gossen, Gary H., ed. 1986. Symbol and Meaning beyond the Closed Community: Essays in Mesoamerican Ideas. Albany: Institute for Mesoamerican Studies, State University of New York.

Graulich, Michel. 1981a. "The Metaphor of the Day in Ancient Mexican Myth and Ritual," Current Anthropology 22: 45–60.

———. 1981b. "More on the Metaphor of the Day and Ancient Mexican Myth," Current Anthropology 22: 438–39.

———. 1983. "Myths of Paradise Lost in Pre-Hispanic Central Mexico," Current Anthropology 24: 575–88.

———. 1984. "Aspectes mythiques des peregrinations mexicas," in Jacqueline de Durand-Forest, ed., The Native Sources and the History of the Valley of Mexico, 24–75. British Archaeological Reports International Series 204. Oxford.

Guzmán, Eulalia. 1958. Aclaraciones y rectificaciones a la "Relación de

Hernán Cortés a Carlos V sobre la invasión de Anáhuac," 2 vols. Mexico City: Libros Anáhuac, Imprenta Arana Hermanos.

Harner, Michael. 1977. "The Ecological Basis for Aztec Sacrifice," American Ethnologist 4: 117–35.

Harris, Marvin. 1977. Cannibals and Kings: The Origins of Cultures. New York: Random House.

Hassig, Ross. 1985. Trade, Tribute, and Transportation. Norman: University of Oklahoma Press.

———. 1988. Aztec Warfare: Imperial Expansion and Political Control. Norman: University of Oklahoma Press.

Hicks, Frederick. 1988. "Gift and Tribute: Relations of Dependence in Aztec Mexico," paper presented at the 12th International Congress of Anthropological and Ethnological Sciences, Zagreb.

Hirth, Kenneth G. 1989. "Militarism and Social Organization at Xochicalco, Morelos," in Richard A. Diehl and Janet Catherine Berlo, eds., Mesoamerica after the Decline of Teotihuacan, A.D. 700–900, 69–81. Washington, D.C.: Dumbarton Oaks Research Library and Collection.

Hocart, Arthur M. 1970 [1936]. Kings and Councillors: An Essay in the Comparative Anatomy of Human Society. Chicago: University of Chicago Press.

Hubert, Henri, and Marcel Mauss. 1964 [1898]. Sacrifice: Its Nature and Function. Chicago: University of Chicago Press.

Hunt, Eva. 1977. The Transformation of the Hummingbird: Cultural Roots of a Zinacanteco Poem. Ithaca, N.Y.: Cornell University Press.

Ingham, John H. 1984. "Human Sacrifices at Tenochtitlan," Comparative Studies in Society and History 26: 379–400.

Karttunen, Frances. 1992. An Analytic Dictionary of Nahuatl. Norman: University of Oklahoma Press.

Katz, Friedrich. 1969. Vorkolumbische Kulturen: Die Grossen Reiche des Alten Amerika. Munich: Kindler Verlag.

Keen, Benjamin. 1971. The Aztec Image in Western Thought. New Brunswick, N.J.: Rutgers University Press.

Klein, Cecelia F. 1975. "Post-Classic Death Imagery as a Sign of Cyclic Completion," in Elizabeth P. Benson, ed., Death and Afterlife in Pre-Columbian America, 69–85. Washington, D.C.: Dumbarton Oaks Research Library and Collection.

———. 1979. "Rethinking Cihuacoatl: Aztec Political Imagery of the Conquered Woman," paper presented at the XLIII International Congress of Americanists, Vancouver, B.C.

———. 1980. "Who Was Tlaloc?" Journal of Latin American Lore 6: 155–204.

———. 1984. "Dioses de la lluvia o sacerdotes ofrendadores del fuego? Un estudio socio-político de algunas representaciones mexicas del dios Tlaloc," Estudios de Cultura Nahuatl 17: 33–50.

————. 1987. "The Ideology of Autosacrifice at the Templo Mayor," in Elizabeth Hill Boone, ed., The Aztec Templo Mayor: A Symposium at Dumbarton Oaks, 8th and 9th October 1983, 293–370. Washington, D.C.: Dumbarton Oaks Research Library and Collection.

Kovar, Anton. 1970. "The Physical and Biological Environment of the Basin of Mexico," in William T. Sanders, Anton Kovar, Thomas Charlton, and Richard Diehl, The Teotihuacan Valley Project Final Report, 1: 13–25, and Appendix A: Major Meteorological Events in the History of the Basin of Mexico, 26–58. Department of Anthropology Occasional Papers in Anthropology 3. University Park: Pennsylvania State University.

Krickeberg, Walter 1956. Altmexikanische Kulturen. Berlin: Safari-Verlag.

Kurtz, Donald V. 1981. "The Legitimation of Early Inchoate States," in H. J. M. Claessen and Peter Skalnik, eds., The Study of the State, 178–200. The Hague: Mouton.

Lehmann, Walter. 1949. Sterbende Götter und Christliche Heilsbotschaft: Wechselreden Indianischer Vornehmer und Spanischer Glaubensapostel in Mexico 1524 ["Coloquios y Doctrina Christiana" de Fray Bernardino de Sahagún aus dem Jahre 1564]. Quellenwerke zur Alten Geschichte Amerikas 3. Stuttgart: W. Kohlhammer Verlag.

León-Portilla, Miguel. 1963. Aztec Thought and Culture: A Study of the Ancient Nahuatl Mind. Norman: University of Oklahoma Press.

————. 1987. "The Ethnohistorical Record for the Huey Teocalli of Tenochtitlan," in Elizabeth Hill Boone, ed., The Aztec Templo Mayor: A Symposium at Dumbarton Oaks, 8th and 9th October 1983, 71–95. Washington, D.C.: Dumbarton Oaks Research Library and Collection.

Lockhart, James. 1982. "Views of Corporate Self and History in Some Valley of Mexico Towns: Late Seventeenth and Eighteenth Centuries," in George A. Collier, Renato I. Rosaldo, and John D. Wirth, eds., The Inca and Aztec States, 1400–1800: Anthropology and History, 367–93. Stanford, Calif.: Stanford University Press.

————. 1992. The Nahuas after the Conquest. Stanford, Calif.: Stanford University Press.

López Austin, Alfredo. 1974a. "The Research Method of Fray Bernardino de Sahagún: The Questionnaires," in Munro Edmonson, ed., Sixteenth-Century Mexico: The Work of Sahagún, 205–24. Albuquerque: University of New Mexico Press.

————. 1974b. "Organización política en el altiplano central de México durante el posclásico," Historia Mexicana 23: 510–50.

————. 1980. Cuerpo humano e ideología: Las concepciones de los antiguos nahuas, 2 vols. Mexico City: Instituto de Investigaciones, Universidad Nacional Autónoma de México.

————. 1989. Hombre-Dios: Religión y política en el mundo nahuatl. Mexico City: Universidad Autónoma de México.

————. 1990. Los mitos del tlacuache: Caminos de la mitología meso-americana. Mexico City: Alianza Editorial Mexicana.

MacNeish, Richard. 1964. The Prehistory of the Tehuacan Valley 1: Environment and Subsistence. Austin: University of Texas Press.

Marcus, Joyce. 1992. Mesoamerican Writing Systems: Propaganda, Myth and History in Four Ancient Civilizations. Princeton, N.J.: Princeton University Press.

Matos Moctezuma, Eduardo. 1987. "Symbolism of the Templo Mayor," in Elizabeth Hill Boone, ed., The Aztec Templo Mayor: A Symposium at Dumbarton Oaks, 8th and 9th October 1983, 185–209. Washington, D.C.: Dumbarton Oaks Research Library and Collection.

Mignolo, Walter D. 1995. The Darker Side of the Renaissance: Literacy, Territoriality, and Colonization. Ann Arbor: University of Michigan Press.

Molina, Fray Alonso de. 1970 [1571]. Vocabulario en lengua castellana y mexicana. Mexico City: Editorial Porrúa.

Moreno de los Arcos, Roberto. 1967. "Los cinco soles cosmogónicos," Estudios de Cultura Nahuatl 7: 183–210.

Nicholson, Henry B. 1966. "The Significance of the 'Looped-Cord' Year Symbol in Pre-Hispanic Mexico: An Hypothesis," Estudios de Cultura Nahuatl 6: 135–48.

————. 1971. "Religion in Pre-Hispanic Central Mexico," in Robert Wauchope, Gordon F. Ekholm, and Ignacio Bernal, eds., Handbook of Middle American Indians, vol. 10, 395–446. Austin: University of Texas Press.

Ortiz de Montellanos, Bernard R. 1990. Aztec Medicine, Health, and Nutrition. New Brunswick, N.J.: Rutgers University Press.

Palerm, Angel. 1975. Obras hidráulicas prehispánicas en el sistema lacustre del Valle de México. Mexico City: Instituto Nacional de Antropología e Historia.

Parsons, Jeffrey R. 1976. "The Role of Chinampa Agriculture in the Food Supply of Aztec Tenochtitlan," in Charles E. Cleland, ed., Cultural Change and Continuity: Essays in Honor of James B. Griffin, 233–62. New York: Academic Press.

Paz, Octavio. 1972. Posdata. Mexico City: Siglo Veintiuno Editores.

Price, Barbara J. 1978. "Demystification, Enriddlement, and Aztec Cannibalism: A Materialist Rejoinder to Harner," American Ethnologist 5: 98–115.

————. 1980. "The Truth Is Not in Accounts but in Account Books: On the Epistemological Status of History," in Eric R. Ross, ed., Beyond the Myths of Culture: Essays in Cultural Materialism, 155–80. New York: Academic Press.

Rands, Robert L., and Carroll L. Riley. 1958. "Diffusion and Discontinuous Distribution," American Anthropologist 60: 274–97.

Read, Kay Almere. 1986. "The Fleeting Moment: Cosmogony, Eschatology, and Ethics in Aztec Religion and Society," Journal of Religious Ethics 14: 113–38.

————. 1991. "Binding Reeds and Burning Hearts: Mexica-Tenochca Concepts of Time and Sacrifice." Ph.D. diss., University of Chicago.

————. 1994. "Sacred Commoners: The Motion of Cosmic Powers in Mexica Rulership," History of Religions, August: 39–69.

Rojas Rabiela, Teresa, coord. 1987. "Y volvió a temblar": Cronología de los sismos en México (de Uno Pedernal a 1821). Cuadernos de la Casa Chata 135. Mexico City: CIESAS.

Rounds, J. 1982. "Dynastic Succession and the Centralisation of Power in Tenochtitlan," in George A. Collier, Renato I. Rosaldo, John D. Wirth, eds., The Inca and Aztec States, 1400–1800: Anthropology and History, 63–89. New York: Academic Press.

Ruiz de Alarcón, Hernando. 1984. Treatise on the Heathen Superstitions That Today Live among the Indians Native to This New Spain, 1629, translated and edited by Richard Andrews and Ross Hassig. Norman: University of Oklahoma Press.

Sahagún, Fray Bernardino de. 1949 [1564]. Coloquios, edited by Walter Lehmann.

————. 1950–1969 [1569]. Florentine Codex: General History of the Things of New Spain, 12 vols., translated by Arthur J. O. Anderson and Charles Dibble. Salt Lake City: University of Utah Press.

Sahlins, Marshall D. 1978. "Culture as Protein and Profit," New York Review of Books, 25 (8): 45–53.

Sanday, Peggy Reeves. 1986. Divine Hunger: Cannibalism as a Cultural System. Cambridge: Cambridge University Press.

Sanders, William T. 1992. "Ranking and Stratification in Prehispanic Mesoamerica," in Diane Z. Chase and Arlen F. Chase, eds., Mesoamerican Elites: An Archaeological Assessment, 278–91. Norman: University of Oklahoma Press.

Sanders, William T., and Barbara J. Price. 1968. Mesoamerica: The Evolution of a Civilization. New York: Random House.

Sanders, William T., Jeffrey R. Parsons, and Robert S. Santley. 1979. The Basin of Mexico: Ecological Processes in the Evolution of a Civilization. New York: Academic Press.

Smith, Michael E. 1984. "The Aztlán Migrations of the Nahuatl Chronicles: Myth or History," Ethnohistory 31: 153–86.

————. 1986. "The Role of Social Stratification in the Aztec Empire: A View from the Provinces," American Anthropologist 88: 70–91.

————. 1996. "The Strategic Provinces," in Frances F. Berdan and others, Aztec Imperial Strategies, 137–50. Washington, D.C.: Dumbarton Oaks Research Library and Collection.

Steward, Julian H. 1949. "Cultural Causality and Law: A Trial Formulation of the Development of Early Civilizations," *American Anthropologist* 51: 1–27.

Sugiyama, Saburo. 1989. "Burials Dedicated to the Old Temple of Quetzalcoatl at Teotihuacan, Mexico," *American Antiquity* 54: 85–106.

Sullivan, Thelma D. 1974. "*The Rhetorical Orations,* or Huehuetlatolli," in Munro S. Edmonson, ed., Sixteenth-Century Mexico: The Work of Sahagún, 79–109. Albuquerque: University of New Mexico Press.

————. 1980. "Tlatoani and Tlatocayotl in the Sahagún Manuscripts," *Estudios de Cultura Nahuatl* 14: 225–38.

————. 1994. A Scattering of Jades: Stories, Poems, and Prayers of the Aztecs, edited by T. J. Knab. New York: Simon and Schuster, Touchstone.

Tezozómoc, Hernando Alvarado. 1944. *Crónica mexicana.* Mexico City: Editorial Leyenda.

Townsend, Richard Fraser. 1979. State and Cosmos in the Art of Tenochtitlan. Studies in Pre-Columbian Art and Archaeology 20. Washington, D.C.: Dumbarton Oaks, Trustees for Harvard University.

————. 1987. "Coronation at Tenochtitlan," in Elisabeth Hill Boone, ed., The Aztec Templo Mayor: A Symposium at Dumbarton Oaks, 8th and 9th October 1983, 371–409. Washington, D.C.: Dumbarton Oaks Research Library and Collection.

Umberger, Emily. 1987. "Events Commemorated by Date Plaques at the Templo Mayor: Further Thoughts on the Solar Metaphor," in Elizabeth Hill Boone, ed., The Aztec Templo Mayor: A Symposium at Dumbarton Oaks, 8th and 9th October 1983, 411–49. Washington, D.C.: Dumbarton Oaks Research Library and Collection.

————. 1996. "Art and Imperial Strategy in Tenochtitlan," in Frances F. Berdan and others, Aztec Imperial Strategies, 85–106. Washington, D.C.: Dumbarton Oaks Research Library and Collection.

Velázquez, Primo Feliciano. 1975. Códice Chimalpopoca: Anales de Cuauhtitlán y leyenda de los soles. Mexico City: Universidad National Autónoma de México.

Willey, Gordon R. 1976. "Mesoamerican Civilization and the Idea of Transcendence," *Antiquity* 50: 205–15.

Wright, Henry T. 1977. "Recent Research on the Origin of the State," *Annual Review of Anthropology* 6: 379–97.

Zantwijk, Rudolf van. 1960. "Los indígenas de Milpa Alta, herederos de los aztecas," *Acción Indigenista* (Mexico) no. 38: 2–3.

————. 1973. "Politics and Ethnicity in a Prehispanic Mexican State between the 13th and 15th centuries," *Plural Societies* (The Hague) 4: 23–52.

————. 1985. The Aztec Arrangement: The Social History of Pre-Spanish Mexico. Norman: University of Oklahoma Press.

————. 1988. "Zijn Azteken en Duitsers ook Mensen: Levensbeschouwing en mensenoffers in twee onafhankelijk van elkaar ontwikkeelde beschavingen." Inaugural lecture, University of Utrecht.

National Socialist Germany

Abel, Theodore. 1938. Why Hitler Came to Power. Englewood Cliffs, N.J.: Prentice Hall.
Ackermann, Josef. 1970. Heinrich Himmler als Ideologe. Göttingen: Musterschmidt.
Anderson, Perry. 1974. Lineages of the Absolutist State. London: NLB.
Arendt, Hannah. 1951. The Origins of Totalitarianism. New York: Harcourt Brace.
Ayçoberry, Pierre. 1981. The Nazi Question. New York: Pantheon Books.
Baird, Jay W. 1974. The Mythical World of Nazi War Propaganda, 1939–1945. Minneapolis: University of Minnesota Press.
Baldwin, P. 1990. "Social Interpretations of Nazism: Reviewing a Tradition," Journal of Contemporary History 25: 5–37.
Bartov, Omer. 1992. Hitler's Army: Soldiers, Nazis, and War in the Third Reich. New York and Oxford: Oxford University Press.
———. 1996. Murder in Our Midst: The Holocaust, Industrial Killing, and Representation. New York and Oxford: Oxford University Press.
Baum, Rainer C. 1981. The Holocaust and the German Elite: Genocide and National Suicide in Germany, 1871–1945. Toronto: Rowman and Littlefield.
Bauman, Zygmunt. 1989. Modernity and the Holocaust. Ithaca, N.Y.: Cornell University Press.
Bein, Alexander. 1965. "Der jüdische Parasit, Bemerkungen zur Semantik der Judenfrage," Vierteljahreshefte für Zeitgeschichte 13: 121–49.
Berenbaum, Michael, ed. 1990. A Mosaic of Victims: Non-Jews Persecuted and Murdered by the Nazis. New York: New York University Press.
Brinkmann, Carl. 1926. "Die Aristokratie im kapitalistischen Zeitalter," Grundriss der Sozialökonomie (Tübingen) 9: 22–34.
Browning, Christopher R. 1992. The Path to Genocide: Essays on Launching the Final Solution. Cambridge: Cambridge University Press.
———. 1993. "Beyond 'Intentionalism' and 'Functionalism': A Reassessment of Nazi Jewish Policy from 1939 to 1941," in Thomas Childers and Jane Caplan, eds., Reevaluating the Third Reich, 211–33. New York and London: Holmes and Meier.
Burleigh, Michael. 1994. Death and Deliverance: "Euthanasia" in Germany c. 1900–1945. Cambridge: Cambridge University Press.
Burleigh, Michael, and Wolfgang Wippermann. 1991. The Racial State: Germany 1933–1945. Cambridge: Cambridge University Press.
Caplan, Jane. 1993. "National Socialism and the Theory of the State," in

Thomas Childers and Jane Caplan, eds., Reevaluating the Third Reich, 98–113. New York and London: Holmes and Meier.

Cecil, Robert. 1975. Hitler's Decision to Invade Russia, 1941. New York: David McKay.

Childers, Thomas, and Jane Caplan, eds. 1993. Reevaluating the Third Reich. New York and London: Holmes and Meier.

Cohn, Norman. 1961. The Pursuit of the Millennium: Revolutionary Messianism in Medieval and Reformation Europe and Its Bearing on Modern Totalitarian Movements, 2d ed. New York: Harper Torchbooks.

———. 1996. Warrant for Genocide: The Myth of the Jewish World Conspiracy and the Protocols of the Elders of Zion. London: Serif.

Conze, Werner. 1954. "Vom 'Pöbel' zum 'Proletariat,' Sozialgeschichtliche Voraussetzungen für den Sozialismus in Deutschland," Vierteljahrschrift für Sozial-und-Wirtschaftsgeschichte 49: 333–64.

Craig, Gordon A. 1982. The Germans. New York: Putnam.

Dallin, Alexander. 1957. German Rule in Russia, 1941–1945: A Study in Occupation Policies. New York: Macmillan.

Dorn, Walter L. 1931. "The Prussian Bureaucracy in the Eighteenth Century," Political Science Quarterly 46: 403–23.

Douglas, Mary. 1966. Purity and Danger: An Analysis of Concepts of Pollution and Taboo. New York: Frederick A. Praeger.

Dronberger, Ilse. 1971. The Political Thought of Max Weber: In Quest of Statesmanship. New York: Appleton-Century Crofts.

Eichberg, Henning. 1986. "The Enclosure of the Body—On the Historical Relativity of 'Health,' 'Nature' and the Environment of Sport," Journal of Contemporary History 21: 99–121.

Elias, Norbert. 1989. Studien über die Deutschen: Machtkämpfe und Habitusentwicklung im 19. und 20. Jahrhundert. Frankfurt on the Main: Suhrkamp.

Faye, Jean Pierre. 1972. Langages totalitaires: Critique de la raison / l'économie narrative. Paris: Hermann.

Fest, Joachim C. 1970. The Face of the Third Reich: Portraits of the Nazi Leadership. New York: Pantheon Books.

Fischer, Fritz. 1967 [1961]. Germany's Aims in the First World War. New York: Norton.

Fornari, Franco. 1975. The Psychoanalysis of War. Bloomington: Indiana University Press.

Fraenkel, Ernst. 1941. The Dual State. A Contribution to the Theory of Dictatorship. New York: Oxford University Press.

Friedlander, Henry. 1995. The Origins of Nazi Genocide: From Euthanasia to the Final Solution. Chapel Hill: University of North Carolina Press.

Friedrich, Otto. 1994. The Kingdom of Auschwitz. New York: Harper Perennial.

Gay, Peter, and R. K. Webb. 1973. Modern Europe to 1815. New York: Harper and Row.

Gay, Ruth. 1992. The Jews of Germany: A Historical Portrait. New Haven, Conn.: Yale University Press.

Gellately, Robert. 1993. "Enforcing Racial Policy in Nazi Germany," in Thomas Childers and Jane Caplan, eds., Reevaluating the Third Reich, 42–65. New York and London: Holmes and Meier.

Geyer, Michael. 1984. "The State in National Socialist Germany," in Charles Bright and Susan Harding, eds., Statemaking and Social Movements: Essays in History and Theory, 193–232. Ann Arbor: University of Michigan Press.

———. 1992. "The Stigma of Violence, Nationalism, and War in Twentieth-Century Germany," German Studies Review, Special issue: German Identity, 75–110.

Gierke, Otto. 1958 [1934]. Natural Law and the Theory of Society, 1500 to 1800. Cambridge: Cambridge University Press.

Girard, René. 1977. Violence and the Sacred, translated by Patrick Gregory. Baltimore, Md.: Johns Hopkins University Press.

Goldhagen, Daniel J. 1996. Hitler's Willing Executioners: Ordinary Germans and the Holocaust. New York: Knopf.

Haas, Peter J. 1988. Morality after Auschwitz: The Radical Challenge of the Nazi Ethic. Philadelphia: Fortress Press.

Halder, Franz. 1962–1964. Kriegstagebuch: Tägliche Aufzeichnungen des Chefs des Generalstabes des Heeres, 1939–1942, 3 vols. Stuttgart: W. Kohlhammer.

Hamilton, Richard. 1982. Who Voted for Hitler? Princeton, N.J.: Princeton University Press.

Haney, Craig, Curtis Banks, and Philip Zimbardo. 1973. "Interpersonal Dynamics in a Simulated Prison," International Journal of Criminology and Psychology 1: 69–97.

Hauschild, Thomas. 1987. "Völkerkunde im Dritten Reich," in Helge Gerndt, ed., Volkskunde und Nazionalsozialismus, 245–59. Munich: Münchner Vereinigung für Volkskunde.

Hayes, Peter. 1993. "Polycracy and Policy in the Third Reich," in Thomas Childers and Jane Caplan, eds., Reevaluating the Third Reich, 190–210. New York and London: Holmes and Meier.

Heiber, Helmut. 1958. "Der Generalplan Ost," Dokumentation, Vierteljahreshefte für Zeitgeschichte 6: 281–325.

Hermand, Jost. 1992. Old Dreams of a New Reich: Volkish Utopias and National Socialism. Bloomington: University of Indiana Press.

Hiden, John, and John Farquharson. 1983. Explaining Hitler's Germany: Historians and the Third Reich. Totowa, N.J.: Barnes and Noble.

Hilberg, Raul. 1992. Perpetrators, Victims, Bystanders: The Jewish Catastrophe 1933–1945. New York: HarperCollins.

Hildebrand, Klaus. 1973. The Foreign Policy of the Third Reich. Berkeley and Los Angeles: University of California Press.

Hillgruber, Andreas. 1981. Germany and the Two World Wars. Cambridge, Mass.: Harvard University Press.

Hitler, Adolf. 1939 [1925]. Mein Kampf. New York: Reynal and Hitchcock.

————. 1953. Hitler's Secret Conversations 1941–1944, translated by Norman Cameron and R. H. Stevens, with an essay by Hugh Trevor-Roper on "The Mind of Adolf Hitler," xiii–xxx. New York: Farrar, Straus and Young.

Höhne, Heinz. 1969. The Order of the Death's Head: The Story of Hitler's SS. London: Stecker and Warburg.

Hollyday, Frederic B. M., ed. 1970. Bismarck. Englewood Cliffs, N.J.: Prentice Hall.

Horkheimer, Max, and Theodor W. Adorno. 1972. Dialectics of Enlightenment. New York: Seabury Press.

Hunczak, Taras. 1990. "The Ukrainian Losses during World War II," in Michael Berenbaum, ed., A Mosaic of Victims: Non-Jews Persecuted and Murdered by the Nazis, 116–27. New York: New York University Press.

Jacobs, Jack. 1989. On the Verge of Apocalypse: German Jewry, Social Democracy, and the Nazi Threat, 1928–1933. Occasional Paper No. 3. New York: Center on Violence and Human Survival, John Jay College of Criminal Justice, City University of New York.

Kampe, Norbert. 1987. "Normalizing the Holocaust? The Recent Historical Debate in the Federal Republic of Germany," Holocaust and Genocide Studies 2: 61–90.

Kater, Michael H. 1983. The Nazi Party: A Social Profile of Members and Leaders. Cambridge, Mass.: Harvard University Press.

Kelman, Herbert. 1973. "Violence without Moral Restraint," Journal of Social Issues 29: 29–61.

Kershaw, Ian. 1983. Popular Opinion and Political Dissent in the Third Reich: Bavaria, 1933–1945. Oxford: Clarendon Press.

————. 1989. The "Hitler Myth": Image and Reality in the Third Reich. Oxford and New York: Oxford University Press.

Kogon, Eugen. 1980 [1945]. The Theory and Practice of Hell: The German Concentration Camps and the System behind Them. New York: Berkley Books.

Koshar, Rudi. 1987. "From Stammtisch to Party: Nazi Joiners and the Contradictions of Grass Roots Fascism in Weimar Germany," Journal of Modern History 59: 1–24.

Kosok, Paul. 1933. Modern Germany: A Study of Conflicting Loyalties. Chicago: University of Chicago Press.

Krausnick, Helmut, ed. 1957. "Einige Gedanken über die Behandlung der Fremdvölkischen im Osten" [Himmler memorandum], Vierteljahreshefte für Zeitgeschichte 5: 194–98.

Kren, George M., and Leon Rappaport. 1980. The Holocaust and the Crisis of Human Behavior. New York and London: Holmes and Meier.

Kühl, Stefan. 1994. The Nazi Connection: Eugenics, American Racism, and German National Socialism. New York: Oxford University Press.

Kumanev, Georgily A. 1990. "The German Occupation Regime on Occupied Territory in the USSR (1941–1944)," in Michael Berenbaum, ed., A Mosaic of Victims: Non-Jews Persecuted and Murdered by the Nazis, 128–41. New York: New York University Press.

Langer, Lawrence L. 1995. Admitting the Holocaust: Collected Essays. New York and Oxford: Oxford University Press.

Laqueur, Walter. 1971. Out of the Ruins of Europe. New York: The Library Press.

Leach, Barry A. 1973. German Strategy against Russia, 1939–1941. Oxford: Clarendon Press.

Leed, Eric J. 1979. No Man's Land: Combat and Identity. Cambridge: Cambridge University Press.

Lewin, Ronald. 1984. Hitler's Mistakes: New Insights into What Made Hitler Tick. New York: William Morrow.

Lichtheim, George. 1970. George Lukács. New York: Viking Press.

Loewenberg, Peter. 1983. "The Psychological Origins of the Nazi Youth Cohort," in Peter Loewenberg, Decoding the Past: The Psychohistorical Approach, 240–83. New York: Knopf.

Lüdtke, Alf. 1995. "What Happened to the 'Fiery Red Glow'? Workers' Experiences and German Fascism," in Alf Lüdtke, ed., The History of Everyday Life: Reconstructing Historical Experiences and Ways of Life, 198–251. Princeton, N.J.: Princeton University Press.

Madajczyk, Czeslaw. 1962. "Generalplan Ost," Polish Western Affairs 3: 391–442.

Maier, Charles S. 1988. The Unmasterable Past: History, Holocaust, and German National Identity. Cambridge, Mass.: Harvard University Press.

Mannheim, Karl. 1953 [1927]. "Conservative Thought," in Karl Mannheim, Essays on Sociology and Social Psychology, edited by Paul Kecskemiti, 77–164. New York: Oxford University Press.

Marrus, Michael R. 1987. The Holocaust in History. New York: Meridian/Penguin.

Mason, Tim. 1981. "Intention and Explanation: A Current Controversy about the Interpretation of National Socialism," in Gerhard Hirschfeld und Lothar Kettenacker, eds., Der Führerstaat: Mythos und Realität, 21–40. Stuttgart: Klett-Cotta.

———. 1993. "The Domestic Dynamics of Nazi Conquests: A Response to Critics," in Thomas Childers and Jane Caplan, eds., Reevaluating the Third Reich, 161–89. New York and London: Holmes and Meier.

Mayer, Arno J. 1988. Why Did the Heavens Not Darken? The "Final Solution" in History. New York: Pantheon Books.

Meinecke, Friedrich. 1950. The German Catastrophe: Reflections and Recollections. Cambridge, Mass.: Harvard University Press.

Merkl, Peter H. 1975. Political Violence under the Swastika: 581 Early Nazis. Princeton, N.J.: Princeton University Press.

Milton, Sybil. 1990. "Non-Jewish Children in the Camps," in Michael Berenbaum, ed., A Mosaic of Victims: Non-Jews Persecuted and Murdered by the Nazis, 150–60. New York: New York University Press.

Mitzman, Arthur. 1973. Sociology and Estrangement: Three Sociologists of Imperial Germany. New York: Knopf.

Mommsen, Hans. 1976. "National Socialism: Continuity and Change," in Walter Laqueur, ed., Fascism: A Reader's Guide, 179–210. Berkeley: University of California Press.

———. 1993. "Reflections on the Position of Hitler and Göring in the Third Reich," in Thomas Childers and Jane Caplan, eds., Reevaluating the Third Reich, 86–97. New York and London: Holmes and Meier.

Moore Jr., Barrington. 1978. Injustice: The Social Bases of Obedience and Revolt. White Plains, N.Y.: M. E. Sharpe.

Mosse, George L. 1975. The Nationalization of the Masses: Political Symbolism and Mass Movements in Germany from the Napoleonic Wars through the Third Reich. Ithaca, N.Y.: Cornell University Press.

———. 1981. The Crisis of German Ideology: Intellectual Origins of the Third Reich. New York: Schocken Books.

———. 1985. Nationality and Sexuality: Middle-Class Morality and Sexual Norms in Modern Europe. Madison: University of Wisconsin Press.

Mühlberger, Detlef. 1980. "The Sociology of the NSDAP. The Question of Working Class Membership," Journal of Contemporary History 15: 493–511.

Mühlmann, Wilhelm E. 1933. "Die Hitler-Bewegung. Bemerkungen zur Krise der bürgerlichen Kultur," Soziologus, Zeitschrift für Völkerpsychologie und Soziologie, 9: 129–40.

———. 1964. Rassen, Ethnien, Kulturen: Moderne Ethnologie. Neuwied/Berlin: Luchterhand.

Neumann, Franz. 1944. Behemoth: The Structure and Practice of National Socialism, 1933–1944, 2d ed., with new appendix. New York: Oxford University Press.

Noakes, J., and G. Pridham, eds. 1995. Nazism, 1919–1945, vol. 3: Foreign Policy, War and Racial Extermination: A Documentary Reader. Exeter Studies in History, 13. Exeter: University of Exeter Press.

Nolte, Ernst. 1969. Three Faces of Fascism: Action Française, Italian Fascism, National Socialism. New York and Toronto: Mentor Books, New American Library.

Payne, Stanley G. 1995. A History of Fascism, 1914–1945. Madison: University of Wisconsin Press.

Peterson, Edward N. 1969. The Limits of Hitler's Power. Princeton, N.J.: Princeton University Press.

Peukert, Detlev J. K. 1987. Inside Nazi Germany: Conformity, Opposition, and Racism in Everyday Life. New Haven, Conn.: Yale University Press.

Pflanze, Otto. 1963. Bismarck and the Development of Germany. The Period of Unification, 1815–1871. Princeton, N.J.: Princeton University Press.

Proctor, Robert N. 1988a. Racial Hygiene: Medicine under the Nazis. Cambridge, Mass.: Harvard University Press.

———. 1988b. "From *Anthropologie* to *Rassenkunde* in the German Anthropological Tradition," in George W. Stocking Jr., ed., Bones, Bodies, Behavior: Essays on Biological Anthropology, 138–79, History of Anthropology 5. Madison: University of Wisconsin Press.

Rauschning, Hermann. 1940. The Voice of Destruction. New York: G. P. Putnam's Sons.

Rebel, Hermann. 1983. Peasant Classes: The Bureaucratization of Property and Family Relations under Early Habsburg Absolutism, 1511–1636. Princeton, N.J.: Princeton University Press.

———. 1991. "Reimagining the *Oikos:* Austrian Cameralism in Its Social Formation," in Jay O'Brien and William Roseberry, eds., Golden Ages, Dark Ages: Imagining the Past in History and Anthropology, 48–80. Berkeley and Los Angeles: University of California Press.

———. 1995. "The Prussian Junker and Their Peasants: Articulation with Kinship of a Tribute-Taking Class," in Jane Schneider and Rayna Rapp, eds., Articulating Hidden Histories, 94–107. Berkeley and Los Angeles: University of California Press.

Reich, Wilhelm. 1975. Mass Psychology of Fascism. Harmondsworth, England: Penguin.

Rich, Norman. 1992. Hitler's War Aims: Ideology, The Nazi State, and the Course of Expansion. New York: W. W. Norton.

Rogowski, Ronald. 1977. "The Gauleiter and the Social Origins of Fascism," Comparative Studies in Society and History 19: 399–430.

Rosenberg, Hans. 1958. Bureaucracy, Aristocracy, Autocracy: The Prussian Experience, 1660–1815. New York: Beacon.

———. 1967. Grosse Depression und Bismarckzeit: Wirtschaftsablauf, Gesellschaft und Politik in Mitteleuropa. Veröffentlichungen der Historischen Komission zu Berlin beim Friedrich-Meinecke-Institut der Freien Universität Berlin, vol. 24; Publikationen zur Geschichte der Industrialisierung, vol. 2. Berlin: Walter de Gruyter.

———. 1978. Machteliten und Wirtschaftskonjunkturen. Göttingen: Vandenhoeck and Ruprecht.

Sabean, David W. 1984. Power in the Blood: Popular Culture and Village Discourse in Early Modern Germany. Cambridge: Cambridge University Press.

Schäfer, Renate. 1962. "Zur Geschichte des Wortes 'zersetzen,'" Zeitschrift für deutsche Wortforschung 18: 40–80.

Schulze, Hagen. 1991. The Course of German Nationalism: From Frederick the Great to Bismarck, 1763–1867. Cambridge: Cambridge University Press.

Sheehan, James J. 1984. "National Socialism and German Society: Reflections on Recent Research," Theory and Society 13: 851–67.

Smith, Woodruff D. 1986. The Ideological Origins of Nazi Imperialism. New York and Oxford: Oxford University Press.

Smolinski, L. 1967. "Planning without Theory, 1917–67," Survey no. 67: 108–28.

Snyder, Louis L. 1976. Encyclopedia of the Third Reich. New York: McGraw-Hill.

Spengler, Oswald. 1919. Preussentum und Sozialismus. Munich: Oscar Beck.

Stern, Fritz. 1974. The Politics of Cultural Despair: A Study in the Rise of the Germanic Ideology, 2d ed. Berkeley: University of California Press.

Streit, Christian. 1990. "The Fate of the Soviet Prisoners of War," in Michael Berenbaum, ed., A Mosaic of Victims: Non-Jews Persecuted and Murdered by the Nazis, 142–49. New York: New York University Press.

Taylor, Peter K. 1994. Indentured to Liberty: Peasant Life and the Hessian Military State, 1688–1815. Ithaca, N.Y.: Cornell University Press.

Theweleit, Klaus. 1989. Male Fantasies, 2 vols. Minneapolis: University of Minnesota Press.

Turner Jr., Henry Ashby. 1985. Hitler—Memoirs of a Confidant. New Haven, Conn.: Yale University Press.

Volkov, Shulamit. 1989. "The Written Matter and the Spoken Word: On the Gap between Pre-1914 and Nazi Anti-Semitism," in François Furet, ed., Unanswered Questions: Nazi Germany and the Genocide of the Jews, 33–53. New York: Schocken Books.

Waite, Robert L. 1952. Vanguard of Nazism: The Free Corps Movement in Postwar Germany, 1918–1923. Cambridge, Mass.: Harvard University Press.

Walker, Mack. 1971. German Home Towns: Community, State and General Estate, 1648–1871. Ithaca, N.Y.: Cornell University Press.

Wallace, Anthony F. C. 1956. "Revitalization Movements," American Anthropologist 58: 264–81.

Webb, James. 1976. The Occult Establishment. La Salle, Ill.: Open Court.

Weber, Max. 1946a [1906]. "Capitalism and Rural Society in Germany," in H. H. Gerth and C. Wright Mills, eds., From Max Weber: Essays in Sociology, 363–85. New York: Oxford University Press.

———. 1946b [1917]. "National Character and the Junkers," in H. H. Gerth and C. Wright Mills, eds., From Max Weber: Essays in Sociology, 386–95. New York: Oxford University Press.

———. 1979 [1894]. "Developmental Tendencies in the Situation of East Elbian Rural Laborers," Economy and Society 8: 177–205.

Wegner, Bernd. 1985. "The 'Aristocracy of National Socialism': The Role of the SS in National Socialist Germany," in Hansjoachim W. Koch, ed., Aspects of the Third Reich, 430–50, 567–70. New York: St. Martin's Press.

Weiss, John. 1996. Ideology of Death: Why the Holocaust Happened in Germany. Chicago: Ivan R. Dee.

Zenner, Walter. 1991. Minorities in the Middle: A Cross-Cultural Analysis. Albany: State University of New York Press.

Index

285–91; and referential semantics, 282; and semiotics, 56–57; structuralist view of, 61–63; and symbolic action, 59–61
custom: as concept, 48

Darwinism, 22, 36; social, 229
Davies, Nigel, 157
Dawson, George, 116–17
DeBeck, George, 99
Degérando, Joseph-Marie, 25
De Heusch, Luc, 192–93
Descartes, René, 25
descriptive integration, 18
Destutt de Tracy, Antoine de, 25, 27, 28, 31, 58
Dick, Chief Adam, 131
Dilthey, Wilhelm, 38–39, 40, 41, 44
Douglas, James, 75
Douglas, Mary, 168, 246
Drucker, Philip, 91
Duby, Georges, 282
Duff, Wilson, 294
Dumont, Louis, 58–59
Duncan, William, 76, 99
Durán, Diego, 135, 148–49, 168, 173, 179–80, 181, 188, 197
Durkheim, Émile, 48, 58, 192; and Saussure, 51–52
Duverger, Christian, 186–87

Eagleton, Terry, 44
Eco, Umberto, 54
Eichmann, Adolf, 248, 250
Einstein, Albert, 231
Elias, Norbert, 254–55, 297; and power, 4–5
Engels, Frederick, 15, 22, 30–35
Enlightenment: and Counter-Enlightenment, 22, 23, 26–30; and French Revolution, 25–26; and Marxian perspective, 30; and progress, 24, 25; and Reason, 30, 38, 64; and study of ideas, 31–32; and universalism, 24; and Volk, concept of, 211, 268
Erdheim, Mario, 140, 295
estate, concept of, 86
ethnography, 70

eugenics: and National Socialism, 240–41. See also race
Europe and the People without History (Wolf), 14–15

fetishism: Marxian concept of, 34–35
Fichte, Johann Gottlieb, 24; and French Revolution, 27; and Volk, 211–12
Florescano, Enrique, x
Fort Rupert, 69, 72, 74, 76, 78, 80, 86, 87, 88, 113
Foucault, Michel, 5
Fox, Richard, 61, 274
Frazer, James, 192, 284
Frederick Barbarossa, 212
Frederick II, 212
French Revolution, 209; and Counter-Enlightenment, 26–27; and Enlightenment, 25–26; and German states, 267–68; and Jews, 243
Friedman, Jonathan, 34
Friedrich-Wilhelm III, 207
Fritzsch, Karl, 250
functionalism, 47–48, 283–84, 291

Gandhi, Mohandas, 61
Geertz, Clifford, 59–60
Gellner, Ernest, 38
General German Workingman's Association, 215
George, Stefan, 230
German Ideology, The (Marx and Engels), 31
Germany: anti-Semitism in, 226, 236, 243, 245, 252–53; capitalism in, development of, 213–17; citizenship in, concept of, 209; and Counter-Enlightenment, 37–38; crises of, 206, 207, 220–22, 226; and French Revolution, 214–15, 267–68; and Jews in German history, 204, 205, 218, 226, 238, 243–44; and Jews in Third Reich, 245–54, 256–57; language of, 209; and militarism in Second Reich, 218–19; and militarism under National Socialism, 241–43, 271–72; and Prussian state, 207–10, 213–16; rulership